THE BEST OF
ANN LANDERS

HER FAVORITE LETTERS OF ALL TIME

ANN LANDERS

Formerly titled WAKE UP AND SMELL THE COFFEE!

Fawcett Columbine   •   New York

A Fawcett Columbine Book
Published by Ballantine Books

All of the columns in this work have been previously published in Ann Landers' syndicated newspaper column.

The do's and don'ts for people who want to help bereaved parents on page 348 were prepared by Lee Schmidt, Parent Bereavement Outreach, Santa Monica, California.

Acknowledgments for previously published material can be found on page 418–19.

http://www.randomhouse.com

Library of Congress Catalog Card Number: 97-90022

ISBN: 0-449-91274-4

Cover photo © Bob Fila/Chicago Tribune

Manufactured in the United States of America

First Ballantine Books Edition: May 1997

10 9 8 7 6 5 4 3 2 1

Dedication

I dedicate this book to my priceless staff: Kathy Mitchell, Marcy Sugar, Barbara Olin and Catherine Richardson. Kathy has been with me for 27 years, Marcy for 22, Barbara, 14 and Catherine, 6. They have saved me from myself more times than I care to remember. Without the loyalty and dedication of such a stellar group, this collection would not have been possible.

A 21-gun salute to my employees who handle the thousands of pieces of mail that arrive daily: Stanley Schall, Susie Harris, Bobbie Nussbaum and Pam Hegarty. Their support is invaluable.

Special thanks to my boss, Richard Newcombe, President and CEO of Creators Syndicate. He is dynamic, generous and my personal candidate for sainthood. And kudos to his right arm, Anita Tobias, who keeps her eye on everything and everybody. And to Mike Santiago, who's always there when we need him. A round of applause to the syndicate's editor, Katherine Searcy, for her eagle eye. And my hat's off to Marianne Sugawara and Mary Ann Veldman for their hard work and dedication. Although Creators is based in Los Angeles, each and every member is as close as my telephone.

Denis Gosselin, editor of the *Chicago Tribune Magazine*, is never too busy to set everything aside and edit my column. He is a pussycat, and I cherish our friendship.

A warm hug to daughter Margo Howard, who has long served as a sounding board. She is extraordinarily perceptive, and I always can count on Margo for an honest opinion.

A word of gratitude to Ava Andrews and Bobby West, who keep my home fires burning. Without this competent, good-natured pair, I could never manage my back-breaking schedule.

Grateful thanks to my twin sister, Dear Abby, who married Morton Phillips. Had she married anyone else, I never would have known Mort's mother, Rosie, who unwittingly supplied the title for this book. Going back more than 55 years, I heard her say many times to her sweet-natured, often silent, husband, "Jay! Wake up and smell the coffee!"

Foreword

The very first column I wrote appeared on October 16, 1955. Here it is:

Dear Mrs. Landers: I've always regarded most marital mix-ups as very humorous—until now, that is, when the noose is tightening around my own neck. We have been married 10 years and have two sons. I like auto racing, but my wife has no interest in it, so I've always gone without her.

I've fallen for a woman with three children who is also very fond of auto racing. Her husband is ignorant and impossible. This may sound corny, but I think she would be a wonderful companion for me. I suppose you think I'm a louse—but I am stumped. I would like to have your advice on this problem.

—Mr. K

Dear Mr. K: Time wounds all heels—and you'll get yours. Do you realize that there are five children involved in your little racetrack romance? Don't be surprised if you wake up one of these days and wish you had your wife and sons back. You are flirting with a muddy track on Black Friday, and the way you're headed, you will get exactly what you deserve.

Dear Mrs. Landers: I have just graduated from grade school, and the boy I like is in the Army. He has written that he will be home on leave soon, but my mother forbids me to see him. I tried to explain that we just want to see a movie and will be home early. Mother says I can't go and that I am too young to know what I am doing. Please help me.

—EV

Dear EV: If you "just graduated from grade school," you are about 13 years old, Chicken. Uncle Sam needs men—you don't. Listen to your mother; she is right. And about that boyfriend—his brains must be AWOL.

Dear Mrs. Landers: I've been married four years, have two children and am expecting a third soon. My husband has been chasing around town with women for the past seven months. When I told him that I was getting a separation, he promised to change his ways and behave himself. I have no money for attorneys' fees, and I cannot work. Shall I try to borrow the money from relatives, or should I wait and see what happens?
—Troubled Wife

Dear T.W.: You have every right to blow a gasket. This character does not deserve a family—as of now. But since he has promised to mend his ways, give him another chance. Try to persuade him to go with you to a marriage counselor. See if, together, you can't find out what's gone wrong with your marriage. Let him know, too, if there is any more extramarital activity, you're giving him the heave-ho.

Dear Mrs. Landers: Two months ago, I met a man who seems very fond of me. He has two jobs, which is the reason he has never called me up on the phone or taken me out. He is very busy. He says he cares for me a great deal, but I see him only once a day when he delivers food at my home. I don't want to rush him into anything. What do you think?
—Steady Reader

Dear S.R.: What this man is delivering to your home sounds like baloney. I have a sneaking suspicion that your back-door Romeo has a wife and a family, plus several other very good "customers." You'd better forget about him and suggest that he leave whatever it is that he is delivering in a convenient place. He ought to stick to his commission as the "bonus" for his sales.

Dear Ann Landers: I am a girl of 14, and I like a certain boy and am sure he likes me, but when it comes time to meet, he gets scared and backs out. I am deeply troubled.

—S.V.

Dear S.V.: Don't worry; he's only a kid. Soon, now, he'll become unscared, and you'll have a chance to find out if you really like each other.

Meanwhile, you can have a lot of good times with other youngsters—boys and girls!

Confidential: Miss E.B.: You are entitled to a life of your own. You have given more than your share to your mother and the rest of the family. Move out of that house before they drive you batty.

————

When I started writing the Ann Landers column, I had no intention of hanging around for 40 years and landing in the *Guinness Book of World Records*, but that's exactly what happened.

I was shot full of luck from day one. When Will Munnecke, vice president of the *Chicago Sun-Times*, suggested that I enter the contest to replace the original Ann Landers, who had died suddenly, I reluctantly agreed. Miracle of miracles, I won the contest. The phrase that came to mind was "Be careful what you pray for. You may get it."

Good fortune smiled on me from the start. Editor Larry Fanning, fresh from San Francisco, was assigned the unenviable job of teaching the new girl how to write an advice column. Larry became apoplectic when he discovered that the new girl had never written a line for publication. In fact, she had never held a job before.

Apparently, ignorance can be an asset. The column took off like a rocket. I had greatly admired Dorothy Dix, the grandmother of advice columnists, but she had been dead for seven years. I had the whole field to myself.

I also was blessed with a generous publisher, Marshall Field IV, plus a succession of editors who promoted me endlessly and allowed me to print letters that dealt with homosexuality and other subjects considered taboo for family newspapers.

I spent 33 wonderful years at the *Sun-Times*. Then, Rupert Murdoch bought the paper. It wasn't long before most of my pals walked over to the *Chicago Tribune*. I decided to join them. The *Tribune* welcomed me and my staff with open arms and provided us with beautiful offices. We soon felt very much at home.

Writing seven columns a week can be a headache, but it's never a bore. I hope this compilation of columns spanning 40 years will satisfy the thousands of readers who, over the years, have asked me to rerun their favorites. Since it was impossible to accommodate them all, I decided to make a collection of *my* favorite columns. And here it is.

Contents

THE BEST OF ANN LANDERS

Love, Marriage and the In-laws from Hell

Have you ever wondered, "Am I in love, or is this just infatuation?" Well, this essay might help you know the difference. After this appeared in print, many readers wrote to tell me it helped them distinguish one from the other.

Love or Infatuation?

Infatuation is instant desire. It is one set of glands calling to another. Love is friendship that has caught fire. It takes root and grows—one day at a time.

Infatuation is marked by a feeling of insecurity.

You are excited and eager but not genuinely happy. There are nagging doubts, unanswered questions, little bits and pieces about your beloved that you would just as soon not examine too closely. It might spoil the dream.

Love is quiet understanding and the mature acceptance of imperfection. It is real. It gives you strength and grows beyond you—to bolster your beloved. You are warmed by his presence, even when he is away. Miles do not separate you. You want him nearer. But near or far, you know he is yours and you can wait.

Infatuation says, "We must get married right away. I can't risk losing him."

Love says, "Be patient. Don't panic. Plan your future with confidence."

Infatuation has an element of sexual excitement. If you are honest, you will admit it is difficult to be in one another's company unless you are sure it will end in intimacy. Love is the maturation of friendship. You must be friends before you can be lovers.

Infatuation lacks confidence. When he's away, you wonder if he's cheating. Sometimes you check.

Love means trust. You are calm, secure and unthreatened. He feels that trust, and it makes him even more trustworthy.

Infatuation might lead you to do things you'll regret later, but love never will.

Love is an upper. It makes you look up. It makes you think up. It makes you a better person than you were before.

How do we know if a relationship is worth pursuing?
When is it time to call it quits?
What irritations should be overlooked for the sake of family harmony?
My mail indicates that more and more people want serious, committed relationships but are having a hard time making it work or finding the right someone. Look over my shoulder to see some of the ways things can get off track.

Dear Ann: I've been going with a wristwatch salesman for 16 months. He takes me to the most expensive places, and last year for my birthday he gave me a beautiful watch.

Something weird is going on, and I can't figure out what's at the bottom of it. His stenographer is overly interested in our personal business. She wants to know where we go, how much he spends and what we talk about.

Last night, I'm sure I saw her following us in her car. The night before, she sat directly behind us at the movies. I asked my boyfriend to explain this. He said he didn't want it to "get around" because it'd be bad for business, but she's his first cousin. He claims she's very competent and he can't tell her off because she might quit. He asks that I be patient and overlook her odd behavior. What do you make of it?

—Shadowed

Dear Shadowed: A watch last year, but *this* year, you're getting the works.

The reason the girl is so interested in what's going on is because your boyfriend has probably been making time with her, too. Plain, ordinary, everyday cousins don't go to such lengths to find out what's buzzin', unless they're kissin' kin, that is.

Tell your watch salesman to unwind himself from this private eye or you'll try to find a boyfriend from a less closely knit family.

Dear Ann Landers: I read something in the paper a while back that gave me an idea. I need your advice on whether to do it. The problem: a husband who would rather go fishing and hunting with the boys than be with me.

The following news story appeared on the Associated Press wire:

A woman in Isanti, Minn., got fed up with her husband's absenteeism. He, too, was a fishing and hunting nut. She ran the following ad on his birthday:

"Husband for sale cheap. Comes complete with hunting and fishing equipment. Also one pair of jeans, two shirts, a Lab retriever and 25 pounds of deer meat. Not home much between September and January or April through October. Will consider trade."

When the first few calls came from interested women, her husband thought it was amusing. But by the second day, the phone was ringing off the wall. He didn't think it was so funny.

A few days later, she ran a second ad saying it was all a joke and she had decided to keep her husband after all. I'd say the little lady scored a victory.

How about it, Ann? Should I do likewise?
—Fifty Pounds of Deer Meat, 30 Quails, 40 Mallards, 20
Trout and 2 Marlins

Dear Woman: How good is your husband's sense of humor? And what about yours? Do you really want to unload the guy? Any chance of your going along at least part of the time? Consider all of the above before you do anything rash.

Dear Ann Landers: My husband is a workaholic. He regularly works on Saturdays and often on Sundays as well. He averages 10 to 12 hours a day. Our three children are grown and doing well. We have purchased annuities for them and our four grandchildren. We give generous gifts of money for birthdays and Christmas and enjoy the fact that we can.

We have two cars, a lovely home, no debts and approximately $1 million in assets. Sound good? Well, we also have no hobbies. We haven't had a vacation in years except for a couple of weekends when we visited our children and their families.

I was a professional woman and worked both inside and outside the home. We are both in our 70s. When does the fun start?

—The Big Q

Dear Q: The fun started for your husband a long time ago. Workaholics would rather work than play, which is why they do it.

Mates of workaholics must make their own fun. If you're in your 70s and haven't discovered that, you're a slow learner, honey.

Dear Ann Landers: Now that the great American home-wrecker (football) is being glorified on all the networks, will you please relay a message to my husband? There is no chance that I can get his attention until after January, but he might listen to you.

Dear Husband: I am fast slipping into a state of depression as I face another season of watching you watch the idiot box as if it is the only thing in life that matters. But, then, I guess it is. I find it quite remarkable that you chat so easily with the players, whom you don't even know (and who never answer you, of course), while I sit there, the woman who has been married to you for 15 years and bore you three healthy, beautiful children, and I could drop dead in front of your eyes and you wouldn't even notice.

I find it fascinating that you can call each and every player by name. You know where they were born and how much they weigh. I am certain you do not know how much your own children weigh, and at this point, I wouldn't bet that you could call them by name.

For the last three Thanksgivings, you have not come to the table to eat with us. Christmas and New Year's, it is the same story. When your children grow up, they will remember that you ignored them. Nature has a strange way of paying people back. When you want their love and affection, they will tell you to get lost.

—The Girl in Your Wedding Picture, Remember Me?

Dear Girl: I'm printing this in the hope that things will brighten up around your house before the holidays. Thanks for writing.

Dear Ann Landers: Please, Ann, be fair. Tell every woman who gripes because her husband watches so much football on TV to button her lip. It so happens the games are played on weekends and holidays, and that's when husbands are home.

How many of those housewives who complain are glued to their sets during the week, watching soap operas? When I was home with the flu, I couldn't get my wife to bring me a glass of orange juice. She was too busy with *General Hospital, Marcus Welby, M.D., The Doctors, Medical Center* and so on.

I say, "Let she who is without sin cast the first stone." What do you say, Ann Landers?

—A Husband Who Watches Football and Could Be Out
Doing Something Worse

Dear Husband: I say you've conveyed two major messages—one in your letter and another in your signature.

The women are going to hate me, but I agree with you. If the worst thing a wife can say about her husband is that he watches too much football on TV, she has a better marriage than most.

It can be hard to figure out exactly what the problem is between men and women.

Dear Ann Landers: I am a 6-foot-2-inch, 180-pound male and considered attractive. I have a master's degree and hold an excellent position. I dress well and work out to stay in shape. I always pick up the lady on time, take her to the best and most interesting place I can afford, and behave like a gentleman. I often hear comments such as "I've always wanted to go there, but no one has ever taken me. Thank you." Or "You are so easy to talk to" or "It's so nice to meet a guy who knows how to treat a lady."

So what's the problem? I never see them again. They thank me for the lovely evening, but when I ask them out a second time, they are "busy." After three rejections, I simply give the lady my phone number and ask her to call me when she has some free time. After 12 years of dating, not one of these women has ever called me back.

When I pressed some of these women to tell me what was wrong, they said, "It's not you, it's me" or "You're just too nice." These are not airheads. Most of my dates are college-educated career women.

Occasionally, I hear news about some of the women I have dated. I cannot count the number who have taken up with guys who are liars, freeloaders or drunks, and some are even physical abusers. I'm beginning to think all women are masochists.

I am tired of hearing that same old complaint, "There are no nice guys." Maybe my letter will help women recognize their self-destructive behavior and the result will be better relationships for all concerned.

—M.F. in Michigan

Dear Michigan: I am stumped. Baffled. Don't have a clue. You sound like the answer to a single girl's prayers.

I'm going to tell you exactly what I told a woman who wrote a similar letter complaining that no man ever asked her out a second time although they all said that she was great company and a lot of fun and that they'd had a terrific evening.

Talk to five people who know you well—good friends, your clergyman, your doctor, people you work with, and some of the women you've taken out. Ask for a totally honest appraisal. If you can't get satisfaction, consider a few sessions with a counselor. It is obvious to me that something about you needs fixing.

Dear Ann Landers: Your mind must have gone on vacation before your body did. That guy who hasn't had a date since his divorce 10 years ago told you he thought women were only interested in a man's looks. You told him he sounded terrific and to hang in there because someday the right woman would come along.

Why didn't you tell him the same thing you tell women who can't get a date—that something about him must turn them off? Here's a list of questions for him:

1. Are you well-groomed? A lot of men who feel they aren't handsome give up on their looks entirely. Do you bathe and change your clothes regularly? Is your hair clean? Are you still wearing the glasses you had in high school?
2. Are you sensible about diet and exercise? A 300-pound couch potato isn't going to attract a lot of women.
3. Do you talk about yourself all evening and never ask a question?
4. Are you informed about world affairs, or do you read only the sports page?
5. Is your idea of a "fun evening" four hours in front of the tube with a six-pack?

6. Are you self-centered and stubborn? Do you insist on having your way and grumble if you don't get it?

7. Can you discuss an issue in a civilized manner and perhaps even admit you were wrong once in a while?

8. Do you come off looking desperate? It's a standard assumption that women want to get married and men avoid commitment, but it's been my experience that often the opposite is true. Most women will be scared off by a man who is too eager to get married, especially if his last marriage was unsuccessful.

Finally, this guy reads the personal ads looking for a woman. Tell him to get a life. He should become involved in church or community affairs, politics, a club or a charity. A man who expects his girlfriend to provide him with a social life is no prize.

—Highly Dubious in Santa Fe, N.M.

Dear H.D.: Right on. Thanks for sitting in my chair today.

Dear Ann Landers: I always thought it was narrow-minded and mean of you to take such a strong stand against lonely-hearts advertisements. I changed my mind today when I read the *Nashville Banner*.

It seems a man named Henry Joneson of Tomahawk, Alberta, Canada, answered an ad in an agricultural publication. The woman who was looking for a companion was Ada Wittenmyer, age 37. Henry, the 50-year-old owner of a 900-acre ranch, was lonesome and thought Ada sounded "interesting." He didn't realize his letters and checks were going to a prison until District Attorney General Kenneth Atkins called and told him that Ada had just been convicted of poisoning her fourth husband. She was already serving a 25-year term for poisoning her third husband—a wealthy Oklahoma rancher she had met through another lonely-hearts ad. Atkins said that when he told him the news Mr. Joneson said, "Oh, Lord."

I hope you will print this letter in your column, Ann, as a warning to others who are lonely. And please accept my apologies for my previous attitude.

—Nashville Reader

Dear Reader: Nothing I might have said could have had the impact of your report. I checked it out with Nashville, and every detail was on target. Thanks for the backup.

Dear Ann Landers: Having been happily married for 34 years, I have tried to set a good example for my four sons, all under age 30. Unfortunately, I have watched two of their marriages end in divorce. Our grandchildren were the real losers.

I know there are two sides to every story, but from the very beginning, there were signs that those marriages were not going to work.

I try not to prejudge the women my sons go out with, but after meeting several of their dates, I decided to give them some advice. Enclosed is a copy of a letter I gave to each of my sons. If you run it in your column, it might help other young men make better choices.

—Dad in Anaheim, Calif.

Dear Dad: Here's your letter, and it's a good one. Thanks for sending it my way.

To My Son

One of the benefits of being a father is being able to give advice. Based on experience and the desire to have only the best for my sons, I offer these observations about selecting a mate for life.

Leave her alone if:

1. She does not know whether hamburger comes from a cow or a pig.
2. She can get her pantyhose off in less than five seconds. It means she has had lots of practice.
3. She has sex with you on the first date.
4. Her parents call you "son" on your first meeting.
5. She smokes but tells you she can quit anytime she wants.
6. She tells you she didn't get her high school diploma because her parents moved frequently.
7. When you ask her where she goes to church, she tells you her high school class once toured the Crystal Cathedral.
8. You suggest a cocktail before noon, and she accepts.
9. She says the words "till death do us part" in marriage vows are outdated.
10. She tells you she has never voted in a presidential election.
11. She works and makes it clear that her money is *her* money and your money is *our* money.
12. She wants a baby soon—to cement the relationship.

Dear Ann Landers: A while back, you printed a letter from "Dad in Anaheim," who made a list of 12 observations to help his sons select a mate.

I am a 32-year-old divorced mother who has learned from her mistakes. I also have some observations to offer my two daughters. I hope you'll print them.

Leave him alone if:

1. He feels cooking and cleaning is "woman's work."
2. He still lives at home.
3. He pressures you for sex.
4. He tells you he "has never felt this way" about anyone else.
5. He drinks before noon or after work on a regular basis.
6. He spends money on himself but has trouble paying rent and utilities.
7. He thinks birth control is your responsibility.
8. He can't seem to hold a job.
9. He frequently needs to borrow money from you.
10. He shows disrespect for his family members or yours.
11. He has never asked for your opinion or advice on anything.
12. You have never heard him say, "I'm sorry."

—Mom in Minnesota

Dear Mom: Your observations are excellent. My female readers really rose to the occasion. Here's another superb response:

Dear Ann Landers: I read those 12 guidelines to help sons choose a mate, and I think some of them are clearly sexist.

No. 3, for example, says to leave her alone if "she has sex with you on the first date." Well, if she had sex, so did he. A male who is so judgmental is no candidate for marriage.

The same goes for the one that says to leave her alone if "she can get her pantyhose off in less than five seconds. It means she has had lots of practice." If the man has had enough experience to set a time limit, he, too, has had too much practice. I wonder how long it took for him to get his socks off, or was he in such a hurry he just left them on?

And No. 8 is absurd. Leave her alone if "you suggest a cocktail before noon and she accepts." What was he doing suggesting a cocktail at that hour in the first place? Does he have a booze problem?

I have no beef with the man's warning signals, but why didn't you point out that some of these red flags also reflected poorly on men?

It is considered perfectly OK for men to have one-night stands, get skunk drunk and want sex on the first date, but women who do this are called tramps.

It's time men were held to the same standard. And it's also time that Dad in Anaheim gave his sons some advice on how they should treat women.

—Faithful Reader in Chicago

Dear Chicago: Thanks for nailing those male chauvinist attitudes. In my opinion, the women's responses made a monkey out of "Anaheim."

Sometimes my readers send me letters that are real knee-slappers.

Dear Ann Landers: You are undoubtedly aware of the revival of the old chain-letter concept in the form of a pyramid.

I thought you might be interested in the one I received for my birthday. I sent it on—in two languages. Here it is to share with your readers.

—Still Laughing in Lima, Peru

Dear Lima: Chain letters are illegal in the United States, but yours is different and involves no money. Thanks for passing it on.

"This chain letter was started by a woman like yourself in the hope of bringing relief to tired, discontented wives. Unlike most chain letters, this one does not cost anything. Just send a copy to five of your female friends who are equally tired. Then, bundle up your husband, and send him to the woman whose name appears at the top of the list. Add your name to the bottom of the list. When your name comes to the top, you will receive 16,748 men. Some of them will be dandies. Have faith, and don't break the chain. One woman who broke the chain got her own husband back. At the time of this writing, a friend of mine has received 183 men. They buried her yesterday, but it took three undertakers 36 hours to get the smile off her face."

Dear Ann Landers: My husband has been pulling a stunt that embarrasses me to tears. When we have company, he puts on a Tarzan outfit (leopard skin over one shoulder and leopard shorts), paints claw marks on himself with lipstick, tucks oak leaves in his hair, grabs a banana and goes up in the tree and waits. When the guests arrive, he starts making chimpanzee noises and swings down on them.

Everyone laughs hysterically, but I am secretly humiliated. Why would a guy in his 30s behave like this? I suspect he is very immature.

—Jane

Dear Jane: Not necessarily. Your husband's exhibitionism has more to do with the satisfaction he gets from the laughter. I suspect he hungers for an appreciative audience and this act is a sure-fire hit.

Dear Ann Landers: I handle your column in *The Washington Post*. Recently I ran across a wonderful poem by Herbert Scott in a book called *Disguises* (University of Pittsburgh Press). I hope you will print it.
　　　　　　　　　—Shelby Coffey [Shelby Coffey is now editor of the
　　　　　　　　　　　　　　　　　　　　　　　Los Angeles Times.]

Dear Shelby: With pleasure. The poem is a hoot. Thanks for your sharp eye.

Frankenstein's Wife
Writes to Ann Landers

Dear Ann, I think I am losing my husband.
He never straps me to the bed anymore,
or fiddles with my parts.
I haven't had a charge in weeks.
Sometimes I think he wants to do me in.
There were intimations of this last week,
when I found water in my oil can.
Am I going crazy?
I have faulty wiring and poor compression,
yet he won't fix anything around my body.
Lately, strange arms appeared beneath the couch,
and a leg under the table,
and teeth in my teacup.
I began to put things together.
And finally, last night, he robbed the grave
of that little tramp
who died down the street.
Should I sever connections?
I would like to make this marriage work.
But where have I failed? I try to keep neat.
Heaven knows, it's difficult with no help
in the kitchen, and nothing to wear,
and vapor lock to contend with.
I think I am pregnant, and he won't pay the bills.
What will I do when they turn off the lights?

Not all relationships are meant to be, and when that's the case, divorce may be inevitable. I didn't always feel this way. Here's what I wrote back in 1960. In retrospect, I find it incredible that I printed what follows:

Dear Ann Landers: You frequently say in your column that a married woman need not put up with a man she no longer cares for. You phrase it this way: "Your husband has to support his children or go to jail."

By such advice, you give the impression that when a wife gets bored, she can throw her husband out and collect support money. In other words, you encourage divorce as "the easy out."

In case you don't know it, Ann Landers, there are already too many man-hungry divorcees on the loose. You don't help the situation by painting glowing pictures of the split home. You do more harm than good, and I wish you'd button your lip on this subject.

—A Four-Year Observer

Dear Observer: Anyone who has read this column for four years should know where I stand on divorce. If you can show me a single column that I wrote which advocates divorce, I will buy you a new car (your choice).

It is the law that a man must support his children. Most states have closed a favorite loophole for irresponsible husbands who simply leave the state to avoid paying support.

I do not believe that a woman should live with a man who abuses her and the children or beats her. In such cases, I recommend separate roofs and child support. This is not the same as divorce. In my book, marriage is forever.

But times change, and so have I. As more women were able to support themselves and their children financially, it seemed unnecessary for them to stay in relationships that were verbally or physically abusive, unhealthy or simply unhappy.

Divorce became so commonplace that I began to wonder if too many people were rushing to divorce for trivial reasons and regretting it later.

In 1993, I asked my readers this question: "Looking back, do you regret having moved so rapidly to be divorced, and do you now feel that had you waited, the marriage might have been salvaged?"

I asked for a yes or no answer on a postcard, but thousands of readers felt compelled to write long letters. I'm glad they did. I learned a lot.

To my surprise, out of nearly 30,000 responses, almost 23,000 came from women. Nearly three times as many readers said they were glad they divorced, and most of them said they wished they had done it sooner.

Here are some samples:

From Bloomington, Ind.: My husband was a boozer and a skirt-chaser, but I stayed with him for the sake of the kids. When I finally threw him out, the kids thanked me. Two years later, I married a terrific man. When I think that I almost missed this part of my life, which is the best, I could die!

Charlottesville, Va.: I divorced my husband five years ago and regret it. My kids miss him, and so do I. He's a lot better than any of the jerks I've dated since.

North Bay, Ontario: Being a staunch Catholic, I thought hard and long before I decided to divorce my wife. (She came after me on two occasions with a kitchen knife and once with a gun.) Our children are now mentally healthy, and I realize I was wrong to have stayed in that marriage "for their sake."

Lenexa, Kan.: I don't regret my divorce. It's the marriage I regret. My parents split when I was 27. I only wish they had done it sooner, too. Children are not victims of divorce; they are victims of unhappy relationships.

Minneapolis: I'm sorry I divorced. The worst pain of my life was seeing a family picture of my children with their dad's other family. I suddenly realized that my kids had a whole other life, and I wasn't part of it. Talk about being heartsick.

Bloomfield Hills, Mich.: Why so many divorces? I believe it is the yuppie mentality at work—the concept that there is something newer and better just around the corner. We trade in people like cars these days. Most marriages today fall apart because the wife has to compete with the women in the workplace. My husband always left the house in the morning looking better and smelling better than he ever did at home. Of course, the inevitable happened. Am I glad I'm divorced? Yes. Life with a cheater is hell.

Vienna, Va.: I am not divorced, but I could have been five years ago. My husband was a faithful, reliable, decent man. I wanted romance and passion. A sensible marriage counselor made me see my life as it really was. Thank heavens.

Chicago: My divorce was good not only for me (I have remarried) but for my ex-husband. He joined Alcoholics Anonymous and now holds a responsible job. We are both better off.

Richmond, Va.: I'm a practicing Sunni Muslim. We have what is called "idaht"—a three-month waiting period before a divorce is final. Both parties have breathing room to learn if divorce is really what they want. After that, they can split or stay together. Most of the time, they stay together.

Dear Richmond: You don't have to be a Muslim to get this braking mechanism. Most states have a waiting period. In Virginia, all couples with children must wait a year for a divorce.

After a While
Veronica A. Shoffstall

After a while, you learn the subtle difference
Between holding a hand and chaining a soul,
And you learn that love doesn't mean leaning
And company doesn't mean security,
And you begin to learn that kisses aren't contracts
And presents aren't promises,
And you begin to accept your defeats
With your head up and your eyes open
With the grace of a woman, not the grief of a child,
And you learn to build all your roads on today
Because tomorrow's ground is too uncertain for plans.
And futures have a way of falling down in midflight.
After a while, you learn
That even sunshine burns if you get too much.
So you plant your own garden and decorate your own soul,
Instead of waiting for someone to bring you flowers.
And you learn that you really can endure . . .
That you really are strong.
And you really do have worth.
And you learn and learn . . .
With every goodbye you learn.

Fortunately, most relationships are loving and healthy. Some just don't work and are better off ended. And then there are those that are downright sick and dangerous.

Dear Ann Landers: I am an 18-year-old college student. Several weeks ago, I attended a fraternity party with "Jeff." We had a lot of fun. When he asked me out a second time and then a third, I accepted.

After the fourth date, I decided I didn't want to go out with Jeff anymore. Frankly, he was becoming very moody and unpleasantly aggressive. He got upset when I told him not to call me anymore and begged for a chance to talk about "what went wrong." I felt I owed him that much, so I agreed.

That get-together turned into a three-hour session of Jeff trying to get me to go out with him again. Fifteen minutes after I got home, the phone was ringing. It was Jeff. More talk. Finally, I hung up on him. He called back immediately. The next day, he called 20 times in a row. I decided to take the phone off the hook. The following week, I had my phone number changed.

I thought I could handle this guy, but when he started to follow me around campus, I became concerned. Twice, he followed me up to my dorm room and refused to leave. My neighbors called security. He has threatened to continue this "as long as it takes" for me to go out with him again.

I have told Jeff in every way possible that I want nothing to do with him and to leave me alone, but I'm beginning to feel uneasy. Please tell me what to do.

—Stressed Out in the Midwest

Dear Stressed: Jeff's persistence suggests that he is obsessed with you. This could prove dangerous. Obsessions are a form of mental illness.

Notify the dean of the college. If he or she suggests that you charge Jeff with harassment, do it. If Jeff threatens to harm you in any way, go straight to the police. In the meantime, do not walk on campus (or anywhere else) alone. I'm worried about you.

Dear Ann Landers: After so many years of reading your column, I never thought I would be writing a letter of my own. But I am in need of help and have faith in what you say.

A year ago, I was separated from my wife. The split was her idea. She has no intention of returning to me. We have a 4-year-old daughter I miss a lot. When my wife left, I was lost and unable to cope with life. I even contemplated suicide. Then, I was introduced to a nice girl. She saw how desperate I was and gave me good advice. She even suggested that I fight for my child—something I had never thought of before. Without her, I wouldn't have made it through the months of suffering. I love this girl and want her to move in with me. My problem is that I am 27 and she is 13. I know this sounds young, but she is very mature for her age. Her mother knows about me—but not her father.

We both want to tell the world that we love each other. Please give me some advice.

—Shorty

Dear Shorty: I don't know what you are short of, but I have a feeling you could be short an important part of your anatomy if this girl's father ever finds out about you.

My advice is: Stop seeing her before you get arrested for contributing to the delinquency of a minor, and get some counseling. You sure do need it, bub.

Dear Ann Landers: I am a man in my early 60s, divorced and retired. My sister is in her late 50s and widowed. We go to bed together twice a week. This has been going on since her husband died eight years ago. Actually, when we were teenagers we fooled around a lot but never had intercourse. This is not a love match, but it is sex, and good sex at that.

We both enjoy these escapades, and they always produce a good night's sleep. No one knows about this, and no one is getting hurt. Or do you think we are fooling ourselves?

—No Name, No City, Please

Dear No Name: Sick, sick, sick. If I had your address, I would send you a get-well card.

You say no one is getting hurt? I disagree. While you and your sister are practicing incest, you are denying yourselves the opportunity to have normal relationships. I am talking about marriage.

The fact that neither of you sees anything wrong with such behavior suggests a moral dead spot that is unnatural and revolting.

Dear Ann Landers: Is it all right for a father to have sex with his daughter if both are consenting adults? I am 37, and my daughter, "Jean," is 20.

My wife passed away two years ago. After she became ill, Jean assumed all the household responsibilities, and we became very close. We live here, just the two of us, and she is a wonderful cook and housekeeper. We have the same likes and dislikes and are compatible in every way.

Jean is pretty and I am still a young man. Rather than move out of a home that she loves and look for a husband (and risk getting AIDS), Jean says she wants to stay with me. We have a wonderful time together. She hasn't dated in several months because she would prefer to be with me more than any of the young men she knows. I love her company and am not interested in anyone else.

Can a man legally marry his daughter? Please do not publish my name as it is a very controversial subject and I don't want to be harassed. P.S. Does the Old Testament say anything about this?
—Mr. X

Dear Mr. X: According to John Beckstrom, professor of family law at Northwestern University Law School, it is not legal anywhere in the United States for a father and daughter to knowingly marry each other. Such a marriage would not be valid. In fact, in many states the father would be prosecuted for criminal incest.

You asked about the Old Testament: The Book of Leviticus makes it abundantly clear that it is a sin to approach "any that is near of kin."

Although you didn't ask for my opinion, Mr. X, I feel compelled to say that you and your daughter sound as if you are two sandwiches short of a picnic. Your letter is one of the sickest I've read in years.

If you want Jean to have a decent life, please get her into counseling and find a woman who is suitable for marriage.

Dear Ann Landers: A group of us were discussing marriage and what has happened to that once-hallowed institution. Several couples expressed the opinion that there are a great many closet disasters around—marriages that are empty, joyless or pure hell—yet nothing is done about them for one reason or another.

A few couples voiced the notion that most marriages are tolerable but even the individuals involved in those marriages would not have picked the same partner if they had it to do over again.

Almost in unison, three males said, "Let's ask Ann Landers." (I was one.) So we are asking you to do another survey. Question: "If you had it to do over again, would you marry the person to whom you are now married?" Sign us

—Eager to Know

Dear Eager: At least a hundred others have written to ask for the same survey. So here's the question and some specific instructions.

Please answer the question: "If you had it to do over again, would you marry the person to whom you are now married?"

Use postcards, if possible. Write either yes or no. State whether you are male or female—and the number of years you have been married.

Sample: Dear Ann: Yes—Female—35.

I will print the results as soon as I get them.

That letter ran on Valentine's Day of 1977. Within 10 days, my office was bombarded with more than 50,000 pieces of mail, and letters continued to pour in for weeks after. The results were published on March 28, 1977.

Dear Readers: Although I requested postcards only, well over 7,000 wrote letters to tell me in detail how wonderful—or how lousy—their marriages are.

Are you ready? Well, there were two sets of responses, and there was a big difference. Thirty percent signed their cards and letters (many gave their addresses).

Seventy percent did not sign. Here are the results of the signed mail: Seventy percent said yes, they would marry the same person again. Thirty percent said no. Of the signed cards and letters, 80 percent came from females and 20 percent came from males.

The unsigned mail told me more than I wanted to know.

Forty-eight percent said yes, and 52 percent said no.

The breakdown according to sex was 70 percent from females and 30 percent from males.

We received 42 postcards from homosexuals who considered themselves "just as married as anyone else."

They were all happy and voted yes.

I couldn't do a thing with the response to my request that readers let me know how many years they have been married. At least half of my respondents were confused and gave me their age. It is obvious that not only Johnny can't read but his parents have the same problem.

Several readers pointed out a fact that could have influenced many women. The survey column appeared on Valentine's Day.

From San Jose, Calif., a wife wrote: "I may feel different tomorrow, but tonight, I am voting no. It's Valentine's Day, and this clown to whom I've been married for 15 years (five children) didn't even give me a card."

A man in Pittsburgh sent two dozen cards (unsigned). On each card, he wrote (in green ink), "I vote *no. She's murder.*"

A woman from San Francisco wrote a letter saying, "I voted no yesterday. I was drunk. My husband is an angel—a lot better than I deserve. Please change my vote to *yes.*"

From Davenport, Iowa: "Female, married 27 years. We are the happiest couple in town. I vote *yes.*" At the bottom of the card, hastily scrawled in pencil, was a word from her husband, who obviously had been asked to drop the card in the mailbox. He wrote, "That's what *she* thinks. I vote no."

Phoenix: "I *did* do it over again—married the same person three times. My marriage to Thelma was annulled by her parents because she was underage. When she turned legal, we were married by a justice of the peace. Two years later we were married by a Catholic priest. She's terrific."

Akron: "I am 12 years old. I read your column every day. My parents got into a fight tonight over how to vote in your survey. My mother said she was voting no because my dad spends too many nights playing backgammon.

"Dad said their marriage was a lot better than most—even with her griping about him playing so much backgammon. He said he would vote yes. The conversation suddenly turned to how much my mother's brother cost my dad in business. I think you'd better put them both down as no."

Oklahoma City: "In the 32 years we've been married, my husband never once told me he loved me—even though I asked him several times. He always answered, 'I'm not the mushy type.' Tonight, he clipped out your column and wrote across it. 'Yes. She is a beautiful person. I'm a lucky man.' I cried like a baby. Make that two yesses from O. City."

This definition of love has been requested by more than 10,000 readers over the years. And it's still asked for every Valentine's Day:

Love is friendship that has caught fire. It is quiet understanding, mutual confidence, sharing and forgiving. It is loyalty through good and bad times. It settles for less than perfection and makes allowances for human weaknesses.

Love is content with the present, it hopes for the future and it doesn't brood over the past. It's the day-in and day-out chronicle of irritations, problems, compromises, small disappointments, big victories and working toward common goals.

If you have love in your life, it can make up for a great many things you lack. If you don't have it, no matter what else there is, it's not enough.

Readers have given me many suggestions on how to make a marriage work. I really enjoyed this one:

Twelve Rules for a Happy Marriage
1. Never both be angry at once.
2. Never yell at each other unless the house is on fire.
3. Yield to the wishes of the other as an exercise in self-discipline, if you can't think of a better reason.
4. If you have a choice between making yourself or your mate look good—choose your mate.
5. If you feel you must criticize, do so lovingly.
6. Never bring up a mistake of the past.
7. Neglect the whole world rather than each other.
8. Never let the day end without saying at least one complimentary thing to your life's partner.
9. Never meet without an affectionate welcome.
10. Never go to bed mad.
11. When you've made a mistake, talk it out and ask for forgiveness.
12. Remember, it takes two to make an argument. The one who is wrong is the one who will be doing most of the talking.

Vows written by a bride and groom can be touching and immensely meaningful. I would like to share with you ones written and read by a young couple who were married in 1984 atop a mountain overlooking Waikiki in Honolulu. These wedding vows, in my opinion, could serve as enduring guidelines for a beautiful life together. Here they are:

BRIDE: We are two individuals who enrich our existence by having a single life and a shared life.

GROOM: We have chosen to marry because we belong not to each other but with each other.

B: We wish the same happiness for each other and will strive to reach harmony, adjusting to the needs of the other while remaining true to ourselves.

G: When things do not go smoothly, we will try to be patient, gentle, understanding, flexible, receptive, open and loving.

B: We will give what is needed—and more.

G: We will take what we need—and no more.

B: We will be faithful because nothing can be stronger or more important than our love.

G: We will be truthful so we may always trust.

B: We will be respectful, for each of us is a special human being.

G: We have been blessed with much love and the capacity to share it. So we plan to share it with a growing country and a growing family.

B: We are friends and shall remain so.

G: We are lovers and shall remain so.

B: We are individuals and shall remain so.

G: We are partners and shall remain so.

B: Who knows what other beautiful facets our relationship will foster?

B and G: For there awaits us all the joy of growing together in a life shared for years to come.

Relationships are not just about husbands and wives, lovers or friends. Sometimes, they are about family—his nosy mother, your flirtatious sister, his freeloading brother-in-law, those unruly stepchildren.

Here are a few letters I have printed that make it clear that some family problems are universal:

Dear Ann Landers: Here are some excellent commandments for in-laws. And please, Ann, feel free to add to this list.

As one who has been through the mill, I can tell you there are many young married couples who need all the help they can get.

Bylaws for In-laws

1. Don't feel that you are entitled to know everything about your married children's lives (who they entertain, what they do every

night, how much money they make, what their friends are up to, etc.).

2. Don't complain that visits with your children and grandchildren are too infrequent. If your son takes you to lunch, don't tell him it should be every month and then call him to make sure that it is. Be content with whatever time he can give you.

3. Don't try to force your married children to spend time with their married siblings. We are old enough to arrange our time together. (My mother-in-law is constantly suggesting that we should entertain my brother and his wife every week. We love them, but neither of us has the time, money or desire to do so.)

4. Don't correct your grandchildren constantly, nor should you expect perfection. Enjoy them. Rearing them is not your job.

5. Don't ask to be included when your married children tell you of some special plans. If they want to include you, they will.

6. Don't criticize your child in front of his or her spouse and don't criticize the spouse. Neither one appreciates this.

7. Don't phone every day unless you are asked to do so.

8. Don't drop in unexpectedly—ever.

9. Do develop your own friendships and your own hobbies. Your children should not be made to feel responsible for entertaining you.

10. Do compliment your child's spouse and say thank you when thanks are due instead of behaving as if a thoughtful gesture took little time and no effort.

Please print this. You could save a lot of marriages.
—Love 'Em, but They're Driving Me Crazy in Kansas

Dear Crazy in Kansas: Great list. I can think of nothing to add. I do feel, however, that these bylaws should not be targeted exclusively for in-laws. Parents could profit from following them as well.

Dear Ann Landers: Yesterday, I looked out of my kitchen window and could have sworn I saw an old cow across the way, munching grass between two houses. I was just about to shout to my husband and tell him a cow had wandered out of the pasture and to go put her back in.

Thank heavens I was interrupted by a phone call.

After a second look out the window, I discovered the "cow" was my mother-in-law wearing saddle pants.

Three weeks ago, I was frightened by the sight of a tramp hanging around the machine shed. It was dusk, and I quickly locked all the doors. A few minutes later, I saw my husband walking toward the tramp. When they embraced, I nearly fainted. The "tramp" was his mother.

To put it bluntly, Ann, the woman looks so down at the heels that it makes me sick. She also scares the daylights out of me. My mother-in-law is 74 years old, has plenty of money to spend and is in good health. What can I do about this revolting situation?

—Fargo, N.D.

Dear Fargo: Nothing. At her age, she is not likely to change. So grin and bear it, honey. I just hope your eyesight remains good. And thank heavens you aren't trigger-happy.

Dear Ann: I am bursting at the seams to say a word to "Fargo, N.D.," the woman who was looking out the window and thought she saw a cow in the backyard. On another occasion, the "cow" looked like a tramp. Both times, it turned out to be her mother-in-law.

My mother-in-law is 77, not the most beautiful or best-dressed woman in the world but certainly the finest.

When our kids were sick or I was down with the flu, "the old cow" was right there, cooking, cleaning and doing the laundry.

In every emergency, "the old tramp" has come through like the angel she is.

Beauty is in the eye of the beholder.

—Helen from K.C.

Dear Helen: You said it, honey.

Dear Ann Landers: When I was first married, I used to clear my throat to get the attention of my in-laws. I didn't want to call them Mom and Dad, or Mother and Father, and I wouldn't have dared to call them by their first names. When I did use "Mom" and "Dad," I was very uncomfortable, even though I liked them both a great deal. But they were not my parents, and I kept searching (without success) for a name that would identify them properly and show love as well.

Now, we have a son-in-law who calls my husband and me by our first names and another son-in-law who calls us "Mr. and Mrs." We are not happy with either. The first is too chummy, and the second is too formal.

Every in-law we have talked to feels as we do except a few people who don't mind being called by their first names. Do you have a solution to this age-old dilemma?

—Nameless and Placeless

Dear N. and P.: In the absence of an ideal salutation (which I am unable to produce), I suggest that each family make up their own. In my own dear family, all four sons-in-law called my father "Mr. A.B." (the initials of his first and middle name). It was the perfect solution.

Did you know that when sisters marry, the husbands of said sisters are not even remotely related? I'll bet you thought the boys were brothers-in-law. Well, so did I—but I know better now. Dozens of readers have told me.

I will explain it as it was explained to me:

Princess Margaret is a sister-in-law to Prince Philip, because she is his wife's sister. But Margaret's husband, Anthony Armstrong-Jones, is no relation whatever to Prince Philip. They are just a couple of nice boys who married sisters.

Figuring out how family members are related is the least of in-law problems. As every couple knows, in-laws can boost or bust a relationship.

Eight Ways In-laws Can Break Up a Marriage

1. When a son or daughter lets you know he or she plans to marry, show open hostility to the person of his or her choice. After all, marriage means less love and attention for parents, and they have a right to resent it.

2. Expect your married children to spend every Sunday and holiday at your home. Act hurt if they have other plans.

3. If your married children have problems with their mates, encourage them to come home to you. Let them know your home is still theirs, no matter what. Listen attentively to all complaints and point out additional faults that may have gone unobserved. Remember, one drop of water after another can wear away a rock.

4. If your married children are having financial problems, rush in with the checkbook. If you are having financial problems yourself, borrow if necessary, but let them know they will never have to do without anything as long as you are around.

5. If a married child has a drinking problem, keep telling him his mate drove him to it. It will make him feel better. Everyone needs someone to blame.

6. If your married child gets an opportunity for advancement that takes him to another city, tell him family life is more important than money, and if he leaves, God will punish him for not obeying the commandment "Honor thy father and thy mother."

7. If there are grandchildren, smother them with gifts. If the parents object, tell them to keep out of it. After all, grandchildren are to spoil. Sneak money to the kids secretly if you have to. They'll love you for it.

8. If your married child has a difference of opinion with his mate, get into the act and fan the flame. Family loyalty is a beautiful thing. If you work at it, you can turn a minor argument into a major hassle and break up the marriage.

Dear Ann Landers: You've covered this a number of times, but here's another point of view to consider.

Let us quit criticizing whomever it is our children choose to marry.

My son, "Don," and his wife, "Sharon," live in another state with their two children. I visit them for five or six days a year.

Sharon is a lousy housekeeper, and I do mean lousy. Don is also a slob. It's up to him to keep the lawn mowed and the garage clean. Both are a disgrace.

I presume Sharon is a good wife. They seem happy. I know she's an excellent mother, involved in every facet of their children's lives. She is also honest and outgoing. I really do love her.

The reason I am writing is because so many parents today seem overly involved in the marriages of their children. I believe this does more harm than good, and I hope you'll back me up.

—A Reader in Monroe, La.

Dear Monroe: I'm with you. And now I wonder how many copies of this column will be mailed to the appropriate people.

Dear Ann Landers: I am about to bail out of a five-year marriage to a woman I love a great deal. The problem—my sister-in-law.

A year and a half ago, my wife's sister, "Rose," was widowed. Her husband was killed in a car accident. They had no children. Since that unfortunate event, Rose has been with us for dinner almost every night and on weekends. She goes with us on vacations and to social events to which she is not invited, but my wife gets her included. I do not dislike my sister-in-law, but I am tired of having her around.

My wife knows how I feel, but she says Rose needs her now and she can't let her down. When I suggested that she (my wife) talk to a counselor about this unusual attachment, she flatly refused and called me crazy. Last night, I told her I was seriously considering divorce because of her sister's constant presence. She slammed the bedroom door in my face. I slept on the couch.

Am I selfish, as my wife claims? I cannot bear the thought of living like this for the rest of my life. Please advise.

—Excess Baggage in N.C.

Dear E.B.: Your wife's devotion to her sister is admirable, but when it begins to threaten her marriage and she refuses to do anything about it, the situation requires a closer look.

Now is the time to find out if your wife prefers her sister's company to yours. I suggest that the two of you make an appointment with a marriage counselor and determine if your marriage is worth saving. If your wife refuses to go, go yourself and get some professional advice.

Dear Ann Landers: I am married to a kind, considerate, thoughtful man. It's the second marriage for both "Ben" and me. We are in our 50s.

Ben's children are in their 20s. He has given them cars and paid their golf fees, and he continues to hand over spending money and buy them luxuries. Nobody works. They are all in college (for which their father pays, of course).

When I point out that his kids are taking advantage of him, Ben becomes sullen and uncommunicative. Our marriage would be perfect if it weren't for this problem. What should I do?

—Clear View

Dear Clear: Lay off. Your husband knows you are right, but he can't help himself. His relationship with his children was established before he met you.

The principal reason for the failure of second marriages is kids. So watch it, dear, lest you become a statistic.

Dear Ann Landers: My family situation is unbearable. My 15-year-old stepdaughter, "Lottie," has been living with my husband and me for 18 months. She left her mother's house by mutual agreement because she could not get along with her mother's live-in boyfriend. Before this, she used to visit us twice a month, and to be perfectly honest, I did not look forward to seeing her.

I cannot say anything good about having this girl around. She is rude and sneaky, has flunked several classes and has no interest in school. Her friends slink in and out of our home and are an unwholesome-looking lot. I have found evidence of pot smoking. To put it bluntly, I am fed up to the teeth with this girl and the way she has disrupted our lives.

My husband's head is buried in the sand. He says, "She is just experimenting. It's a stage she is going through. She only yells at us to show off to her friends." Ann, I wasn't raised this way. I barely speak to Lottie, and I am losing respect for my husband. I have tried therapy, but neither my husband nor Lottie will go.

I think Lottie should go back to her mother. I don't want to break up my family, but I can no longer tolerate this girl's daily tirades. Our home is like a war zone.

I'm sure Lottie doesn't want to leave. She has her daddy conned. My husband says his ex-wife is not fit to raise their daughter. Where do I go from here?

—Losing It Fast

Dear Losing It: Lottie is clearly in charge, and this has got to stop. You must insist on family counseling, which means all three of you. Believe it or not, the girl wants an authority figure to take control.

I urge you to deep-six the therapist you were seeing. It sounds like he or she was zero effective. Good luck.

Dear Ann Landers: My new husband, "Dave," and my 21-year-old daughter, "Barbara," have become buddies. I think the way they dress around the house is entirely too suggestive. Dave wanders around in his jockey shorts, just like he did when he lived alone. At night, Barbara will flounce around in the living room, or even in our bedroom, wearing only a towel or an oversized T-shirt and perfume. I've voiced my disapproval, but neither sees anything wrong. Barbara tells me she sees more at her coed college dormitory. Dave says, "I'm wearing the same thing people wear at the beach."

Maybe I'm prudish, but their underwear is *not* swimwear. Almost everything is visible in these outfits. My first husband never left the bedroom unless he was fully dressed. Shouldn't there be even more modesty between Barbara and her stepfather?

—Worried in New Jersey

Dear Worried: Barbara sounds like a seductive little wench, and your husband has popcorn where his brains belong. Tell your daughter to knock off the striptease, and let your husband know you will not tolerate any more semi-nudity.

Dear Ann Landers: My wife and I have been married for 16 years. In that time, I have watched her children from a previous marriage grow to adulthood. I have been present at the births of 10 grandchildren.

Here's my problem. I love my wife's children dearly, and I tell them so frequently. However, I have yet to witness any show of affection from any of them. Instead, I get subtle reminders that I am not, after all, their real father. It has reached the point where I wish no further contact. My heart has been broken too many times. My wife says I am being silly. What do you think?

—Stepped-on Dad in Calif.

Dear Dad: Your wife knows you better than I do, so I would accept her assessment.

Cool it, Dad. Apparently, your stepchildren are uptight and unable to show affection. I feel sorry for them. They will miss so much joy in life. I suggest that you settle for what there is and don't push for more.

Dear Ann Landers: With the ever-increasing number of blended families, some of your readers may have the same problem I've been experiencing: how to address new relatives other than by first name.

I have invented some words that could be incorporated into the language. They may take a little getting used to, but after a while, they will come naturally. This is what I propose:

Stepson—ston
Stepdaughter—staughter
Stepfather—stather or stad

Stepmother—stother or stom
Stepgrandfather—stampa
Stepgrandmother—stamma
Stepbrother—strother (or stro if you are close)
Stepsister—stister or stis
Stepcousin—stousin (or stuz if you are close)
Stepaunt—staunt
Stepuncle—stuncle

What do you think about this, Ann? Once you get the hang of it, it could be terrific.

—Ray C., Tulsa

Dear Ray: I am aware that new words are added to the language on a regular basis, but somehow, staughter and stampa don't quite do it for me. As for stuncle, I wouldn't touch that one.

Just because the idea didn't grab me, Ray, doesn't mean that some of my readers won't warm up to it. So, on behalf of those who want to try it out, I thank you.

Dear Ann Landers: Here's a new one for you. First, let me say I am divorced and the father of three wonderful children. I love them very much, and I try to spend as much time with them as possible. At present, I am with them about three days a week.

Recently, my ex-wife asked that my present wife, "Babette," watch the children every day after school while she works. This means until 6:30 in the evening. It seemed like a great idea to me since the children get along very well with Babette, and our home is a pleasant and familiar place to them.

The problem is that Babette believes that she should be paid the same as any other child-care provider because she is performing a service for which my former wife has paid others in the past.

My former wife feels that Babette is obligated to watch the children for free because they are, after all, my children and she is now my wife.

Babette says it's not so much the money but the idea that my ex-wife is just trying to take advantage of her.

I love my children and am in the middle of a battle between these two women who are not crazy about each other to begin with. Do you have a solution?

—Between a Rock and a Boulder in Colorado

Dear Rock or Boulder, whichever seems more comfortable: I can understand Babette's resentment because she feels your ex-wife is taking advantage of her. However, in my opinion, she should be willing to take care of the children without being paid. After all, they are your kids, and she is their stepmother, not just a person sent by an employment agency.

I suspect this may be Babette's way of sticking it to your first wife. Not only is her behavior ungenerous, but if she loves you, such mean-spiritedness will not do much to enhance the relationship. Is there an unbiased third party who can talk to Babette?

When I printed that letter, I had no idea it would create such an uproar. Stepmothers and ex-wives all over the country wrote to let me know how they felt. A radio talk-show host did an entire show around this column. Here's the follow-up I did on it:

Dear Ann Landers: I couldn't believe your answer to "Between a Rock and a Boulder in Colorado." The writer wanted to know if it was fair to ask his wife, "Babette," to take care of his children from a previous marriage. Babette said OK, but she wanted to get paid. The ex-wife insisted she should do it for free. You agreed.

Taking care of three children every day from 3:30 through dinner is a huge responsibility. You said asking to get paid might be Babette's way of sticking it to the ex-wife. I believe it's the other way around. It's the ex-wife's way of sticking it to Babette. It looks to me like the ex is looking for free child care. And *you* fell for it. Dumb-dee dumb dumb.
—Been There in Auburn, Ky.

Dear Been There: You would not believe the avalanche of mail I received on this subject. Keep reading:

Dear Ann: You blew it. Would you ask your mother, father, sister or brother to watch your three kids on a regular basis, 15 hours a week, without offering to pay them? And if Babette *does* resent this, as she rightfully should, how will she treat these kids? Don't print my name, please. I prefer to be
—Anonymous in Colorado

The most spirited responses came from the listeners of a Los Angeles–based radio call-in show hosted by Dr. Laura Schlessinger. Dr. Laura sent me dozens of responses. Here's a sampling:

From Karen in Calif.: Ann Landers is *wrong*. Time is money. You get nothing for nothing these days. Babette should be paid for watching those kids.

XYZ: Ann is right. The second wife should *not* be paid. If Babette has no interest in children, she should not have married a man who has three.

Gina D.: I thought slavery was abolished in 1863, or did the Emancipation Proclamation not include wives? Babette should be paid in cold, hard cash.

Erica: You don't pay parents for watching their own children. This is the family Babette became a part of when she married. She is a step-mother, not a baby-sitter. Blood is thicker than water.

Eileen P.: My vote is against Ann and for Babette. Why doesn't the father change *his* work hours so he can do some baby-sitting? After all, they are *his* kids, not Babette's.

Mary D.: I agree with Ann. How are these kids going to feel when they learn that Babette is being paid to take care of them? Has anyone thought of that?

Hershey, Pa.: Maybe the husband and the ex-wife would consider deducting the cost of child care from the support payments. That way, everybody gets a break.

Kimberly in San Diego: All three are idiots—Babette, her husband and the ex-wife. No one seems to want the kids. They are more concerned with money. Too bad. I feel sorry for those children.

Rancho Santa Margarita, Calif.: It would be nice for the kids, and good for the marriage, if Babette took care of the kids, but she is not *obligated* to do so. To ask to be paid is downright tacky. The ideal solution would be as follows: "Pay" Babette by putting money into the kids' college funds. It would be the same as outright payment but less crass, plus, the kids wouldn't have to know that Babette was paid to be with them.

So, dear readers, you've just read an ounce of responses off a glacier. Make up your own minds. I'm sticking to my original response. Babette should *not* be paid.

2

Columns from the Bedroom

The Other Woman
Judith Viorst

The other woman
Never smells of Ajax or Spaghetti-O.
And was bored with Bob Dylan
A year before we had heard of him.
And is a good sport about things like flat tires and no hot water.
Because it's easier to be a good sport
When you're not married.

The other woman
Never has tired blood.
And can name the best hotels in Acapulco
As readily as we can name detergents.
And wears a chiffon peignoir instead of a corduroy bathrobe.
Because it's easier to try harder
When you're not married.

The other woman
Never has to look at Secret Squirrel.
And spends her money on fun furs
While we are spending ours on obstetricians.
And can make a husband feel that he is wanted.
Because it's easier to want a husband
When you're not married.

After that poem appeared, I received this in the mail:

> I am the Other Woman.
> I also smell of Ajax, ammonia and Kitty Litter.
> I wasn't bored with Bobby Dylan.
> I hadn't heard of him, either.
> I am a good sport about flat tires. I call AAA. I'm expected to be
>   a good sport.
> Because I'm "still looking."
> The best hotels in Acapulco are listed in my guidebook.
> I wear a terrycloth bathrobe.
> I've never owned a peignoir.
> I'm not trying harder.
> Why should I? I'm not married.
> I spend money on real fur—a couple of purring cats.
> I have also spent money on obstetricians—two children I raised
>   alone.
> Why do I make your husband feel wanted?
> I can't answer that. I can only ask—
> Were things so perfect before I came along?

When it comes to cheating, I have readers on every side of the issue. Look at this:

Dear Ann Landers: Why has no one described the Other Man? He is everywhere. Places you'd never suspect. I know him well. My wife knows him even better.

The other man is never seen in the morning unshaven, with hair disheveled, in a ratty bathrobe, groping for his glasses. He appears in the morning (at work) or in the evening at a favorite rendezvous, looking perfectly groomed and very appealing.

The Other Man is not puttering around the house in torn trousers and an old shirt, trying to fix the plumbing or a garage door or a leak in the roof. No hint of perspiration from mowing the lawn or washing the car. He smells of cologne, toothpaste and aftershave.

The Other Man is always in a good mood. When he is with you, he is out for a good time. He leaves his worries at home.

The Other Man invariably has a wife who has back trouble or is emotionally disturbed, frigid and a terrible nag. She doesn't understand him and talks of nothing but bills, unmanageable kids, bothersome relatives and things that are depressing. But he can't leave her to marry you—for a while—because of financial circumstances, the children, his aging mother, his religion or his boss. His list of excuses is endless.

The Other Man doesn't care that he has caused his wife untold hours of anguish, that she has become a guilt-ridden nervous wreck, confused and unsure of herself. He doesn't give a thought to the fact that his children have heard rumors or sense something is terribly wrong in the family. He is having a great big round ball—concerned only with himself, his pleasure and his ego, in spite of what he has led his playmate to believe. Do you know him? Look again.

—Watching

Dear Watching: Thank you for an insightful description. It's bound to hit a lot of people where they live—or at least visit.

Dear Ann Landers: You have printed several letters over the last few years to the Other Woman. How about one to the Other Man? Here it is:

Hello there, sucker.

You fell in love with my wife, which is OK with me. I can understand how it happened because 29 years ago I fell in love with her, too.

Here are a few things you ought to know if your intentions are serious:

That smile of hers that you think is so wonderful cost me $3,000 plus $75 every two months for maintenance.

The upkeep on her hair is $300 a month. If she wants to change the color, add another $75. I'm sure you enjoy dancing with her, but be prepared for bills from her chiropractor ($35 a visit, twice a month), and her podiatrist costs about the same.

She's a great little dresser, isn't she? Well, the bills from the shops run about $1,500 a month. This doesn't include shoes. (She and Imelda Marcos have a lot in common.)

She complained because I was never home, and she had a right to. But I was working two jobs six days a week to keep her in the style to which she had become accustomed.

I'm not bitter, although I did get used to her after 29 years. Actually, I owe you a lot. When she dumped me, I quit my second job, and life is a lot easier.

One more thing: About that trip you two took to watch the whales off Martha's Vineyard—I wrote the credit card company and told them I'm not paying for it because I wasn't there.

—Color Me Gone in Hackensack

Dear Hack: Feel better after unburdening yourself? I hope so.

Dear Ann Landers: This letter is from the Other Man. I am addressing my remarks to the husband of the woman I love. The relationship I enjoy with your wife is the most precious thing in my life. She is a gem. But somehow you never noticed. How long did you think you could ignore her before she felt an emptiness in her life and a need to do something about it?

You claim to be a "family man," but everything else comes first—business is at the top of your list. How you love to travel to meetings and conferences. Then there's golf and hunting with the boys. (Good for business.)

She is the one who cooks dinners for your relatives and chauffeurs the kids to all their activities, takes them to the emergency room in the middle of the night and listens to them when they have problems.

You are never around during a crisis. Your timing is perfect.

The real trouble started when you couldn't find time to listen when she wanted to tell you how unhappy she was. It was then that she came to me—a nervous wreck with nobody to talk to.

Our friendship began because I listened. Within six months, we were in love. I would marry her in a minute, but she says she just couldn't do that to her family. It would be too disruptive, too painful to too many people. So, we keep stealing golden moments, and I am grateful for every one.

I showed her this letter, and she said, "Mail it if you want to. He'll never recognize himself. He thinks he's perfect." So, here it is. Meanwhile, I hope you never wake up, you idiot.

—Half a Loaf in Greenwich

Dear Half a Loaf: Maybe he won't wake up, but I wouldn't be surprised if a few thousand husbands around the globe felt a twinge of discomfort when they read your letter. You may have done more good today than you know, buddy.

In 1991, I printed a letter that brought in so much mail that I devoted two columns to it. The original letter was from "Florida Wreck," whose husband of 17 years fell in love with an old flame at his high school reunion and ran off with her. Here's what my readers had to say about that:

Dear Ann Landers: I couldn't sleep tonight if I didn't tell you what was on my mind after reading the letter from "Florida Wreck."

My own experience has a similar ring. My husband left me after 17 years of marriage for a girl who was *still* in high school. He took to wearing her school letterman's jacket and started behaving like a teenager.

I tried to be patient, thinking if I gave it time, he would see how foolish he was. Well, it didn't work out that way. He became nuttier and nuttier, and finally when he asked for a divorce, I was ready to give him one.

It has taken me five years to heal, but I know now when the right man comes along I will be free of excess baggage and ready to make a new life for myself. If I can do it, "Florida Wreck" can, too.

—Wendy in Pomona

Dear Ann Landers: I'm an American living in Taipei, Taiwan. I read your column in the *China Post.*

I hope "Florida Wreck" sees this because at age 38, I was hit with the identical problem. The only difference is that it was my wife who went back home to attend her 20th reunion and during that weekend decided that she was in love with a guy she used to go with. I couldn't believe it when she came home and asked for a divorce.

After three weeks of pleading, I agreed to the divorce if she would give me sole custody of our two children. She agreed. Seven months later, she was back home, on her knees. The guy had decided to stay with his wife and family. In the meantime, I had met a beautiful young woman who loves my children and adores me. We are going to be married in October.

—A True Fan

Dear Ann Landers: I want to help "Florida Wreck" by telling her what happened in our family. It should give her strength and hope. My father is now going through his fourth divorce. He left my mother for his secretary. He then left the secretary for the woman who sold him their condo. That marriage lasted less than three weeks when he fell in love with the assistant to the doctor who was giving him a hair transplant. He is divorcing her to marry his aerobics instructor. His former wives have formed a "support group" to help each other. I can truthfully say they are all in better shape emotionally than he is. Sometimes it takes some real knocks to put life in the proper perspective. "Florida" could emerge stronger and wiser from the wreckage.

—Toronto

Nowadays, we don't need to be face-to-face to have affairs of the heart—we can have affairs via machine.

Dear Ann Landers: Please warn your readers that there is an insidious monster about to pounce on the American people. It will destroy more marriages and lives than anything the world has ever known.

Thousands of lonely souls, both men and women and even some children, are seeking friendship by talking via computer. My wife and I bought modems last spring. "Ellen," an efficient typist, logged onto the computer frequently and was gung-ho for it. I was less interested.

Ellen became friendly with a group of people on a computer bulletin board and began exchanging e-mail. She was particularly chummy with one man. They exchanged home phone numbers and began calling each other at four o'clock in the morning.

When the computer junkies planned a trip to Nevada, I went with Ellen. While I was losing money at the casino, Ellen was making love to her on-line Romeo in his hotel room.

When we returned home, my wife packed her clothes and her laptop computer and left me for this man. I have spoken with her since and begged her to come home, but she refuses. We have been married 17 years.

Let this be a warning to all married couples who intend to buy a computer with a modem. Be sure to take good care of your spouse's physical needs before, during and after the purchase.

—Outmaneuvered in Arizona

Dear Arizona: I am certain computers have fostered some romances that led to the altar. Your relationship, however, must have been quite fragile. To blame an electronic device for breaking up a marriage is a bit of a reach.

Your last sentence identifies the real culprit. I hope Ellen comes home and gives you another chance. You sound as if you've learned your lesson.

Dear Ann Landers: I was stopped cold by that letter from "Out-maneuvered in Arizona," whose wife left him for a computer lover. My son's wife just left him for her cybersex lover. Maybe she wasn't very happy before, but it's a tragedy when a woman walks out on her husband and three small children for a stranger. There's going to be a lot more of this sort of thing, Ann. Just you wait and see.

—Rochester, Minn.

Dear Minn.: I don't need to wait. I am seeing it right now, and it's sad. Want to look over my shoulder?

From Sacramento: My husband (I'll call him Romeo) met Juliet on a chat line. The next thing I knew, he was on his way to Las Vegas for a little romp with his new on-line friend. Before he left, he went into hock for a new Mustang so he could show off.

Chico, Calif.: The Internet can be addictive. It also can be danger-ous and destructive. People suddenly become whoever they wish to be, hiding behind a piece of electronic equipment. I met three men on the Internet, and each one turned out to be a phony.

Tulsa, Okla.: My wife became acquainted with a man on the East Coast via her computer. It was just "fun" at first, but when she began to stay up until 3 a.m. sending and receiving messages, I knew our mar-riage of several years was in trouble.

Chicago: I discovered my husband's secret life when I decided to check out some of the numbers on his Internet bill. Maybe I'm just an old-fashioned, low-tech girl in a crazy, juiced-up high-tech world, but I told him flat out to knock off the fun with strangers in cyberspace or I was walking. He promised to quit the on-line flirting, but I'm still going to keep my ears and eyes open.

Juneau: Computer chat lines can become every bit as addictive as co-caine. I have been hooked on both, and it was easier to get off coke. I left my wife and family for my cyber-vamp, and within three months I discovered she was a nut who had broken up three marriages before she almost wrecked mine. I'm back home now, in counseling, and thank God my wife was able to forgive me.

It appears that the electronic geniuses have hatched a potential monster. Those who are currently flirting on the Internet should be aware that it can lead to serious long-term trouble.

It has been said that sex takes up less time and causes more trouble than any other single activity. My mail supports this allegation.

Curiosity on the subject abounds. Ignorance is rampant. Every day at least a dozen readers want to know, "What is normal bedroom behavior?"

I must answer that question with yet another question: "Who gets to decide what is 'normal'?" Please continue to read with an open mind.

Dear Ann Landers: When you read my problem, you'll know why I can't ask anyone else.

I've been going with this perfectly lovely woman who is 27 years old, teaches high school English and sings in the church choir. After several months of courting, we decided to have sex. She informed me that in order for her to have complete satisfaction, I must wear my motorcycle helmet to bed.

I did as she suggested, but it was quite uncomfortable for me. She, however, had a great time.

Just how kinky is this? I hope to marry the woman and would not like to carry on this way forever. Can you help me?

—Mr. D. in Nevada

Dear Mr. D.: I'd say it is a bit weird but no crazier than some of the other stuff that shows up in the daily mail. If this pleases your lady, continue for a while, then suggest that *she* wear the motorcycle helmet. Perhaps when she discovers how uncomfortable it is, she will give up on the idea.

Dear Ann Landers: I'm sure your column has done a lot of good and that you have helped thousands of readers over the years, but I wonder if you realize the harm you do when you print letters that give people crazy ideas. For example: that letter from the man whose sweetheart asked him to wear a motorcycle helmet to bed to "heighten the excitement."

My husband saw that letter and decided it would be a great turn-on if I put on my ice skates before retiring last night. (I was a professional skater 20 years ago when we met.) I told him he was out of his mind, but he kept nagging and begging until finally I gave in. Not only did my skates rip the bed sheet and the mattress, Ann, but I gave my husband a nine-inch gash on his leg. I had to drive him to the emergency room for stitches at 11:30 at night. We were ashamed to tell the doctor how it happened.

So please be aware when you print some of those letters that there are an awful lot of nuts out there. Sorry to admit that my husband was one of them.

—Past Revisited in Palm Springs

Dear Palm Springs: Sorry about the leg wound. I trust, however, that my column does more good than harm or I would not have lasted this long.

Dear Ann Landers: I would like to know how you and your readers feel about couples showering together. Is there a lot of this going on?

After 20 years of a fairly good marriage, showering together has become a major bone of contention. My husband watches more TV than I do. He tells me that he has seen dozens of couples in the shower together and they seem to be having a wonderful time. "Henry" thinks I am completely out of sync, because the few times we tried showering together, I didn't care for it at all.

We have a standard-size tub with a shower. There is no room for anything larger. We are both average-size people. When Henry and I shower together, he gets the warm water and I get the damp steam. Frankly, I do not think there is anything sexy about this sort of togetherness.

I have always looked forward to a warm bath as a wonderful opportunity to relax at the end of a hectic day. I love the solitude and don't need any company when I'm in the tub. Also, showers wreck my hair. Am I alone in this? And please, Ann, one more thing: I already changed Henry's name, so don't change it to something else or you just might hit his real name, and he would kill me.

—All Wet in Binghamton, N.Y.

Dear Wet: I'm a tub girl myself. In fact, it's one of my favorite places to read the mail.

If Henry enjoys showering with you, be a good sport and go along with it. You can take a bath later. The least Henry can do, however, is change places once in a while so you get the hot water and he gets the steam.

How about it, readers? If you've tried it, did you like it? If not, why not?

Dear Ann Landers: When you asked your readers how they felt about showering together, I knew I had to write.

My wife and I (married 27 years) have enjoyed showering together since our honeymoon, which is when we first tried it. But please tell your readers the setting must be exactly right. By mutual agreement, there must be no answering of the phone or doorbell. The lights must be off, and a candle on the sink should supply the only light.

Showering together can be an erotic and soul-satisfying experience, guaranteed to relieve tension, mend any quarrel and diffuse anger. No way could this be done in a bathtub. Leave my name out if you print my letter. I'm well-known in this city.

—Seattle

Dear Seattle: I'm glad joint showering works so well for you and your wife. Not everyone shares your enthusiasm. Read on:

From Vancouver, British Columbia: You sure know how to make trouble, Ann. When my husband, who always reads your column, saw the letter about couples showering together, he said, "Let's try it tonight, hon." The only time I have to myself is when I can get in a hot tub, soak to my heart's content and escape from the kids. Well, the big baboon insisted I try the shower, so I did. It didn't do a thing for me, but he is crazy about it. There goes my relaxation.

Port Huron, Mich.: My husband weighs more than 300 pounds, and I'm a good 220 plus. There is no way we could both fit into the tub together, so we take showers when the yearning for water-soaked togetherness takes over. My husband enjoys it more than I do. In fact, I'm happy when the hot water gives out. Last night he told me he is going to buy me a larger water heater for my birthday. Needless to say, I am thrilled. (In a pig's eye.)

Fort Lauderdale: That column about couples showering together brought back a terrifying memory. The first time my husband got into the shower with me, I was a bride. My back was to the door, and I didn't hear him enter the bathroom. I thought he was a burglar, screamed and fainted in his arms. I've hated showers ever since.

Morristown, N.J.: My husband is 6 feet 4 inches. I am 5 feet 11 inches. We can't fit into the tub together because our legs are too long. When we take trips and stay in hotels, we always ask for a room with a large tub. They look at us as if we are nuts. If anyone in your reading audience wants to know where the largest bathtubs in the United States and Canada are located, we can tell them.

Wausau, Wis.: I would like to give some guidance to the woman who complained that her man got all the hot water and she got the steam. Get a handheld shower nozzle. We installed ours ourselves. If you are a klutz, a plumber can do it in 10 minutes. And if you're worried about your hair, buy a shower cap, lady.

Right after I printed those letters about couples showering and bathing together, it seemed as if the readers wanted to write about nothing else. Here's what followed:

From Chicago: That kinky idiot who wants his wife to shower with him is a perfect example of what's wrong in our society. Every semblance of privacy has been stripped away from women. I am tired of sick people who are obsessed with sex. No wonder the world has become a sewer.

Longview, Wash.: My grandparents are of Japanese descent. They used to tell us about the family baths in their homeland where discussions were held on every conceivable subject and three generations had a wonderful time. Such a thing would be impossible today. Maybe that's what's wrong with the world.

Kalamazoo, Mich.: I married a lovely guy who treats me beautifully, caters to my needs and is really a love. But he's a bit of a mama's boy, which I knew from the day I met him. On our honeymoon, he suggested that we bathe together. It sounded like a fun idea, so I said, "OK," climbed in first and got the bubbles going. Lo and behold, here he comes with his rubber duck! I had to bite my lip to keep from laughing. We've been married many years and are extremely happy. He's an executive in a big company and travels for his firm. That rubber duck goes everywhere with him, and I've never said a word. Obviously it's linked to his childhood and gives him a feeling of security, which is just fine with me.

Morristown, N.J.: When my husband and I built our home six years ago, he said I could do it any way I wanted but he would like to design the bathroom. Guess what he told the architect? "I want a great big shower stall in the master bath—big enough for two, with six shower heads!" At first I thought he was crazy, but later I began to see the wisdom in it. Whenever we have a little spat, we make up in the shower. It's better than marriage counseling.

Has your sex life gone from wow to pfftt? If so, don't be depressed. You are not alone.

Back in November of 1988, I asked my readers, "Has your sex life gone downhill after marriage? If so, why?"

The results of my survey said more about the state of marriage than you may want to know.

I received 141,210 responses. They came from every state in the union and every province in Canada. Letters and postcards arrived from Tokyo, Bangkok, Korea, Mexico, Germany, Bermuda, the Virgin Islands, Puerto Rico, Panama, South Africa, Guam and Taiwan. It's the same story the world over.

More males responded than females (52 percent). The ages ranged from 17 to 93. I received 27 responses from homosexuals. There were letters in French and Spanish. A reader from Brooklyn wrote in Yiddish. Obviously I hit a raw nerve.

The verdict was clear. Eighty-two percent said sex after marriage was less exciting. The adjectives that turned up most frequently were: boring, dull, monotonous and routine. The message came from both men and women. The percentage of disenchanted females was almost identical to the male vote.

Although I asked for postcards, more than half of the faithful wrote letters. One from Bangor, Maine, was 23 pages long. A woman from El Dorado, Kan., apologized: "I know you asked for postcards, Ann, but this is a small town, and a lot of folks know my handwriting."

Why the decline in sexual enjoyment after marriage? There was a cafeteria of reasons. Take your choice. A great number of men echoed the resentment of a 42-year-old from Minneapolis. He wrote: "Good sex is the bait women use to hook men. Once they land the sucker, they don't want to be bothered. Suddenly he's an animal."

A man from Spokane said sex went downhill when he and his wife married and made love in bed. "It was much better in the car," he said.

Many women who said their sex lives were better before marriage cited the same reason as this 37-year-old woman from Chicago: "It's a matter of energy. It just isn't possible to be the Playgirl of the Month after shagging two preschoolers and a hyperactive 7-year-old all day. I hate to blame it on the kids, but those are the facts, Ann."

A woman from Sault Ste. Marie, Mich., sent me before and after (marriage) photos of her husband. It was apparent that he had gained a great deal of weight. "He couldn't help losing his hair," she wrote, "but nobody needs six bottles of beer a night and second helpings of everything. That belly of his killed our sex life."

Poor hygiene was mentioned in many downhill marriages. A 44-year-old woman from New Orleans wrote, "My old man takes two baths a year—spring and fall. The smell of soap would be a real turn-on."

A man from Boise crowed: "Our sex life is fantastic. We never married, but we have been together 25 years. I believe marriage ruins sex, and so does my sweetie. Why? Because after you get what you want, the challenge and excitement are gone. We are taking no chances."

I found the results of the survey disturbing. These people said more than they realized. Those who were unfulfilled described something beyond the bedroom scene. They were talking about the state of their marriages.

Dear Ann Landers: You printed a letter from a woman who had showered, brushed her hair, put on a pretty nightie, dabbed perfume all over and waited in vain for her husband to make a move. When he did nothing, she said, "It was humiliating for me to ask him to make love to me, but I did. He told me he was tired and rolled over and went to sleep."

I have a suggestion for that woman and all others with the same problem. When a man says he is too tired, be sympathetic. Say, "I know you are, dear. Lie on your stomach and let me give you a nice relaxing massage . . ." Get some cream or lotion—any kind will do—and give him a wonderfully loving back rub, working your fingers up and down his spine, onto his shoulders and neck, using a circular motion. The quality and variety of the massage is limited only by your imagination. Chances are very good that the back rub will make him realize he wasn't as tired as he thought.

A woman who wants love sometimes needs to be aggressive. She should not wait until her husband comes to her. So, I say to you wives out there, it is high time you got busy and made an effort to get what you want, need and is rightfully yours.

—Successful in Ore.

Dear Ore.: Hurray for letting married women know that physical intimacy from a spouse is not a privilege, it's an entitlement. I heartily recommend your approach.

A woman once wrote and asked me, "What can I do about a man who just rolls over and goes to sleep?" I told her, "Wake him up. If he growls, 'Can't you see I'm sleeping?' respond with, 'Yes, dear, but you're such a marvelous lover, and I really do need you.' Almost any man will respond if you turn on the heat."

In 1966, I printed two letters from businessmen who were too tired for sex. They certainly stirred up a hornet's nest.

Dear Ann Landers: I've had it to here with wives who complain their husbands are dead (or half dead) sexually and that they feel unwomanly and unloved. Why don't these whining females stop thinking about how *they* feel and give some thought to how their husbands feel?

The problem of the "neglected" wife is more prevalent among people in the higher income brackets. Why? Because the greater the economic pressure, the less energy a man has left for romance.

The 8-to-5'er leaves his troubles at the office or at the garage or the store. But the aggressive young guy who is clawing his way up is a different story. He has to have eyes in the back of his head to see who is trying to knife him. Every decision must be right because one wrong move could land him out on the street. Organizational footwork can leave a guy completely drained.

So what happens? He comes home exhausted, and his wife considers it a personal insult if he doesn't become instantly aroused at the sight of her bending over the kitchen stove.

If she should suggest something, and he says he's too tired, she locks herself in the bathroom and cries for hours. She is positive (a) he no longer loves her, (b) her life as a woman is finished, (c) he has another dame someplace. It has always struck me as interesting that a woman has the born right to be too tired, but a man—*never!*

So, what happens to the husband who struggles to get ahead and isn't sure he's making it? His wife lets him know he isn't making it at home either, and he becomes doubly depressed. More conflict, more guilt, more anxiety—and finally total incapacitation.

You won't print this letter because you always take the woman's side, but I feel better for having written it. Now you can throw it on the floor, babe. Thanks.

—Wall Street Warrior

Dear Warrior: Your letter was too good for the floor. You make sense, boy. Now, read on:

Dear Ann Landers: Do you know why so many women complain about insufficient physical attention from their husbands? Well, I can tell you. It's because their timing is lousy, that's why.

Most men come home from work about 6 p.m., exhausted from fighting with employees, associates, bosses and the worst kooks of all—customers. The minute he hits the door, the kids are on him. Gloria needs a new dress for a party. Junior wants an electric guitar. All through dinner, the kids are campaigning and the little woman is in there backing up the kids.

When dinner is over, the wife starts on what *she* needs. "The washer broke down today. It'll cost so much to get it fixed we really ought to buy a new one." "My mother needs an operation. You know who is going to have to pay for it." "The living room rug is so shabby I'm ashamed to have people in. I saw a real bargain advertised in the paper. . . ." All this chatter goes on and on until the lights go out. And then—zowie! In two seconds, the husband is supposed to turn into a sex maniac.

This has happened so many times at our house that I'm sure it happens in thousands of other houses. So stop sending people to doctors, Ann. Tell the wives to improve their timing and they won't be so frustrated.

—Veteran of Domestic Wars

Dear Vet: You and Warrior must be reading each other's mail. And thanks to you both for your contribution to my mail today.

Dear Ann: What a rotten trick you pulled on every love-starved wife in America. I wonder if you know how much trouble you caused. My Lochinvar has been giving me the old routine: "I'm dead tired beating my brains out making a living for you and the kids—blah blah blah." I've been saying it is not normal for a man who is 38 years old to be too tired for love no matter how hard he works at his job. Then, you come along with your lousy column and take *his* side. He has talked of nothing else for two days. Why don't you retire?

—Mad

Dear Ann: I wish I could trade places with Wall Street Warrior's wife. She doesn't know how lucky she is. My husband thinks sex is the answer to everything—tension, sleeplessness, worry, headache. Where he got this crazy idea, I'll never know, but it has been the bane of my existence for 15 years. I wonder if I'm the only woman in the world who is married to such a nut. Ask around, will you?

—Paducah Shimmy Queen

Dear Ann: Please tell "Warrior" he is an ignorant boob. When will men learn that sex and love are not the same thing? A simple "I love you," a warm caress or a sweet kiss on the cheek would keep most hardworking, floor-scrubbing, baby-tending wives happy for a week. In fact, a little affection *without* sex as the objective would be darned welcome. Women get tired, too, you know.

—Madeline

Dear Ann: "Veteran" had a lot to say about women, most of it rubbish. Funny how some men can be so smart when it comes to business and so stupid when it comes to the female psyche. Veteran complained because his wife's timing was poor. Even the dumbest wife knows that the only way to get anything extra out of a husband is to nail him when he feels romantic. Any wife who tries to get a new vacuum sweeper or a new rug out of the old man by explaining that she *needs* one is out of her mind.

—Been There and Back

Dear Ann: Why don't men wise up? The reason women attach so much importance to sex is because it's the only method of communication open to us. Men don't talk anymore. They turn on the TV or bury their noses in the paper or just fall asleep. The only way a wife can win the battle for her husband's attention is to use her strongest weapon.

—Chickadee

Dear Ann Landers: Where do all the tired men come from? When I was single, I never ran into a man who was too tired for anything. What is there about the marriage ceremony that creates such exhaustion? If you know, will you please let me in on it?

—Lollypop

Here is the best and most incisive response I had. It's for all Wall Street Warriors:

Dear Ann Landers: I have been married to a Wall Street Warrior for over 20 years, so I feel qualified to speak about the successful business or professional man who willingly (perhaps eagerly) sacrifices his husband-father role in exchange for the exhilaration and the rewards of the marketplace.

These men would not have it any other way. The excitement of the daily battle on the professional front or the money front is sufficiently ego-warming and stimulating that they don't need anything else to fill their lives.

Because their values are warped (this happened long before marriage), these men lack the true understanding of what a husband-wife relationship ought to be. If his wife becomes cold from waiting, or if a wife resorts to a part-time replacement because she is lonely, the Warrior couldn't care less. He is relieved that he doesn't have to bother with her because he has already discovered younger and more fascinating substitutes in his work, in the cities he visits—on business, of course.

Sex to him has nothing to do with love. He doesn't even try to kid himself, as women often do. Intimacy outside of marriage means fun with no commitment. Moreover, it's a great morale booster for the middle-aged male who wonders if he's losing his punch.

The Warrior lives in a world of work, and he adores it. Even his play must in some way be related to his work. A wife and children do not belong in this world. Anyone who cannot contribute to his battle gains is relegated to the periphery.

No one will ever persuade me that a lack of interest in the marriage bed stems from working too hard. This bit of folklore was invented by a man who must have known better. And anyone who regards this problem as a problem of the rich had better think again. It exists at every economic level. The man who has spent himself elsewhere and is tired when he comes home got that way because he chose to.

After years of loneliness and soul-searching ("Where did I fail?"), I confess that I wish I had married another kind of man. I would gladly forgo my large home, the cars in the garage, my fine furs and jewelry and the club memberships in exchange for a husband who would attend church with his family, show some interest in our children and be available for the little confidences that can make marriage the special relationship that God intended it to be. Just sign me

—Lost: One Home Front; Gained: Much Insight

Husbands could learn a lot from these angry wives who roasted, toasted and broiled their "money-hungry," power-mad, egocentric Wall Street Warriors

for expending their energies on the financial and professional battlefield and leaving nothing for the home front.

Sometimes you have to ask yourself that well-known Ann Landers question: Would your life be better with him or without him?

Dear Ann Landers: Several weeks ago, because neither my husband nor I had been sleeping well in our shared double bed, I moved into the guest room. Since then, he has hinted that he'd like me back in his bed, but I've been ignoring him. After 35 years of marriage, I'm tired of sex and prefer to sleep alone.

Last week my husband told me that if I wasn't willing to be a wife to him in every sense of the word, he was going to leave. This is the same man who told me several years ago that when I'm in his bed I should know what to expect.

I explained, for the 50th time, that I've lost interest in sex because our relationship is meaningless and empty and I no longer love him. He replied: "That's ridiculous. A wife does not have the right to say no unless she has a good reason, and not feeling like it isn't good enough."

He wants me to go for counseling so someone can "help me understand." He says that if I go twice, he will go with me the third time.

Ann, is it wrong for me to want control over my body and refuse to use it as a bargaining chip to keep a man I'm not sure I want? Am I being unreasonable when I refuse to have sex with him just because he's my husband? Please comment.

—Ceiling Zero in Pa.

Dear Zero: There's more trouble here than just your husband's sexual appetite. The real problems between you two are rooted elsewhere, and I suspect they are of long standing.

Your husband sounds like a man who needs to control people. You say you aren't sure you want him. If you do, please tell me what for. Your marriage sounds like a nightmare. Ask yourself: Would your life be better with him or without him? If the answer is with him, get some counseling and hold him to his word to go with you the third time.

Dear Ann Landers: This is in response to "Ceiling Zero," the Pennsylvania woman who did not want to sleep in the same bed with her husband, so she moved into the guest room. (He had told her that if she was in his bed, she should know "what to expect.")

My husband and I have no problem with sexual incompatibility, but we do have a mutually satisfactory sleeping arrangement that Pennsylvania might consider.

For the first few years of our marriage, I slept without covers on 17 inches of a 54-inch double bed. My husband was a restless sleeper and sprawled horizontally across the bed and hogged the blankets.

My solution was to redecorate. I bought two twin beds. They each have their own covers, are made up separately and then pushed together. With one bedspread, it looks like a king-size bed.

Now, after almost 50 years of marriage, we both like our sleeping arrangement and nobody feels exploited. Pennsylvania and her husband seem to be thoroughly confused about sex, sleep, night and bed—things that are not necessarily related.

A sexual act can take place on the kitchen floor or under the dining room table as well as in a number of other locations in the house. It can occur during the day or night. Sleep, however, generally occurs in bed and usually at night.

Your advice to seek counseling is right on target. Sign me
—Sleeping Beautifully in California

Dear Sleeping Beauty: If all the women who wrote to complain about their marital sleeping arrangements were laid end to end, they would be much more comfortable.

Twin beds pushed together, as you described, is the ideal solution for couples who want to be close, but not all night every night.

Dear Ann Landers: I am desperate for advice and hope you can help. My husband no longer finds me sexually attractive. For the past several years, he has made love to me only when I've asked.

I admit that I'm not as beautiful as I once was, but I'm not repulsive either. I have scars from a surgery, which I try to conceal with pretty nightgowns and soft lights, but he said the scars don't bother him.

I've tried discussing the problem, but he insists there's nothing wrong. He says he still loves me and that he finds me attractive. I've begged, remained silent and cried. He told me a while back that a woman shouldn't be aggressive, so I decided to wait for him to make the first move. I'm still waiting. Next month, it will be two years since we made love.

I went to a therapist who said my husband may be suffering from depression or some physical problem. I asked my husband to go for a physical, but he refused. When he saw the bill from the therapist, he became angry with me for discussing our personal life with "a stranger," and he refused to speak to me for three days.

When I look in the mirror, I see a 48-year-old woman who will probably never again have intimate contact with a man. This makes me overwhelmingly sad. I've tried to count my blessings because he is otherwise a good husband and I do love him. Am I being selfish to want more? Do you think I will be able to adjust to abstinence? What should I do?

—Zero Self-Esteem in Chicago

Dear Chicago: First, recognize the fact that it is your husband who has the problem, not you. I can understand why you think he is selfish and inconsiderate, but please be aware that he may be clinically depressed.

Obviously you want to stay married, so I'm going to make a suggestion that will probably bring in a ton of criticism. A woman of 48 is too young to forget about sex. So, if your husband refuses to satisfy you, then satisfy yourself. Since AIDS has appeared on the scene, I am recommending this alternative, which can be a lot better than nothing. I don't want to hear from clergymen telling me it's a sin. Self-gratification is how almost everyone discovers his or her sexual self. There is nothing sinful about it.

Dear Ann Landers: Bless you for having the courage to suggest self-gratification to the 48-year-old woman whose husband hasn't touched her in two years. I am nearly 80 now, and my youth flashed before my eyes when you said you didn't want to hear from any clergy saying it's a sin.

When I was 13, our preacher gave me a book to read. It said boys who masturbate would become bald, diseased and insane, lead a life of crime and end up in hell. When my sexual urges became overpowering, I did indeed indulge in what they called in those days "self-abuse" and suffered tremendous anxiety and wretched feelings of guilt. Every morning, I woke up wondering if I had gone insane during the night or developed some outward sign that would let the world know of my "unpardonable sin."

That terrifying misinformation carried over to my adult life, and it took a long time before I could be a loving husband. Now that I am older and wiser, I see what horrendous damage was done to the youth of our day by hypocritical clergy who surely must have experienced the same urges in their younger days.

Hurray to you for having the courage to say it in print and remove the burden of guilt suffered by millions of healthy, normal people, both young and old.

—Raleigh, N.C.

Dear Raleigh: When I wrote that response, I didn't think it was particularly heroic. It just seemed to be a simple truth that needed to be said. Thousands of readers, however, saw it quite differently. Read on:

From Seattle: Bravo! You are sure to get a ton of mail from the Bible Belt denouncing your advice to the woman whose husband has not approached her sexually for two years. Ignore them, please. Millions of others will applaud your courage. These days, when there is so much sexually transmitted disease, especially AIDS, it's the ideal solution. I could not respect you more.

Denver: I'm a 43-year-old man and have not had sex with my wife for six years.

Since 1982, she has had three miscarriages and a hysterectomy. Sex, to her, is a burden and makes her feel inadequate. "Mary" is a marvelous person, and I love her dearly. We have a fine relationship and get along beautifully. I would never look for a sex partner outside of marriage, and she has told me that counseling is out. So, the answer for me is self-gratification. I'm sure it's the answer for millions of other males, even though they would never admit it.

Fort Dodge, Iowa: *The Mayo Clinic Family Health Book* (1990) backs you all the way. Here's the passage: "Masturbation is normal and healthy. It is a way to release sexual tension, give yourself pleasure, savor sexual fantasies and curb impulses to engage in sexual activity that may not be appropriate. In adulthood, deprivation of regular sexual outlets leads to an increase in masturbation in both sexes. As an occasional sexual variant, it is common in emotionally healthy adults after marriage but is more frequent during periods when the sexual partner is absent or ill. Only when masturbation is routinely preferred to intercourse or so frequent that it becomes an indication of an incapacity for sexual gratification with a partner is it considered to be abnormal in adulthood."

Dear Ann Landers: "Kay" and I have been married for 40 years. We are semiretired and have five grown children who are on their own. We are comfortable financially, active in the community and by all outward appearances happily married.

My problem is that there is no closeness in our relationship—meaning no sex. We went for counseling about this four years ago. Kay admitted that the problem was hers, and after several sessions, things were better. Now we are back to Square One.

We have had no intimate relations for the last 18 months. All my attempts to get close to Kay come to naught. Our religious beliefs do not permit sex outside of marriage, and I am becoming extremely frustrated. Although I've been tempted to have an affair and suffer the consequences, I've decided not to go that route. I'm afraid I couldn't handle the guilt.

My last attempt to get back to a normal relationship was a coupon book for "One little hug," "One little kiss," "One big kiss," "One evening meal at a place of your choice," "One romantic night in front of the fireplace," "One day trip to the place of your choice" and a few others. I gave her this coupon book as a Christmas gift along with several other gifts. I thought it was a unique idea. To date, she hasn't mentioned it.

I don't know what else to do, Ann, and I'm very unhappy with the situation. Any suggestions?

—Married but Lonesome in Wisconsin

Dear M. but L.: You sound like the kind of man a lot of women would kill for. Too bad you're running on empty at home.

Tell Kay you are frustrated and unhappy with the way things are and that you want to go back for more joint counseling. If she refuses, perhaps you should consider a trial separation. Drastic? Yes, but it sounds as if the marriage needs a serious jolt, and this might do it. Good luck.

Once I printed a letter from a woman who signed herself "Content in Montreal." She and her husband were in their late 50s. They played golf, took frequent vacations and counted themselves among the happily married. Twelve years before, they had given up sex.

"Content" said she was sure that they would be considered off if not abnormal, if people knew. She asked how many other married couples enjoyed a full life without sex. I said I'd ask. And I did.

The mail on this subject knocked my office for a loop. More than 35,000 people responded, and guess what? More than 65 percent of the couples older

than 60 who wrote, and 75 percent of the couples older than 70, had very lit-
tle or no sex and didn't miss it. It became clear that men of all ages are far
more interested in sex than women are, and an amazing number of women
in all age groups consider sex a duty or a nuisance. They pretend to enjoy it
and fake orgasms to keep their men happy. Some couples give up on sex in
their early 30s while others still enjoy it in their 80s. But enough from me.
Let's look at the mail.

From Dallas: My wife and I are both 62. We have not had sex in 15 years, and we don't miss it. Instead of sex, we hug, kiss, pat, squeeze, wink and tell jokes. We love each other and get along a lot better than our married children, who are sexaholics. They have asked us not to call them weekends because they don't want their lovemaking interrupted, yet they argue and fight all the time and show no respect for one another.

Los Angeles: I am 89. My wife is 91. We have been married for 65 years. I don't remember when we last had sex, and neither does she. On my 85th birthday, I asked her if she'd like to "celebrate." She said, "What if I get pregnant? What would you do?" I said I'd notify *The Guinness Book of World Records.* She didn't think it was a bit funny, and I haven't brought up the subject since.

Hillsdale, Mich.: I am 60. My husband is 70. I never cared for sex, but my husband, who has been over the hill for at least five years, insists on trying. Sometimes his efforts last an hour and I am exhausted. He thinks you are very smart, Ann. I wish you'd do a column on this and tell the old goats to give up on sex when their batteries have gone dead.

New York: When my husband turned 50, he told me he was impotent and suggested that I find myself a lover. I said I wasn't interested. Two years later, he was hit with a paternity suit. No sex at home doesn't necessarily mean no sex.

Portland, Maine: My husband and I are both 33. After our third child was born, we agreed not to have any more sex. We bought a stationary bicycle for the bedroom, joined a health club and are very happy.

Grand Rapids, Mich.: My wife and I are 50 and more in love now than we were at 22. Our lively sex life adds a magical dimension to our marriage. Physical intimacy is truly a life enhancer. Life without sex would be like spring without flowers.

Houston: My husband and I have been married 26 years. We had three children, wore out a couple of mattresses the first five years and decided we'd had enough. We have Bible study, the Masonic lodge, Eastern Star and crossword puzzles. If you print this letter in your column, please don't publish our name. Our parents are still alive, and they would be mortified. Thank you.

Dear Ann Landers: May I add something to the no-sex-after-marriage flap that drew so many fascinating comments?

Be sure that the fire is out of both furnaces before you decide to give up sex for crossword puzzles, a stationary bike in the bedroom or any of the other dumb substitutes mentioned by one nutty reader. I made the mistake of not doing that, and my husband became involved with a widow who was my best friend. A word to the wise is sufficient.

—Concord, Calif.

Dear Concord: Thanks for the testimonial. I trust that you got back in the ball game and eliminated the substitute hitter.

Sex can break up marriages, but it can also keep them together.

Dear Ann Landers: "Baffled in Tulsa" complained that her husband said the reason he stayed with her all those years was because the sex was so good. My guess is her husband is going through his mid-life crisis and she doesn't know a compliment when she hears one.

When marriages go on the rocks, the rocks are usually in the mattress. The vast majority of husbands want more sex than they get. Studies show that men think about sex an average of 6 times an hour, or about 750 times a week, not counting dreams. Compare that figure with this one: The average married couple has sex 1.5 times a week.

Have you ever heard of a man leaving his wife and family for another woman because she is a great cook or a fabulous housekeeper? Men leave their wives because they want more and better sex. Let's face it, "Tulsa" kept her husband because she is good in bed. She should be proud of herself and appreciate her husband's frank, truthful compliment.

It might be useful for her to seek out and talk to a woman who didn't think sex in marriage was that important and ask that woman how happy she is with her separation, divorce and singleness. "Tulsa" could then ask her how important the other things were on which she worked so hard.

—Baffled in South Bend

Dear Baffled: Thanks for a letter that reflects more truth than poetry. I couldn't have said it better myself.

Dear Ann Landers: Fat is killing our marriage. When D. and I walked down the aisle, he was only a few pounds overweight. I pledged to quit smoking if he would promise to slim down. I have not touched a cigarette since our wedding day. D. has gained 50 pounds. He is a great guy. We enjoy each other, our children and our lives. But those mounds of fat are coming between us. He doesn't understand why our sex life isn't what it used to be. I try, but I'm turned off by those rolls of fat around his middle. Even his kisses leave me cold because his jowls are flabby. I decided a long time ago not to nag since I don't want to hurt him. I fix proper meals and keep no fattening snacks around the house, but I can't padlock his mouth when he walks out the door. Please help me, Ann.

—Lovely Man but Too Much of Him

Dear Lovely: You are wise not to nag. It won't help. Your husband knows he needs to lose weight and probably hates what he has done to himself, but the man has a problem. Your best bet is his doctor. When did your husband last have a checkup? This you can nag him about. It won't hurt his vanity. Make the appointment, and enlist the doctor's help. You'll get it. Obesity is hard on the heart and is one of the major contributing factors to high blood pressure. Tip the doctor off to suggest Weight Watchers or Overeaters Anonymous. Both are excellent, and they're in the phone book. Good luck to you.

Dear Ann Landers: The woman I married two years ago was Rubenesque, or should I say "heavy"? I've always been interested in large women; I'm one of the many males in this country known as "chubby chasers."

"Isabelle" went on a strict diet last year at the instigation of her girlfriends, and she is now as skinny as a rail. I am no longer interested in her sexually.

She knew when I married her that I liked obese women, so I've concluded that she is more interested in pleasing her girlfriends than me.

Isabelle weighed 180 pounds when we married and she looked fabulous. Now she weighs about 105 and looks like she has tuberculosis. I gave her an ultimatum that unless she gains at least 50 pounds I am leaving. She is shocked and angry.

Please put out the word that plump women are very desirable to some men, and if a woman is heavy when she gets married, she should stay that way.

—Love Those Love Handles in Philadelphia

Dear Philadelphia: The only mention of love in your letter appears in the signature, and that reference has more to do with sex.

Full-figured women will be delighted with what you have written, but I wonder about a relationship based solely on weight. It sounds pretty light to me.

Here are a few of the most common questions I've been asked about sex:

Is oral sex wrong . . . or kinky?

No. The desire to have oral sex is an instinctive drive. It is not, as some people believe, deviant behavior learned from pornographic movies and magazines. No sexual act between married adults is kinky provided it is not painful. Open communication, discussion and experimentation will let each couple know what brings the greatest erotic pleasure. If one of you wants oral sex and the other does not, discuss your objections with a therapist who specializes in sex problems. If, after a genuine effort, you still do not feel comfortable with oral sex, your husband—or wife, as the case may be—should respect your wishes.

Any individual who wants oral sex for him or herself and is not willing to reciprocate is selfish and exploitive.

To what extent can one share fantasies with another?

There are no hard and fast rules. It depends on the taste, sense of humor, self-possession and emotional strength of the people involved.

Fantasy sharing is an option, not an obligation. There is no all-purpose formula for what ought to be shared or how. Given the fact that most people are ashamed and guilty about their fantasy lives, it is likely that fantasy sharing in most relationships will be minimal.

Slow, gradual, tasteful, witty sharing of daydreams is probably a sign of a healthy development.

Is it OK to fake an orgasm?

One reader wrote that she'd been faking orgasms for years, and now she wondered if she should confess to her husband that she had been pretending. She went on to say that their sex life was good and she didn't feel cheated but she felt guilty. My reply was simple: If it ain't broke, don't fix it.

What does it mean when a woman enjoys sex but rarely has an orgasm? Is there something wrong with her?

No. Many women who are sexually active do not climax more than half the time. Some women never do. If you find sexual intercourse pleasant and fulfilling, orgasm is not important. My advice is: Quit counting. Enjoy yourself.

Does a man have to have an orgasm to get a woman pregnant?

No. Even without orgasm, a few drops of semen can seep into the vagina, and if the woman is in her fertile phase, pregnancy is possible.

Is it dangerous to have sexual intercourse during pregnancy?

Most obstetricians approve of sex during pregnancy up to two weeks before delivery, unless there is some medical problem. If the woman has gained a great deal of weight, she should ask her doctor about various positions that will be satisfying to both her and her husband.

If the physician recommends abstinence or restraint in sexual activity for a certain length of time before or after delivery, the condition should be explained to both husband and wife, thus avoiding unnecessary strain on their relationship. The couple should also be encouraged and possibly helped to communicate openly with each other about their sexual feelings and desires. Alternative forms of sexual gratification can be recommended. Oral-genital sex and manual stimulation can be satisfying and rewarding without physiological ill effect.

If you are ill, it is perfectly OK to decline the invitation.

Can a nursing mother become pregnant?

Although nursing does lower hormone levels and sometimes prevents pregnancy, don't count on it. As a method of birth control, it can be risky. There *are* children born 11 and 12 months apart. Often it is the result of believing that old wives' tale that a nursing mother can't get pregnant.

Is there a sex life after hysterectomy?

Many women have this fear. As one woman wrote:

"Doctors have told me I need a hysterectomy. I have been warned by woman friends that this operation will put an end to my sexual desire. I am only 41 years old and would hate to think of life without sex. Please tell me if these stories are true."

Every gynecologist and obstetrician I have consulted tells me there is no medical reason for this to occur. True, if the ovaries are removed, the loss of hormonal output can reduce the excitement level in some women, but this can be remedied by taking estrogen. (Females who have had cancer or are at risk should not take estrogen.) Many women say doctors are unsympathetic when they tell them they have lost "that old feeling" after surgery and are furious that they were not told of these consequences in advance. So, I went to the psychiatrists and psychologists. This is what I was told: Women whose sex lives are negatively affected by a hysterectomy may be suffering from a psychological problem that prevents them from having pleasure. This is particularly true of females of childbearing age, who may subconsciously feel that the loss of their reproductive organs has left them less of a woman. Women who have been reared to believe that sex is only for procreation may feel that since they can no longer have babies, they do not deserve to enjoy sexual pleasure. I recommend counseling for any woman who, after a hysterectomy (or tubal ligation), believes that her sex life is over.

Does a woman's sex life end after menopause?

One reader wrote, "I used to enjoy sex. But now at age 54, I find that sex is actually painful. Can anything be done about this?"

Dr. George M. Ryan, an obstetrician-gynecologist in Memphis, says discomfort may be due to an estrogen deficiency that causes dryness in the vaginal area. This is normal for women your age. Your gynecologist can prescribe estrogen pills and a vaginal cream. One caveat, however: A slight risk of developing endometrial cancer may be present among women who take estrogen. It goes without saying that a woman who has had cancer should *not* take estrogen in any form. The same applies to pregnant women. These women should use a lubricant.

What can be done about premature ejaculation?

One woman whose husband has this problem wrote: "It frustrates him and makes me angry. I know he can't help it, but it's hell to be left dangling." Years ago, Masters and Johnson developed a technique a wife can use to help her husband hold off. Your gynecologist should be able to describe it to you. If he or she doesn't know about this technique, you might consider switching gynecologists or consulting a sex therapist.

Here's a letter on the subject:

Dear Ann Landers: My husband and I have been married for 14 months. I am realistic enough to know that no marriage can be perfect. Our problem is sex.

There were signs of trouble just before we married. He seemed to have lost interest in being intimate. I told myself it was too much stress. He was taking on a new job that involved a move to another state. After a while, I realized that I had been making too many excuses for him.

We had a frank talk, with me asking him, point-blank, "Don't you find me attractive anymore?" He replied, "It's not *you*, it's *me*. I just don't have the urge." His response didn't help much.

When we do make love, it's over before I know it. I am never satisfied. He is always apologetic and says, "I'm sorry. I'll try to do better next time." The "next time" is four or five weeks later, and it's the same story.

I'm feeling resentful. Here I am in my mid-20s and starving sexually. I hate to think of spending my whole life this way.

I can't risk a letter coming to the house, so, please, Ann, print your reply. I would be ever so grateful.

—Unfulfilled in the East

Dear Unfulfilled: I spoke with Dr. William Simpson about your problem. He is the director of the Center for Sexual Health at the Menninger Clinic in Topeka, Kan. Dr. Simpson said, "The key sentence in your letter is 'When we make love, it's over before I know it.' Your husband presents himself as having a lack of sexual desire, but his primary problem is premature ejaculation. Every time this happens, he feels like a failure. To escape humiliation, he performs as seldom as possible. This is one of the more easily treated sexual dysfunctions."

Your husband needs to see a certified sex therapist or sex counselor.

Dear Ann Landers: I have been reading your column since I was an eighth grader in Cheyenne. You opened my eyes about a lot of things, and I always believed every word you wrote. I still do. And now I need some advice.

I don't know how to put this in words that you can print, but I will do my best because I am desperate and can't ask anybody else.

I am a 21-year-old guy, 5 feet 11 inches tall, and I weigh 170 pounds. I am considered pretty good-looking and am normal in every way. What I am trying to say is that I have the same sexual drives as all the other guys, but from looking around in locker rooms, I can see that I am not as well-endowed.

I have dated a couple of very nice girls, but I broke up with them because I was afraid to get intimate. To be truthful, Ann, I am scared to death that I wouldn't be able to please a woman. That would be so damaging to my self-esteem that I am better off not trying.

This problem is wrecking my life, and I don't know what to do about it. I have seen ads in sleazy magazines for men who have this problem—powdered reindeer horns, crushed seeds from Samoa and salves from India—but I don't believe they work. Is there anything legitimate that does work? Maybe hormone shots or some kind of injections with silicone? Thanks a million. I'll sign this

—Shortchanged in Wyoming

Dear Wyoming: You couldn't have written at a better time. I just heard from a woman in Portsmouth, N.H., who speaks precisely to the problem you are worried about. Here it is:

Dear Ann Landers: It's difficult to believe that you have never received a letter in praise of the modestly endowed male and how he often turns out to be the most satisfying lover of the lot. Since no such letter has appeared, I hope you'll print mine.

I've had eight partners (three were husbands) over a period of 25 years. These men were, I believe, a fairly good sampling of what is out there. From my experience, I can tell you that lovemaking with the man who was the least spectacularly endowed was by far the most fulfilling. He was also the most exciting. Why? Because he was responsive, sensitive, caring, romantic and considerate.

What too many men fail to understand is that sexual pleasure is generated in the mind. The brain is the most important sex organ of all. That's where everything happens—or fails to happen.

I hope that you will one day discuss this in print. There is entirely too much emphasis on size these days. This goes for women's measurements as well. Because you are famous for "telling it like it is," I hope you will have the courage to print my letter. It would be a public service.

—Anonymous, Of Course

Dear Anonymous: Thank you for validating that provocative phrase "Less is more." You have educated a great many people today and given comfort and encouragement to an equal number of insecure men.

Bless you for writing a letter that will lay to rest some myths and help bolster the confidence of many.

Dear Ann Landers: Thank you, thank you for your wonderful response to that man who was concerned because he isn't well-endowed. You said, "Less can be more." What a fabulous response. A locker-room-type pecking order based on "endowments" can play havoc with a male's self-esteem and be downright dehumanizing. Those feelings of inferiority, unfortunately, can last a lifetime.

Your sensible and reassuring comments made a lot of males feel better about themselves. Thanks from all of us.

—Salem, Ore.

Dear Salem: It was good of you to write. So did many others. And would you believe I heard from more women than men? Read on:

Dear Ann Landers: I was married to a bona fide stud for eight years. He was extremely proud of his "endowments" and considered himself a real prize. This man couldn't stop reminding me that I was very lucky to have him. Meanwhile, our sex life was hell. I dreaded going to bed at night, and he was always after me.

Things went from bad to worse, and finally we were divorced. Then I met "Andy," who was wonderfully kind, considerate and thoughtful. I was relieved to discover that he was modestly endowed. This man is marvelously satisfying in every way, and I have never been happier.

—New Orleans

From Cleveland: "Shortchanged in Wyoming" needs to know that being well-endowed has absolutely nothing to do with love and loving. I've been with several men, both before and between marriages, and I can attest to the fact that the most generously endowed were the worst lovers, and the least endowed were the best. Almost without exception, the big guys thought that all they had to do was be there because they were "God's gift" to females. These men were invariably the most self-centered, egotistical and, I might add, the least satisfying.

Elgin, Ill.: It seems that "Shortchanged" is mostly short on confidence. I, too, am somewhat undersized, but no woman ever complained or ran from my bedroom laughing. Most women are too preoccupied with their own inadequacies the first time around. Chastity is in style again, thanks to AIDS, so no longer will there be the broad sampling that created a climate for all sorts of comparisons. This is a big plus for men and women, who can now assess one another's compatibility in a much more rational manner.

Seattle: I have been sexually involved with at least 20 men. Please, Ann, tell your readers that size doesn't mean a thing if you really care about the man you're with. What matters is gentleness, generosity, consideration and just plain decency. Without exception, the men who had the most modest equipment were the most satisfying. I married one of them.

Salt Lake City: Your recent column in the *Salt Lake Tribune* had the heading: "Underendowed Males Can Be the Best Lovers." Let me state from personal experience as an overendowed male, we can be the worst lovers.

I don't wish to appear immodest, but I have had more than my share of female lovers, and almost without exception, they complained that sex was uncomfortable or downright painful. If a surgical procedure for penile reduction were possible, I would be a willing candidate. As you said in your column, Ann, less is more.

Dear Ann Landers: I have been a widow for nine years. My husband was a big, well-built man and a wonderful lover. My first romance after his death proved to be a poor choice, and I ended the relationship. The intimacy, however, was extremely gratifying.

The man I've been seeing for over a year treats me beautifully, and we have many mutual interests. I could be perfectly content with "Bart" for the rest of my life except for one thing: I do not enjoy his lovemaking.

The first time we made love, I was so disappointed that I seriously considered breaking up with him, but his winning ways made me change my mind. I'm trying to convince myself that his personality and fine qualities outweigh his inadequacy in the bedroom, but I'm not having much success. After all, it's not his fault that he isn't well-endowed.

Lately, Bart has been talking about marriage. My family and friends think he's fabulous and tell me how lucky I am. Meanwhile, I find my life becoming more and more entwined with his. People are beginning to think of us as "a couple."

I love Bart, and I would really miss him if we should part. But how do I handle this sex thing? He is not fully aware of how I feel, and I don't want to hurt him by saying anything. I'm sure he believes he is a good lover. I've faked enthusiasm to boost his ego. He tries all sorts of variations and tells me how important it is to please me, but nothing seems to help. There's not much he can do about his anatomy. What do you suggest?

—A Wisconsin Woman

Dear Woman: You say the problem you are experiencing with Bart is a matter of size. In that regard, what is, is—but with proper instruction, Bart can compensate for what you perceive to be a serious inadequacy.

To pass up the chance to marry this man for the reason you stated would be sheer lunacy.

When it comes to sex, my readers want to know what's spicy, what's kinky and what's what. Read the next few letters and decide for yourself:

Dear Ann Landers: My wife and I have been married 20 years. We have two sweet children and consider ourselves very fortunate. Our problem is one we cannot discuss with our minister. It is very important that we have an answer and can think of no one better qualified than Ann Landers.

My wife believes that sex anywhere but in the bedroom is sinful according to the Bible. I say a change of setting can add extra pleasure and so long as there is complete privacy it is perfectly moral.

The place I have in mind is the car. We have a garage with a sturdy lock on the door. No one could possibly get in.

We are good Christians and want to know what the Bible says about this. Can you contact a religious scholar?

—Strictly Confidential in Kentucky

Dear Strictly: Since the Bible predates the automobile by a couple thousand years, there is no point in bothering a Christian scholar.

If you will settle for my opinion, here it is: It's perfectly all right for a married couple to make love anywhere they choose, provided it is private, safe and reasonably comfortable.

Dear Ann Landers: I was interested in the letter from the man who wanted to make love in the car. His wife felt guilty and wanted to know if it was proper. You said so long as it was private, not dangerous and reasonably comfortable, it was nobody's business.

I married one in a million. She was totally uninhibited, willing and eager to make love any place at any time. I must say we dreamed up some mighty exciting situations. We traveled quite a bit, and it was not unusual for us to pull off the road in the middle of the day if we ran into a wooded area, a sandy beach, a calm lake or an inviting motel. On occasion, when the mood came upon us and none of the above was available, we used the car.

This kept up until we were in our 60s, when my beloved wife passed away. I always felt as if we had the healthiest sex life of anyone I knew because we never stopped turning each other on. Sex was always unpredictable, imaginative and fun. Our sexual compatibility spilled over into all areas of our lives, and we were divinely happy. Just call me

—Beautiful Memories

Dear Beautiful: How lucky you were to find each other. It was a perfect match. Lots of readers will be envious—especially the man who wrote the next letter.

Dear Ann Landers: My wife and I have been married 14 years. I thought I was getting a prize when I married "Joan" because she was a virgin. Now I'm not so sure.

We make love every Saturday morning at precisely the same time, in the same bed and in the same way. Any suggestion from me that we should try a bit of variation brings a firm rebuke from her: "It isn't decent! It isn't moral. Are you crazy?"

Ann, I am not a kook, nor am I interested in far-out stuff. I am just bored with the same, mechanical routine. Can you suggest something that might help?

—Milwaukee, Wis.

Dear Milwaukee: I don't know what you mean by "variation." That word can cover a wide range of activities.

Go to a bookstore and browse around for just the right book to give your wife. Read it and underline the parts she needs to see. Stay away from hard-core pornography. Select a high-quality sex manual. There's a world of difference.

Dear Ann Landers: A while back, you printed a letter from a woman whose husband wanted to spice up their lovemaking. He insisted on tying her hands and feet with silk scarfs. She refused, saying it was "sadistic." You called him "kinky."

Bondage can be fun. My girlfriend and I have enjoyed it for years. Sometimes we reverse roles. She is the binder, and I am the bindee. There is no slapping, hitting or clothespins on the breasts. The key words are "mutual consent."

We play another game called "Make Believe." We take turns making up situations to act out. For example: I pick her up in a bar and pretend that she is a hooker. We play our respective roles, and it's very stimulating. Another scenario: She is a lonely working woman who is spending yet another evening alone, wondering why romance has eluded her. An attractive man shows up to repair the furnace. Your imagination can take over from there. Granted, these games are not for everyone, but they can enhance lovemaking to an incredible degree.

—Hedonist in Woodland Hills, Calif.

Dear Woody: The mail on that subject was mind-boggling. I had no idea so many people in the United States and Canada were tying each other up. The final word from here is: Whatever turns you on is

OK so long as there is mutual consent, no whips, no chains and no inflicting of severe pain.

Dear Ann Landers: My husband and I have been married for a little over a year. We have a baby and are extremely happy.

"Mel" has a hobby he started when he was a little boy. I knew about it before I married him, so I am not complaining. He likes to dress up in women's clothes. I told him it was OK with me as long as he didn't do it in my presence.

Since the baby came I've been home a lot, and this has created a problem. Mel hasn't been able to dress up, and it has made him irritable and short-tempered. I asked him why he needs to do this, and he says he doesn't know. Last night, I took the baby to my mother's so Mel could dress up. When I came home, he was watching TV wearing a blond wig, a beautiful sequined gown, high heels and a feather boa. He looked better than a lot of women I know. He also does a fantastic job of applying makeup. I thank the Lord that our baby is too young to remember his father in that get-up.

Why would a man want to do this? He is definitely not a homosexual and is the most manly-looking guy I know.

—Mel's Wife, U.S.A.

Dear M.W.U.S.A.: I checked with one of the country's foremost authorities on cross-dressing. He asked that his name not be used because several years ago when I named him he was swamped with mail. Dr. X said there are many types of transvestites. Most are married and have children. He made it clear that while some are homosexuals, many are straight.

When questioned about their first cross-dressing experience, almost all say it was a woman who put them in girl's clothes, usually to humiliate them. Also, cross-dressers almost invariably view their fathers as cold, distant, powerful and uncommunicative. The yearning for acceptance becomes so intense that it creates an erotic sense of frustration. Dressing up provides an emotional release.

Some transvestites say they started to dress like girls because their sisters were "Daddy's favorite" and they felt that if they were girls they would get special treatment, too.

Accept the fact that this behavior is deep-seated and almost always irreversible. Since he told you about it before marriage, try not to be judgmental.

Dear Ann Landers: It was with great interest that I read your enlightened reply to Mel's wife about cross-dressing.

Since I have been a cross-dresser for years, I can tell you there is a great deal of ignorance on this subject, and not many people want to listen to correct information. They would rather harbor their preconceived notions.

I have battled this thing all my life, and no way can I stop it, Ann.

I am normal in every respect except this one. I love to dress like a woman, and nothing will ever change that.

I am a minister's son, a college graduate, a Vietnam vet, a Boy Scout leader, happily married for 12 years. We have two children who are fine students, and I am considered a good citizen.

My wife thinks cross-dressing is weird and has told me she will not tolerate it in her presence. I respect her too much to defy her wishes.

Early in our marriage, she insisted that I see a psychiatrist. The doctor informed me that he sees nothing wrong, weird or harmful in what I do so long as I do it in private.

I want to thank you, Ann, for helping me and millions of other cross-dressers feel less guilty and freakish.

—Ann Fan Forever in California

Dear Forever: There are a great many misconceptions about cross-dressers, the principal one being that they are all homosexuals. The purpose of this column is to educate, and that is what I try to do. Thanks for noticing.

Dear Ann Landers: I'm an attractive 23-year-old woman with a great job, money in the bank and a wonderful fiance. You'd think I haven't a worry in the world, but I'm a nervous wreck because I don't know how to tell my fiance about my fetish.

When I'm feeling really stressed or tired, I dress and act like a baby. I have adult-size diapers, rubber pants, baby pajamas, etc. I put these on, feed myself baby food from a jar and drink juice from a bottle. Then I fall asleep with a pacifier and a "blankie."

This soothes me because I imagine I'm being taken care of by a loving father. I wake up in the morning refreshed and ready to take on my responsibilities.

I've had this fetish since childhood. I was an only child, and my mother died when I was very young. My father raised me on his own.

He worked long hours, so the only real chance we had to talk was at night. The first thing he did when he came home from work was diaper me because I wet the bed. I stopped the bedwetting at age 12, and that was the end of a lot of attention from my father. I would occasionally wear a diaper under my pajamas, but after Dad caught me, he threw the diapers away and I no longer wore them.

I am perfectly normal except for this kinkiness, but I know I can't keep it from my fiance forever. I just can't muster the courage to tell him, and I'm desperate for help. Please advise.

—Twenty-three-year-old Baby in Ohio

Dear Ohio: First, you are not alone. Several males as well as females have a baby fetish. In fact, a few years ago I saw five grown men on a talk show in rompers and baby bonnets, waving rattles and drinking milk from baby bottles. They all declared that dressing in baby clothes relieved tension and gave them a feeling of contentment and well-being.

Psychiatrists with whom I checked said infantilism is not harmful, but spouses should be told before marriage about this fetish so there will be no surprises.

P.S. A father who diapers his daughter until the age of 12 has a geranium in his cranium. But that's another letter.

Dear Ann Landers: Can a person be "addicted" to pornography? My boyfriend seems like the most clean-cut guy in the world. You'd never guess he was a trash addict.

Despite his choir-boy appearance, "Jeff" has been buying these magazines since adolescence. (He is now 25.) He kept his collection hidden from me, and I stumbled across it only recently. When I confronted him with the magazines, he became angry and defensive and insisted it was a better outlet than having affairs. Later he said he was ashamed of himself but he just can't help it.

It hurts that Jeff doesn't seem satisfied with me. We are very compatible sexually, even though I'm not nearly as well-endowed as the women in his magazines. I can't help but feel that he is comparing me to them, though he denies it.

I don't want to break up with Jeff, and I can't make him stop buying that trash. I've suggested therapy, but he refuses to consider it. I really love the guy and feel I'd be losing a lot if I left him. Please tell me what's going on and what I should do about it.

—Ohio Quandary

Dear Ohio: Jeff's problem is immaturity. He never outgrew the adolescent stage when he got turned on by what he perceived to be "forbidden pictures."

Don't let this become your problem. It's his. And stop comparing yourself to the "girlies." (Many of them have had breast implants, and photographic lighting is extremely flattering.) Let Jeff fantasize. Hopefully one day he'll grow up, lose interest in the paper dolls and settle down to real life.

Dear Ann Landers: For 15 years, I've been fighting a porno war with my husband. A battle ends and I think I've won, but a few months later I find more filthy magazines. I'm not talking about *Playboy* or *Penthouse*. I mean the XXX-rated trash that makes me sick to my stomach. He then started with 8mm movies, VCR tapes and swingers catalogs. But what upset me more than anything was finding a pen and pad stuck in a catalog and little stars next to some bimbo's name.

When I confronted "Jack," he said it's normal for a man to be interested in these things and that he would never write to any of those women.

Ann, I don't know how to deal with this. I feel so hurt and angry when I find this trash. I used to snoop to see what he was up to, but I don't anymore because it's too painful. The stuff is everywhere—in the car, the basement, just name it.

I thought our sex life was wonderful for him as well as for me, but apparently I'm mistaken. Am I overreacting? Is this behavior normal for a married man in his late 30s?

—Lost in a World of Dirt

Dear Lost: Stop feeling inadequate because Jack finds this garbage exciting. We now know that pornography lovers are addicted.

Snooping and throwing out his "toys" won't help. Accept this oddity as beyond your control, because it is. Porn addicts need counseling.

Can a totally monogamous couple get herpes? Yes. Read on:

Dear Ann Landers: I am 45 years old. My husband and I have been married for 26 years. We have three beautiful grandchildren. Our life hasn't been all peaches and cream, but for the last 13 years, I thought things were pretty OK.

"Hank" is in the Army National Guard. He signed up when he was 30 years old. He is now 44. He was deployed in December 1990 for Desert Storm and was gone for six months.

He returned in June, and things were fine until February. Then Hank developed some sores on his genitals. We went to see a doctor together, and the diagnosis was full-blown genital herpes.

I accused him of being with someone while he was in the war, which he denied vehemently. Now I have found out that the first outbreak of herpes usually occurs 2 to 26 days after having had sex, which would mean Hank was with someone here in the States.

We've been through a living hell ever since that visit to the doctor. I've contacted several other doctors and called the herpes hotline. The information I've been able to gather points to the same thing: Hank must have had sex with someone else.

Of course, I was tested also. The reports were negative, which was no surprise to me, because I've never been with anyone else. Even Hank's sister, who is an R.N., wants to know why he won't fess up. I need to know the truth, no matter how much it will hurt. It's the lie that's killing me.

Now I find myself questioning every move he makes. I love Hank very much and don't want to divorce this man. I need your help.

—Trouble in Toledo

Dear Toledo: My medical consultants say it is possible, though not likely, to get herpes through skin-to-skin contact that is nonsexual. Since you want desperately to keep your marriage together, go with the long shot and accept his word as the truth.

I hope you have talked with your gynecologist about how to protect yourself from getting infected. If not, do so *at once*.

Dear Ann Landers: This is in response to "Trouble in Toledo," whose husband of 26 years contracted genital herpes.

I am 24 years old and have been married for one year. If my husband weren't so understanding, I probably wouldn't be married now. Three months after we became engaged, I was diagnosed with herpes.

Before I met "Bob," he practiced safe sex, and I was less careful and more promiscuous. Because we'd been friends for a very long time, he knew about my past and accepted me in spite of it. Bob is the only man I've ever been faithful to.

I was terrified that he would think I'd been fooling around. It killed me that after finally turning my life around, something out of the past might destroy my future.

I asked my doctor how I could have gotten herpes since I was faithful to my fiance. She explained that I had probably had the virus before and something stressful had caused it to flare up.

Most men wouldn't have believed that, but Bob had faith in me. We must live with an outbreak from time to time but have learned to manage. Of course, we're being very careful so he won't be infected.

My husband is a rare person, and I plan to hang on to him for the rest of my life.

—Sacramento, Calif.

Dear Ann Landers: Two years ago, I became ill with high fever, chills and severe genital pain. The diagnosis was genital herpes. At the time, my husband and I had been married 15 years. He was the only sex partner I'd ever had in my entire life. He showed no symptoms. Life in our household was hell. Thanks to the help of several doctors, we learned a lot about genital herpes.

1. Since my husband had other sex partners before our marriage, he could have contracted it then. Some people have such a mild case that they don't even know they have herpes. Nevertheless, they become carriers. Years later, they may have another mild (unnoticed) outbreak and pass on the virus.

2. Condoms do not protect against herpes because the virus is in the entire genital area.

3. If a sex partner with a cold sore performs oral sex, he or she can infect a partner.

4. I am a nurse, so I could have picked it up while tending a patient. I am meticulous about hand washing, but that is no guarantee.

We still don't know how I got genital herpes. I have had two flare-ups since the initial outbreak. My husband has never had a symptom. I have *never* had a sex partner other than my husband.

Please tell "Trouble in Toledo" that I believe her husband completely. I know he could have contracted herpes without having an extramarital affair because that is what happened to me.

—New Orleans, La.

Dear N.O.: Thanks for the backup. I have received many letters from readers who wanted to vouch for "Toledo's" husband because they, too, had had the same experience. My readers, bless them, are loyal not only to me but also to each other.

Dear Ann Landers: Thank you for printing the letter from "Trouble in Toledo," whose husband of 26 years is experiencing an outbreak of genital herpes. She wanted to know if it was possible for her husband to have contracted herpes without having had an affair. You said it was unlikely but possible.

The American Social Health Association would like to offer some additional insights into this woman's situation. Symptoms of herpes usually develop within 2 to 20 days after contact with the virus, although it may take far longer. In some people, the herpes virus causes a first attack so mild that it goes unnoticed. In other words, it is possible "Trouble's" husband had a primary outbreak so mild that he carried a dormant infection for several years without knowing it, and the stress of serving in Desert Storm may have caused the virus to reactivate.

Sometimes people contract genital herpes from contact with a cold sore during oral sex. (They never consider this the source of genital herpes because they don't associate cold sores with the herpes simplex virus.) There are many explanations, including the ones you suggested to "Trouble." Problem is, it's often impossible to know.

Many thousands of your readers have genital herpes, Ann. For all of them, the issues surrounding this infection are deeply felt and complicated. Please tell them that help is available. The American Social Health Association provides pamphlets, tapes, books, telephone counseling and referral services to people concerned about herpes.

For free, confidential information, please ask your readers to send $1 (for postage and handling) to: ASHA, Department HRC, P.O. Box 13827, Research Triangle Park, NC 27709.
—Peggy Clarke, executive director, American Social
Health Association

Dear Peggy: Your letter is going to be a boon to thousands of readers who had no idea what to do or who to turn to. Thanks for all the good you did today.

Dear Ann Landers: You recently printed a letter from "Wisconsin Woman," whose husband has genital herpes. She said that by abstaining from sexual contact during her husband's outbreaks, she has remained free from the infection.

It is important to point out that scientists now believe people infected with genital herpes release substantial amounts of infectious virus even while displaying no physical signs of the infection. This is known as "asymptomatic shedding." That means people with herpes can transmit the virus even when no symptoms are present.

Some researchers suspect that as many as 60 to 70 percent of new cases of herpes result from sexual contact with an infected person during periods of asymptomatic shedding. Please make this clear to your readers so they will understand that they cannot rely on the absence of physical signs of herpes as a guarantee that they will not be infected.

Data presented in October 1994 at the 34th Interscience Conference on Antimicrobial Agents and Chemotherapy in Orlando, Fla., showed that asymptomatic shedding could be reduced by 95 percent through daily treatment with acyclovir, an antiviral drug currently used to treat herpes. Scientists, however, cannot yet say for certain if this also prevents infection.

You have an excellent track record of informing readers about genital herpes, Ann. With more than 30 million Americans infected with this virus, those not infected may unknowingly continue, like "Wisconsin Woman," to place themselves at risk. Please keep giving us solid information.

—North Carolina Reader

Dear N.C. Reader: Thank you for yet another opportunity to educate my readers. Those who have herpes should also know they can live very nearly normal lives by following a few simple guidelines. The key, of course, is acyclovir, truly a miracle drug that has changed the lives of millions.

Dear Ann Landers: I'm a 20-year-old college sophomore who lives in a coed dorm with 300 other students. Last year, I met a really neat guy from another school at a party. I made the mistake of sleeping with him on the first date. I thought he liked me a lot and would ask me out again. I was wrong. I'm sure he considered me a pushover.

I wish I could chalk this up to experience and forget it, but I can't. He gave me genital warts.

Ann, I'd never even heard of genital warts, but now I've become an expert. It's one of the most common sexually transmitted diseases around. Too bad it doesn't make the headlines like AIDS, though it is highly contagious. You can use a condom and still get genital warts. Once you have the virus, it is in your system for years. Without treatment these warts can cause cellular changes that could progress to cervical cancer. If you're pregnant, you can pass the virus on to your unborn child.

Ann, I'm scared to death. I can't concentrate on school. I'd give anything to be healthy again. My folks are supportive and I'm thankful for that.

And what about the guy I was with? He's out there, still scoring. I don't care what happens to him, which is not very nice, but I feel sorry for the girl he will probably charm the pants off of this weekend.

Please tell your readers that this disease is serious stuff. It can be deadly. No sex is worth the price I'm paying.

—Hurting Alone

Dear Alone: I can understand your bitterness, but your attitude is almost as destructive as the genital warts. This doesn't have to ruin your life. HPV (human papillioma virus), the virus that causes genital warts, is both treatable and manageable.

I hope you are seeing a competent gynecologist. Treatment may not eradicate the pesky things, but you'll feel a lot better. Please educate yourself. Thank you for writing. I wish you the best of luck.

Do people ever get too old for sex? Not if they remain in good health. Sexual activity can continue into the 80s and 90s.

Dear Ann Landers: You have printed several letters from older people who say they enjoy sex, but not as frequently as they did in their younger years. I am pleased to tell you that such is not the case with me.

My wife died a few years ago. I was 67. Several months later, I met an extremely intelligent divorcee with a fantastic figure. We are very close to the same age.

I courted her for several months, and we became lovers. On New Year's Eve, 1982, one of us suggested we put a dollar in an envelope each time we became intimate. We agreed to spend the money in 1983 on something foolishly extravagant. (On January 5, there was already $3 in the envelope.)

On New Year's Eve, 1983, the envelope contained $174. My partner accused me of shorting the envelope by at least $30. I considered the accusation a compliment, gave her the entire amount and told her to treat herself to something ridiculous. What does this do to your statistics, Annie old girl?

—Zippy in Sacramento

Dear Zippy: It calls for a revision on the upside. Thanks for the input, Romeo.

Dear Ann Landers: I have a dear friend who is driving me crazy. I will call her "Tillie." She and her husband just celebrated their 57th wedding anniversary. They are both 79.

Tillie is upset because her husband's sex drive has slowed up. She says she is sure he isn't seeing another woman because he is never out of her sight. I tried to explain that time takes its toll, but she says she hasn't lost a darn thing in that department and wonders why he has. Can you explain it?

—Confidentially Speaking in New England

Dear Confid: A 79-year-old male should not be expected to perform sexually like he did when he was 22.

It's nice that Tillie doesn't think she's lost a darned thing in that department, but I suspect maybe her memory isn't as good as it used to be.

Dear Ann Landers: Premarital sex and extramarital sex are frequently dealt with in your column. Lots of advice there. But what about postmarital sex? It's almost like no one cares to advise adults as to how they should program their sex lives in the later years. How would Ann Landers advise on this one?

After 30 years of a good marriage, I lost my wife. After 32 years of an equally good marriage, my lady friend lost her husband. We are both in our early 60s, long past child-bearing age, so we don't have to worry about pregnancy. And, yes, we are having sex, but morally, we are committing adultery.

Abstinence is not the answer because the hormones are still raging and we enjoy this aspect of our relationship a lot. Somehow I can't believe the Creator intended for people to stop loving and living after performing their duties as spouses and parents. I find it hard to understand why people in their golden years must refrain from enjoying their sexuality to the fullest. Can you explain this?

—Hot to Trot in Sioux Falls, S.D.

Dear Hot: Your relationship is not adulterous since your spouses are deceased.

A strict fundamentalist would judge you guilty of fornication, since you are having sex outside of marriage. If either of you feels guilty about this, talk to your clergyman. If not, it's nobody's business.

Dear Ann Landers: Please address yourself to the growing problem of healthy, middle-aged men who are impotent.

As a divorcee in my early 40s, I have encountered three dead batteries in the last two years. You cannot imagine the disappointment when a woman gets worked up in anticipation of an exciting experience only to have him confess, shamefacedly, "I can't."

I just received an anguished phone call from my cousin, who recently went through that nightmare. Her gentleman friend was extremely attentive for several months and appeared to be well-adjusted and healthy. The romantic weekend in Bermuda they had anticipated for so long was a disaster. He "couldn't."

If these males know they are unable to perform, why do they put a woman through the embarrassment and frustration? And how do you account for what appears to be epidemic? Is there any way these men can be helped?

—Unfulfilled in D.C.

Dear Un: Many impotent males hope the problem is temporary and the magic of the moment or the excitement of a new partner may somehow produce a reversal.

According to Dr. Domeena Renshaw, a psychiatrist and an authority on sexual dysfunction at Loyola University of Chicago, male impotence is not a new problem. It is simply being discussed more openly.

Men who are impotent should be checked by a urologist to make certain there is no physical problem. If there is none, they need to seek the help of a psychologist or a sex therapist. Also, they might give some thought to their alcohol consumption. Impotence can be caused by too much booze. While one or two drinks may help a male overcome his inhibitions, three or four drinks can render him nonfunctional.

Over-the-counter sleep remedies also can deaden the libido. When high blood pressure pills are the culprit, a switch to another type of medication often solves the problem. A caring physician who is willing to take the time and trouble to work with you can do wonders.

Dear Ann Landers: I am a 70-year-old woman and have two male friends, one in Colorado, age 72, another in Oregon, age 69. I lament the fact that both men, though attractive, interesting and successful, are impotent. Unfortunately, they become defensive instead of acknowledging it and seeking help.

These men had long, happy marriages, as I did. I would love to find a man who could be a husband to me physically as well as emotionally, and I wonder if anything can be done about these two.

Thanks, Ann. I will always be your number one fan.

—Languishing in Virginia

Dear Va.: We spoke with Dr. Irwin Goldstein, professor of urology at Boston University School of Medicine. He said about 30 million American men between 40 and 70 suffer from impotence. After the physical aspects of impotency are treated, the psychological problems must be addressed.

There are four available therapies to treat impotence: medication, vacuum devices, bypass surgery and penile implants.

Medication involves injecting the penis with a drug just before intercourse. It has an 80 percent overall success rate and is generally not hazardous when performed after thorough training.

Dr. William Fitch of the Impotence Information Center in Minnesota informed us about the vacuum pump device, which is completely external and works for most men. It costs about $300 and lasts indefinitely.

The bypass is a surgical procedure best for men under 40 whose impotence is caused by injury to the artery that supplies blood to the penis. The success rate is about 70 percent to 75 percent.

Implants are 90 percent successful but involve invasive surgery and are recommended only when all other therapies fail.

If the two gentlemen are not interested in any of the above, I hope you realize that there can be a great deal of satisfaction in holding, caressing and just touching. There's actually a name for this. It is "outercourse."

Dear Ann Landers: I am in love with a man who is middle-aged (as I am), and we have been going together for almost a year. He is very affectionate but has made no effort to become intimate, although he has hinted strongly that he would like to marry me.

At first I thought he was refreshingly old-fashioned and respected him for it. Later I decided he was extremely shy. Now I am almost certain the man is impotent. Please tell me how I can let him know this sexual dysfunction would not make a particle of difference to me. I believe when you sincerely love a man, you accept him as he is.

Many marriages have plenty of sex but fall apart because love and trust, kindness and respect are missing. To share this man's life and fall asleep in his arms every night would be enough for me. The bond created by intimate caressing and tender words can be much more meaningful than the consummated act between people who don't care about one another. How can I let him know my feelings without putting him on the defensive?

—Knowledgeable in Sarasota

Dear Sara: Tell him, as you told me, exactly how you feel. If he has the qualities you described, he will be thrilled. And it will put the relationship on a much more secure and honest footing.

Dear Ann Landers: I hope you will print this letter for "Unfulfilled in D.C." Along with being "Unfulfilled," she is also unsympathetic and uncaring. There was no mention of how many live batteries D.C. had encountered in two years, only that she had run into three dead ones. Could it be that her charger is on the fritz?

My advice to D.C. is this: If you want a fulfilling relationship, be patient, caring and helpful. You will be surprised at how responsive a dead battery can be.

—A Live One

Dear Ann Landers: My husband's battery went dead 12 years ago when he had surgery for a malignant prostate. While we no longer have sexual intercourse, our love life is as good as ever. Maybe better.

There's a lot of cuddling and kissing and tenderness. I find it completely satisfying and don't miss sexual intercourse one bit.

—Happy at Home

Dear Ann Landers: My husband (age 37) has become impotent and refuses to admit anything is wrong. He says, "I just don't feel like it."

What can a woman do when her husband won't acknowledge that he has a problem? It has made me desperately unhappy because our sex life used to be wonderful. Now he is distant and sullen. A urologist assured him that there is no physical problem.

Please help me. I don't know where else to turn.

—Desperate in Denver

Dear Denver: An avalanche of information on impotence has appeared in the last eight years. The experts once thought this problem was 90 percent stress-related. Today they say about 40 percent is caused by anxiety and emotional problems. They now believe the major culprits are alcoholism, diabetes, vascular or neurological irregularities, prostate and urological problems and medication for high blood pressure and heart trouble.

Impotence need not be viewed as a disaster. A great deal of pleasure can be experienced by being loving and innovative. Moreover, when the pressure to perform is removed, a man often does better.

According to Dr. William Simpson, director of the Center for Sexual Health at the Menninger Foundation in Topeka, Kan., your husband is probably suffering from inhibited sexual desire. His distancing may be a defense against humiliation. Dr. Simpson suggests that he see a certified sex counselor or sex therapist.

Dear Ann Landers: You have printed many letters on the active sex lives of people over 70. There has been so much lying on this subject that I'm sick to death of it.

Let's face it. People get arthritis, bad knees and bum backs. The testosterone level begins to diminish after age 45, so what's the big deal? Why all the subterfuge? Let's have a little more truth in advertising, please.

—Davis, Calif.

Dear Davis: I guess "denile" is more than just a river in Egypt. Keep reading for another perspective from British Columbia:

Dear Ann Landers: One of your female correspondents from Huntsville, Ala., stated with the ring of authority, that when a man's battery runs down, the reason is almost always "psychological." She then added sarcastically, "This is the line you've been peddling for years, Ann. Give me a break."

A great many women are dumping impotent partners these days not because their batteries are run down but because they won't do a darned thing to recharge them. Perhaps too many nonperforming males think nothing can be done about it. They are wrong.

When a man retains his desire but loses his ability to perform, it's not all in his head. It's a malfunction of some sort. Age alone does not cause impotence.

If a man is otherwise healthy, his impotence can be remedied in a variety of ways. Please, Ann, tell these males to go see a really good urologist who is up on the latest. If they want help, they can get it.

P.S. A man whose wife has died and who has been celibate for a period of time will almost certainly fail the first time he tries with another woman. This condition is temporary and calls for patience and encouragement.

—Vancouver

Dear Van.: I've told readers for years that impotence can be treated, but once more won't hurt. Thanks for the opportunity.

Dear Ann Landers: Several weeks ago, my husband had a severe attack of indigestion. He believes it was a mild heart attack and has been afraid to have sex ever since.

I have tried to explain that he has nothing to worry about. I remember reading in your column that sex is OK even if a man has had a heart attack. In fact, it might be beneficial.

If I say anything, I am a dummy, but he thinks you hung the moon, kiddo. Please help me out.

—Nervous in Nevada

Dear Nevada: Your memory has served you well. Too bad you didn't save that column. What's more, according to the Harvard Medical School Health Letter (March 1986), a widely quoted Japanese study provided more valuable information on this subject.

Investigators analyzed the autopsy records of 5,000 people who had died suddenly. Of this group, 34 had died during intercourse. Of the 34, 30 were with someone other than their spouse, and the partner was, on the average, 18 years younger. Moreover, all had blood alcohol levels in the range of intoxication.

The conclusion I draw is that extramarital affairs with a much younger woman after boozing it up can be lethal.

Contact your husband's physician. The man needs to hear from an authority that sexual activity, even after a heart attack, can be physically as well as psychologically beneficial.

In November of 1984, I published a letter from a woman who wrote the following: "If you were to ask 100 women how they feel about sexual intercourse, I'll bet 98 percent would say, 'Just hold me close and be tender. Forget about the act.' If you don't believe it, why not take a poll?"

I replied, "You're on." I then asked the women in my reading audience to send a postcard or letter with a reply to the question "Would you be content to be held close and treated tenderly and forget about 'the act'? Reply yes or no and please add one line: 'I am over (or under) 40 years of age.' No signature is necessary."

Well, dear readers, I received more than 90,000 responses. The mail room looked like a disaster area. We had to put on extra help. The employees worked double shifts and weekends, yet the mailbags seemed to multiply like rabbits. And the mail came from everywhere.

I believe the intense interest in this poll makes a statement about what goes on behind closed doors in the bedrooms of the world. It also says something about communication and fulfillment (or the lack of it) among great numbers of couples—both married and unmarried—who are having sexual relations.

Seventy-two percent of the women who responded said they would be content to be held tenderly and forget about the act. Was I surprised at the outcome of the poll? Yes—but not very. I could have guessed the way it would go. But I never dreamed that more than 90,000 women would be moved to express themselves on this highly intimate subject. Nor would I have predicted the percentages or the passion with which so many women described their sex lives.

The greatest revelation, to me at least, is what the poll says about men as lovers. A 32-year-old from Atlanta put it this way: "He insists on getting his satisfaction, so why shouldn't I have mine?"

Clearly, there is trouble in paradise.

From Columbus, Ohio: I am under 40 and would be delighted to settle for tender words and warm caresses. The rest of it is a bore and can be exhausting. I am sure the sex act was designed strictly for the pleasure of males.

Anchorage: I am under 40 (26 to be exact). I want three children, so obviously I need more than conversation. After I have my family, I would happily settle for separate rooms. Sex doesn't do a thing for me.

Westport, Conn.: I vote *yes*. My husband is a diabetic and hasn't been able to perform for 10 years. I would have voted *yes* 20 years ago.

He never bothered to satisfy me when he had his health. His illness was a blessing.

Kansas City: I'm 55 and vote *yes*. The best part is the cuddling and caressing and the tender words that come with caring. My first husband used to rape me about five times a week. If a stranger had treated me like that, I would have had him arrested.

Chicago: I don't want either his tender words or the act. My husband became impotent from alcoholism 10 years ago. The only word I'd like from him is goodbye, but the bum won't leave.

Helena, Mont.: *No.* I am 32. To say that touching and tender words are sufficient is like settling for the smell of freshly baked bread and ignoring the nourishment it provides. Such people must be crazy.

Texarkana: *Yes.* Without the tender embrace, the act is animalistic. For years, I hated sex and felt used. I was relieved when my husband died. My present mate is on heart pills that have made him impotent. It's like heaven to be held and cuddled.

Washington, D.C.: *Yes, yes*, a million times *yes*! I would love to be spoken to tenderly. It would be enough. My boyfriend never says a word. If I say anything, he says, "Be quiet. You're spoiling things."

Eureka, Calif.: I'm 62 and voting *no*. If my old man were over the hill, I would settle for high school necking, but as long as he's able to shake the walls and wake up the neighbors downstairs, I want to get in on the action. And I'll take an encore anytime I can get it.

A man wrote to say his wife was no longer interested in sex. He said she thought this was perfectly normal because of my survey back in 1984, which showed that 72 percent of women prefer being held close and treated tenderly to "the act." He added, "That's why so many men are out looking for the other 28 percent."

The man asked me to put this question to my male readers: "How many of you males would settle for being held tenderly and be willing to forget about 'the act'?"

The response was overwhelming. I received 67,588 replies. Out of the 67,588, only 5,600 males, almost all over 60 years of age, said they were willing to settle for cuddling and forget about "the act." Here's a sampling:

From Dallas: The older I get, the longer it takes, but I won't settle for cuddling until that's *all* I can do.

Lafayette, Ind.: Any man who would settle for holding his wife tenderly is getting some action somewhere else.

Dallas: Being held tenderly is much more romantic than "the act." Any animal can perform the act, but only a loving person can experience the thrill of being held close. It says far more than words.

Des Moines: Settle for being held tenderly? Are you kidding? No way. I am 74. My wife is 70. My sweetie pie is 55.

Chicago: After four children, my wife cut me off. I lived like a monk for three years, and then I met a beautiful woman who was as unfulfilled as I was. Now it's the Fourth of July every week.

Bloomfield Hills, Mich.: The greatest pleasure is to *give* pleasure. I'm sorry for men who don't know this.

Springfield, Mass.: Any doctor will tell you an active sex life helps men stay healthy. I'm hot to trot at 76.

Omaha: I'm a widower with arthritis. The doctor says I should keep active. Sex is better than the NordicTrack.

St. Louis: Bag "the act." Two hours of cuddling vs. 30 seconds of sweat? I didn't have to think twice.

Tulsa: What's with these people who just want to be held? Are they dead? My wife said "No more" after our only child was born, so I found a fabulous "friend" who has made me very happy.

Miami: My wife claims that holding her close is nothing more than "upper persuasion for a lower invasion."

San Francisco: I married a nun—"There will be nun of this and nun of that"—so I hunted up an old flame.

Porterville, Calif.: Don't those fools know that being held tenderly can lead to "the act"? It always does in our house.

Kansas City: I'll answer for my husband. He doesn't do either. So where does that leave me? Up that well-known creek.

Worcester, Mass.: You once wrote, "Use it or lose it." I'm using it, and it's terrific. I'm an 82-year-old widower. (Please don't print my name. I have all I can handle.)

Washington, D.C.: Time has taken its toll. I'm reminded of that wonderful line by Justice Oliver Wendell Holmes, "Oh to be 70 again." (I'm 83.)

Montreal: I am settling, though not by choice. My "get up and go" got up and went.

Anchorage; Springdale, Ark.; Florence, Ala.; Midvale, Utah; Phoenix; Fort Wayne; New York and Boston, the same response: *Hell no.*

Newport News, Va.: We've been married 47 years, and neither of us has ever strayed. Our love is complete.

Charleston, S.C.: This world has gone sex crazy, and TV is to blame. Sex should be for procreation, not recreation. The Bible doesn't say anything about cuddling. I'm 52 and unmarried.

Los Angeles: It is better not to cuddle if you don't intend to go all the way. Something unexpected can happen, as many girls in my school have learned. (Age 17.)

Springfield, Ill.: I still have the urge to merge, but high blood pressure medication has slowed me down a lot. My wife is very understanding and satisfies my needs.

Portland, Maine: Have you heard that sex is now a misdemeanor? The more dey miss da meaner dey get.

Carbondale, Ill.: Cuddling without sex is like holding a baseball season ticket that states you must leave every game in the sixth inning. I vote *no*.

Odessa, Fla.: Lack of sex at home is why we have massage parlors, dating services, call girls, topless bars and prostitution. Men want more than being held tenderly. Wake up out there.

Brisbane, Australia: Anyone who would settle for being held tenderly is looking for nothing but companionship. I suggest he buy a dog.

Hemet, Calif.: My wife, 80, is terminally ill in a convalescent home. I see her and hold her hand every day. Yes, if I could have her on our big, clean bed and cuddle her just one more time, I would be happy to die with her.

Mobile: My wife is 59. I am 60. We have been married 41 years. Our sex life was once very satisfying, but no more. Now I am permitted "access" every Monday between 6 a.m. and 6:15—by the clock. This may explain why so many older men are interested in younger women.

New York: After a year of marriage, my wife said, "Let's just cuddle." The following day, I suggested that we go to her favorite restaurant. When we got there, I told her we weren't going to be seated. Instead, we would just stand by the kitchen and smell the food. (We are both 40.)

Deep River, Ontario: Getting my wife to have sex is like pulling teeth. I seriously considered visiting a house of prostitution, but this is a small town, and I don't know if there are any such places here.

Dear Friend: This is Ann talking. I checked with the municipal department in Deep River (no listing for the Chamber of Commerce), and you are right. She said, "No houses of prostitution here—that we know of."

For more information on impotence and sexual dysfunctions, contact:

American Association of Sex Educators, Counselors and Therapists
P.O. Box 238
Mount Vernon, IA 52314-0238

For more information on sexually transmitted diseases, contact:

American Social Health Association
P.O. Box 13827
Research Triangle Park, NC 27709
(800) 230-6039

National STD Hotline
(800) 227-8922

How I wish I could speak personally to each and every parent and say, "It is not your fault if your daughters and sons don't save their virginity for the wedding bed. That decision will be theirs."

Parental guidance and exemplary role models are helpful, but the Pill has changed everything. Also, there is peer pressure, advertising, movies, TV and highly seductive music. Today, in terms of physical maturation, a 13-year-old is where a 16-year-old was 40 years ago. Better nutrition and medical care have made the difference. The urge to engage in sex hits teenagers three years sooner. The juices are flowing, and the circuits are overloaded. The bodies are ready, but the emotional equipment often is too frail to handle a sexual relationship. Once they become sexually active, they don't quit.

How can you prevent your children from taking the same route? You can't. You can only try to establish an honest relationship and instruct them on how to prevent venereal diseases, AIDS and pregnancy. You can also explain the difference between sex and love and emphasize the beauty of saving oneself for marriage.

Parents should not write their children off if they choose to go in another direction. Nor should they feel guilty if their children ignore good counsel and get into trouble.

In my opinion, all this sleeping around is sad. It has very little to do with love and caring. I liked it better the other way. But we cannot turn the clock back. Parents do not have the last word. Each individual, in the final analysis, is responsible for himself or herself.

Dear Ann Landers: I want to share with you what I consider a rare piece of wisdom. It is called "Teenage Lament," by Nancy Curtis:

> The new morality—and freedom.
> From classes—what a drag!
> From Mom and Dad—always arguing.
> From homework—senseless hours.
> From discipline—useless.
> From church—a bore.
> From conformity—a hangup.
> I'm my own woman now.
> Made so by one decision.
> One hour of love and pleasure.
> Free now to look at my cheerleading sweater hanging in the closet.
> My books and basketball schedule resting on the shelf.
> My material for a prom formal—never made—as it sits amid the
>   remnants of the fabric left over from my maternity tops.
> My medals from band and choir, forsaken in the clutter of a
>   jewelry box.
> My friends passing by my window.
> Laughing over the gossip column in the school paper
> And giggling over who will be the next to experience
> The new morality—and freedom.
> For cleaning—what a drag!
> For him—always arguing.
> For ironing—senseless hours.
> For dishes—useless.
> For cooking—a bore.
> For sex—a hangup.
> Oh God, if you are there,
> Please let someone take this crying baby off my hands
> And let my feet dance once more.
> I am so old. And I was never young.

Dear Friend: I'm grateful for this touching poem. (Are you listening, students? The silence is deafening.)

Back in 1959, I advised a young girl not to marry. She was pregnant, and her parents were urging her to wed a very reluctant boy. Here's what my readers said:

Dear Ann Landers: Do you believe in fate? Well, I do—now. That letter in your column on whether or not a young man should be forced to marry a girl appeared just in time to decide a crushing problem for us. Now, we feel we're doing exactly the right thing.

Your words "an unwilling groom makes a poor husband" made a lot of sense. When we showed it to our daughter, she said, "Ann's right. I know in my heart Nick doesn't want to marry me. That settles it."

You'll never know what a favor you did us, Ann Landers. For the first time in months, there is peace and contentment in our home. The baby will be put up for adoption through an agency, and our daughter will start life over in another city. God bless you.

—Grateful Folks

Dear Ann Landers: Are you tetched in the head or what? How can you advise a young girl to have a baby out of wedlock?

Whether or not the parents are madly in love is of little importance when a baby is on the way. Your advice in this case stank.

—Alabama Reader

Dear Ann: Good for you. I had a shotgun wedding, and I've wished a million times since that the gun had been pointed at me, not him, and that someone had pulled the trigger.

I knew Jack didn't want to marry me, but my parents insisted. My mother kept harping, "Every child is entitled to a name. Nothing else counts now."

I was only 17, a nervous little girl, ignorant and scared. I thought Mama knew best. Besides, I had brought so much shame on the family, I couldn't hold up my head—much less give them an argument.

I've been miserable for 10 long years. I know now I would have been much better off facing the situation alone. Jack has never been a husband or a father, and I'm going it alone anyway.

—Anna

Dear Ann Landers: You ought to be tarred and feathered. The idea—advising an expectant mother not to marry! After I read that advice, I got my bifocals out to make sure my eyes hadn't played tricks on me.

Romantic love is just a lot of nonsense anyway. No matter what people get married for, the romance doesn't last beyond a few months at best. As one wit put it, "Marriage is the cure for the intoxication known as love." So, they might as well get married to give a child a legal name. It's a better reason that most.

—X-Pert Sal

Dear Ann Landers: I was one of those foolish girls who let my folks push me into marriage because I was in a family way at 17. My boyfriend told me if he was forced to marry me, he'd make me sorry. He's kept his word.

He has told our son, who is now 9, that he had to marry me and has warned the boy against getting mixed up with women like his mother. The poor child is too young to know what he's talking about, but he'll know someday. I've had to work since the boy was 5 weeks old because my husband says his money belongs to him. Divorce is against our religion. My life is ruined and I'm only 26.

Your advice is excellent, but it came too late for me.

—Miserable

A note to all who wrote on this subject: The mail has been running 35-to-1 in favor of not forcing a marriage. Almost everyone who wrote has had firsthand experience. Thank you all for letting me know how it looks from inside the lodge. Your letters are deeply appreciated.

———

Dear Ann Landers: We are having discussions in our Sunday religious instruction class. The subject under debate is "Should Sex Education Be Taught in Schools?"

Most of the kids I have talked to are for it. I am against it. I feel that a subject as intimate as sex should be taught at home, by parents. Do you agree?

—Against It

Dear Against It: Sex education *should* be taught at home by parents. But too many parents are abysmally ignorant.

Some parents are incapable of discussing sex with their children because they are inhibited by age-old taboos instilled by *their* parents.

To those who are against sex education in schools, I say this:

It is foolish and unrealistic to tell teenagers to stop thinking about sex. They *are* thinking about sex, and they are going to continue to think about it. What they need is correct information so they will know *how* to think about it. Nine out of 10 teens who write to me about sex problems say they cannot communicate with their parents, which is a sad commentary, indeed.

When the information is not available at home, school is the next best place to learn.

Dear Ann Landers: I am absolutely heartbroken. My 16-year-old daughter has just been diagnosed with a very severe case of herpes.

I am beside myself and totally shocked. "Melissa" has had plenty of sex education, and we have had many talks about safe sex and condoms. When I asked her how this happened, she said she had no idea. Of course, Melissa would not tell me who she got it from. I did insist, however, that she inform the boy at once that he has a contagious disease. I hope and pray she knows who he is and that he wasn't one of several.

Please give me some advice as to how to deal with this nightmare. Melissa does not want to share this information with a therapist, and I don't dare tell my husband. He would hit the roof.

I am sick inside, not only for my daughter but because of the ramifications of this affliction, which she will have for the rest of her life. I am also upset with myself because there must have been something I failed to get across to her. I am . . .
—Worried Sick and Feeling Guilty in Pasadena

Dear Pasadena: Cancel the guilt trip, Mother. This is *not* your fault. Herpes is not a death sentence. Thousands of people who have it live normal lives. There are now highly effective drugs that can keep this infection well under control.

Melissa needs to be educated. I recently printed the address of an organization that your daughter should know about. Here it is again: For free, confidential information about herpes, call the American Social Health Association/Herpes Resource Center at (800) 230-6039.

———

Dear Ann Landers: A while back, you wrote a column about the lines guys give girls when they want to break down their resistance. It made a terrific impression because five of those lines had been tried on me.

I have a younger sister who needs to see that column. I wish I had saved it. Please run it again.

—Molly in New Brunswick

Dear Molly: That column was the result of my asking teenage girls to tell me the lines that were used on them. I received more than 18,000 responses. Here it is—thanks for asking:

From Sharon, Pa.: What are you afraid of? Don't be a baby. It's part of growing up.

Louisville, Ky.: If you really loved me, you would. That's the way people express their true feelings. It's been going on since the world began.

Honolulu: It's very painful for a guy to be in this condition and not get relief. You got me all heated up. If you're any kind of woman, you'll take care of me.

Marshalltown, Iowa: It will be good for your complexion. You should have seen mine before I did it. Honest, it's better than any medicine.

Carbondale, Ill.: You're the most exciting chick I've ever met in my whole life. I have never wanted anybody the way I want you.

Fort Lauderdale, Fla.: Life is so uncertain. Who knows whether you will be alive tomorrow? It would be awful if you died in an accident without experiencing the greatest thrill of all.

Mexico City: You're awfully uptight. Sex is a great tension-breaker. It will make you feel relaxed.

Gatineau, Quebec: I want to marry you someday, and we should find out if we are sexually compatible.

Rochester, N.Y.: I've heard rumors you're a lesbian. If you aren't, prove it.

Nassau, The Bahamas: I promise we won't go all the way unless you want to. I'll stop whenever you say.

Harrisburg, Pa.: You have nothing to worry about. I'm sterile.

Toronto: I know you want it as much as I do, but you're afraid of your reputation. I swear I will never tell anybody. It will be our secret.

Shrewsbury, N.J.: It isn't sex I'm after. I'm really in love with you. If you get pregnant, I'll marry you.

Durham, N.C.: You have the body of a woman. Mother Nature meant for you to have sex. You're ready for it.

I also received some letters from boys. Here are the lines the girls used:

Garden City, N.Y.: I've been seeing a psychiatrist. He says I'm too inhibited. He has advised me to have sex.

Greenwich, Conn.: I have terrible monthly cramps. The doctor said sex would be helpful. Of all the guys I know, you're the one I want to help me with this medical problem. [P.S. The guy said "No."]

Dear Ann Landers: I have a ridiculous problem, and I am plenty disgusted with myself. I can't talk to my parents because I'm too ashamed. You are the only one I can turn to.

I am male, 16 years old, and as you will soon discover, I'm a rotten kid. I have a double hernia caused by masturbation. I can't take a chance on receiving a letter from you so I am begging you to give me some advice through the column.

—No Good

Dear Friend: Where in the world did you get the idea that a hernia can be caused by masturbation? Self-manipulation is a normal part of growing up. About 99 percent of all normal boys and 90 percent of all normal girls first become aware of their sex drives by experimenting in this manner.

If you are having physical discomfort in the groin, I urge you to see a doctor at once. Your ignorance is appalling, son. And what is even more frightening is that there are millions of kids running loose who know as little as you.

One of the most interesting letters I printed was the Know Thyself Question-naire sent in by some teenagers in Memphis. It certainly was the talk of the town. Since then, I've received many "updated" versions, but the original, printed in 1967, really tells it like it was back then:

Dear Ann Landers: The teenagers here in Memphis think you are tuned in to our world like no other adult. You must get a ton of mail from teenagers, or you must talk to a lot of kids because you really have the word. Just to keep you posted, I am sending a copy of a question-naire that has been floating around our high school. Nobody knows for sure where this thing got started, but the kids in my crowd, both guys and dolls, think it's pretty good.

I would like your opinion of this questionnaire, and I know you will level. Please don't suggest I take it home and get my mother's views. If she saw it, she would faint, and we'd have to call the doctor. Here it is:

Know Thyself Questionnaire

(Score the number indicated for each "yes" answer)

1. Ever gone out with a member of the opposite sex?	4
2. Ever been kissed?	4
3. Ever been French kissed?	4
4. Ever been kissed while in a reclining position?	5
5. Ever gotten or given a hickey?	3
6. Ever been kissed in your pajamas?	2
7. Ever been kissed against your will?	2
8. Ever parked for more than an hour?	5
9. Ever said, "I love you"?	3
10. Ever said, "I love you" to more than one person?	3
11. Ever gone steady?	4
12. Ever been picked up by a person you never saw before?	7
13. Ever played strip poker with a member of the opposite sex?	5
14. Have you gone all the way?	10
15. Have you had the desire to go all the way but managed to keep from it?	2
16. Have you ever made a member of the opposite sex cry?	4
17. Has a member of the opposite sex ever made you cry?	4
18. Do you smoke?	2
19. Do you drink?	2
20. Ever passed out from drinking?	6
21. Ever lied to your folks about where you went or with whom?	8
22. Ever smoke pot?	7
23. Ever taken an LSD trip?	10
24. Ever consider the pregnancy route so your folks would have to let you get married?	10

SCORE CHART

9 or under	Queer or something
10 to 15	Pure as the driven snow
15 to 25	Passionate but prudish
25 to 35	Normal and decent
35 to 45	Indecent
45 to 55	Headed for serious trouble

55 to 60	In terrible shape
60 or over	Condemned
	Signed—Normal and Decent

Dear N. and D.: I can't evaluate this questionnaire because each questionnaire should be evaluated on the basis of the individual scoring. Let me say it's darned interesting (though somewhat gamey), and I appreciate your sending it to me.

I have always advised my readers to be tolerant of homosexuality. I will admit, however, that when I first began writing about homosexuality back in the early '60s, I followed the American Psychiatric Association's view that homosexuality was a deviant psychiatric disorder.

Over the years, I have revised my opinion. I now believe homosexuals are born, not made, and that something in their genetic makeup predetermines sexual orientation.

The next step is for society to accord homosexuals the same respect and tolerance as everyone else.

Here are some of the letters I've received on the subject:

Dear Ann Landers: I am glad to see you are printing some decent information on homosexuality. I am pleased, too, that you are publishing sensible letters from homosexuals. As a lesbian, I can tell you there are plenty of kooks in our segment of society, as in others. Whenever you separate people into groups, you are bound to get some nuts. This goes for lawyers, doctors, teachers, homosexuals, creeps, poets, Women's Lib—yes, even newspaper columnists.

The principal desire of lesbians is to be accepted as human beings, to be allowed to hold jobs, to be paid commensurate with their abilities and to be left alone by straight people who view them as freaks. You can't believe some of the questions I have been asked by supposedly intelligent people. For example, a man I work with (he knows about my relationship with another woman, who is employed by our firm) recently asked, "Which one of you is the guy?" Such misconceptions make my blood boil.

You are doing a great deal to lift the veil of ignorance, Ann, and I hope you will continue to do so.

—The Ladder

Dear Ladder: I'll continue to try. Thank you for writing.

Dear Ann Landers: I have read several letters in your column from people who despise homosexuals. What do they want from us? Would they be satisfied if we were all locked up, isolated from society? Or would they prefer that we simply be shot at sunrise?

Why don't people realize that the only difference between homosexuals and heterosexuals is what we do behind closed doors? We don't worry about them. Why should they worry about us? My roommate and I frequently entertain mixed couples, and we have many interesting friends. We are honorable people. We don't play with girls, pretending to be straight, dragging them around to parties as cover. We believe this is cheap and dishonest.

The notion that gay boys are all limp-wristed and swishy is absurd. Many homosexual males with whom I am intimately acquainted are extremely masculine in appearance, dress and mannerisms. They work at being masculine to avoid detection.

I am acquainted with homosexuals who are successful doctors, lawyers, teachers, clergymen and politicians. They are in every walk of life. The closet queens in the professions as well as politicians must be circumspect, however, because they are subject to blackmail. Isn't this shameful?

A year of psychiatric therapy has helped me to accept myself as I am. I now know that I don't need the friendship of anyone who views me as a freak. I hope and pray that one day *all* people will be judged on the basis of what they contribute to humanity and how they treat their fellow man. Wouldn't that be wonderful?

—Written in Beaumont, Mailed in New Orleans

Dear Friend: Yes, it would be wonderful—and I predict that one day it will come to pass.

Dear Ann Landers: Bisexual women not only freak out their husbands, they freak out other women.

I didn't know such females existed until a couple of years ago. Out of a clear blue sky, a woman I had known for years suddenly confessed that she was in love with me—and had been for a long time. I didn't know how to act. I was shocked and dumbfounded, totally unprepared for such a confrontation. Apparently, I was too naive to get the signals she had been sending out. What's more, the whole thing seemed revolting. Needless to say, I terminated our friendship then and there.

I don't want a recurrence of this unpleasant episode, yet how do I avoid it? I am 35 and have never been married. I was shy as a teenager and didn't date much. I never learned how to attract men and probably never will. I am busy with my work and reasonably happy. While I would like a man, I won't die if one doesn't come along.

How can I avoid future advances of this kind? Once in a lifetime is enough, thank you.

—An Old Maid but Plenty Straight

Dear Straight: You didn't invite that advance, and you may well get another. Your best protection is to be alert to women who buy you gifts for no reason, who suggest taking a trip together and who get onto the subject of lesbianism.

Since kissing and hugging among straight women is so commonplace in our culture, this is not much of a clue unless you feel it is excessive. Then, of course, you cool it.

The moment you suspect something is out of kilter, split. It serves no useful purpose to show disgust or revulsion and create an ugly incident.

Dear Ann Landers: Do I have the right to ask my older sister if she is gay? There are many telltale signs that lead me to believe she is.

"Lisa" was a member of a sorority for four years and lived in the sorority house with some very masculine-looking girls. Very few of the girls in that sorority went out with guys. I can't believe they never got asked. My guess is they enjoyed each other's company more.

My sister never dates. At present, she is awfully close with a woman friend. They spend nights at one another's homes and are on the phone constantly. One doesn't make a move without the other.

Both my brothers and I think something is strange. Should I ask "Lisa" the question straight-out?

—A Doubting Sister in a N.Y. Suburb

Dear Doubting: How would it change your life if she is or isn't? If Lisa were a lesbian and wanted to go public, she would.

The tone of your letter suggests you would talk to her in an accusatory or judgmental way. This could create tremendous resentment and permanent alienation—especially if she is straight. My advice is M.Y.O.B.

I received a letter in September 1989 from a homosexual who signed himself "Waiting for Justice in Chicago." He wrote, "At the present time, no state will allow two people of the same sex to obtain a marriage license. Isn't it about time homosexuals were given the same options that heterosexual couples enjoy? This is discrimination of the most blatant kind in a country that claims to believe in freedom, equality and liberty."

I told "Waiting for Justice" I doubted that we would see the legalization of same-sex marriages in our lifetime and then invited my readers to drop me a line and let me know if they were for homosexual marriages or against them.

I received more than 55,000 responses. The tally ran about 2-to-1 against same-sex marriages. Keep reading, and you will learn how Americans and Canadians feel about this controversial issue. I must say that I am deeply troubled by the viciousness and lack of compassion of so many correspondents.

From Grosse Pointe, Mich.: You want an answer? I'll give you one. The way you stick up for queers is disgusting. But I am not surprised, seeing as how you are an ultra left-winger, a Jew and a woman. And while I'm at it, I would like to say that San Francisco, which is 50 percent gay, is the armpit of America.

Saginaw, Mich.: I cast my vote for legal recognition of same-sex couples. I am gay, my wife is straight, and we have been married 25 years. The love and understanding of this wonderful woman have kept me away from temptation. I know deep down, however, that if I could have been legally married to my first love, I would have had a glorious life in harmony with my true nature.

Philadelphia: I am the father of two sons. One is gay. I want equal rights for both boys. Put me in the "for" column.

Long Beach, Calif.: We are against legalizing homosexual relationships. It is wrong to encourage these sick people who are killing themselves and infecting others because of their filthy lifestyle.

Santa Rosa, Calif.: I work at a hospice and never cease to be moved by the unselfish love and devotion these males have for one another. Such beautiful relationships ought to have the dignity of legal recognition.

Chicago: History is repeating itself. The gays are where the blacks were 35 years ago. Who would have thought back then that we would have black mayors in dozens of our country's largest cities?

Louisville, Ky.: I'll go to Leviticus 20:13: "And when a man lies down with a male the same as one lies with a woman, both of them have done a detestable thing. They should be put to death without fail."

Detroit: Have those dumb clucks in San Francisco who passed the domestic partners legislation figured out what will happen when the "partnership" goes sour? Will these partnerships end up in "divorce court"? That's all we need—to let those fruitcakes who want to cut loose jam our courts.

Eau Claire, Wis.: I vote no. The notion that members of the same sex should have the rights and privileges of normal couples is outrageous. I am not a religious fundamentalist, but I believe that homosexuality is morally wrong. Those faggots should go back in the closet where they belong.

Baton Rouge: It is time Americans stopped being afraid of (and feeling threatened by) people who are different. This goes for members of minority groups, those who are physically handicapped and individuals whose sexual preference is not that of the norm. As far as I'm concerned, same-sex couples should be allowed to marry.

Chicago: The family unit is the core of civilization. This means parents and children. When homosexuals can be biologically altered so that they can produce a child, I will vote yes. Until then, I'm voting no.

Charleston, W.Va.: If society had not placed such a stigma on homosexuality, I would have been able to face myself as I truly am instead of living a lie, marrying a wonderful woman and messing up her life.

Lubbock, Tex.: Homosexuality is against the law of nature, God and Texas. Remember that commercial, "It is not nice to fool Mother Nature"? Well, that's what the perverts are trying to do, and it doesn't work.

Raleigh, N.C.: Marriage? I wouldn't go that far, but since I have been in a monogamous same-sex relationship for 10 years, I certainly would like to see a tax break. I am in the 30 percent bracket because I am considered single. My significant other and I are just as much "married" as many of our friends, yet we get none of the tax advantages.

Dear Ann Landers: Lately, I have read several of your columns concerning teenage sex, and the question has been raised: Who are the more aggressive, boys or girls? I don't know how it was in your day, but I can tell you that the girls of our generation are much more sexually aggressive than the boys.

Ann, I am an 18-year-old high school senior and a member of the football and basketball teams. I am gay.

My parents and most of my schoolmates, both guys and girls, are aware of this, and I am comfortable with myself. I cannot understand why the girls who know I'm gay still hit on me. They phone at all hours of the night, mostly with sexual invitations. My mother has asked a couple of the more persistent ladies to please stop calling. She told one, "My son is not interested in you."

The kids at school accept me the way I am. Once in a while, one of the guys will give me a hard time, but I have no problem dealing with that. The girls are another story. Just yesterday, one of them told me that she could "straighten me out" if I would give her the chance.

I have a very special friend who is a student at the local university, and we are together a lot. We look like the jocks of the year and are very happy with each other. He also gets lots of offers from young ladies, and neither of us can understand it.

Will you please make it clear that gay guys are not interested in members of the opposite sex?

—Leave Us Alone in Santa Barbara

Dear L.U.A.: You made it a lot clearer than I could, and I thank you. After this letter appears in the *Santa Barbara News-Press*, I doubt that you will have any more trouble with girls hitting on you.

Dear Ann Landers: I read that two genetic researchers, Dr. J. Michael Bailey at Northwestern University in Illinois and Dr. Richard Pillard of the Boston University School of Medicine, have turned up some convincing evidence about homosexuality based on studies of identical twins. The results have established that genes may play a major role in whether a person is gay or straight.

Since there is now scientific evidence that homosexuals are born that way and their lifestyle is not something they choose, do you think people will be less hostile to and more tolerant of homosexuals? Please respond in the paper. This is a subject that a great many people are interested in and need to know more about.

—Covina, Calif.

Dear Covina: Valid information is always a plus. I think that if people believed homosexuality was not merely an alternate lifestyle but the result of genetics, there would be less hostility toward the gay population.

Many straight people believe homosexuality is a curse and that gays are miserable. Some homosexuals may agree with them. I, however, have heard from gays who consider homosexuality a "special bonus." So let's settle that question once and for all. I'd like to ask the gay community how it feels about this.

Write either "Yes, I'm glad I'm gay," or "No, I would rather be straight." I will announce the results in a few weeks.

This survey was taken in 1992. I was not surprised at the answer most gave, but the volume of mail was astonishing. The count was 75,875 responses, with 30-to-1 saying, "Yes, I'm glad I'm gay."

I asked for postcards only, but thousands of gays and lesbians wrote letters. It was a busy time—and an enlightening one.

Here are some sample responses:

From San Francisco: What a question! If I had a choice, I'd be straight, white, possibly Swedish, 6-feet-1-inch tall and Protestant. My life would be easier, but I am not sure that an easy life is always the best life.

Chicago: We have four children. One of our sons is gay. He is the brightest and most sensitive, caring and thoughtful of the four. We often wondered if being gay made the difference and have concluded that it did.

Detroit: Am I glad I'm gay? You've got to be crazy. I've been beaten up, spat on and discriminated against in the job market. Who would choose this?

Columbus, Ohio: Yes, I am glad that I'm gay, but one thing I regret is that it took me 20 years to admit it to myself and 45 years to be open about it.

Oakland: Actually, I am bisexual, and I choose to be so. Since I was lucky enough to be presented by nature with two options, why not take both?

Harrisburg, Pa.: I have known since I was 7 years old that I was different. I am an adult now and have been in a rewarding relationship for more than five years. I do not push my preference on anyone and ask only that people not persecute me for being who I am. God alone is my judge.

Portland, Ore.: For the first 36 years of my life, I wanted desperately to be straight. I married and became the father of two beautiful children. I am a successful attorney. When I turned 40, four years after my divorce, I tried to straddle the fence—straight by day and gay by night. It didn't work. Finally, I met a terrific man, and we are extremely happy. So, Ann, to answer your question, "Yes, I'm glad I'm gay," because that's who I am.

Charleston, S.C.: Everyone knows black people don't choose to be black, but that doesn't prevent discrimination. Do you honestly believe if people accepted the fact that homosexuals were born that way, it would make a difference? I don't.

Lexington, Ky.: Am I glad I'm gay? My response is an unqualified yes. It's wonderful to know that there are people out there who would happily kill me because of my sexual orientation. I am delighted that the government discriminates against me at tax time and I can't file jointly. I'm ecstatic that I'm barred from serving my country in times of war. I'm overjoyed that all major religions reject my lifestyle. I love it that I could lose my job if the truth were known. Best of all, it's great to be viewed as an outcast by one's own family. This is what it means to be gay.

Louisville: Yes, Ann, I'm glad I'm gay. Thank you for asking. But being gay is a very small part of who I am. I'm a teacher and a football coach. I play classical music and a good game of tennis. I'm a gourmet cook. I can ski, and I can sew. I am active in my church and a volunteer at our local shelter for the homeless. I don't believe in labels. Let's just say I am human.

Boston: I'm 32 years old, the chairman of a multimillion-dollar, high-tech company. And yes, I'm gay. Several weeks ago, I attended a meeting of a group called the Greater Boston Business Council. I walked into the ballroom of a Hilton hotel and couldn't believe my eyes—more than 200 professional gay men and women. If I hadn't known where I was, I would have sworn it was a meeting of the Chamber of Commerce. We are your doctors, lawyers, shopkeepers, bus drivers, waiters and florists. But best of all, we look, walk and talk like everyone else. There are many more of us in the closet than out, but it's becoming much easier to be open, thank the good Lord who made us all.

Royal Oak, Mich.: Yes, I'm gay, now 73 years old, and it's been a difficult life. I knew that being gay was beyond my control from the beginning. I prayed about it and finally accepted it. I figured if God made me this way he must have had a reason. I never felt comfortable with a woman. It was impossible to think of a woman in a sexual way. I tried a few times when I was in the Army during World War II and just couldn't. So when they now say it's in our genes, I know it's the truth. I'm glad I'm not married because I wouldn't want to bring a son into the world who might have to struggle as I have.

Chicago: Are gay people happy? Actually, some of us are, despite the fact that we live in a society that calls us "sick," "depraved" and "evil." With those labels, it's not easy to maintain self-esteem. If straight people have a problem with my being gay, that's their hang-up, not mine. I also find it fascinating that some of the most vicious gay-bashers are closet gays themselves. People who are sure of their own sexuality are willing to live and let live.

And now, dear readers, this is Ann: It is my firm conviction that homosexuality is not learned behavior, it is genetic. It can be suppressed but not altered.

3

Children: A Mixed Blessing— His, Hers and Ours

A Child's Plea to His Parents

Give me more than food to nourish me. Give me the warmth and the security of your love.

Let me enjoy all five senses. Give me plenty of things to look at, to feel, to smell, to listen to, to taste. And even some things to break.

Teach me to take my turn. Watch me play so you can see how I am trying to work out my problems and what I am up against.

When you tell me to do something, please tell me why I should do it. Let me feel that I am a contributing member of the family. And be sure to include me in making the family plans when you can.

Please don't keep me your baby when I want to feel grown up. Don't transfer your fears to me. I have enough of my own to cope with, and I don't need any more.

Help me not to act when I am angry. But don't make me so afraid of showing anger that I lose my capacity to feel strongly about anything.

Let me learn bit by bit to bear pain, and to want things but to be strong enough to postpone gratification of certain feelings I am not yet ready to experience.

Let me try out my new powers as my body develops—to creep, to stand, to walk, climb, jump and run when I am ready. Don't limit the natural needs of my body because you have some unresolved hang-ups.

Give me a little corner in the house that is all mine and nobody else's. I need moments of peace and quiet that cannot be invaded by anyone.

Give me my share of consideration and attention. I must know that every day, even if for just a few moments, I am the only one you are thinking about and loving.

Let me ask any question that pops into my head. Don't make me ashamed for having asked it, even if it seems stupid. And give me as honest an answer as you can. If you don't know the answer, please say so. It's good training to hear someone say, "I don't know, but I will try to find out for you."

Be patient with me when I don't do things very well at first. Remember I have so many things to learn and almost everything takes some practice.

Let me bear the consequences for whatever I do. I need to be punished as well as rewarded. And when you punish me, make sure the punishment fits the "crime."

Above all, grant me, without reservation, your debt to me—unconditional love. For if I know it is there, I will be able to give the same to my children, and they will be able to give it to their children.

—Your Child

The Child's Plea contains some lovely bits of wisdom. It is an excellent guide for rearing gentle, independent, loving children.

———

The following declaration of independence is something I saw taped to my granddaughter's refrigerator in Minneapolis. It really hit my funny bone. Sorry I can't give credit to the author. Anyone who has a child under 3 years of age will see that youngster in the lines that follow:

Toddler's Creed

If I want it, it's mine.
If I give it to you and change my mind later, it's mine.
If I can take it away from you, it's mine.
If it's mine, it will never belong to anybody else, no matter what.
If we are building something together, all the pieces are mine.
If it looks just like mine, it is mine.

As any parent knows, children can be both a delight and a handful. Sometimes things don't work out the way we plan. Parents can only do the best they know how and hope their love and care will produce loving and caring people.

In some cases, problems can start in infancy. And of course, the problems don't go away when our children are grown and independent.

Here are some of the issues that have come up over the years:

On November 3, 1975, a young married couple wrote to say they were undecided as to whether to have a family. They asked me to solicit opinions from parents of young children as well as from older couples whose families were grown. "Was it worth it?" they wanted to know. "Were the rewards enough to make up for the grief?" The question, as I put it to my readers, was this: "If you had it to do over again, would you have children?"

Well, dear friends, the responses were staggering. Much to my surprise, 70 percent of those who responded said no.

Here are some excerpts from the most fascinating (and disturbing) mail I had received in a long time:

From Fargo, N.D.: My husband and I were married for eight years before we had our first child. Within four years, we had three. (The third one was a mistake.) Then, I had my tubes tied, and my husband had a vasectomy—just to make sure. We both agree our happiest years were before we had the kids. They have brought us a lot of heartache and very little pleasure. If we had it to do over again, we'd have remained childless.

—Rather Die than Sign My Name

Tampa, Fla.: I am 40, and my husband is 45. We have twin children under 8 years of age. I was an attractive, fulfilled career woman before I had these kids. Now I'm an overly exhausted, nervous wreck who misses her job and sees very little of her husband. He's got a "friend," I'm sure, and I don't blame him. Our children took all the romance out of our marriage. I'm too tired for sex, conversation or anything else.

—Sign Me Too Late for Tears

Chippewa Falls, Wis.: As the mother of six, I can tell you my life would have had no meaning without my children. Sure, there are runny noses, chicken pox, arms in slings, fights, loads of laundry and sky-high grocery bills, but when I tuck them in at night, I thank God I've been so richly blessed.

—Worth the Pain

New York: I've lived for 70 years, and I speak from experience, as a mother of five. Was it worth it? No. The early years are difficult. Illness, rebellion, lack of motivation (we called it shiftlessness and laziness in our day). One was seriously disturbed—in and out of mental hospitals. Another went the gay-lib route. Two are now living in communes (we never hear from them). Another has gone loony with the help of a phony religious leader who should be in jail. Not one of our children has given us any pleasure. God knows we did our best, but we were failures as parents, and they are failures as people.

—Sad Story

Chicago: Should you have children? It depends on what you want them for. Do you want a child who will be everything you weren't? Someone whose achievements you can brag about? Do you want company in your old age? Forget it. Have children only if you can give them unselfish love and expect nothing in return. Only then will you have a fighting chance of turning out emotionally healthy individuals who will appreciate and respect you and themselves.

—Been There

Dear Been There: There's still hope for mankind as long as there are human beings like you around. May your tribe increase.

————

Dear Ann Landers: I was married in 1955. It's been four years, and I want a family. The problem is my husband. Before you jump to conclusions, let me assure you he's a perfect specimen of manhood. He feels it would be an injustice to bring children into this crazy world.

He reads everything available on nuclear warfare. I'm practically an authority on radioactivity myself. Some of the articles make me wonder if I'll get out of bed in the morning.

I admit he has a point, but I hate to think of going through life without a family. Is it wrong to bring children into a world equipped with weapons of total destruction? What are your views?

—Woman on the Beach

Dear Woman: Life is for the living. Since the beginning of time, every age has been a dangerous one. Today, we are concerned with nuclear warfare. Fifty years ago, they worried about the mortality rate of infants and mothers.

Beware the merchants of doom and gloom. They've been peddling their wares for centuries. Mustard gas was a terrifying weapon in World War I, but that didn't stop your grandmother, did it?

I suspect hubby is using the atomic age as an excuse. He's immature and afraid to face the responsibilities of fatherhood.

Make it plain you don't buy his theory. And instead of scaring yourselves to death with tracts on the horrors of war, visit friends who have loving, healthy children. Perhaps this will open your husband's eyes to his selfish, shortsighted, sick approach to life.

Dear Ann Landers: More and more doctors and parents agree that early intervention is the key to controlling or correcting physical challenges, such as cerebral palsy. To assure early intervention, parents must know what warning signs to look for. Many of your readers have babies or young children, and you can help them by printing this information.

The Pathways Awareness Foundation in Chicago publishes a brochure for parents with babies. This brochure enables parents to detect a physically challenging condition early in a child's life, so the condition can be treated as soon as possible. It includes pictures that show the difference between a normally developing child and one with physical difficulties, making it easy for parents to spot a problem and consult with their doctors.

Parents who frequently notice the following signs in their infants should consult their pediatricians at once:

Inability to lift head or push up on arms by 3 months of age
Stiff or rigid legs
Pushing back or away with head
Flabby or limp body posture
Stiff, crossed legs at 6 months
Inability to sit up without support by 8 months
Using only one side of the body or only the arms to crawl

When physical problems appear, the following behavioral problems may be additional warning signs:

Extreme irritability
Failure to smile by 3 months

Feeding difficulties
Persistent gagging or choking when fed
After 6 months, tongue pushes soft food out of mouth

Children with physical challenges can lead more independent, more productive lives when treatment is sought early. That's why the Pathways Awareness Foundation brochure and knowing the signs to look for are so important.

If you wish more information on this subject, get a free copy of the Pathways brochure. Send a self-addressed, stamped envelope to Pathways Awareness Foundation, 123 N. Wacker Dr., Chicago, IL 60606, or call (800) 955-2445.

—Dr. H. Garry Gardner, president, Illinois Chapter,
American Academy of Pediatrics

Heaven's Very Special Child
Edna Massimilla

A meeting was held quite far from Earth!
It's time again for another birth.
Said the Angels to the Lord above,
This Special Child will need much love.

His progress may be very slow.
Accomplishment he may not show.
And he'll require extra care
From the folks he meets down there.

He may not run or laugh or play;
His thoughts may seem quite far away.
In many ways, he won't adapt,
And he'll be known as handicapped.

So let's be careful where he's sent.
We want his life to be content.
Please, Lord, find the parents who
Will do a special job for You.

They will not realize right away.
The leading role they're asked to play.
But with this child sent from above.
Comes stronger faith and richer love.

And soon they'll know the privilege given
In caring for their gift from Heaven.
Their precious charge, so meek and mild,
Is Heaven's Very Special Child.

Dear Ann Landers: I read your column regularly, and although I don't always agree with your advice, I think you have a lot of common sense when it comes to raising children.

I have a perplexing problem with my 18-month-old son. He is a very active child, large and strong for his age. Just recently, he began playfully hitting me. I would tell him, no, and that would be the end of it. In the past two weeks, however, his playful hitting is beginning to get to me. He climbs up in my lap says, "Hi, Mommy," then whacks me right in the face.

I believe in spanking as a last resort, and I have spanked him a couple of times for doing this, but it hasn't solved the problem. In fact, he has been hitting me even more.

The strange thing is that he never hits anyone but me. This whole thing has put a terrific strain on my patience.

Can you offer a solution?

—Worried

Dear Worried: First, stop hitting the child. It only teaches him that you can inflict pain, and as you have already discovered, it's no deterrent. When the youngster belts you, tell him again, in a very firm manner, "No—you must not hit anyone." Then put him in a chair and make him sit there for 30 minutes—no TV, no toys, no books, nothing to amuse him. Thirty minutes will seem like an eternity to an 18-month-old. This punishment conveys the message that hitting is unacceptable and you are in control. And that is what you need to get across.

After this letter appeared, several readers told me that 30 minutes is far too long for a child so young. They suggested 10 to 15 minutes would be more appropriate. I agreed and said so.

One letter that I printed provoked a huge response from my readers. Read on to see why:

Dear Ann Landers: What do you think of a 30-year-old father who, on his son's second birthday, pushes his son's face into the birthday cake while 20 people are watching? Then, with a big grin, the father proceeds to videotape his child's stunned response and the tears that follow.

For several weeks, the little boy knew that his birthday was coming. He kept repeating words like "birthday" and "two," while holding up two little fingers. He had looked forward to the party with such joy, and to have it end like that was heartbreaking. I was so upset that I left without saying goodbye.

I am the child's grandmother. What would you have done?

—*Milwaukee Journal* Reader

Dear Reader: No loving father could have done such a thing. Beneath that "joke," there is genuine hostility.

I would not have left the party. I would have stayed, comforted the child and told his father in no uncertain terms that I didn't see anything funny about pushing his son's face into a cake—that it was cruel and disgusting.

P.S. I wonder if he was one of those grooms who shoved the wedding cake in his bride's face, a "custom" I find equally deplorable and highly suspect.

Dear Ann Landers: I wept when I read the letter from the Milwaukee grandmother of a 2-year-old whose father had pushed the boy's face into his birthday cake and then videotaped the child's stunned response. I'm afraid that little guy is in more danger than your response indicated.

The father is clearly a bully who probably suffers from low self-esteem. As his son matures, the peril to that youngster will increase. Will you please advise the grandmother to stay as close to the situation as possible and suggest that she be less reluctant to intervene? That father's behavior certainly sounds like child abuse.

—Ruth, Glastonbury, Conn.

Dear Ruth: The outpouring of sympathy and support for the boy was enormous. When I read his grandmother's letter, my heart ached for him, but I didn't anticipate the tremendous amount of mail that letter would generate. Read on:

From Brooklyn: The letter about the 2-year-old boy whose father pushed his little face into his birthday cake made me cry. It's bad enough that the grandmother left without saying a word, but where was the kid's mother, for heaven's sake? And how about the rest of the clan? Didn't anyone have the courage to speak up? Some family!

Groton, Conn.: I am a 57-year-old grandfather and not the bleeding heart type, but I shed tears when I read about that helpless child, his face smeared with ruined birthday cake, while that heartless jerk of a father videotaped. May the good Lord stand by this boy and speed the years until he is able to get away from that awful man.

Lexington, Ky.: About that slob of a father. You called it hostility. I call it greed. Thanks to those TV shows that give big prizes for videotaping such things, thousands of mean-spirited, money-hungry apes are running around with cameras taking advantage of anyone who happens to be in an embarrassing situation. I'll bet that father was trying to get some footage that would win a prize.

Sacramento: If a father can do that in front of people, what does he do when nobody is looking?

Dickinson, N.D.: That little boy will never trust his father again. And those goofy relatives who just stood around need a thump on the head to instill some caring and compassion.

Appleton, Wis.: We live in Appleton, which is not much of a drive to Milwaukee. Will you please hurry and send me that father's address? I would like to go to his house and paste him one in the mouth.

The following appeared in the Laurens, Iowa, Sun through the courtesy of Jim Gale. I hope it will make people stop and think.

A Letter from a Father to All Who Drive

Dear Driver: A few weeks ago, I saw a little girl struck by a car when she tried to cross the street. Her father raced toward her, swept her up in his arms and held her close as she struggled against the certainty of death.

I saw all the plans he had made for her future fade into nothingness. A look of despair came over his face. I could only offer a prayer that such a thing would never happen again—but I knew it would and more hearts would be broken.

Today, my 6-year-old daughter started off to school. Her cocker spaniel, Scott, watched her leave and whined his doubts about the value of education. Tonight, we talked about her very first day. She described the girl with yellow curls who sits in front of her and the boy across the aisle who makes faces and the teacher who has eyes in the back of her head. As I write this letter, my adorable little girl is sound asleep, with her big doll, Paddy, in her arms.

When Paddy gets broken, I can fix the cut on her finger or the bump on her head, but when my daughter starts across the street, Mr. Driver, she is in your hands.

It is not possible for me to be with her at all times. I must work to pay for her home and food and education. So I am asking you to look out for her. Drive slowly past schools and intersections. And remember that sometimes children run from behind parked cars.

Please don't kill my little girl.

—A Father

Here are some rules for protecting your children:

1. Keep your child next to you at all times while shopping, even if it means a harness.
2. Never leave a child in a locked or parked car. A tot can easily be tricked into unlocking the door.
3. Tell your child that if you become separated to go directly to a checkout counter and say to the clerk, "I am lost."
4. Adults, please do not ignore the plight of a lost child, no matter how busy you are. Take the youngster to a sales person. You would want your child or grandchild to be helped in that manner.

In every batch of letters, there is at least one from a parent asking how to ease the hostility between siblings. Here's a letter that says it best:

Dear Ann Landers: I hope you can stand reading one more letter about siblings who grew up hating each other. Both my husband and I had parents who pitted their children against one another and made it impossible for us to be close.

I was determined that competitiveness would never separate my own two children when they were growing up. When their adolescent squabbling turned mean-spirited, I stepped in and helped them learn how to settle things before they destroyed each other.

This worked pretty well until one day when they were in their early teens. They had been quarreling and hurting each other all day, and I was sick of it. I became angry and blew my top. "You must become better friends," I said, "because, God willing, you will both live a long time. I will be gone, and your father will be gone, and all your teachers and many of your friends will be gone. There may be only the two of you left, and you will remember what you were like as children.

"Nobody else will remember the Christmases you had, the tree house you built, the day you learned to ride a bike, the fun you had trick-or-treating, the teacher you loved in the third grade and the kittens born in the laundry. There will be only the two of you, and you had better love each other now because 60 years from now, only you will remember all the wonderful experiences you shared and those memories will be golden."

They both became very quiet, and I thought perhaps they were too young to understand. But it must have made an impression because they have never squabbled or tried to hurt each other after that. I wish my parents had explained to my sister and me, 40 years ago, that sibling rivalry is natural but brothers and sisters who are not good to each other lose something precious.

—Lucille in St. Louis

Dear Lucille: What a beautiful sermon! This is one column I hope will go up on thousands of refrigerators and under dinner plates.

P.S. One way to make sure your children will grow up to hate each other: Show favoritism and keep repeating, "Why aren't you as smart as your brother (or sister)?" Such remarks are guaranteed to create lifelong animosity. If you want your children to love each other, teach them to respect one another and to help each other succeed. It's the basis for true friendship.

Dear Ann Landers: I have twin girls, 2 years old. Please forgive a mother's pride, but they are very pretty and loaded with personality. Of course, they attract a great deal of attention wherever they go. People stare, poke each other with elbows and say, "Look at the twins." My daughters are aware of the furor they create and revel in it.

How did you and your twin, Dear Abby, react to the staring, whispering and finger-pointing when you were growing up? Was it annoying? Was it fun? Did it have any impact on the way you thought about yourselves? Did it make you more reclusive or more outgoing?

What advice do you have for a mother who is trying to raise twin girls to be normal, well-adjusted human beings?

—H.H.U. in Miami

Dear Miami: My sister and I were almost always the center of attention from the day we were born. As if being twins weren't enough, I was born with two teeth and my sis had one. No one could ever accuse us of being "reclusive."

Since our mother dressed us alike from infancy until we were married (a double wedding, of course, with identical gowns and bridal veils), no one could miss us.

The wonderful thing about being a twin is that you are never lonely. There is always someone to talk to. And talk we did, nonstop for 21 years. Then marriage provided each of us with a new set of ears.

The awful part of being a twin is that you are never alone. There was no opportunity for quiet introspection and honest self-appraisal. Granted, the "togetherness" was great fun, but it denied us the opportunity to develop as individuals. We would never escape the image of the sister act.

In retrospect, we grew up surprisingly unspoiled, although we traded on our twinship shamelessly, a natural and easy thing to do. We also got into a great deal of mischief. What one couldn't think of the other one could.

My advice to mothers of twins is this: Do not, repeat not, dress your twins alike. Treat them as individuals, not halves of a single unit. Encourage them to have different friends. If possible, send them to different schools. If that isn't possible, try to put them in different classes.

Do not make your twins feel guilty if they fail to stick together on all issues. Encourage them to be independent and have their own point of view.

Be impartial, and always remain neutral when they have their battles. Don't take sides.

Never compare one twin with the other, and do not permit relatives or friends to make comparisons.

Be aware that sibling rivalry is natural and with twins it is intensified.

Not until my daughter Margo was born did I realize what a remarkable (and heroic) woman my mother was. I have thought many times that God must have a special place at his right hand for the mothers of twins. Especially if the twins are anything like my sister and me.

Here's a poem for all parents to remember:

To My Grown-up Son
Alice E. Chase

My hands were busy through the day.
I didn't have much time to play
The little games you asked me to.
I didn't have much time for you.
I'd wash your clothes, I'd sew and cook,
But when you'd bring your picture book
And ask me please to share your fun,
I'd say: "A little later, son."
I'd tuck you in all safe at night
And hear your prayers, turn out the light,
Then tiptoe softly to the door . . .
I wish I'd stayed a minute more.
For life is short, the years rush past.
A little boy grows up so fast.
No longer is he at your side,
His precious secrets to confide.
The picture books are put away,
There are no longer games to play,
No goodnight kiss, no prayers to hear . . .
That all belongs to yesteryear.
My hands, once busy, now are still.
The days are long and hard to fill.
I wish I could go back and do
The little things you asked me to.

As children grow and change, so do their problems. Instead of worrying about their first day of school, we find ourselves worrying about their first kiss—and other intimacies.

Dear Ann Landers: Our son is 12 and of normal weight and height. But I am concerned about his genitals. They are still the size of a toddler's. His 6-year-old brother is larger than he is. "Ed's" gym instructor says that he takes a lot of kidding.

I have taken this boy to a pediatrician and an endocrinologist. They both laughed the matter off and said, "Don't worry, Mom, he'll have plenty of girlfriends." I don't appreciate that kind of response. It seems to me that a joke is being made of something that is very serious.

I am deeply concerned, Ann. This boy's self-esteem is low enough without being ridiculed about his manhood. Furthermore, I know how important it is to be able to have a satisfying sexual relationship.

Ed is a sensitive child, and I really do worry that this problem may ruin his life. I don't know who to talk to about this now that two doctors have laughed about it and made me feel foolish. Can you help?
                                                    —No Name in Illinois

Dear Illinois: Although the pediatrician and the endocrinologist meant to reassure you, they could have been more supportive. It should, however, be a relief to know the child has no physical problem and is just undersized.

Please be careful not to transfer your anxiety to the boy. This could be extremely damaging.

Sex therapists tell us that size has very little to do with satisfaction. Also, what appears to be undersized in the flaccid state can be much larger when there is an erection. And remember, he is only 12 and may be a late bloomer. So, cool it, Mom. A lot can happen in the next five years.

The readers were not in agreement with my response. Did they think the problem was well-handled? Not on your tintype.

Dear Ann: What the devil is the mother of a 12-year-old boy doing examining his genitals? That poor kid. If his life is ruined, it won't be due to a lack of generosity in the area of sexual endowment but the overbearing intrusiveness of his mama.

I am the mother of a boy who will be 12 in a few weeks. I bowed out of his hygiene and bathroom activity six years ago with excellent results. Respecting children's privacy is a key ingredient in helping them to develop self-esteem and respect for others. You didn't lay this out as clearly as you could have.

                                            —P.L.M., Williamson, Ga.

From Melbourne, Fla.: That was one of the most miserable answers you have ever given. Several years ago in Iran, where the soil was highly deficient in zinc, many boys had substandard genital organs.

Doctors who were interested in the problem put them on zinc, and the boys became normal for their age group.

—Col. William H. Frederick

Louisville, Ky.: If a man were to comment on the sexual development of his 12-year-old daughter, he would be considered a sexual abuser, arrested, jailed and ordered to stay away from the child. How long is that mother going to be permitted to inspect her son's genitals? Until he is 17? Or maybe 20? By that time, the boy will be a major league sicko, and it'll take years of therapy to straighten him out. It's the mother who has the problem, not the boy. As you say, "Wake up and smell the coffee."

—Anonymous

Somewhere in Kentucky: Tell that 12-year-old kid he has been blessed. I'm 80 years old and have known several women whose lives were made miserable by men who were over-endowed. Son, you have at least one small thing to be thankful for. Count your blessings.

—Little Willie

Here's a guaranteed recipe for a rotten kid:

Dear Ann: Because of my husband's business, I am subjected to the cocktail circuit more than I want to be. It seems the principal topic for discussion is "our crazy, mixed-up kids."

Those who have no nutty offspring to talk about feel strangely deprived. Here is a superb recipe for creating one. After observing several nieces and nephews, as well as the progeny of my friends, I can attest to its authenticity:

Start with one child.

Add a little hot air—Two hours of "when I was your age" will get a rise out of him.

Stir in some sarcasm—It will bring out the bitter flavor.

Fill with bad examples—preferably your own. Instruct the child how to lie about his age so you can sneak him into the movie at half price. Take "souvenirs" from restaurants and hotels. Towels are nice. Pillow cases are better.

Season with indifference—Most families have a lot of "I don't give a damn what you do so long as you don't bother me" lying around.

Sift in some indecision—Not being able to decide what you stand for will give your child that subtle, no-texture, no-substance look.

Add a dash of alcohol—Drink in front of them, behind them and all around them. They will then get the impression it's a normal and natural part of life. And be sure they see you take a belt when the going gets tough. In a crisis say, "Jeez, I need a drink!" They will then get the idea that the way to deal with a problem is by getting bombed.

Toss in a few pills—This will teach your children there are chemical solutions to all problems. They should get the idea early in life that nobody has to suffer because there is a capsule or a tablet made to order that can protect them against any kind of disappointment, failure or discomfort.

Let simmer until ready to boil—Ignore all symptoms of your child's anger, anxiety or fears. If you pretend they don't exist, they will disappear.

Beat regularly—It's your job to see that the children shape up. Reasoning takes too long, and sometimes they don't know what you're talking about. (Too young or too stupid.) A crack across the mouth is easily understood.

Bake in the heat of your own temper—Being screamed at will give your child that "fresh" quality. It will also make *him* a screamer, which will make him very popular with his peers, teachers, colleagues and bosses.

Omit God—Teach your kid early that sleeping, golf or tennis is more important than going to a place of worship. On special occasions (severe illness or death), you may have to mention God, but don't overdo it. God is to be used only in case of emergency.

If you follow these instructions, you are sure to have a problem child of your very own to discuss at cocktail parties—just like everyone else.

—I Prefer Plain Cooking Myself

Dear Cookie: Now that's what I call a dynamite recipe. I hope nobody tries it because there are already too many unhappy, maladjusted children out there.

Some parents must feel they've gotten through the Terrible Twos only to be confronted with the Terrible Teens:

Dear Ann Landers: What can a mother say to a 14-year-old girl who is spoiled, disobedient and disrespectful and who screams, "I know I'm a rotten kid, but it's your fault. You raised me."

I raised her, all right. Her father was too busy playing golf, going fishing and traveling to sales conferences. He never could spare the time to give me a hand with this girl. I need an answer, Ann.

—Tongue-Tied Mother in Appleton, Wis.

Dear Mother: Untie your tongue, and tell your daughter, "Yes, I raised you, and I'm sorry I didn't do a better job. If you don't like the way you are, then make something better of yourself. People can change if they are willing to work at it. Be my guest."

Dear Ann Landers: Your answer to "Tongue-Tied in Appleton" bothered me. It was good, but I think that mother needs more help.

I have a few suggestions for the mother that will ease a tense and unhappy situation:

1. Never engage in a shouting match with your daughter. If she screams, bite your tongue, lower your voice and say anything you feel compelled to say in a voice only slightly above a whisper. If you can't manage that, tell her quietly that you will discuss the subject with her when you are calmer. Then do it.
2. Never let her reduce you to tears. You are an important person, too. When she gets out of hand, send her to her room, deprive her of a privilege, but don't let her defeat you.
3. Let her know you love her. Tell her the next time she rages at you that there is nothing she can say that will cause you to stop loving her. You may not like her behavior, but she is your daughter and you are committed to loving her, so let her know she might as well stop trying to alienate you. (Don't worry, there will be times when you can't stand her, but remember, you're probably not lovable all the time, either.)
4. Touch her a lot. This is important! When she's glued to the TV and you pass by her chair, reach out and pat her. Give her lots of hugs, and don't be put off by her groans or pulling away.
5. Try not to criticize too often. Suggest if you must, but don't be on her back about every little thing. Save your "nos" and "don'ts" for the biggies, and *make them stick!*

6. Stop blaming your husband for not spending time with her. If he is stand-offish and gone a lot, that is his problem—and his loss. You are responsible for your relationship with your child, and you cannot control anyone else's attitude or behavior.

7. When you reprimand her (if you must) in your newly acquired quiet voice, choose good language. Example: "I find your offensive behavior unacceptable." It will be far more effective than "You are a rotten kid."

Remember that 14 is a tough age. It's not easy to grow up, and this baby you rocked in your arms is finding it more difficult than it was in your day. Don't worry about what other people think.

Listen to *her*. No matter what she says, all she wants is for you to love her.

—Mother of Four Who's Been There

Dear Mother: Thank you for those excellent guidelines. Mother-daughter relationships are never easy, for a wide variety of reasons. Any mother who says, "My daughter never gave me a moment's trouble or a single heartache" is not leveling.

I honestly believe that it is not possible for a daughter to completely understand or appreciate her own mother until she has a daughter of her own.

Dear Ann Landers: My husband was deeply moved by this letter, which he received from our 13-year-old son last Father's Day. Perhaps you would like to share it with your readers. It is so refreshingly honest and full of wisdom.

I asked "Jimmy" if I could send this letter to you. He replied: "Heck no. I would die if my name were printed in the paper." When I told him I would ask you not to print his name, he said, "OK, but don't tell the relatives."

So, here it is, Ann. My husband had a hard time holding back the tears when he read it, and so did I.

—No Name in Omaha

Dear Omaha: Thank you for sending your son's letter. It is truly one of the sweetest letters I've ever read. I'm sure my readers will love it:

Dear Dad: I wish I had some money so I could buy you a neat present for Father's Day, but I am broke, so please let this letter be your present.

Even though you don't wear a suit and tie to work like Tommy's dad, I wouldn't trade you for anything. Tommy's dad brings work home from his office every night and even on weekends. They never go to the zoo or play ball in the park or go fishing off the pier.

I like the way you talk to me when I am down. You always make me see that things aren't so bad and that they will get better, which they always do. I like the way you don't let me get away with much. Sometimes I act mad when I don't get my way, but deep down I am glad you are strict. I would be scared to death if you let me do anything I want.

I like that you and Mom agree on the rules around here. At Tommy's house, if his mom says he can't do something, he goes and asks his dad because he knows his dad will say OK just to get rid of him. And then there is a fight. Kids hate it when their mom and dad fight.

I like the way you tell me the truth about everything. When I grow up and have kids, I want to be just like you.

Yours Truly—Jimmy

Twelve Rules for Raising Children

Remember that a child is a gift from God, the richest of all blessings. Do not try to mold him in the image of yourself, your father, your mother, your brother or your neighbor. Each child is an individual and should be permitted to be himself.

Don't crush a child's spirit when he fails. And never compare him with others who have done better.

Remember that anger and hostility are natural emotions. Help your child find socially acceptable outlets for these feelings, or they may be turned inward and create physical or emotional problems.

Discipline your child with firmness and reason. Don't let your anger throw you off balance. If he knows you are fair, you will not lose his respect or his love. Make sure the punishment fits "the crime." Even the youngest child has a keen sense of justice.

Present a united front. Never join with your child against your husband or your wife. This creates emotional conflicts and generates destructive feelings of guilt, confusion and insecurity.

Do not give your child everything his little heart desires. Permit him to know the thrill that comes from earning something. Do not deny him the greatest pleasure of all, the satisfaction that comes with achievement.

Do not set yourself up as a model of perfection. This is a difficult role to play 24 hours a day. You will find it easier to communicate with your child if he knows that Mom and Pop can make mistakes, too.

Don't make threats in anger or glowing promises when you are in a generous mood. Threaten or promise only what you can deliver. To a child, a parent's word means everything. If he loses faith in his parents, he will have difficulty believing in anything.

Do not smother your child with gifts and lavish surprises. The purest and the healthiest love expresses itself in day-in, day-out discipline. Consistency builds self-confidence, trust and a strong base for character development.

Teach your child that there is dignity in hard work, whether it is performed with a shovel or with delicate fingers that hold surgical instruments. Let him know that a useful life is a rewarding one and that a life of ease and pleasure-seeking is empty and meaningless.

Do not try to protect your child against every blow and disappointment. Allow him to get a few lumps. Adversity strengthens character and makes us compassionate. Trouble is the great equalizer, the common denominator of living. He is bound to have some trouble in his life. Let him learn how to handle it.

Teach your child to love God and to love his fellow man. Don't *send* your child to a place of worship—*take* him there. Children learn from example. Faith in God can be his strength and his light when all else fails.

Dear Ann Landers: I don't think I have ever read anything in your column that was printed elsewhere, but I hope you will make an exception in this case, because the enclosed is something every parent should see. The following was reportedly prepared by the police department of Houston, Texas.

Twelve Rules for Raising Delinquent Children

1. Begin with infancy to give the child everything he wants. In this way, he will grow up to believe the world owes him a living.
2. When he picks up bad words, laugh at him. This will make him think he's cute. It will also encourage him to pick up "cuter" phrases that will blow off the top of your head later.

3. Never give him any spiritual training. Wait till he is 21, and then let him "decide for himself."

4. Avoid use of the word "wrong." It may develop a guilt complex. This will condition him to believe, later, when he is arrested for stealing a car, that society is against him and he is being persecuted.

5. Pick up everything he leaves lying around—books, shoes and clothing. Do everything for him so he will be experienced in throwing all responsibility onto others.

6. Let him read any printed matter he can get his hands on. Be careful that the silverware and drinking glasses are sterilized, but let his mind feast on garbage.

7. Quarrel frequently in the presence of your child. In this way, he will not be too shocked when the home is broken up later.

8. Give a child all the spending money he wants. Never let him earn his own. Why should he have things as tough as *you* had them?

9. Satisfy his every craving for food, drink and comfort. See that every sensual desire is gratified. Denial may lead to harmful frustration.

10. Take his part against neighbors, teachers and policemen. They are all prejudiced against your child.

11. When he gets into real trouble, apologize for yourself by saying, "I never could do anything with him."

12. Prepare for a life of grief. You will be apt to have it.

Dear Ann Landers: A while back, you printed a letter from the mother of a teenage girl asking that you emphasize the importance of saying no. I am the mother of a 17-year-old boy who wants you to know that you're a little out of date. The problem isn't the boys; it's the girls.

Our son, "Johnny," gets at least three phone calls a night from girls. Some are as late as 11:30. You would not believe how aggressive those girls are. One drives over in her own convertible and offers to help him with his homework. I've heard him tell her that he really doesn't need any help, but she hangs around anyway. She wears spandex tops and short shorts with absolutely no underwear.

A few weeks ago, my husband had a talk—not the first—with Johnny about sex. Johnny is not sexually active yet but says he doesn't know how much longer he can hold out. He claims the girls carry condoms and put so much pressure on the guys that they almost feel they have to give in. One girl told him that any guy who has not had sex by the time he's 17 must be gay.

So please, Ann, stop worrying about the girls. These are the '90s. Direct your concern to the guys who are virtually being hit over the head and dragged into the back seat.

—Southern California Mom

Dear California Mom: Thanks for the update. Yours is not the first letter conveying this message, but it's the most graphic. Any other mothers of teenage boys want to comment?

Dear Ann Landers: I almost fell over when I read the letter from "Southern California Mom."

I am an American mother who has lived and worked in Germany for the U.S. Army for nearly 20 years. I have a very attractive 17-year-old son who has a difficult time escaping from the girls who have been chasing him since he was 15; not only American girls, but Italian, German and Turkish, as well.

Several days ago, my son and I returned from shopping, and a girl had fallen asleep in front of our door waiting for him. He was embarrassed to death.

Girls call him at all hours of the night. Several have cried on my shoulder about how much they love him and asked me if I thought they stood a chance. Their brazenness never ceases to amaze me.

At one point, I became concerned about my son's cool and heartless attitude toward these girls, but I changed my mind after we had a long talk. He explained that just once he would like to go out with a girl and have a nice dinner and some intelligent conversation without being pawed and propositioned. If you print this letter, Ann, no name please. He would be upset that I wrote to you, but I wanted California Mom to know that she is not alone.

—International Mom

Dear International Mom: I can't believe the volume of mail on this subject. Here's another one that puts the problem into its proper historical context:

Dear Ann Landers: "Southern California Mom" writes of teenage girls who phone her 17-year-old son late into the night and hang around "wearing spandex tops and short shorts with absolutely no underwear."

That letter brought to mind the observations of Martin Luther while teaching at the University of Wittenberg in 1544:

"We have a great horde of young men here from all countries. The girls are getting very bold. They run after the fellows into their rooms and chambers and wherever they can, offering them free love. I hear that many parents have ordered their sons home."

It's obvious, Ann, that some things don't change much across half a millennium.

—T. A., Fountain Valley, Calif.

Dear T.A.: Thanks for the research. The more things change, the more they stay the same.

Dear Ann Landers: I was interested in the letter from "California Mom," whose 17-year-old son was disgusted with super-aggressive, sex-crazy girls. When our third son was born, a friend said to me: "You are lucky to have boys instead of girls. You don't have to worry about them getting pregnant." What a joke. We worry instead about our sons getting herpes, genital warts and maybe AIDS from girls who are plain out of control. I've found notes in my 16-year-old son's pockets that made me blush.

—Indianapolis

From Meridian, Miss.: Aggressive girls? You'd better believe it. I can't bring myself to repeat the messages they leave on our answering machine: imitations of orgasms, etc. Our son is only 15.

Palm Springs, Calif.: I don't know if it's the trash on TV, the movies or what, but by the time the girls in this town get to high school, they've done everything in the book. We are sending our 15-year-old son to military school.

Greenwich, Conn.: After reading what several girls wrote in our 16-year-old son's yearbook, we feel like putting him in a cage until he's 21. Apparently, four-letter words are part of their normal vocabulary.

Oxnard, Calif.: My teenage son was propositioned by two girls who taped roses with sexy notes to the windshield of his car in the school parking lot. A third girl wrote her phone number on his hand in ink when he was clearing dishes in a fast food place. With this kind of pressure, I worry about how long he can hold out.

Hannibal, Mo.: I caught a 13-year-old girl throwing pebbles at my son's bedroom window at 1:30 in the morning. Where are the parents of girls like this, I wonder. It's scary.

Flint, Mich.: Our 16-year-old son has been getting seven and eight letters a week from a 14-year-old girl who lives in Iowa. She puts lipstick kisses all over the envelopes. He has not written to her since October, but she won't give up.

Washington, D.C.: A 16-year-old girl sent our 17-year-old son a $900 wristwatch and a gold ring for Christmas with a card saying, "We're engaged." He sent both gifts back. Her mother then wrote to me and said: "Your son hurt my daughter's feelings. When he returned her gifts, she cried all day. That young man needs to learn some manners." Can you believe it, Ann?

Dear Readers: I would believe anything now. I've heard it all.

Marian Wright Edelman's advice to her three sons is so superb that I want to share some of it with you. Here are a few excerpts from her book, The Measure of Our Success—A Letter to My Children and Yours *(Beacon Press):*

There is no free lunch. Don't feel entitled to anything you don't sweat and struggle for.

If you see a need, don't ask, "Why doesn't somebody do something?" Ask instead, "Why don't I do something?" This world needs more shepherds and fewer sheep.

Never work just for money or power. They won't save your soul or build a decent family or help you sleep at night.

Don't be afraid of taking risks or being criticized. If you don't want to be criticized, don't say anything, don't do anything and don't be anything.

Don't be afraid to fail. It's the way you learn to do things right.

Remember that your wife is not your mother or your maid but your partner and your friend. Raise your sons to be fair to your own and other people's daughters and to share parenting and household responsibilities. Teach them to clean up their own mess, pick up their own towels and clothes, take their dishes off the table and put things back where they belong for the next person.

Be honest. Struggle to live by what you say. Be moral examples for your children. If you lie, they will lie, too. If you snicker at racial jokes, so will they.

Teach them good manners. "Please" and "thank you" are very important words. Being considerate will take them farther in life than any college degrees.

Let's be clear on the fact that tobacco and alcohol are killing more people than cocaine. It's time for consumers to speak out and put a stop to the marketing of sickness and death to our children.

Be confident that you can make a difference. Don't get overwhelmed. Sometimes when I become frantic about all I have to do, I stop and remind myself to take each day as it comes and to break the formidable challenges into manageable pieces.

Never think life is not worth living, no matter how hard it gets. Harriet Beecher Stowe wrote, "When you get into a tight place and everything goes against you and you think you can't hang on a minute longer, don't give up, for that is the time and place the tide will turn."

Choose your friends carefully and stay out of the fast lane. You were born God's original. Try not to become someone else's copy.

Remember that you are in charge of your own attitude. The only person you can control is yourself.

You have a role to play every minute of the day. Have you ever noticed how one example, good or bad, can prompt others to follow? How one illegally parked car can give permission for others to do likewise? How one racial joke can fuel another? How one sour person can ruin a meeting? Well, the opposite is also true. An anonymous sage correctly said, "The world needs more people who do not borrow from integrity to pay for expediency, whose handshake is an ironclad contract, who are as honest in small matters as in large ones, who know how to win with grace and lose with dignity."

Dear Ann Landers: I am hoping you will print this letter, not for my sake, but to help your young readers who are having trouble at home and think their lives are lousy.

I've spent the last four years as a runaway living on the streets of Los Angeles. I was never happy at home. I didn't like it when someone in my family told me what to do. I fought with everybody. I wish I had listened. Now I realize they were trying to help me because they loved me.

Every day in Los Angeles has been a battle for my survival. Before I had spent a month out here, I was into prostitution. I was only 14 years old. I've done a lot of drugs, lived under bridges and slept in alleys off Hollywood Boulevard. I've eaten out of dumpsters behind restaurants and fallen in with psychos and winos. It's a miracle that I'm still alive.

Actually, I shouldn't say it's a miracle because my luck ran out. I just saw a doctor and was given a death sentence. I'm now 18 years old, I'm seven months pregnant and I have AIDS.

I'm writing this letter to tell other kids that no matter how bad things are at home and how tough you think your life is, it's 100 percent better than it would be on the streets. Stay where you are, and work things out.

If you feel like you need a break from your family, go visit a friend or take a 10-day backpack trip, but don't run away. There are already thousands of kids out here who are in the same spot I'm in, and Lord knows how many there are in other cities. Please don't add to that number. Stay home no matter what. I wish I had.

—Too Late for Me

Dear Too Late: Your letter is sure to make an impact on some of those kids who are now where you were four years ago. It should give you some solace to know that by writing to me you have saved some lives. If you think I am overstating the case, let me assure you that I am not. I know my readers. Please know that you are in my prayers.

Dear Ann Landers: Four years ago, I had to discipline my son. From that came a lengthy discussion about our father-son relationship. When the boy told me he did not feel I always treated him fairly, I asked him to sit down and write out what he thought were the most important attributes of a good father. To my surprise, he was gone less than 10 minutes and returned with this list.

Over the past four years, I have looked it over several times and felt that for a lad in the 10th grade, he showed a great deal of insight. I'm sending it to you, Ann, because I now realize that it was the turning point in our relationship. If you think it may have value for others, please feel free to run it in your column.

—An M.D. in Atlanta

Dear M.D.: I would say that for a 10th-grader, your son showed extraordinary maturity. Thanks for sending it on. I am pleased to share it with my readers.

Attributes of a Good Father

1. Listen to both sides of an argument, and respect the opinions of the other person.

2. Accept the fact that every child doesn't have to be "normal."
3. Don't always judge by actions. Consider the motives behind them.
4. Work to increase strengths in the relationship, as well as improve the weaknesses.
5. Don't be overly protective.
6. Consider the harshness of the punishment as compared with the seriousness of the "crime."
7. Recognize that I want to be treated like an adult.
8. Emphasize my good points instead of dwelling on the bad.
9. Don't push a child into doing things he doesn't want to do simply because the father would like to do them himself.
10. Realize not everyone has the same abilities and the same ideas of what's important.

I believe it's a lot harder to grow up straight and strong today than it was when I was a teenager (in the Stone Age, of course). There weren't as many permissive parents in those days, nor was there the easy availability of drugs, guns and extra money. And we didn't spend thousands of hours in front of a TV set. If I sound like a museum piece, I apologize, but this is the way I see it—and I've been a close observer for a very long time. There's a lot of wisdom in the following essay:

Recipe for Becoming a Dropout

Take one child who has had some tough breaks. Mold into a chip on the shoulder. Press firmly into a tough shell of refusing to accept guidance. Add a heaping cup of hostility. Fold in equal amounts of arrogance and anger.

Mix well, and take the easy way out. Add regular dashes of the wrong friends. Sift in the refusal to listen to people who know what they're talking about.

Stir vigorously with shortsightedness, excuses for not doing homework and refusals to accept help. Sprinkle with a thick coating of caring more for what's cool than for what's right. Finally, cover with a thick layer of blame. There is always plenty to go round.

This casserole is called Adolescent Surprise. If you're surprised, you don't get it. If you get it, you're not surprised.

Dear Ann Landers: I'll bet anything your editor or publisher will not have the guts to print this. The worst that could happen is some people might choke on their morning coffee. The best that could happen is hundreds of kids might get shocked into good behavior and avoid the nightmare of jail.

With the arrival of summer, more teenagers get into trouble. The kind of "trouble" I'm referring to is assault with a weapon, dealing in dope, burglary and murder. For kids who are considering any of the above, here is what jail is like:

You are locked up in a cage, surrounded by killers and thieves. Jail food is horrible. You can eat it or go hungry. You are watched carefully and strip-searched often. You will probably be homosexually raped by sex-starved criminals.

Little conflicts will become life-and-death matters. You will learn every trick in the book from the real "experts"—which will make it tempting to return to a life of crime when you get out.

Once released from prison, you will discover that ex-cons can't vote, enter the military or hold public service positions. Few ex-cons can find a decent job.

The police will knock on your door first if a crime is committed in your neighborhood. Even if you are not guilty, you will get panicky every time you hear a siren, wondering if they are coming for you.

If you have a potential jailbird at your house, the next time he or she gets in serious trouble, try this punishment: Lock the teenager in his or her room with nothing except a blanket and a chamber pot from Friday night to Monday morning. Feed him a rotten meal.

Convey the message that this is very much like solitary confinement in most reform schools or juvenile detention facilities in almost every state. If this sounds cruel, let me assure you two days in "jail" at home is a lot easier to take than five years in prison.

—Caring in Chicago

Dear Caring: You lose. Here's your letter and I am willing to bet not a single editor will censor a word of it. Thank you for telling it like it is.

The following is a letter from a parent to a daughter or son. I hope my teenage readers will realize that it's especially for them.

My Darling Daughter (or Son): Ever since you were a baby, knowing where you were meant knowing you were safe. You grew from being safe in the house to being safe in the yard, on the block, in the neighborhood and now in the whole world. Knowing you are safe is still my major concern.

Remember when you were little and came home from school and I wasn't there? You called all the phone numbers you knew. When I finally got home, you said in your most grown-up voice, "Where have you been?" You weren't meddling, you were frightened. When you didn't know where I was, your security was threatened.

I don't mean to be nosy. I want to give you as much freedom as possible. But the only way I can do this is if I know where you are and when you'll be home. My responsibility for you will end one day, and my insecurity will also be gone. In its place will be confidence and love. Asking where you are going and when you'll be home is mom-talk. It really means, "I love you, and I hope you'll be safe." Your answer, translated from child-talk, means, "I love you, too."

—Your Mom

Dear Mom: You've expressed the thoughts of millions of parents of teenagers today, and I thank you.

Dear Ann Landers: I'm a high school senior who is very concerned about the way kids my age drive. Some of these crazy drivers are my pals and I worry about them.

The following story was part of our reading assignment in a criminal justice class.

Please print it, Ann. It could save some lives.

—*Newsday* Reader in Long Island

Heaven Can Wait

It takes 7/10ths of a second to kill a person in an automobile crash. Studies at Yale and Cornell universities provided a dramatic split-second chronology of what happens when a car rams into a tree at 55 m.p.h.

At 1/10th of a second, front bumper and grillwork collapse.

At 2/10ths of a second, the hood crumbles, rises, smashes into the windshield and grillwork disintegrates.

At 3/10ths of a second, the driver is sprung upright from his seat, his broken knees pressed against the dashboard, the steering wheel bends under his grip.

At 4/10ths of a second, the front of his car is destroyed and dead still, but the rear end is still plunging forward at 55 m.p.h. The half-ton motor crunches into the tree.

At 5/10ths of a second, the driver's fear-frozen hands bend the steering column into an almost vertical position and he is impaled on the steering wheel shaft. Jagged steel punctures his lungs and arteries.

At 6/10ths of a second, the impact rips the shoes off his feet. The chassis bends in the middle, and the driver's head is slammed into the windshield. The car's rear begins its downward fall as its spinning wheels churn into the ground.

At 7/10ths of a second, the entire body of the car is twisted grotesquely out of shape. In one final agonizing convulsion, the front seat rams forward, pinning the driver against the steering shaft. Blood spurts from his mouth. Shock has frozen his heart.

He is now dead. Grisly to contemplate, and all so unnecessary. The difference between death and arriving at your destination safely is simply a matter of thinking about the consequences.

Recklessness is foolish. Drive carefully and live.

Dear Ann Landers: I am a mother of three children and have had it up to here with quizzes that are supposed to show whether I am a "good parent." My answer is, "I am as good a parent as I can be," and I mean it. My husband and I love each other (the Rev. Theodore Hesburgh's first rule). We do things as a family.

We take an interest in our children's school projects and activities. We don't spoil them with gifts or privileges.

They work for spending money. They aren't disciplined with a strap. We use the "talk-it-out" approach.

What then is my gripe? Simply this: As they get older, they become more surly, more irresponsible and more disobedient. They quarrel among themselves, whine, sulk and complain. I used to enjoy doing things for them, but now I find it neither satisfying nor rewarding.

I know we are not alone, Ann. Our friends tell us, "If you think they are a handful now, just wait a couple years." Maybe if the kids would try a little harder, more parents would be able to answer "yes" to that survey you ran recently—"If you had it to do over again, would you have had children?" Here's a quiz for *them*—for a change:

1. When did you last hug your mom without wanting something?
2. When did you last make an attempt to be especially pleasant to your dad without asking him to fix something?
3. Do you say hello to your parents' friends and treat them with respect?
4. Do you take pride in your home, or do you leave yogurt cups in the living room and the spills for someone else to clean up? How about the yard? Did you leave your new football out in the rain all night?
5. How about the car? Can a person sit down without getting stuck to a wad of gum? Speaking of the car, when was the last time Dad had to pull over to the curb or the shoulder of the road because of the yelling or fighting in the back seat?
6. When did you last tell your mom that the dinner was good and that you appreciate the effort she puts into cooking for you?
7. Are you on time when Mom or Dad offers to drive you somewhere or pick you up? Are you where you are supposed to be, or do they have to look for you?
8. When was the last time Mom or Dad had to bring a forgotten lunch or a book to school? Do you ever say thanks for this?
9. When did you last do what you were told without asking why or saying, "Wait a minute" or "Do I have to?"
10. Are you proud of your mom or dad? Their manners? Could they be proud of you?

Please, kids, we love you. We could have a wonderful time together, but it's a two-way street. You have to do your part.

—Florida Mom

Dear Mom: Millions of eyes will see your letter and the quiz. It's sure to make many parents feel less alone.

Your complaints are par for the course. It may also connect with a few million kids out there who need to shape up. Thanks for the input.

Dear Ann Landers: I have been reading a lot lately about the stress our children are under these days. I say, baloney.

You are about my age, Ann, and I'll bet you will agree that we had it a lot rougher than the kids have it today.

The Depression was so awful I don't know how we lived through it. There wasn't enough food in the house to feed us five kids. If the neighbors hadn't helped, I think we would have starved.

There were no jobs. Both Mom and Dad took any little piece of work they could find. I remember when Dad put in three days at a coal yard and was paid in coal, which he was darned happy to get.

Kids today don't know what it is to be hungry. A lot of them get fed breakfast and lunch in school at government expense, which means by us taxpayers, of course.

When Franklin D. Roosevelt became president he started the Civilian Conservation Corps, which was a godsend. What a brilliant idea! It not only helped rebuild our country but provided millions of young people with jobs. I was one of them. How many kids today would be willing to work that hard? Darned few, I'll bet.

I look at my grandchildren, Ann, and they are cream puffs compared to what we were. They have it so much softer, it isn't even funny. I'll bet you agree with me. Please print my letter, and let me know what you think.

—A Feisty Michigander

Dear Feisty: Here's your letter, but I can't say I agree with you that kids today have it a lot easier than we did.

The problems they face are worse than poverty. In fact, I believe growing up in the Depression gave us motivation and survival skills that today's young people don't have. To put it another way, they have the disadvantage of too many advantages.

Today's children must deal with the reality of nuclear weapons that could incinerate them overnight. And they are going to have to figure out how to revitalize the environment. In some parts of the country, you must go to a museum to see what a butterfly looks like. The air is polluted, the rivers and lakes are dying and the ozone layer has holes in it.

When I was growing up, we never used to lock the doors at night. Today, everything is locked up, and in spite of the locks, alarms and security systems, the number of muggings, rapes and murders that occur in even the best neighborhoods is appalling. Crime is rampant.

As a teenager, I never heard of cocaine or crack. A few of the musicians smoked "reefers," but teenagers didn't touch them. Today, there's speed and angel dust and crack and gang violence and murders that are clearly drug-related. There are billions of dollars to be made dealing dope, and some teenagers want part of the action.

AIDS is something else we never heard of. And it's a death sentence. The sexually transmitted diseases in our day could be cured with penicillin.

I haven't even mentioned the mania for body-building that has created steroid junkies. This is a dangerous drug, and young people are going bananas over it. Also, the craze to be pencil-thin has produced an astonishing number of anorexic and bulimic teenagers.

I'm glad I have lived the greater part of my life. I wouldn't be 20 again for all the tea in Sri Lanka. I just pray that my grandchildren and yours will be able to pick their way through the mine fields of the '90s and into the 21st century.

"Feisty Michigander" was convinced that the older generation (mine) had it a lot rougher than the kids today.

I disagreed, citing the threat of nuclear war, pollution, crime, drugs, gangs, AIDS and so on. That exchange really turned the readers on. Here's a sampling of some high-octane mail:

Dear Ann Landers: As one of the so-called "cream puffs" of American youth, I offer a different portrait of what today's spoiled teenager is like.

I am the eldest of four in a blue-collar home. Five years ago, our father walked out on us. Mom hadn't worked in 20 years. We lived on peanut butter and homemade biscuits until she finally got a job as a cook and cleaning woman. It's true that there is no Great Depression today, but there might as well be for those of us who have been victimized by divorce.

—A Teenager in Virginia

From Sheboygan, Wis.: You are right when you say the horrendous problems of today's teens are mind-boggling. The bomb hangs over them by a hair, and the globe has become a sewer. But at the heart of the matter is morality. No matter what happens, each person is responsible for his or her actions. Unlike you, Ann, I would love to be 20 again.

Portsmouth, N.H.: Thanks for your column comparing today's kids with the youth of the Depression years. I know several high school kids who are working two jobs. I see them all the time, too tired to stay awake in class. And what are they doing with the money? Plenty, but

they certainly are not saving it for college. They are supporting a secondhand car or a motorcycle and buying records and tapes, VCRs,
makeup, funky clothes and junk food.

Pensacola, Fla.: I'm a 15-year-old who can tell you it's no fun to be a
teenager today. In my crowd, if you don't do drugs, you are weird. Last
month, a "good" kid at our school hanged himself. Guns seem to be
everywhere. When you were a teenager, Ann, were you afraid of getting shot? Well, I am.

Stoughton, Wis.: If "Feisty Michigander" thinks children today have
it soft, he should visit a shelter for the homeless and see 2-year-olds who
don't smile, 3-year-olds who can't talk and 4-year-olds who don't know
how to play. Maybe instead of whining about his tax dollars buying
breakfast and lunch for schoolchildren, he should visit their homes and
see what they're eating for dinner. For many of these youngsters, subsi-
dized school meals are the only decent food they ever get.

Detroit: I agree that the pitfalls for the young are deadlier today.
We didn't have much in the way of material things—no TV or
electronic toys, no designer clothes—but it was safe to play games
outside, to jump rope, play hopscotch and skate. We used our imagination and made things from scratch. The girls sewed doll clothes,
and the boys made scooters and skateboards. We had plenty of exercise compared to the couch potatoes of today. And we actually walked
to school! We were also taught respect for parents, the police and
teachers. If we got in trouble in school, we were in plenty of trouble
at home. Times have sure changed and, I'm sorry to say, not for the
better.

Dear Readers: Again, you've proven that there's lot of wisdom out
there.

When it comes to having children, everyone has an opinion.

Dear Ann Landers: The enclosed came in the mail. Attached was
your column on childless couples. We happen to have six children. We
also have a sense of humor. If you do, you'll print the letter. It's signed
"Author Unknown," and it goes like this:

There is nothing sadder than a childless couple. It's heartbreaking to
see them stretched out, relaxing around the swimming pool, sun-tanned

and miserable, trotting off to Europe like lonesome fools. What an empty life! Nothing but money to spend and time to enjoy it!

They miss all the fun of doing without for the children's sake. How selfish they become, buying what they want and doing as they please. Everyone should have children.

No one should be allowed to escape the rewarding experiences that accompany every stage of parenthood. Those all-night vigils, the coughing spells, drunken babysitters, saturated mattresses, midnight rushes to the hospital, separating little brothers and sisters when they try to kill each other.

I pity the couple without children to brighten the cocktail hour. The little darlings have a way of brushing a martini from your hand and massaging the potato chips into the rugs. And what fun when they fight you for the olive! The little scuffles in the presence of guests make for a well-rounded life. And an early breakdown.

The *real* satisfaction comes later. Those thoughtful discussions when the report card reveals your prodigy is one step below a nitwit. Then the hours of arguing. You try to pin it on his side of the family. He tries to pin it on your side of the family.

But children are worth it all. The warm feeling the first time you took the boy hunting. He didn't mean to shoot you in the leg. Remember how he cried? He was so disappointed that you weren't a deer. The limp is with you to this day.

Nothing builds character like practicing self-control. And what better practice than watching the warm smile of a lad with the sun glittering on $500 worth of dental braces—ruined by peanut brittle.

The childless couple lives in a vacuum. They try to fill the lonesome hours with golf, bridge, trips, civic affairs. Sometimes the tranquility and extra money is enough to drive you crazy!

All you have to do is look at these empty, unfulfilled shells to see what the years have done to them. He looks boyish, unlined, rested. She is slim, well-groomed and youthful. It isn't natural.

If they had kids like the rest of us, they'd be beat-up, gray, wrinkled and nervous wrecks, too.

—San Francisco

Dear Friends: Many thanks for sending on what will be a yuk for some and a yawn for others. I could write a 10-page rebuttal, but I won't. I can't refrain from one comment, however. Those "cocktail hours" enjoyed by childless couples age them a lot faster than half-a-dozen kids.

Here's a column I wrote to help those parents who have tried their best and need words of encouragement. It's one of my most-requested pieces:

Dear Ann Landers: What wisdom, consolation or advice can you give parents in their 50s who have worked hard to achieve the American dream, loved their kids and tried to give them the best world ever? We are also the unhappiest.

Many of our children are on drugs, unemployed dropouts, migrants, drifters, angry with the world, hostile toward us and out of joint with society. How much and for how long should parents pay, in terms of self-recrimination, worry, disappointment and financial support? How can we enjoy the years that are left to us now that we have more money and fewer business pressures and are still in fairly good health?

It's heartbreaking to see our kids maladjusted, disoriented and unable to cope. We can't help but feel we are to blame. After all, they are our sons and daughters. We raised them. Where is the cutoff line? Do you have any answers?

—Meant Well Parents

Dear Meant Well: To you and the thousands of other parents who are miserable because of "what you have done" to your children, I say this: Stop beating yourselves. You did the best you could with the tools at hand—inexperience, clay feet, the works. No one knows why some children turn out to be champions in spite of parents who provide precious little emotional nourishment, while other kids—loved, wanted, tenderly nurtured, with all the so-called advantages—turn out perverse, estranged and unable to cope.

I have come to believe in the genetic factor that has been ignored by many behavioral "experts." We all inherit our nervous systems, and if the nervous system is fragile, it places severe limitations on what a person can tolerate. Certain individuals are born survivors. They can withstand life's harshest blows and emerge the stronger for it. Others crumble in the face of minor adversity. The same fire that melts butter can make steel strong.

And let us not overlook personal responsibility. I am sick of hearing children blame their parents for their messed-up lives. People with all sorts of handicaps can and do make it in this demanding and competitive world.

For those who are hooked on dope, there are drug-abuse centers with trained personnel, eager and waiting to help. For individuals who need professional counseling, there are mental-health clinics. The self-help groups do a remarkable job—and they are free: Alcoholics Anonymous, Gamblers Anonymous, Recovery, Inc. The list is endless.

Enough of this "You damaged me, now take care of me" nonsense. It's a copout. Parental guilt laid on by our kids is so thick you can cut it with a knife. It serves no purpose except to perpetuate financial and emotional dependence and create a climate of hostility, punishment and ultimate failure. God helps those who help themselves.

It's OK, Son. Everybody Does It!

When Johnny was 6 years old, he was with his father when they were caught speeding. His father handed the officer a $5 bill with his driver's license. "It's OK, son," his father said as he drove off. "Everybody does it."

When he was 8, he was permitted to sit in on a family seminar, presided over by Uncle George, on how to shave points off an income-tax return. "It's OK, kid," his uncle said. "Everybody does it."

When he was 9, his mother took him to his first theater production. The box-office man couldn't find any seats until his mother discovered an extra $2 in her purse. "It's OK, son," she said. "Everybody does it."

When he was 12, he broke his glasses on the way to school. His Aunt Francine convinced the insurance company that they had been stolen and collected $27. "It's OK, kid," she said. "Everybody does it."

When he was 15, he made right guard on the high school football team. His coach showed him how to block and at the same time grab the opposing end by the shirt so the official couldn't see it. "It's OK, kid," the coach said. "Everybody does it."

When he was 16, he took his first summer job at the neighborhood supermarket. His assignment was to put overripe tomatoes in the bottom of the boxes and the good ones on top where they would show. "It's OK, kid," the manager said. "Everybody does it."

When he was 18, Johnny and a neighbor applied for a college scholarship. Johnny was a marginal student. His neighbor was in the upper 3 percent of his class, but he couldn't play right guard. Johnny got the scholarship. "It's OK," they told him. "Everybody does it."

When he was 19, he was approached by an upperclassman who offered the test answers for $3. "It's OK, kid," he said. "Everybody does it."

Johnny was caught and sent home in disgrace. "How could you do this to your mother and me?" his father asked. "You never learned anything like this at home." His aunt and uncle also were shocked.

If there's anything the adult world can't stand, it's a kid who cheats.

Well, you say, now the kids are grown and living on their own. It seems life still has a few surprises in store for us:

Dear Ann Landers: We are middle-income parents faced with a problem that is plaguing many other parents. For want of a better term, I'll call it the problem of the "returnees."

"Returnees" are young adult children we thought were happily married, permanently settled in their homes or apartments and able to manage financially without any help from us.

Now, at long last, we parents can finally (hallelujah!) live our own lives. Right? Wrong. The adult child arrives, suitcases in hand, carrying a pet (or a child) and announces that he/she is getting a divorce and returning home.

Ann, these days, a great many adult children run back to Mama and Papa and are sure that "the folks" will support them as they did before they married. Many of us are just barely making ends meet, and it's a real struggle.

How can parents protect themselves from children who return to the nest and expect to be treated as children when they are in their 30s and 40s?

—S.G., Uniondale, N.Y.

Dear S.G.: How can parents protect themselves against adult children who return home after a failed marriage? There is no way, except to just say, "No."

This seems awfully hard-hearted, however, and it seems to me that temporary shelter is not too much to ask, especially if there was brutality or abuse. Parents do their children no favor, however, if they permit ongoing freeloading. Since every situation is different, there is no pat solution. Each case must be evaluated on the basis of its own merit.

Dear Ann Landers: I have four children who are successful in their marriages and careers. I have always tried to treat them in an even-handed way when it comes to matters such as college tuition and loans for home purchases. It has been my policy to charge a modest rate of interest for the loans in order not to favor one child over the other.

Recently, my oldest daughter asked for a two-year loan to help finance a larger home. Both she and her husband have good jobs, but they wanted to avoid using non-liquid assets. In making her request, my daughter said she had never felt that a parent should charge interest and she wanted her loan to be interest-free. This made me uncomfortable, but I agreed to the loan and said I would consider making it interest-free.

Shortly after, my daughter called to ask for the money. As in the past, I mailed her a check accompanied by a note to sign and return to me.

That note was an agreement to pay interest. I included a repayment schedule. To my surprise, she cashed the check and returned the note with the reference to interest crossed out. Subsequently, she has been making her monthly payments to me on principal only.

In a recent visit to her home, my daughter and I discussed the situation, but we were unable to resolve the issue.

She contended that I had encouraged her to believe I would not be charging interest. I told her I was sorry about the misunderstanding, but my position should have been clear when she received my check and the note requesting her signature.

Is my loan policy unreasonable? How would you handle this?

—Carl in Akron

Dear Carl: For openers, I would never charge a child of mine interest on a loan. Since it is your money, however, you have every right to do with it whatever you wish.

Apparently when you told your daughter you would consider her request to get the loan without interest, she assumed you had agreed to honor her request. She should not have crossed out the reference to the interest, however, without checking with you to make sure her assumption was correct.

Since it is your policy to charge your children interest on loans, this young woman should pay it, just as the others have.

Dear Ann Landers: My husband and I are fuming over the unbelievably dumb response you gave to that father in Akron. His daughter wanted an interest-free loan from Dad to buy a larger home because she didn't want to liquidate any of her assets. Well, unless her father took the money out of his non-interest-producing mattress, he lost money on the deal.

My siblings and I have also used "The Bank of Dad" on occasion, but never, even when offered, would we consider an interest-free loan. One of the problems with our society today is that too many people expect something for nothing, and here you are, encouraging it. We're betting Ann Landers is going to hear plenty about this one.

—Marc and Terri in North Carolina

Dear M. and T.: You win that bet. I am catching it from readers as far away as Tokyo. Since I have no defense, I shall plead temporary insanity. Read on:

From Chicago: Ann, please, please, adopt me! I sure can use an interest-free loan. I am married and have two children, with a third one on the way. We live in a small one-bedroom house and must move to a bigger place. Unfortunately, my credit rating isn't so terrific, which means I'm not "bankable." Tell "Carl in Akron" I'd be happy to pay him 11 percent interest.

—Steve

Houston: Please be advised that there are potentially serious tax implications for failing to charge interest on a loan to family members or anyone else. In 1984, it was written into the Internal Revenue Code that any gift over $10,000 is taxable. So please, Ann, don't be telling people it's OK to lend children unlimited amounts of money without charging interest. That father should be aware that he could be hit with a gift tax.

—W.F.C.

Nashua, N.H.: I cannot believe your holier-than-thou, bone-headed response to the father whose daughter wanted an interest-free loan. I come from a large family. My brothers and I have borrowed money from our parents and from each other. We all pay the same rate of interest the money would have earned had it been left undisturbed in a savings account.

—R. and K.C.

Dallas: May a reader in her 80s comment on your recent advice regarding lending money to children interest-free? It is a grave disservice to children to be deprived of the pleasure of making it on their own. What's more, I know of some elderly people who have indulged their children foolishly and now they don't have adequate money to live decently in retirement. Will their children be willing to help them? I doubt it.

—Been There

North Bay, Calif.: I am an adult child who recently borrowed a substantial sum from my widowed mother. Although she is very comfortable financially, I know she did not take that money out of a cookie jar. It came from a money market account or some investment that was earning interest. Although my mother didn't request it, it would be unconscionable of me not to pay her interest. I cannot believe your response.

—Cathy

Toronto: Relatives are the first to let you down when it comes to repaying loans. More breakups and bitter feelings have resulted from lending money than any other single act.

—J.R.

Dear J.R. and all others who wrote: From the looks of the mail, I really laid an egg on that one. Forty thousands readers can't be wrong. Charge the kids interest, folks.

Dear Ann Landers: In a recent column, you told "Carl from Akron" that you would never charge a child of your interest on a loan. Pray tell, why not?

Most parents feel that charging their children a modest rate of interest on a loan is a generous favor, which indeed it is. Your statement encourages kids to get as much as they can for nothing.

You also neglected to take into account that giving an interest-free loan deprives children of the opportunity to tap into their own ingenuity and learn how to take care of themselves. And, I might add, a modest charge for interest discourages frivolous requests and encourages self-reliance and better family relationships.

—Been There in Falls Church, Va.

Dear Va.: I received a heavy response to this subject, which I've covered before. Almost nobody supported me. Read on for additional clobbering:

From Newark, N.J.: Time and again you've made the point, "What people get for nothing is rarely appreciated." How come you have abandoned that philosophy? I'm surprised and disappointed.

Seattle: Borrowing from a parent saves the cost of loan fees, credit checks and appraisal fees. Why should we expect our parents to forgo interest on their hard-earned money so we can save a few more bucks?

Enid, Okla.: I don't know about Carl, but my mother has her extra money invested in certificates of deposit and collects interest. If she withdraws from those CDs early, there's a penalty. Most people don't have a lot of extra cash sitting around.

Hamilton, Ontario: Every time my husband and I borrowed money from his family, we paid an interest rate 1 percent lower than the bank would charge and 1 percent higher than they could have gotten from a bank certificate of deposit. All his siblings had the same deal. In *my* family, it was a different story. My parents gave a sizable interest-free loan to my sister to buy a house. When my brother and I asked for the same deal, we were refused. This caused a lot of animosity in the family and some bitterness toward our sister.

Munich, Germany: If Carl's kids can afford to buy a bigger home, they should be able to pay their father the going rate of interest on the loan. Wake up, Ann!

Schenectady, N.Y.: When we borrowed money to buy a home, we paid my mother-in-law interest. We learned later that her other children had also borrowed but did not pay interest. When I asked my mother-in-law about this, she said, "You offered. They didn't." We felt ripped off, and things haven't been the same since.

Erie, Pa.: We spoiled our kids, and now they are spoiling their kids worse. An interest-free loan was the beginning.

San Bernardino, Calif.: Interest-free loans give kids a false idea of what life is about. There are 10 "children" over 25 years old on our block who are still living at home. Too much "help" can be crippling.

Hollywood: We charged our 14-year-old son interest on his first loan of $150. He wanted to buy a motor for his go-cart. He signed a contract and made a payment every Saturday. Years later, he worked 40 hours a week while attending college and law school and is now a successful attorney. He thanked us for the way we raised him and said, "I'm going to raise my kids the same way." What a reward!

Dear Ann Landers: All my life, people have asked me if I'm of mixed race.

At the age of 35, I'm ready to find the answer to that question.

My parents separated immediately after I was born. My father insists that when he was away on a Navy assignment, my mother had an affair. I am deeply hurt that he does not believe I am his biological daughter.

I approached my mother about this several months ago because I have many physical characteristics that are clearly biracial. She became very angry and cursed me for raising such an "insulting" question. Since that time, our relationship has been very tense. I'm afraid if I bring up the subject again, she may stop talking to me permanently.

I want to end this estrangement, Ann, but I also want to know the truth. Am I blowing this out of proportion? What can I do?

—No Name, No City

Dear No Name, No City: I contacted Illinois Masonic Hospital in Chicago, which has on-site DNA paternity testing, and this is what I learned:

To get a completely accurate result, you would have to be tested, and so would your father and mother. The cost of the test is $600. It takes two to eight weeks to get the results. The test is 100 percent accurate if the man is not the father and 99.9 percent accurate if he is.

If the mother is not tested, there is a 0.8 percent chance of a false positive.

You are going to have to decide whether you want to risk your mother's wrath by going ahead with the testing. From what you have told me, I doubt that she would cooperate.

If you decide to be tested, are you prepared for the repercussions should the tests reveal that your father's accusations were correct? I hope you will consider all the ramifications before you press hard to pursue the truth.

Adoption

Not flesh of my flesh
Nor bone of my bone,
But still miraculously my own.
Never forget for a single minute,
You didn't grow under my heart,
But in it.

Adoption has become a controversial issue. Many states have changed or modified their laws to allow adopted children to search for their birth parents and vice versa.

Those of you who are regular readers of my column know that I am not in favor of such searches unless both the adult adopted child and the birth parents agree to be found. While medical history is important, disrupting the lives of others in order to satisfy one's curiosity can be very damaging.

I am saddened by the thought that many children waiting to be adopted will languish in foster homes or state-supported orphanages because potential parents are afraid to risk having the child wrenched from them at a later date by the birth parents. And who can blame them?

Dear Ann Landers: You have often addressed the subject of adopted children searching for their birth parents. A recent letter mentioned the cheap media sensationalism covering these reunions and how some adoptive parents are made to feel like "interim" parents, waiting for a now-mature birth mother to show up.

You said it is unfair to generalize about birth mothers and that "many suffer a lot" when they give up their children. That statement is a gross generalization in itself. Adoption does not always mean a cute, cuddly 3-day-old infant delivered into the arms of a waiting couple by a grieving-but-proud unwed teenager.

Our adopted daughter, who came to us when she was 4 years old, was the victim of profound sexual abuse and severe neglect by both her parents. The difficulties in raising such a child are enormous. Many have emotional, physical and neurological problems as well as learning disabilities, which are often the result of drug abuse during pregnancy.

What am I going to tell my daughter, now 7, when she starts to ask questions about her "real" mother and father? So far, I've explained that not all parents are able to care for and love a child, and that it's better to find a mommy and daddy who can. That story will do for a while, but before long, she's going to ask questions that demand specific answers.

Should I tell her that her parents lost three other children to the courts and never bothered to try to get them back? That they sneaked out of town one step ahead of the law and have been on the run ever since?

What is my child going to find if she begins a search for her birth parents? They could be dead from a drug overdose or in jail. Could she ever hope to understand or cope with knowing what kind of people they really were?

I've given this dilemma a great deal of thought and have concluded that, for these kids, no answer is the best answer and no search is by far the best option. I am not signing my name for obvious reasons.

—Sacramento Parent

Dear Sac: As you probably know, I do not recommend these searches, based on the heartbreaking experiences I've been privy to over the years. In all fairness, however, I should tell you that some searches have resulted in happy reunions.

As for what to tell your daughter when she gets old enough to become profoundly inquisitive, the naked truth is always better than the best-dressed lie.

Dear Ann Landers: Since the courts have changed the laws so that "sperm parents" may now re-enter the lives of the children they discarded, why not add some requirements that would ensure a level playing field?

The adoptive parents should present an itemized bill to the "sperm parents" to cover all expenses incurred in raising and caring for the adopted child. This would include charges for the daily 24-hour babysitting, loving, caring and nurturing the adoptive parents gave so willingly. When the total amount has been paid, the "sperm parents" may then re-enter the life of the child they discarded.

I wonder how many "sperm parents" would still feel the need to contact their adopted child if they had to meet these financial requirements. Not many, I'll bet. The laws regarding adoption are a mess, and I am

—Sad in Illinois

Dear Illinois: I agree wholeheartedly. The Baby Richard case in Chicago created a great deal of resentment when a 4-year-old adopted child was forced to be returned to his natural father.

Anyone who saw the TV coverage of that badly handled case will vouch for the fact that the biggest loser is Baby Richard. In my opinion, that Illinois Supreme Court decision was a disgrace. Now that sealed adoption records can be opened, fewer children will be adopted. So again, the losers are the children.

Many people fear having their lives disrupted and are concerned that the law provides no protection. According to the National Council for Adoption, several laws are in place, depending on which state you live in.

Twenty-seven states currently have a mutual consent registry. The Uniform Adoption Act recommends this method of finding an adopted child or birth parent. The registry provides a non-intrusive way for adult adoptees and birth parents to waive the right to privacy if they want to be found.

The 27 states are: Arkansas, California, Colorado, Delaware, Florida, Idaho, Illinois, Indiana, Iowa, Louisiana, Maine, Maryland, Massachusetts, Michigan, Montana, Nevada, New Hampshire, New York, Ohio, Oregon, Rhode Island, South Carolina, South Dakota, Texas, Utah, Vermont and West Virginia.

Searches are not the only area of dispute. Readers often ask me, "When should I tell my child he or she is adopted?" Many have put off informing the child and are wondering if perhaps they should just keep quiet.

The adage "What you don't know can't hurt you" is a meaningless collection of words. Ignorance is far more dangerous than truth.

Children should be told they are adopted or stepchildren as soon as they're old enough to know what the words mean. Better to grow up with the knowledge than to run the risk of hearing it from an outsider.

Unless you plan to raise your child under a glass bell, you can be sure someone who knows the story will one day tell him. And learning it from someone else could shatter his confidence in you forever.

Dear Ann Landers: It happened again today. My two sons and I were in a shopping mall, and a total stranger felt the need to comment on the fact that my boys don't look anything alike.

Apparently, my 6-year-old decided it was time he explained the difference. "I'm adopted," he said. "That's when you have the same family, but not the same face."

I'm thankful that this child doesn't let these rude remarks get to him. Any comment, Ann?

—A Mom in Highland Lakes, N.J.

Dear Mom: That was an extremely intelligent response to a very dumb remark. Thank you for sharing.

Another controversy concerns allowing parents to adopt a child of another race. Here are some columns I printed on this subject back in 1972. My position hasn't changed:

Dear Ann Landers: You have printed many letters on adoption in your column. I have read letters from adoptive parents, adopted children, unwed mothers who gave up their babies and even unwed fathers. But you have never printed a letter from a white couple who has adopted a child from a minority race.

My husband and I plan to adopt a biracial child, and we are running into unbelievable opposition. Both his parents and mine are against it. Many of our friends say we are crazy and that we are looking for trouble. Frankly, we have given up trying to explain. They refuse to listen.

Please tell me, Ann, are we foolish to want to give our love to an innocent child who starts out in life with two strikes against him? These little ones of mixed parentage are not wanted by most people. They are, in a very real sense, handicapped. We want the challenge. We feel we are equal to it. Will you give us a word of encouragement, please?

—From Iowa

Dear Iowa: You sound like a couple of beautiful, selfless, gutsy people with a great deal of love to give. The child who finds a home with you is fortunate. In my book, you two rate a 21-gun salute for your courage.

Dear Ann Landers: About that white Iowa couple who were adopting the baby boy of an interracial union, they may be God's own, as you say, but I question their judgment.

Americans are still a race-conscious people. These parents would do well to consider the problems the child will face. Will he be looked down on by both blacks and whites? What will the attitude of the neighbors be? Are they well enough integrated so that he will have access to both black and white friends?

Parents who want to adopt "any child" should realize that children aren't poodles. There's more to it than providing "a good home." A child must grow into adulthood prepared to live in the real world.

—Mrs. E. in McComb, Miss.

Dear Mrs. E.: The questions you raise are provocative, and there are no easy answers. Since that letter appeared, I have been bombarded with expressions of love, hate, praise, condemnation and concern. Name it, and I've had it. Here are some samples of what the mail has been like lately:

From Ohio: God bless that couple with the courage to adopt an interracial child. The folks down South won't be so happy about this prediction, but within 150 years, America will be predominantly brown.

Indiana: You suggested a 21-gun salute for that Iowa couple. I suggest you save the salute for the kid, if he survives. It's a rough world out there, and whether you like it or not, Archie Bunker is the new American hero, and people love him.

Edmonton, Alberta: I am a 12-year-old girl. I just read a book about a couple who took 12 children of mixed parentage into their home, and they are as happy as can be. Anyone who thinks brown skin or different-shaped eyes make a person inferior needs educating.

Washington, D.C.: How much experience with interracial children have you had, Ann Landers? We adopted a Vietnamese child five years ago, and she has put us through hell. The girl has been in a mental hospital for over a year and is still very sick. Our own children are normal and healthy, and we rue the day we opened our hearts and our home to this foreign girl.

Minnesota: Four years ago, we adopted a Korean boy. He has brought us a world of joy and happiness and has taught our two sons kindness and unselfishness, and we thank God daily for him.

Alabama: You Northerners have a lot to say about brotherly love and racial equality. God made people different colors for a reason. Birds of a feather belong together. If your granddaughter marries a black, you deserve it.

Hartford, Conn.: A spokesman for the Greater Hartford Association of Black Social Workers says, "Black children should be placed with black families. White families cannot provide the experience that will enable a black child to survive in what is a 'racist society.' Children face enormous burdens during their growing-up years even under normal conditions. This special situation is an added burden to the child and the parents." I read this in *The Hartford Courant* two days after your column appeared. It sounds reasonable to me.

So, dear readers, there you have it. In my opinion, the overall results of what happens to biracial, and black and brown-skinned children who are adopted by white families will not be known for at least 15 years. I'm betting there will be many triumphs and many disasters. Those who try it need unusual courage, emotional stability and an infinite capacity to love. If they succeed, the rewards are tremendous.

For more information, contact:

National Council for Adoption
1930 17th St. NW
Washington, DC 20009
(800) 333-NCFA

4

I Love Pets, but an Iguana in the Bathtub?

Some of the funniest, saddest, oddest and most touching letters I've received have been about people and their pets.

Take a look at these creative critters:

Dear Ann Landers: My problem may sound as if the boys at Yale are pulling your leg again, but every word of this letter is absolutely true.

Is it possible for a bird to get sexually excited when he sees a human being of the opposite sex undressing?

I have a very close friend with whom I spend the night occasionally.

Whenever I get ready for bed, she moves the parakeet's cage from the guest room (where I sleep) into the closet. I always thought this was rather peculiar, but I never said anything. Last week, I decided to mention it to her.

She became irate and insisted that birds become sexually excited at the sight of undressed humans of the opposite sex. Is this true or not?

—Never Saw a Bird Blush

Dear Never: Your hostess' concept of what turns on our feathered friends is strictly for the birds. (The cuckoos, that is.) She is projecting her own prudishness onto the parakeet. He hasn't the faintest idea why he is being stashed in the closet. Go along with the nonsense, dear. It costs you nothing.

Dear Ann Landers: I am writing to tell you about my four amazing dogs. They play the piano.

Ginger is an apricot toy poodle who plays "Tea for Two" with her right paw. Pepper, another poodle, can play the C-major scale with his right paw. He also sings while I play the harmonica.

Rusty, who is Pepper and Ginger's pup, plays the pentatonic scale with his left paw, and Gigi, an apricot toy poodle, plays the C-major scale.

These dogs do several other tricks and have been entertaining people in nursing homes, in schools and at private parties for several years. I have tried to get them on national television, but I guess I just don't know the right people.

To my knowledge, they are the only piano-playing dogs alive. Can you suggest a way to get them a bigger audience?
—John Buby, Tallahassee, Fla.

Dear John: I do not book animal acts, but maybe I can help by printing your letter. Perhaps Johnny Carson or David Letterman or Arsenio Hall might be interested. If you're in the phone book, John, maybe you'll get a call. Good luck.

Dear Ann Landers: I know people write to you with all kinds of questions, so I wasn't surprised when that man from Tallahassee asked you to help him get an agent for his dog act. I remember he has some apricot toy poodles named Ginger, Gigi and Pepper, and they play the piano. He said they are the only piano-playing dogs in the world, which I can believe.

You told him that booking animal acts was not your line of work and suggested that maybe Johnny Carson or David Letterman might give him a break. Within a few days, those very same poodles appeared on a TV show (not the shows you mentioned) and performed very well. I'll bet they get some bookings.

Since you helped that guy, maybe you can do something for me. I have a couple of wire-haired terriers that sing. I play tunes on the fiddle like "Sioux City Sue" and "How Come You Do Me Like You Do Do Do," and the dogs harmonize like the Supremes. Everybody deserves one big break in life, and this could be mine. How about it, Annie old girl?
—Longtime Admirer in Arlington Heights, Ill.

Dear Admirer: Since that column appeared, "Annie Old Girl" has heard from a woman in Phoenix who has a horse that does multiplication tables, a man in Fort Worth whose three cats do ballet numbers, and a woman in San Juan, Puerto Rico, with a parrot that can swear in five languages. Please, folks, no more letters about your talented pets. I am sure they are all wonderful, but I can't help you.

But still they come.

Dear Ann: I don't see anything so unusual about a dog who sings. We have a pet squirrel who plays the drums. We started out to teach him by letting him pound the drums with a nut in each paw. Now he doesn't even need the nuts. He just pounds away, and his sense of rhythm is as good as some professionals.

—Pittsburgh

Dear Ann Landers: We have a 13-year-old rat terrier who says, "I want out." I am not claiming she says anything except that one sentence. But she does say it very clearly and only when she wants to go out, so I believe she knows what it means. More than one guest has turned white as a sheet when he heard our dog speak. Please print this. Thanks.

—Nuts for Dogs

Dear Ann: Our dog, Heinz (57 varieties), says, "Howdy, partner," "Vas you dere, Cholly?" and "Goodnight, all." It all started when Heinz sneezed and my husband said: "Gesundheit." We almost fell over when the dog repeated after him, "Gesundheit." We have tried to teach Heinz to say other words, but for some mysterious reason, he refuses. I guess you can say we have a talking dog, too.

—Covina, Calif.

Dear Ann Landers: Our schnauzer speaks Italian. He says, "Mama Mia," "Grazie" and "Bella Signora." When he hears "Arrivederci Roma" on the radio, he puts his head between his paws and cries. The kids have tried to teach the dog Latin, but so far no luck. We will let you know if they succeed. Print this letter if you want to, but please don't give away the name of our city. Many local people know about our dog, but we don't want our home to become a tourist attraction. Thanks.

—Proud of Him

Dear Ann: We've all heard jokes about parrots that yelled out dirty words when the minister came to call. But have you ever heard of a dog that did the same thing? Well, my husband has a warped sense of humor, and he taught our boxer some terrible words. After three embarrassing experiences with company, I gave the dog to my sister, who lives on a farm. Now I can relax for the first time in two years.

—Mrs. M.M.

There's always a letter from a comedian. Here's an example:

Dear Ann Landers: Our son's dog, Sampson, has a vocabulary of two words. When asked, "What's on the top of the house, Sam?" he answers, "Roof!" When asked, "What's on the outside of an oak tree?" he replies, "Bark!"

What is even more incredible about Sampson is that he can read. I saw proof of this with my own eyes when we were walking through a park last summer. Sam saw a sign on a park bench that said, WET PAINT. So he did.

—Bragging in Florida

Dear Bragging: Big deal. We once had a Mexican chihuahua who didn't need any signs. He always knew when he was on expensive carpeting—and that's where he "went."

Some letters about animals are unusual but informative. I learn something new every day—and not long ago, I seemed to be majoring in cows:

Dear Ann Landers: Some good friends of mine insist that cows sleep standing up and that it is possible to sneak up from behind and tip them over.

I asked my dad about this, and he thought it was the funniest thing he'd ever heard. When he finally stopped laughing, I asked if it was really possible to tip over a cow. He replied, "Absolutely not. Somebody's kidding you."

Will you please tell me if there is such a thing as "cow tipping," or are my friends pulling my leg?

—Flora in Cincinnati

Dear Flora: We checked with LuAnne Metzger, farm curator of Chicago's Lincoln Park Zoo, who assured us that cows sleep lying down. She also said, "It is not a good idea to try to tip a cow over because they do kick, and the results could be extremely unpleasant."

We then checked with Doug Houghton, assistant dean of students at Iowa State University. The Department of Dairy Sciences said cows sleep lying down but can "doze" standing up. The dean said he had heard of cow tipping but thought it was just a gag to get kids out in the pasture and leave them stranded, like "snipe-hunting" in the '60s.

We then called the University of Wisconsin. The administration there echoed the sentiments of the faculty at Iowa State. A better authority, however, the students in a fraternity house, said cow tipping is a common form of recreation, and it takes about four husky students to tip over a cow. Our source added, "So far as we know, the cows don't get hurt, but they do get pretty darned mad."

Dick James of Verdon, Neb, past president of the Nebraska State Dairy Association, said cows do not have a sense of humor and do not enjoy being knocked over. Such stress can result in reduced milk production and poor growth.

The word from here, students, is this: If you want to go in for tipping, tip the waitress, but leave the cows alone.

Dear Ann Landers: I am the mother of two small children. I have a job outside my home. All of this keeps me extremely busy. I have never had the time or felt a real desire to write to you before today.

An outraged reader recently wrote to you about global warming and the so-called greenhouse effect. Please read the enclosed story from the San Bernardino *Sun* in California.

"University researchers will strap gas-measuring equipment to cows to find out how bovine belching might be contributing to the greenhouse effect. Washington State University researchers will get $70,000 a year for three years from the U.S. Environmental Protection Agency to determine how much methane cows and other cud-chewing animals make when they belch."

I never would have believed it if someone just told me about this. It sounds like some of the sensational garbage that you might see in a supermarket tabloid.

Ann, please tell me this isn't true. I hate to think our Environmental Protection Agency is throwing away money on such an absurd research project. If they would like some suggestions for their $70,000, I'd like to remind them of the homeless and hungry people in our country.

—Redlands, Calif.

Dear Red: We spoke with Al Ruddy, associate director of News and Information Services at Washington State University. He said: "The news story is true. Although this might seem like a foolish expenditure, it's not. Here's why:

"There are two primary gases involved in the greenhouse effect: carbon dioxide and methane. Methane traps radiation in the Earth's atmosphere, and its production is increasing about 1 percent every year. The three primary sources of methane are wetlands, rice fields and cattle. Cows belch four to six times a minute and produce about 15 percent of all our methane. If man wishes to use natural gas as a source of fuel, it will necessitate releasing more methane into the atmosphere. Before we can safely do that, we must find out how much methane is produced already."

Clear? Well, I hope so, because Al Ruddy did his darndest to simplify it for me.

Our pets depend on us to take care of them and see that they are supervised properly. Here are a couple of letters that should be read by pet lovers everywhere:

Dear Ann Landers: We went to visit my brother-in-law and his wife last weekend, and I am still shaking from the experience.

My sister-in-law told us when we arrived that we would have to share the children's bathroom because the bathroom connected to the sun porch where we were to sleep was not usable. No other explanation was given.

After I unpacked, I went into the adjoining bathroom just to wash my hands. I almost died of fright. There was a 5-foot alligator in the bathtub. I ran downstairs and asked my sister-in-law what that thing was doing in there. She was very cool about it and said the kids had been given an iguana by their uncle last year, and it had just kept growing.

I asked what they planned to do with it, and she said they'd probably give it to the zoo as soon as they could talk the children into parting with it. She also said it was harmless and I was silly to be so upset.

I didn't get much sleep that weekend, and I still shake when I think of it. Having an alligator in an adjoining room is not my idea of a restful weekend. Please tell me if something that looks like a crocodile is harmless and if an iguana can grow that big. (It must have weighed 30 pounds.) No one in Grand Rapids has ever seen one of those things.

—Fraidy Cat

Dear Cat: Your sister-in-law gave you the straight goods. Iguanas can grow to be 5 feet long. I think it's criminal that animals are sold to the public as novelty toys for kids. Thousands of baby chicks and bunnies suffer the same sad fate at Easter time. Most people don't know what to do with the chickens and rabbits when they grow up.

That poor iguana was not meant to flop around in a bathtub. I hope your sister-in-law takes him to a zoo soon. Please tell her I suggested it. Animals have rights, too.

Dear Ann Landers: This is in response to the letter from "Fraidy Cat," regarding the bathtub-prone iguana. While I agree that a tub is no place for one, I disagree with her opinion of them as pets. I am the proud owner of a precious 5-foot-long-and-still-growing green iguana.

Sebastian Bach Jr. is the light of my life. He is a wonderful animal full of spunk and personality, as cuddly and lovable as any cat or dog. "Junior" is easy to maintain, cheap to feed and potty-trained. He's also spoiled rotten and lives like a king. If given the love and attention they deserve, iguanas thrive in a domestic habitat and can grow from 5 feet to 9 feet in length.

I've had Junior since infancy. He sleeps in a bed with his own heating pad, pillow and blanket. Many people fear reptiles and label them "harmful" because of their appearance. But looks can be deceiving.

A word of caution to parents of small children. If you have a male iguana, get it "fixed." Although a tame iguana is harmless, an "excited" male is another matter. I recommend consulting a vet who specializes in reptiles.

—S.K., Junior's Mama, Stockton, Calif.

Dear Mama: Thanks for the briefing. I'd rather have a cat.

Dear Ann Landers: You've printed many letters about whether to keep the toilet lid up or down.

Our parrot, Clark, shinnied up the rear of our toilet tank onto our bathroom counter—his favorite roosting spot when we are in or near the bedroom. While putting the groceries away, I was distracted. When I returned to collect Clark, I discovered him—stiff, wet and shivering—floating on his side in the toilet bowl. He was glassy-eyed and appeared to be suffering from severe exhaustion. Clark has one clipped wing and only one foot with a full quotient of toes, so he doesn't balance very well under the best of conditions.

My husband and I rushed Clark to the animal clinic for emergency anti-stress drugs and oxygen. He stayed overnight in the incubator and recovered sufficiently so that we were permitted to take him home the following afternoon.

From now on, you can be sure the toilet seat lid will remain closed in our house.

—Learned the Hard Way in Miami

Dear Miami: Several readers wrote to tell me they were stunned to discover rare creatures in their toilet bowls. I mean beavers, rats, skunks, a raccoon and even a snake. Others reported that their cats and dogs nearly drowned in their toilets. A pediatrician wrote to say children have been known to drown in the darned things. So, folks, the verdict is clear—the toilet seat and lid should be down at all times when the toilet is not in use. Case closed.

Dear Ann Landers: As a podiatrist and animal lover, I feel an obligation to tell you that an alarming number of children are being bitten by dogs. The misery and potential disfigurement can be awesome.

I have treated many adults who have been bitten on the foot and ankle, but bites inflicted on children are the most upsetting. Seventy percent of these victims are bitten by the family pet or a dog known to them. We are not talking about rabid strays, Ann. These dogs are Spot and Fido, members of the family. Parents, dog owners, children and guests, please take heed of the following:

1. All dogs have the potential to bite. They react aggressively to teasing, rough play and threatening sounds or behavior. Puppy or full-grown, they are capable of biting, especially when food or jealousy of a new baby is involved.

2. There is no such thing as a dog that is so wonderful it can be trusted with children. Every dog, no matter how well-trained, can become jealous of a child and bite. And some children provoke dogs, especially if they think no one is looking. It is never safe to leave children unattended with an animal.

3. Also, please be a considerate host, and do not insist that your pet remain in the room if your guest tells you, "I am afraid of dogs." Leave the psychology to professionals, and get the animal out of there.

4. When approaching an oncoming stray or a strange dog, follow the old rules: no direct eye contact, no running, no arm flailing and no unnecessary jerky movements that could be perceived as a threat to the animal. Instead, speak in the dog's direction in a high-pitched but soothing voice, "Good girl, good boy, good dog," etc.

5. Do not fail to immunize your dog so, if the worst happens, further complication of the wound by rabies infection won't occur. Low cost and/or free vaccinations are available, but you must find them by calling your local ASPCA chapter or animal shelter.

Please print this letter, Ann. I'm sure it will do a lot of good. There is information here that needs to be repeated time and time again.

—M.Z.T., Brooklyn

Dear Brooklyn: Here's your letter. I'll bet you prevented hundreds of dog bites by taking the time and trouble to write. Bless you.

A Dog's Plea
Beth Norman Harris

Treat me kindly, my beloved friend, for no heart in all the world is more grateful for kindness than the loving heart of me.

Do not break my spirit with a stick, for though I might lick your hand between blows, your patience and understanding will more quickly teach me the things you would have me learn.

Speak to me often, for your voice is the world's sweetest music, as you must know by the fierce wagging of my tail when the sound of your footstep falls upon my waiting ear.

Please take me inside when it is cold and wet, for I am a domesticated animal, no longer accustomed to bitter elements. I ask no greater glory than the privilege of sitting at your feet beside the hearth.

Keep my pan filled with fresh water, for I cannot tell you when I suffer thirst.

Feed me clean food that I may stay well, to romp and play and do your bidding, to walk by your side and stand ready, willing and able to protect you with my life, should your life be in danger.

And, my friend, when I am very old, and I no longer enjoy good health, hearing and sight, do not make heroic efforts to keep me going. I am not having any fun.

Please see that my trusting life is taken gently. I shall leave this Earth knowing with the last breath I draw that my fate was always safest in your hands.

Dear Ann Landers: This short story is based on my own experience and I think it will touch anyone who has ever owned a pet. I wrote it with tears in my eyes. Will you please print it?
—Chuck Wells, Palmyra, N.Y.

Dogs Don't Have Souls, Do They?

I remember bringing you home. You were so small and cuddly with your tiny paws and soft fur.

You bounced around the room with eyes flashing and ears flopping. Once in a while, you'd let out a little yelp just to let me know this was your territory.

Making a mess of the house and chewing on everything in sight became a passion, and when I scolded you, you just put your head down and looked up at me with those innocent eyes, as if to say, "I'm sorry, but I'll do it again as soon as you're not watching."

As you got older, you protected me by looking out the window and barking at everyone who walked by.

When I had a tough day at work, you would be waiting for me with your tail wagging just to say, "Welcome home. I missed you." You never had a bad day, and I could always count on you to be there for me.

When I sat down to read the paper and watch TV, you would hop on my lap, looking for attention. You never asked for anything more than to have me pat your head so you could go to sleep with your head over my leg.

As you got older, you moved around more slowly. Then, one day, old age finally took its toll, and you couldn't stand on those wobbly legs anymore. I knelt down and patted you lying there, trying to make you young again. You just looked up at me as if to say you were old and tired and that after all these years of not asking for anything, you had to ask me for one last favor.

With tears in my eyes, I drove you one last time to the vet. One last time, you were lying next to me.

For some strange reason, you were able to stand up in the animal hospital; perhaps it was your sense of pride.

As the vet led you away, you stopped for an instant, turned your head and looked at me as if to say, "Thank you for taking care of me."

I thought, "No, thank *you* for taking care of me."

Dear Chuck: What a beautiful tribute. Every person who has loved a pet will be deeply moved by what you have written. There is a moral here that should not be overlooked. When your faithful pet becomes old and sick, and life is no longer fun but rather a painful burden, do your friend one last kindness. Relieve him or her of the misery. It's the last great act of compassion you can perform.

Dear Ann Landers: A long time ago, you ran a letter from a boy whose dog had died. He wanted to know if dogs went to heaven. It would be a big help, he said, if he were sure that when he died, his dog would be up there waiting for him.

As I recall, you consulted several clergymen. Most said animals do not have souls, and therefore, they would not go to heaven. One kind Congregational minister replied that he wasn't sure but he didn't see anything wrong with telling the youngster that he would probably see his dog in heaven because everything up there is "perfect."

Several days ago, I read a column on that very subject by Rev. Dale Turner, who writes for a Seattle paper. I am sending a condensed version in the hope that you will print it.

—A Seattle Reader

Dear Seattle: Thanks for a real heart-warmer. I loved it. Here it is:

Looking back across the years, I see how important dogs have been in my life. I had been an ordained minister only a few weeks when I received a call from an 8-year-old boy. His dog had been killed by a car. "Mr. Turner," the lad sobbed, "do you do funerals for dogs?"

I didn't know quite how to respond, but I recalled the Scriptures' affirmation of God's knowing when even a sparrow falls. I replied, "Why not?" and I conducted a little ceremony for the boy's pet. He was very pleased and then asked, "Is my dog going to heaven?" I wasn't prepared for that question, but my love for animals got me through it. I'm sure I made the child feel better.

Several years later, I had my own personal experience that provided the answer I had never been sure of.

Our wonderful dachshund, Gretta, died, and we were eager to bring another dog into our home. We went to the pound to get the dachshund whose photo had appeared in the paper. By the time we arrived, it had been claimed. Another puppy, sensing our mission, poked her nose through the wire fence. The look in her eyes seemed to say, "Please pick me." We did. And we named her Pick.

Whenever I came home, Pick was there to greet me. I'd say, "Pick, you've got it made. Other animals work for their keep. A canary sings, cows give milk, chickens lay eggs, but you don't have to do anything but hang around."

After 14 years, Pick became very sick, and there was nothing to be done except put her out of her misery. With a heavy heart I drove her to the vet's, who did what had to be done. I then went back to my study and wept for hours.

A few days later, a parishioner who knew of my grief sent me this poem. It healed my sorrow. Perhaps it will help others. I'd like to share it:

I explained to St. Peter,
I'd rather stay here,
Outside the pearly gate.
I won't be a nuisance,
I won't even bark,
I'll be very patient and wait.
I'll be here, chewing on a celestial bone,
No matter how long you may be.
I'd miss you so much, if I went in alone,
It wouldn't be heaven for me.

5

Straight Talk About Cancer, AIDS and Other Health Problems

I have often joked that one day I might be arrested for practicing medicine without a license, but one of the most valuable services my column provides is to inform my readers about medical problems.

It's not what I know but who I know that has given me access to the finest medical brains in the world. My involvement with the Harvard Medical School, which began in the late '60s, was the magic key.

I have received countless letters from grateful readers telling me they first recognized the symptoms of an illness by reading about it in the column. Through the years, I have kept my readers apprised of a wide variety of medical problems—some serious, some trivial, but all helpful. Here's a letter from 1975:

Dear Ann Landers: Since you frequently remind your readers that emotional problems can create physical problems, I am sending the findings of Dr. Thomas H. Holmes, a psychiatrist at the University of Washington School of Medicine in Seattle. He listed 43 events that create emotional stress in order of their impact.

Dr. Holmes' theory is that any change, pleasant or unpleasant, can create susceptibility to illness. He advises against making several consecutive changes in living patterns when one has a choice. Such changes, he said, should be postponed or canceled. Here is the list and scale of impact:

| | SCALE OF |
EVENTS	IMPACT
Death of a spouse	100
Divorce	73
Marital separation	65
Jail term	63
Death of a close family member	63
Personal injury or illness	53
Marriage	50
Fired at work	47
Marital reconciliation	45
Retirement	45
Pregnancy	40
Sex difficulties	39
Gain of new family member	39
Business readjustment	39
Change in financial status	38
Death of close friend	37
Change to different line of work	36
Change in number of arguments with spouse	35
Mortgage over $10,000	31
Foreclosure of mortgage or loan	30
Son or daughter leaving home	29
Trouble with in-laws	29
Outstanding personal achievement	28
Wife begins or stops work	26
Begin or end school	26
Trouble with boss	23
Change in residence	20
Change in schools	20
Mortgage or loan less than $10,000	17
Change in number of family get-togethers	15
Christmas	12

—Your Seattle Friend

Dear Seattle Friend: My thanks for a fascinating contribution. Interesting that going to jail creates 10 stress points less than getting a divorce—and only 13 more than getting married! I'll bet some convicts would disagree.

Dear Ann Landers: I have a problem, and I hope you can help. Ever since I was a little girl, my hands have gotten tremendously sweaty whenever I've been unsure of myself or felt inadequate. I remember when I played in piano recitals, the piano keys had to be wiped off during intermission.

This has been a problem my entire life. I would be very grateful if you could suggest something that might help me. No name or city, please, just

—A Super Sweater in Kentucky

Dear Super Sweater: I very rarely mention a brand name in the column, but I have recommended Drysol for heavy perspiration in the past and will do so again. This product, available by prescription only, has solved the sweating problem for many when everything else failed. Good luck.

Dear Ann Landers: Thank you so much for printing the information about the American Enuresis Foundation. It was a lifesaver for me. Our 9-year-old son had been a chronic bed-wetter for years. The problem had lowered his self-esteem to the point where he would not spend the night at a friend's house.

We tried medication and reducing fluids before bedtime, both of which were ineffective. We had seen several doctors, and none was helpful.

When I saw your column, I immediately wrote the American Enuresis Foundation. To make a long story short, we ended up with a 30-day program and a safe electronic monitoring device. This proved 100 percent effective. We now know that our son has a sleep disorder and he needed to be trained to wake up from his deep sleep to go to the bathroom.

Thanks again for bringing the American Enuresis Foundation to our attention.

—Dry and Happy in Alabama

Dear Ala.: I appreciate your letting me know the program worked for your son. Many wrote to say it worked for their children, too. Unfortunately, many elderly people also wrote, not aware that this organization is for bed-wetters, not incontinent folks.

Please be aware that the program is expensive because it is tailored to the individual. For more information, send a long, self-addressed, stamped envelope to: American Eneuresis Foundation, P.O. Box 33061, Tulsa, OK 74153-1061.

Adults who suffer from incontinence should see a urologist and find out if there's an organic problem. (In older women who have had children, the complaint is not uncommon. A surgical procedure is often the answer for them.)

If there is no organic problem, the solution might be a special medication. Involuntary action can sometimes be controlled by exercise and/or drugs. By all means, check it out with a doctor.

For more information, contact:

Simon Foundation for Incontinence
P.O. Box 815
Wilmette, IL 60091
(800) 23-SIMON
(708) 864-3913
(Support and advocacy group for people suffering from incontinence)

Dear Ann Landers: I have been married to this woman for 18 years. She has a lot of good qualities, but her temper is fierce. When she gets really crazy, she bites me. I never thought much about it until I read an article in the paper about how dangerous a human bite can be. Please print the facts so people who bite will stop it.

An official in the New York City Health Department started to keep track of human bites, along with animal bites, in 1977. He said he was just amazed to discover that more than 900 people in a single year reported that somebody bit them.

Most bites occur during fights. Hands and fingers are bitten more than any other part of the body.

Occasionally, a person gets bitten accidentally, like during a sports event, but almost all bites are the result of aggressive behavior.

More people bite between March and August, with June being the peak month. Saturday is the most popular day for getting bit. Teenagers and young adults do the most biting.

Knuckles are the most common location for bites. This usually happens when someone is hit in the mouth. All human bites should be seen by a physician if the skin is broken. Victims who do not seek medical attention within 24 hours may be in serious trouble from a human bite because it can produce massive swelling and cause severe pain. I hope I have helped draw attention to a subject most people don't pay much attention to, but they should. Sign me

—Lucky to Be Alive

Dear Lucky: Thanks for giving me a letter that my readers can sink their teeth into. Some of the facts you came up with will be news to millions of people.

Dear Ann Landers: I met a very attractive guy about a month ago. He was introduced to me by my cousin. We are all 17 years of age. Something happened last Saturday night that just about blew my mind. Please tell me what to do.

This cousin, her steady, the attractive guy (I'll call him Phil) and I went to a movie. Right in the middle of a sad scene, when it was so quiet in the theater you could hear a pin drop, Phil stood up and yelled out some of the dirtiest words I've ever heard. All the while, he was throwing his arms around like a crazy man. I tried to get him to sit down and be quiet, but he paid no attention to me. In no time at all, the manager of the theater came over and told Phil he would have to leave. I didn't want Phil to go alone, because I was afraid he was off his rocker—so we all left together. When we were walking to the parking lot, Phil said he didn't feel well and wanted to go home. So we took him home, and I haven't heard from him since.

Please, Ann, tell me what this is all about.

—Grossed Out in Denver

Dear Denver: My guess is that Phil has Tourette's syndrome. This illness is often misdiagnosed as an emotional problem. We now know it is a hereditary disorder involving the central nervous system. Tourette's usually begins between the ages of 2 and 14. The patient blinks his eyes, makes odd faces, jerks his head and shoulders and utters sounds (or says words) that are most inappropriate. These acts are involuntary and cannot be controlled.

As for you, Denver, now that you know the boy is ill, I hope you will be compassionate and share this information with him, in case he and his parents are unaware that he has a medical problem that is treatable.

Dear Ann Landers: When our son was 5, he started to blink his eyes a lot. I mentioned this to his pediatrician who said, "Just ignore it." A year later, "Joey" began to shrug his shoulders and fidget a great deal. "Just nervous tics," the doctor assured me. "He'll outgrow it."

These symptoms and others would come and go. I almost went crazy trying to protect Joey from anything that might produce stress. I took the boy to three other pediatricians and was told I should not be concerned because there was nothing to worry about.

After doing some research on my own, I insisted that our pediatrician refer Joey to a pediatric neurologist. Sure enough, the diagnosis was Tourette's syndrome. The boy was put on medication and has dramatically improved.

Ann, I'm writing to you because half the people I've met whose children have Tourette's syndrome told me they first became aware of this illness when they read about it in your column. You had correctly diagnosed Tourette's syndrome from the description in a letter of someone's behavior. You then listed what types of things to look for.

Will you please tell parents again that if their child develops tics or engages in repetitive blinking, shoulder shrugging, grimacing, tensing muscles, throat clearing, belching, sniffing, humming, etc., they should contact the Tourette Syndrome Association for information. Send a large, self-addressed, stamped (75 cents) envelope to: The Tourette Syndrome Association, 42–40 Bell Blvd., Suite 205, Bayside, NY 11361, or call (718) 224-2999. Thank you.

—Longtime Reader

Dear L.T.R.: That original column diagnosis was made several years ago, and I am still hearing about it. The symptoms were so obvious to me that I felt safe in labeling the problem.

The credit should go to the many fine physicians who have gone out of their way to send me material and keep me informed.

Dear Ann Landers: Our 21-year-old son recently had a mole removed from his neck. It turned out to be stage-three melanoma, which is a deadly cancer. "Hal" had seen a dermatologist three years before and had some benign moles removed from his back. At the time, the doctor took a picture of the mole on his neck, measured it and said it should be watched.

Hal did not return to that doctor. Time passed, and my son met a new dermatologist socially and made an appointment. He removed the mole on the initial visit and had it biopsied. It turned out to be cancerous. My son has had a second surgery and is beginning interferon treatments next week.

What I want to share with your readers is this: A lack of knowledge about melanoma can be fatal. We now know that age is not a factor. All moles with a raised surface should be watched. If a mole becomes larger or seems to be changing in character, you should see a dermatologist. It could be a deadly malignancy.

Fortunately, the odds are in my son's favor, but at 21, it is frightening to know you had something on your skin that could have killed you.

—Shirley in Bakersfield

Dear Shirley: Your letter will save some lives. Thank you on behalf of all the people you helped today.

Sometimes, people send in their "miracle cures." A reader who cured warts with a banana peel generated a lot of mail.

Dear Ann Landers: I was very much interested in that letter about removing warts because I have been plagued by dozens of them for years.

Your correspondent described the miraculous use of a banana peel, but no details were given. Does one rub the peel on the warts periodically or tape the peel on? Is it the inside of the peel that does the job or the other side? Please, Ann, be more explicit. I will try anything that might help me get rid of these pesky things.

—Myrtle Beach, S.C.

Dear Myrtle: I'm not sure how to apply the peel, and it probably doesn't matter, but the mail on this subject has been fascinating. Keep reading.

Dear Ann: Thirty years ago, when I was 9, I had about 20 warts on my left hand. Grandma came to visit around Christmas, and when she saw the warts, she said, "We can get rid of them by magic." She took a piece of bacon, rubbed the warts and said, "Tonight when the moon comes out, we are going to toss the bacon over your left shoulder, and the warts will disappear." I thought she must be a little nutty but decided it was worth the try. Three weeks later, the warts were gone, and I haven't had one since.

—Newport News, Va.

From Wilmington, N.C.: When our daughter was a preschooler, she developed several warts on her fingers. I took her to the pediatrician, who advised me to buy a roll of gauze, a roll of medical tape and a bottle of castor oil. I was instructed to soak the gauze in castor oil and wrap the warts for two weeks, changing the dressings twice a day. The doctor said the oil would "suffocate" the warts and they would drop off. That's exactly what happened within 15 days.

Aberdeen, S.D.: Anyone who wants to get rid of warts should take megadoses of vitamin C. Warts are caused by a virus, and when the vitamin C tackles the virus, the warts disappear.

Escondido, Calif.: Forty years ago, I had dozens of warts under my fingernails. The pain drove me crazy. I went to a dermatologist who tried medication, cauterization, surgery and finally vitamin A injections. The warts would disappear and then grow back. I moved to Dallas and saw another dermatologist who tried liquid nitrogen. Bravo! In three weeks, the warts on my hand were gone, and so were the plantar warts on the bottoms of my feet.

Taipei Post Reader in Taiwan: Anyone who wants to get rid of warts should rub 20 pennies on the warts and then give the coins to a beggar. This has been done in our family for many years and has never failed to work.

Oxnard, Calif.: The mysterious disappearance of warts is no mystery to me though many people seem baffled by it. I believe in the power of positive thinking. People can "will away" warts by the sheer belief that they are able to do so. My grandmother proved it by "curing" five of us kids. All she said was "Hocus-pocus—go away, warts." And they did.

Sioux Falls, S.D.: Anyone who wants to get rid of warts should pick a growing green dandelion, apply the oozing white sap to the warts and let it dry for two days. It never fails.

Philadelphia: After I spent $250 on dermatologists, my janitor bet me a dollar he could get rid of my warts in 10 days. He cut a raw potato in half, rubbed the juice on the warts, and on the 11th day, I paid up.

Dear Ann Landers: An estimated 37 million Americans suffer from arthritis. While often dismissed as "just arthritis" or, as they say on

TV, "minor aches and pains," arthritis is our country's No. 1 chronic disease.

Nearly 200,000 American children suffer from some form of juvenile arthritis. At least half of the population over 65 is affected. Many disabling forms of arthritis strike between the ages of 20 and 40, the crucial years for establishing families and careers. This condition not only causes pain and stiffness but diminishes the quality of life and can lead to disability, disfigurement and premature death.

Too many people think that because there is no cure for arthritis, nothing can be done to treat it. That is a false assumption. There are things that can be done to control it, and the Arthritis Foundation can help. It has many programs, including some self-help courses, exercise classes and patient forums.

For free information on how to cope more effectively with arthritis, contact the Arthritis Foundation, P.O. Box 7669, Atlanta, GA 30357-0669, or call the toll-free Arthritis Foundation Information Line at (800) 283-7800.

Please, Ann, let people know it's not "just arthritis," and that help is available.

—Marilynn J. Cason, chairman, Arthritis Foundation,
Illinois Chapter

Dear Marilynn: You did, and I thank you.

Don't skip this column because you think it doesn't apply to you. In a few months (or years), you may wish you had read it.

Dear Ann Landers: I am a 58-year-old woman and have just been diagnosed with osteoporosis. I went to my doctor because I was having a lot of pain in my back. In addition to the pain, I noticed that I had lost almost 2 inches in height, and my back, starting at the neck, is beginning to hunch over. It turns out that two of the bones in my spine have not only broken but have collapsed and are deteriorating.

My doctor told me I have some of the risk factors for developing osteoporosis, which I didn't know. For instance, I didn't know that since my mother had osteoporosis, I was more likely to get it.

My mother, at age 71, suffered a severe hip fracture that left her permanently disabled. Before this happened, she was active, energetic and young for her age. Today, she is old and frail, uses a walker and can no longer garden, do housework or go out with her friends. She is very dependent on me and my brother, and we worry that the next step will be a nursing home.

I am sure you can understand how upset I am. I have a demanding job and need to be healthy so I can continue to take care of my family responsibilities. What I haven't told you is that I have two daughters who now have a grandmother and a mother with this dreadful disease.

My doctor has given me a program that will help me prevent additional fractures. But she also has made it clear that there is no cure for osteoporosis. Once bone mass is lost, it cannot be replaced. On a brighter note, she believes that if I follow my treatment plan, my bone loss will occur at a slower pace.

Ann, I am writing to ask your help. Please tell me where I can get the most reliable information on how to prevent osteoporosis and how I can keep from breaking more bones. I need this information not only for me but also for my children and grandchildren. I want to start early to help them avoid what my mother and I are now going through. When my doctor told me I had osteoporosis, I set out to learn everything I could about the disease, but I have had trouble finding information.

Because this is such a common problem, Ann, there must be millions of people like me who need to be informed. Please help us.

—Concerned in Nashville

Dear Concerned: I'm glad you wrote. This is a subject that needs a great deal more visibility. Most people think osteoporosis is a disease of the elderly. This is not true. It can strike women as early as the mid-30s, and men are also at risk.

Too many young people today are into a lifestyle that will ensure an even greater incidence of osteoporosis in the future. Teenagers and preteens should be educated about this illness and told: Don't smoke, limit alcohol consumption, eat a balanced diet rich in calcium, and exercise regularly. Women at midlife should see their doctors about their bone health.

Medical experts I've consulted believe that osteoporosis is both preventable and treatable. An excellent organization that can give you the entire picture is the National Osteoporosis Foundation, P.O. Box 96616, Washington, DC 20077-7456. Write for information and send a large, self-addressed, stamped envelope.

Dear Ann Landers: I got into a discussion with the girls at work about sleeping habits. I happened to mention that I always wear underpants to bed. Everyone was shocked. (I have been married for 18 years.)

Am I eccentric, crazy or "hung-up"—as they all seem to think? I never gave this matter any thought until it came up in this morning's conversation. Do you have any statistics on how many married women sleep in underpants? Please respond to

—Oddball in Ohio

Dear Ohio: I have never heard of any surveys on the subject, but it is a safe assumption that most women (single and married) do not sleep in underpants. Those who do are not necessarily wacky, however. It is probably a habit acquired in childhood.

Dear Readers: Remember the woman who slept in her underpants? Well, now we have a new angle, which I feel obliged to share. Please stay with me and learn something. This letter came from Boston:

Dear Ann Landers: For three consecutive years (1974–76) I developed cystitis—a bladder infection. But not until after the third miserable bout did I ask myself some questions. Here I was, an otherwise healthy woman in her 50s, getting this infection regularly. Why?

I figured out a "possibility" and called my urologist. He was flabbergasted that I had been wearing underpants to bed since childhood. To compound the problem came the '70s, when it was considered fashionable to wear pantyhose and slacks everywhere.

I no longer wear underpants to bed and have had no more bladder infections. I believe this information could be helpful to others—especially if you could get the backing of a good urologist. Why not ask one?

—Wiser with Age

Dear Wiser: I took your suggestion and contacted Dr. Joseph J. Kaufman, one of the country's most distinguished physicians. He is chief of urology at the University of California School of Medicine. Here is Dr. Kaufman's response:

Dear Ann Landers: "Wiser" makes a good case for not wearing underpants to bed.

Cystitis among women is extremely common at all ages. It is generally accepted that the reason for this is the relatively poor tissue defense mechanisms and the tendency for bacteria to colonize in the moist areas of the genitalia.

Bubble baths, sexual activity, the use of sanitary napkins and tampons, and the wearing of underpants to bed may be suspect in a patient who develops recurring lower-urinary-tract infections.

Perhaps urologists have not been as aware as they should be of the higher incidence of cystitis among women who wear underpants to bed. It certainly would seem that underpants would favor the growth and migration of bacteria among women who have a tendency to have bacteria colonize in the genital area.

Incidentally, I am sure your male readers will be pleased to receive this news. Sincerely yours,

—Joe Kaufman, M.D.

Dear Joe: Thanks on behalf of the women you've helped today— and the men, as well.

Dear Ann: I have a rather delicate problem, and I hope you can help me. My wife is 55 and has always enjoyed excellent health. She had surgery several weeks ago, and I believe she enjoys talking about her operation far more than she enjoyed her good health.

When we have guests or are out in company, she takes the floor and bores everyone to kingdom come with the details of her operation. She carries the gallstones in a bottle and has them handy in her purse. I've told her this is in poor taste, but she says it makes "interesting conversation." Am I wrong?

—The Mouse

Dear Mouse: There's nothing more boring (and in worse taste) than a person who grabs the floor for an "organ recital." Those who get knee-deep in details of their aches and pains don't realize that the audiences couldn't care less. If your wife's crowning achievement in life has been to produce a few gallstones, I send her my deepest sympathy.

Dear Ann Landers: I saw a news story on TV that said residents of a "nice" neighborhood had discovered an hours-old baby in their driveway, wrapped in a duffel bag. Next to the infant was a note saying: "I'm so sorry. I'm only 14 years old."

Ann, I want that young girl to know that I'm sorry, too. Her baby was another missed opportunity for my husband and me and others like us. Why don't these girls realize that it costs a birth mother nothing to place her child with an adoption agency? If she tells her minister or school counselor that she can't keep her child, she can be assured of help in finding it a loving home.

Three years ago, my husband and I decided to have a family. We assumed that we would have no trouble. We were wrong.

We tried for ten months and then went to a fertility specialist. We worked with her for another nine months without success and were then referred to a reproductive endocrinologist.

My husband has tested "normal" since the beginning. I have been poked, prodded, pushed and probed, have had injections and laser treatment, and was finally told I had endometriosis and polyceptic ovarian disease.

Now we've been informed that my insurance will no longer cover infertility treatment, diagnosis or drugs. The next step is a drug that will cost $8,000, with only a 45 percent chance of success.

To the 14-year-old girl who wrapped her child in the duffel bag: Someone will want and need your newborn. To the others who might do something like this: Please don't jeopardize the health of your baby by not placing it in the hands of people who will help you and know how to contact couples like us.

I'm sorry about the circumstances which led that girl to give up her child and equally sorry that I can't have that baby.

—Infertile in Indianapolis

Dear Indianapolis: Thanks for a letter that could change lives. For those who need help with infertility, send a long, self-addressed, stamped envelope to Resolve, 1310 Broadway, Somerville, Mass. 02144-1731.

A reader asked if I knew a sure cure for hiccups. I offered an old-fashioned remedy that has worked for me for many years. (Sip a glass of water very slowly, stopping after each hiccup, breathe deeply and hold your breath for a slow count of 10.)

I invited my readers to share their "cures" with me but warned that they must be 100 percent fail-safe. Within a few days, I was swamped with dozens of guaranteed gimmicks to stop hiccups. I cannot vouch for these suggestions because, happily, I do not get hiccups very often and have not tried them myself. But, for what they are worth, here they are:

From Jackson Heights, N.Y.: This method works when everything else has failed. We swear by it in our family. Using both hands, stick your fingers in your ears. Take a deep breath. Have someone hold your nose while he (or she) gives you a drink of water.

Miami: My dad hiccupped for eight hours straight. He had tried several suggestions from friends and relatives without success. Finally, someone said, "Drink a few gulps of carbonated soda." He did, and the hiccups stopped at once.

Ashtabula, Ohio: My grandmother learned this hiccup stopper from her grandmother, and I am teaching it to my grandchildren. It can be fun! Cut three holes the size of half-dollars in a paper bag. Put the bag over your head and breathe deeply 20 times. The hiccups will have disappeared.

Chicago: I am 60 years old now, but I remember a sure cure for hiccups that was given to the class by our fourth-grade teacher. She always kept a jar of sugar in her desk drawer. Whenever someone got the hiccups, Miss Swanson would put a teaspoon of sugar on that person's tongue and let it melt. By the time the sugar was gone, so were the hiccups.

Riverside, Calif.: When everything else has failed, this will work. If you can stand on your head, do it. If you can't stand on your head, put your head between your knees. Close your eyes as tight as you can, take a deep breath and recite "Mary Had a Little Lamb" or "Little Bo Peep."

Halifax, Nova Scotia: My great-aunt's hiccup stopper has worked for us like a charm these last 25 years. Make a fist, and bite the knuckle of your little finger. Take a deep breath, and hurry up and bite the next, then the next, then the next, and then the thumb. By the time you bite all your knuckles twice, you are cured.

Cincinnati: This cure is not only 100 percent effective but delicious. Take a tablespoon of peanut butter and keep it in your mouth, making no attempt to eat or swallow it. As the peanut butter disappears, so will the hiccups.

Tacoma, Wash.: No one knows why this works, but it has never failed me or anyone else who has tried it. Fill a glass with water, cover it with a clean handkerchief. Drink the water through the hankie. No sipping, no holding of the breath. The hiccups will disappear as if by magic.

Emporia, Kan.: This hiccup cure must be done in private because it looks so goofy. Open your eyes as wide as you can. Stick out your tongue—all the way. Reach for the ceiling—really reach. Try to sing "The Star-Spangled Banner." Of course, you can't do it with your tongue sticking out, but if you make the sounds, that is good enough. By the time you get to "the rockets' red glare," the hiccups will be gone.

So there you have it, dear readers. If one gimmick doesn't work, try another. Good luck!

Dear Ann Landers: Please help dispel a myth that people always become jaundiced when they get hepatitis. Most people are shocked to learn from a doctor or blood bank that they have or had hepatitis B or C because they don't recall being sick or turning yellow. Hepatitis can lead to cirrhosis and cancer of the liver. Forty percent of the people diagnosed with these viral infections have no history of exposure and don't know how they acquired them.

Hepatitis B and C can be spread by sharing razors, toothbrushes, nail files and needles used by an infected person. Hepatitis B is frequently transmitted through various sex acts and is 100 times easier to catch than AIDS.

You can't tell by looking at people that they are infected. Many infected people don't even know themselves. Unfortunately, the liver is a non-complaining organ and doesn't give any warning that it is in trouble until the damage is far advanced.

We need your help to stop the spread of these two treacherous diseases. Hepatitis tests are not included in a routine blood test and must be specifically requested. Safe and effective vaccines for hepatitis B can provide protection from unexpected exposure for 10 years or more. Newborns, infants and especially adolescents should be vaccinated according to recommendations by the Centers for Disease Control and Prevention.

Please tell your readers that they can get more information by sending a self-addressed, stamped envelope to the Hepatitis Foundation International, P.O. Box 222, Cedar Grove, NJ 07009 or calling (800) 891-0707. Thank you.

—Thelma King Thiel, chairman and CEO, Hepatitis
Foundation International

Dear Thelma King Thiel: Thanks for your informed input. What you have written is sure to save some lives.

Dear Ann Landers: I am in sympathy with the long-suffering physician's wife who wrote to say her husband had to give up going to church on Sunday because he was constantly pestered by people who wanted curb-stone opinions and free medical advice.

A dear friend of mine solved the problem in this manner: The town bore, who was notorious for chiseling everything and anything, collared this good-natured doctor at a cocktail party. She pulled him into a corner and began to describe in detail the shooting pains in her hip and leg.

The doctor looked her square in the eye and in his most professional way said, "Undress."

That did it. The woman has never gone near him since.

—Wandering Texan

Dear Texan: I'm glad it worked for him, but I wouldn't recommend this technique for everyone. Some women would be only too happy to take him at his word.

Dear Ann Landers: Almost 12 million people in the United States have diabetes, and half of them don't know it. All of these millions are at risk for heart disease, kidney disease, blindness and even death, if not treated.

Today (March 20, 1990) is the day the American Diabetes Association (ADA) has devoted to public awareness. During this Alert, ADA chapters and affiliates in more than 800 communities around the country will try to reach people who are unaware that they are at risk for or already have this illness.

Diabetes knows no boundaries or limits. It is an equal opportunity disease that affects people regardless of age, sex, race or financial status. Among blacks, Hispanics and American Indians, diabetes is occurring at an alarming rate.

Local chapters of the ADA sponsor diabetes awareness programs and blood-glucose screenings and distribute information including the American Diabetes Alert risk test.

The Alert risk test is designed to help people determine if they are at risk of getting diabetes. Those who suspect they have diabetes should see a doctor immediately. If detected early, it can be managed throughout a lifetime.

Here's the test. Add your score.

1. I have been experiencing one or more of the following symptoms on a regular basis:
   a. excessive thirst—YES 30
   b. frequent urination—YES 30
   c. extreme fatigue—YES 10
   d. unexplained weight loss—YES 30
   e. blurry vision from time to time—YES 10
2. I am over 40 years old.—YES 10
3. I am at least 20 percent over my ideal weight.—YES 20
4. I am a woman who has had more than one baby weighing over 9 pounds at birth.—YES 20
5. I am of American Indian descent.—YES 10
6. I am of Hispanic or black descent.—YES 10
7. I have a parent with diabetes.—YES 10
8. I have a brother or sister with diabetes.—YES 20

If you scored 30 to 50 points, you probably are at low risk for diabetes. But don't just forget about it. Especially if you're over 40, overweight or of black, Hispanic, or American Indian descent.

If you scored over 50 points, you may be at high risk for diabetes. You even may already have diabetes.

This test is meant to educate and make you aware of the serious risks of diabetes. Only a medical doctor can determine if you have diabetes. Want more information about diabetes? Contact your local American Diabetes Association.

Thanks, Ann, for helping us alert Americans to the risks and dangers of diabetes. It is vital that we get the word out, and you are the one who can do it.

—Sterling Tucker, chairman of the board,
and Sherman M. Holvey, M.D., president,
American Diabetes Association

Dear Mr. Tucker and Dr. Holvey: Glad to help. Now let's hope the readers will follow through.

In 1973, I suggested that my readers send for a booklet on hypertension. One reader wrote, "That column accomplished something I'd been trying to do for years—get my husband to have his blood pressure checked. Thanks to that column, he finally went to a doctor. His blood pressure was so high, he was on the verge of a stroke. I'm sure you could save more lives if you ran it again. [signed] Grateful Forever"

So, dear friends, here it is:

Dear Readers: This month marks the 18th year of my career as Ann Landers. We've gotten to know each other pretty well. You've blessed me, damned me, been delighted with some of my answers and disgusted with others. When you've cried on my shoulder, I've comforted some of you and told others to turn off the waterworks and stop wasting the natural resources.

On occasion, you've persuaded me that my advice was wrong and I've reversed myself. But I've been right more than I've been wrong—and with good reason. I tap the best brains in the country for my answers.

Since a great many physical complaints are closely related to emotional problems, I've prevailed upon some of the country's most distinguished physicians to be my consultants. With the help of these specialists, I've been able to alert 54 million daily readers to what's new in health care. Some of you have written to say I may have saved your lives. When I ran the column urging you to send for the American Cancer Society's free booklet on breast self-examination, nearly half a million women wrote to the national headquarters in New York or to their local Cancer Society offices. Thousands of women did find lumps. Most of them were benign, but some were malignant. Because they were discovered early, hundreds, maybe thousands, of women will live another 40 years and dance at the weddings of their grandchildren.

I am going to ask you again to send for a free booklet that could save your life. It deals with a disease that most of you will be shocked to learn strikes one out of every 10 Americans. I am talking about hypertension—commonly known as high blood pressure.

Over 23 million Americans have high blood pressure. Half of these sick people don't know it because usually there are no symptoms. The person who does have symptoms—headaches, dizziness, fatigue, low sex drive in the prime of life—is lucky because he just might go to a doctor before he suffers a stroke, gets a heart attack or is stricken with blindness or kidney failure.

High blood pressure strikes the rich and the poor, the tense and the relaxed, the old and the young. If you are black, you are twice as likely to have it, and more susceptible to the consequences than if you are Caucasian or Asian. If you are a woman on the Pill, you run a greater risk of developing high blood pressure than if you used some other method of birth control.

How can you protect yourself against this killer disease or deal with it if you do have it? The first step is to educate yourself, and that's why I am urging you to write for the free booklet. It not only will tell you what to do, but it will give you assurance that almost every case of high blood pressure can be controlled with medication.

What you read here today might save your life or the life of someone dear to you. So move already—and God bless.

—Ann Landers

For the latest information on high blood pressure, contact:

Citizens for Public Action on Blood Pressure and Cholesterol Inc.
P.O. Box 30374
Bethesda, MD 20824

Cancer is one of the most frightening words in the English language. Over the years, I have written several columns about this devastating illness. Here are a few that my readers considered the most helpful.

Dear Ann Landers: Thank you for saving my life. Last year, May 6 was a Sunday. Sundays are busy for me, but thank God I wasn't too busy to read your column. On that day, you published the warning signs of cancer.

One of the seven signs was hoarseness. I had quit smoking only a week before, and my throat still bothered me. I went to our family doctor on Tuesday. He immediately sent me to a throat specialist. Four days later, I had a malignant tumor removed from my larynx. After 35 radiation treatments, I was declared "cured" and in excellent health.

I am alive today because I read your column. No way would I have connected hoarseness with cancer if it hadn't been for you. Please publish the seven danger signals again. There must be others who need to be alerted.

May God bless you for the wonderful work you do. I send my sincere thanks and my love.

—B.F., Midway City, Calif.

Dear B.F.: It was generous of you to want to help others as you have been helped. Here again are the seven warning signals that could mean cancer:

1. A change in bowel habits.
2. A sore that does not heal.
3. Unusual bleeding or discharge.
4. A thickening or lump in the breast or elsewhere. (Men should check testicles every month.)
5. Persistent indigestion or difficulty in swallowing.
6. An obvious change in a wart or mole.
7. A nagging cough or hoarseness.

Dear Ann Landers: On the morning of my mammogram last August, I opened the paper to your column. The first letter was from a woman who had breast pain and was told not to worry about it because painful lumps were not cancerous. The writer found out later that her painful lump was indeed cancer.

I, too, was having breast pain, although I could feel no lump. My doctor had recommended that I get a mammogram when I turned 35. Because of the pain, I scheduled the mammogram a month before my 35th birthday.

My mammogram showed a suspicious area too small to be felt. It was biopsied, and I was diagnosed with breast cancer. Although the tumor was very small, the cancer had spread to two of my lymph nodes. I've since had a mastectomy and am now taking chemotherapy.

I have read many articles saying that mammograms have little or no benefit to women under 35. My personal experience has shown this to be untrue. If I had waited until I was older, it could have been a fatal mistake. I was fortunate to have had pain to clue me in that something was wrong. I wonder how many women have breast cancer at a young age and have no idea it is there. I feel certain that the mammogram saved my life.

Please tell your readers that mammograms can benefit them even if they are under 35. Breast pain or lumps should never be ignored no matter what the age. Sign me

—Been There in Alabama

Dear Alabama: Many thanks for a letter that is sure to save lives. Among my millions of readers, several will surely follow your advice and, by so doing, live to a ripe old age.

Dear Ann Landers: I am writing about your column on breast cancer in which you stated, "One out of eight women will get breast cancer."

I believe these statistics are often used to distort opinions when pulled out of context. While some women may need to be frightened into getting regular checkups and mammograms, there are a great many others who don't appreciate the anxiety caused by incomplete data.

Would you please print the following from the *Women's Health Letter*? It presents a more realistic picture. Thank you.

—Longtime Reader in Keller, Texas

Dear Longtime Reader: Here's the piece from the *Women's Health Letter* (published by Planned Parenthood), which certainly has merit. I hope, however, that it will not lull some women into a false sense of security and make them feel that it is not necessary to have mammograms regularly. This could be a fatal mistake.

Redefining the Scary Statistics

If you've been following the news about breast cancer, you probably have the phrase "one in eight" branded in your brain. This is what experts say is your risk of getting the disease. This figure does not, however, refer to your immediate risk. In other words, it doesn't mean that in a roomful of eight women, one of them will get breast cancer at any given moment in time, says Mary Daly, M.D., director of the family risk assessment program at Fox Chase Cancer Center in Cheltenham, Pa.

"The figure refers to a woman's general risk of getting breast cancer sometime in her lifetime if she lives to be 95," says Daly. A chart developed by the National Cancer Institute indicates women have different risks at different ages and the risk rises the older you get.

Here's a more reasonable thought to hold on to: If you are not at high risk, you are more likely *not* to develop breast disease. And please consider this: While the overall rate of breast cancer is on the upswing in women under 50, the death rate is going down in this age group.

If you're among the 20 percent of women in the high-risk group— you have a mother, sister or daughter with breast cancer, or there is ovarian, uterine or colon cancer in your family—consider seeing a risk counselor. The counselor will put together your risk profile based on your family history, interpret studies, suggest medical tests and screening and put into perspective less important risk factors such as early menstruation, late menopause, having no children or no children until after age 30, alcohol consumption and dietary fat.

You may learn, for example, that your risk is lower if your relative developed breast cancer after 50 and had it only in one breast. But even if there is a clear family history of breast cancer, you have a better than 70 percent chance that you'll beat the disease if you get treatment early, says Daly.

A 20-year-old woman has a one-in-2,500 chance of developing breast cancer. At age 30, it's one in 233. At age 40, it's one in 63. At age 50, it's one in 41. At age 60, it's one in 28. At age 70, it's one in 24. At age 80, it's one in 16. And at age 95, it's one in eight.

Dear Ann Landers: Women are told repeatedly to get checked for breast cancer because if it is caught early, there is a good chance of being cured. A less well-known fact is that men can get breast cancer, too. Although it occurs in only one in 2,500 men, it's something to think about.

Most doctors do not check for breast cancer when they examine their male patients. An alert young doctor asked me how long I had had the small lump near my right nipple. I told him it had been about four years and I had never paid any attention to it. He did a biopsy, and it turned out to be skin cancer. Minor surgery was performed, and the tissue was sent to a lab for analysis.

To the surgeon's surprise, the result showed that I had two types of cancer. The hospital cancer board said I needed a mastectomy because one of the cancers was "infiltrating lobular carcinoma," a rare form of cancer in males.

After three more opinions, I was told that surgery was the only way to be sure the cancer was eradicated. So I had a mastectomy, and thank God, they got the cancer in time.

I am writing this letter to let men know that they, too, can get breast cancer—and should be aware of lumps or any noticeable changes in that area. Please, Ann, print it.

—J.C., Tujunga, Calif.

Dear J.C.: I hope every male who reads this column will pay attention to what you have written. When you get your annual physical, guys, take this column along. You'd be surprised how much physicians learn from their patients.

Every so often a letter hits close to home:

Dear Ann Landers: Ten days ago, I had a breast removed, and I want to tell the world how lucky I am.

I was terrified when during a routine examination the doctor said, "You have a lump here. We'd better do a biopsy and find out what it is." Immediately, I thought of all the women I knew who had died of cancer. I was filled with panic and fear.

When the biopsy revealed a malignancy, I was sure my life was over. I checked into the hospital that same day for the removal of a breast.

The first thing I remember after coming out of the anesthetic was the doctor saying, "We caught it very early. You are going to be good as new."

Eight days later, I left the hospital wearing a prosthesis given to me by a group called Reach for Recovery—an organization for women who have had breasts removed. (I never knew the group existed.) These women meet regularly. Their purpose is to help new "members" lead a normal life. You can't imagine the lift I got when the club representative called on me. Her visit gave me renewed strength and hope.

I will return to work—exactly 19 days after the lump was discovered. I feel marvelous. At 48, I look forward to a long and happy life. I consider myself a lucky woman. Lucky because I refused to let anything interfere with my annual physical checkup and therefore caught the malignancy very early. Lucky, too, because my doctors were observant and talented. Lucky that I have a wonderful husband who has let me know the disfiguring operation in no way diminishes his love for me. God is good.

—S.L.D.

Dear S.L.D.: As I read your letter, I thought, "This could have been written by my sister-in-law." When I came to the signature, I discovered it was. Thank you, Sylvia.

Prostate cancer seems to be on the rise. There is disagreement among doctors as to the best method of treatment. I believe my readers should have all the facts in order to make the best decision. Here are both sides of the argument:

Dear Ann Landers: Please print something again about the importance of having a PSA (prostate-specific antigen) blood test to detect prostate cancer. One of my dearest friends recently died from this terrible disease, and a relative is now bravely fighting it.

Every year, 35,000 men in the United States die from prostate cancer. If it is detected early enough, it can be cured. Every male 40 and over should have an annual physical examination. After 50, men also should have a simple PSA blood test to detect prostate cancer that the doctor cannot feel during a digital exam. The PSA test can be done in a doctor's office. Please tell your readers, Ann. It could save lives.
—Your Faithful Reader in Fort Worth

Dear Fort Worth: We spoke with Dr. Jerome Richie, surgeon in chief in the division of urology at the Brigham and Women's Hospital in Boston. He said your information is correct. The PSA is the most accurate and predictive prostate cancer test. Dr. Richie cautioned, however, that the PSA can produce false negatives and false positives, and he recommended follow-up testing. In other words, don't rely on a single test.

Dr. Richie also emphasized that men with a family history of prostate cancer should have an annual digital examination and PSA starting at age 40 instead of 50.

Remember, early detection will increase the chances for survival. To my women readers, I say, if you love the man in your life, nag him until he makes an appointment.

Dear Ann Landers: As a physician and researcher at the National Cancer Institute, I was surprised to read your column recommending the PSA test to screen for prostate cancer. That column wandered into one of the biggest medical controversies of our time.

Numerous professional organizations and advisory groups, including the U.S. Preventive Services Task Force and the American Academy of Family Physicians, have recommended against using the PSA for screening men who have not shown any symptoms. It is important to understand that many prostate cancers do not need treatment. Unfortunately, although we are getting much more proficient at diagnosing prostate cancer, we are not very good at distinguishing the prostates that need treatment from those that are best left alone. Ten-year follow-ups of patients with prostate cancer who received *no* treatment showed very similar outcomes to those who were treated. Treatment of prostate cancer is associated with a significant incidence of both incontinence and impotence. A small number of men die from the treatment.

Clinical trials are currently taking place to determine the effectiveness of the PSA test. Hopefully, these trials will settle the ongoing debate. Until then, please, Ann, let your readers know that a conservative approach is best for some.

—Otis W. Brawley, M.D., National Cancer Institute,
Division of Cancer Prevention and Control,
Bethesda, Md.

Dear Dr. Brawley: There is a great deal of controversy among physicians on this subject, and since I printed another point of view, I felt obligated to print yours.

Readers can now discuss this with their own physicians and make up their minds. Thank you so much for writing.

One of the single most important columns I have ever written was in 1971 when I asked my readers to support the National Cancer Act:

Dear Readers: If you are looking for a laugh today, you'd better skip Ann Landers. If you want to be part of an effort that might save millions of lives—maybe your own—please stay with me.

Who among us has not lost a loved one to cancer? Is there a single person in my reading audience so incredibly lucky that his life has not been changed in some way by this dread disease? More Americans died of cancer in 1969 than were killed in the four years of World War II. Of the 200 million Americans alive today, 50 million will develop cancer. Approximately 34 million will die of it. Cancer claims the lives of more children under 15 years of age than any other illness.

How many of us have asked the question, "If this great country of ours can put a man on the moon, why can't we find a cure for cancer?" One reason is that we have never launched a national campaign, a united effort, against this killer disease. Another reason is money. The funds designated for medical research in America are grossly inadequate. Government grants for medical research have virtually dried up. The lion's share of the tax dollar is going to defense.

The following statistics shook me. They tell an interesting (and shameful) story about the priorities in this country. In 1969, for every man, woman and child in the United States, our government spent:

$125 on the war in Vietnam
$19 on the space program
$19 on foreign aid
89 cents on cancer research

Soon a bill will come before the U.S. Senate that calls for the establishment of a National Cancer Authority. This bill, S-34, will be sponsored by Senators Edward Kennedy and Jacob Javits. The proposed National Cancer Authority would be an agency similar to the National Aeronautics and Space Administration (NASA), which put men on the moon. This Conquest of Cancer bill demands that the highest priority be given to devise better methods of prevention, diagnosis and cure of cancer at the earliest possible date.

Today, you have the opportunity to be a part of the mightiest offensive against a single disease in the history of our country. If enough citizens let their senators know they want bill S-34 passed, it will pass.

I urge each and every person who reads this column to write to his two senators at once—or better yet, send telegrams. The senators for Illinois are Adlai Stevenson III and Charles Percy. Address your letter or telegram to: Senator ____, Senate Office Building, Washington, DC 20510.

Your message need consist of only three words. "Vote for S-34." And sign your name, please.

No one can do everything, but each of us can do something. It is entirely possible that this one small act could reshape the lives of millions. Get moving. My telegrams to Senators Percy and Stevenson went out last night.

Thanks—and God bless.

I was counting on my readers to come through, and you certainly did. Here is what happened:

Dear Readers: Thank you for your magnificent response to my suggestion that you wire or write your senators in support of S-34, the

Cancer Conquest bill. An unprecedented blizzard of letters has hit Washington. The already overworked secretaries who must answer the mail have posted signs saying, "Impeach Ann Landers!" They quietly concede, however, that the response is heartwarming. Judging from the telegrams and letters already received, it is estimated that that single column will generate a million pieces of mail.

I am immensely grateful that President Nixon has announced his support of some of the principles of S-34. The battle will not be won, however, until legislation passes both houses of Congress establishing a National Cancer Authority and making the conquest of the disease a specific national goal. It will not be enough merely to utilize the existing machinery for cancer research.

The existing machinery has been around since 1937, and it is a jungle of red tape. The proposed National Cancer Authority would be an agency similar to the National Aeronautics and Space Administration, which put the first man on the moon. If we stay with "the existing machinery," it is doubtful that we will reach our national goal.

Your wires and letters in support of S-34 are letting Washington know we want a sharp realignment of priorities. We are no longer going to remain silent while medical research picks up the crumbs from the table after the military has finished its gourmet meals. The answers to the scourge of cancer can and will be found. I say a massive, unified assault on this killer disease is long overdue.

The National Cancer Act was signed by President Nixon in 1971, with $100 million going directly to cancer research.

What Cancer Cannot Do

Cancer is so limited . . .
It cannot cripple love,
It cannot shatter hope,
It cannot corrode faith,
It cannot destroy peace,
It cannot kill friendship,
It cannot suppress memories,
It cannot silence courage,
It cannot invade the soul,
It cannot steal eternal life,
It cannot conquer the Spirit.

For more information, contact:

American Cancer Society
1599 Clifton Road NE
Atlanta, GA 30329
(800) ACS-2345

Reach to Recovery
American Cancer Society
1599 Clifton Road NE
Atlanta, GA 30329
(An organization for women who have had mastectomies)

National Cancer Institute
(800) 4-CANCER

What appears below is from a 1992 Department of Health and Human Services report. No frills. No baloney. Just the facts.

About 1 million Americans are now infected with the HIV virus that causes AIDS. In the last ten years, more than 200,000 Americans have been diagnosed with AIDS. Approximately 64 percent of them have died. Worldwide, an estimated 8 million to 10 million people are now HIV-infected.

The average time between HIV infection and the development of full-blown AIDS is ten years. Although engaging in male-to-male sexual contact and intravenous drug use remain the highest risk factors, heterosexual transmission is showing the greatest rate of increase.

In the United States, AIDS is now the second-leading killer of men 25 to 44 years old and the fifth-leading killer of women in the same age group. It has hit some minority populations the hardest. More than one fourth of those diagnosed with AIDS are black, and 16 percent are Hispanic.

As of December 1991, there were 40,362 reported cases of AIDS among men and women 20 to 29 years old. There were 789 cases of AIDS reported among people 13 to 19 years old. The most disturbing fact in this report is that the incidence of HIV infection is growing rapidly among teenagers.

In spite of efforts by the government, the medical community, and civic-minded groups, high-risk behavior among U.S. teens is widespread. More than 40 percent of high school students polled say they have had multiple sex partners. Although condom use has increased significantly, only one third of the sexually active teenagers say they use them.

It should be noted that only latex condoms can provide protection against sexually transmitted disease. And condoms are not 100 percent effective: They can leak, break, or come off.

The two most common forms of transmission are sexual intercourse—anal, vaginal and oral—and the sharing of needles. The virus also can be acquired through blood transfusion. Such occurrences have been rare since 1985, when careful screening of blood began.

HIV is not transmitted through casual contact—by kissing, by touching door handles, phones, drinking fountains or toilet seats, or by getting an insect bite.

At this moment, there is no vaccine to protect a person against the HIV virus and no cure for AIDS. A massive effort, however, is in progress in research laboratories all over the world.

The drugs AZT and ddI have proven successful in delaying the onset of AIDS, improving the quality of life dramatically for some AIDS sufferers and extending their life expectancy.

What can you do to protect yourself against AIDS? Do not share needles. Have a monogamous relationship with a person who is healthy and totally trustworthy.

Dear Ann Landers: Last night, I had sex with 4,097 people. Impossible, you say? You're wrong.

I'm a divorced woman who has had a faithful lover for quite some time. Last night, I had too much to drink, and like a crazy fool, I had sex with a man I had seen several times at our tennis club. He admitted having sex with eight "perfectly respectable" female partners over the last year.

I worked a chart backward the same as in our tennis seeding. I took those eight women and assumed that they also had slept with eight men each and each of those eight men had had sex with eight women, etc.

By using simple arithmetic progression, after only three series, I realized that I had been exposed somewhere along the line to 4,096 persons, plus one.

How can I assume that there was no one in that family tree who was not an AIDS carrier, if only through a blood transfusion? I understand that there are 10,000 carriers in our state alone. How do I know I haven't been "seeded," and I don't mean tennis?

From now on, I am sticking to my lover and hope to make him my husband for life. I pray he never will have to pay a price for my having exposed myself to 4,097 people. Sign me

—Scared

Dear Scared: You have focused on the aspect of AIDS that makes it such a terrifying disease. Add to the nightmare this horror: A person can have the AIDS virus without knowing it and infect a partner.

More and more, it appears that the only way to ensure staying healthy is abstinence or a monogamous relationship with someone who is perfectly safe.

Dear Ann Landers: I am a successful executive woman. A year ago, I applied for life insurance. I was required to take an HIV antibody test (a so-called AIDS test).

To my complete shock, it came back positive.

I am not a prostitute. I am not promiscuous. I am not and have never been an intravenous drug user. I am not a member of a minority group. I am not indigent nor am I homeless. I have not slept with a bisexual.

I am a suburban, non-smoking, non-drug-using, successful American woman. I don't fit any of the stereotypes that ignorant people have designated for those infected with the HIV virus. I got HIV from a man I am in love with and have been seeing for five years. He is not homosexual or bisexual. He has never used intravenous drugs. He had no idea he was carrying the virus. He believes he may have been infected about six years ago by a woman with whom he had a brief, meaningless relationship.

We are both in excellent physical condition, and we look terrific. In my ignorance, I thought people who carried the AIDS virus looked emaciated. I now know it can take years for HIV infection to progress to AIDS. Researchers are learning more about this disease every day. There are many reasons to have hope.

Luckily, after seeing several doctors who knew nothing about AIDS, I found a brilliant, informed physician. He has given me hope and the will to live. I am also seeing a caring, supportive psychologist who has helped me tremendously. Until I found these educated professionals, I contemplated suicide daily for several months.

AIDS has become a party joke. People who would never kid about cancer, cerebral palsy, mental illness or tuberculosis think AIDS is fair game. They don't realize I could be their sister, friend, co-worker, niece, daughter or cousin. They treat AIDS differently because it is sexually transmitted.

Please, Ann, print this letter to sensitize people to the hurt they cause when they make thoughtless comments. Many of us look like everybody else.

—Looking for Two Miracles in New England

Dear Ann Landers: I am in desperate need of the truth. Recently, my boyfriend died of AIDS. I took the test, and my results were negative. I know I have to take the test again in six months.

My question to you is this: If I test negative for one year, is there any chance of testing positive 5 or 10 years down the road?

The counselor advised me that the test was accurate and if I tested negative after a year, it would mean that I didn't catch the virus from my boyfriend. However, I have been told by others that the virus can hide in your system and you will not test positive for years. That means I must take the test every year for the rest of my life.

Please consult your experts so I can know the truth and stop torturing myself about this.

—Confused in N.Y.

Dear Confused: I checked with Dr. Jerome Groopman, Recanati Professor of Immunology at Harvard Medical School and one of the country's most respected authorities on AIDS. Here is his response:

The current tests for HIV are highly accurate. The false negative rate is less than 1 in 1,000.

More than 90 percent of people who are infected with the AIDS virus will test positive three months after exposure, 99.9 percent will test positive at six months and at 12 months, it's 100 percent. There is no need for yearly testing if an individual tests negative at 12 months.

If the test results are unclear, seek consultation with a specialist who can perform other tests for antibodies or the virus itself.

Here's more information on how you can protect yourself:

Dear Ann Landers: Everybody is terrified of AIDS. You have said repeatedly that the only safe sex is *no* sex. You have also said that this is not realistic for some and have suggested condoms.

How reliable are condoms? I'm a sexually active 33-year-old male. I've had condoms break, leak and come off. How can you recommend them?

—On Tenterhooks in Tennessee

Dear Tennessee: The only 100 percent reliable way to avoid AIDS through sexual contact is to stop having sex. Most people will not give up sex, so they should protect themselves as best they can.

I turned your letter over to Dr. David Satcher, director of the Centers for Disease Control and Prevention in Atlanta. Here are his comments:

"Scientific evidence demonstrates that latex condoms, when used consistently and correctly, are highly effective in stopping HIV, the virus that causes AIDS. The Food and Drug Administration requires manufacturers to test every batch of condoms made. The FDA also regularly tests condoms to be sure they meet stringent quality standards. Samples representing millions of condoms have shown that the average batch tests better than 99.7 percent defect-free.

"The FDA and other researchers have shown that latex condoms are an effective barrier to viruses, including HIV and the much smaller virus, hepatitis B. In one set of laboratory tests, the FDA subjected condoms to unrealistically strenuous conditions, such as virus concentrations 100 million times higher than found in infected people. Even under these conditions, researchers concluded that condoms would reduce exposure to the virus by 10,000 times.

"Two recent studies have been conducted with a total of 550 couples, in which one person was infected with HIV, and the other was not. Among those who did not use condoms or did not use them every time, 11 percent became infected. But among the 294 couples reporting consistent condom use, 1 percent became infected—none out of 123 couples in one study and three of 171 couples in the other.

"Those three infections could have been caused by user errors. When condoms slip, break or leak, user error—not product failure—is usually the problem. Also Vaseline or mineral-oil based lubricants will erode latex.

"Refraining from sexual activity is the only sure way to prevent HIV infection. However, latex condoms are highly effective when used consistently and correctly."

Not everyone who tests positive for AIDS actually has the disease. False positives can and do occur—and for a variety of reasons:

Dear Ann Landers: In March 1991, I went to an anonymous testing center for a routine HIV test. In two weeks, the results came back positive.

I was devastated. I was 20 years old and doomed. I became severely depressed and contemplated a variety of ways to commit suicide. After encouragement from family and friends, I decided to fight back.

My doctors in Dallas told me that California had the best care for HIV patients, so I packed everything and headed west. It took three months to find a doctor I trusted. Before this physician would treat me, he insisted on running more tests. Imagine my shock when the new results came back negative. The doctor tested me again, and the results were clearly negative.

I'm grateful to be healthy, but the 18 months I thought I had the virus changed my life forever. I'm begging doctors to be more careful. I also want to tell your readers to be sure and get a second opinion. I will continue to be tested for HIV every six months, but I am no longer terrified.

—David in Dallas

Dear Dallas: Yours is truly a nightmare with a happy ending, but don't blame the doctor.

The moral of your story is this: *Get a second opinion. And a third.* Never trust a single test. Ever.

Dear Ann Landers: I took my annual physical exam and was horrified when the results came back and I tested positive for HIV. I am a 24-year-old woman who has never had sex with anyone.

I returned to my doctor in a state of panic and was retested. The results were negative. It seems the flu shot I had gotten two weeks earlier produced the false positive. Please tell your readers about this again. It scared the living daylights out of me.

—Davenport, Iowa

Dear Davenport: According to the Centers for Disease Control and Prevention in Atlanta, it is indeed possible for a flu shot to create falsely reactive test results with the Elisa test.

It is always best to get retested. The Western Blot test is more specific and will rule out the false positives.

Dear Ann Landers: You printed a letter from a woman who found out that a recent flu shot had caused her to test positive for HIV. There are many reasons a person may receive a false positive when testing for AIDS. A recent vaccination is just one of them. Rheumatoid arthritis and pregnancy (if you've been pregnant before) may also result in a false positive.

Thank you for educating the public on health matters that could mean the difference between life and death.

—Nurses PRN, Flu Center, Denver

For more information, contact:

Centers for Disease Control and Prevention National AIDS Hotline
(800) 342-AIDS
Spanish-speaking: (800) 344-7432
TTY for the hearing impaired: (800) 243-7889

The CDC has developed a brochure (in English and Spanish) on how to use a condom properly. Free copies are available by calling (800) 342-AIDS.

6

Mental Health:
To the Edge and Beyond

We now know that mental illness can be treated with a combination of medication and therapy. Today, there is no longer any need to suffer with untreated mental illness.

I have done what I could to educate my readers on this subject as you will see from the letters that follow:

Dear Ann Landers: I am a patient in a mental hospital. I know I am ill, just as a person who has pneumonia is ill. I know, too, that my illness is temporary and that I am getting better. One day, I will be a useful citizen and perhaps even contribute something to society.

I am writing this letter in the hope that people who have friends and relatives in mental institutions will have a better understanding of the mental patient and his needs. More than anything, we need to know we are not forgotten.

On the Fourth of July, we were served a lovely chicken dinner, and there was a movie afterward. I would gladly have exchanged the dinner and the movie for just one visitor. I have a daughter, grandchildren, brothers, sisters and cousins, but no one dropped by to say hello.

I'm not the only person who waits week after week for a visitor. It's as if our people are ashamed of us and don't wish to remember we are here. We patients discuss this often—never in a self-pitying way, only with a feeling of sadness because others do not understand.

The staff here is wonderful. What grand people they are—but we are so many, and they are so few. They do what they can, but nothing builds morale like a visit with family or friends. These links with the outside, more than anything else, speed a patient's recovery.

Please print this letter. It is too long, I know, but perhaps you can trim it so it will fit in the paper. You could help so many by passing this word. God bless you.

—A Patient Patient

Dear Patient: Thank you for your beautiful letter. Yes, it's about twice as long as most letters that appear in this column, but I couldn't bear to cut a word of it. So here it is—as you wrote it.

Depression strikes more than 17 million Americans each year. Unfortunately, fewer than half the people with depression actually seek treatment. Depression can result in serious disturbances in every aspect of life. Unlike sadness or "the blues," depression does not respond to good news and can last for months or years if left untreated.

Dear Ann Landers: How does a person know if he is depressed? I realize it isn't possible to be happy all the time, yet I fear my bout with "the blahs" or "the blues" is more intense than what the average person experiences.

Please describe the symptoms of depression so I can have a better understanding of what goes on with me. I feel isolated and inadequate.

—OK Today but Worried About Tomorrow

Dear Worried: Millions of Americans suffer from severe depression, according to the National Institute of Mental Health, so if you are severely depressed, you are not alone.

Dr. John Kane, who heads the depression clinic at the Long Island Jewish Hillside Medical Center, listed the common warning signals of severe depression in an interview with Olive Evans of *The New York Times*.

Here they are:

1. Feelings of sadness and hopelessness ("I will never be better").
2. Loss of the "pleasure capacity," the ability to enjoy anything.
3. Loss of interest in sex.
4. Loss of appetite (or overeating).

5. Insomnia (or sleeping too much).
6. Anxious or restless behavior (or apathy).
7. Difficulty in concentration, remembering things and making decisions.
8. Becoming upset by small things.
9. Feelings of worthlessness ("I'm no good").
10. Withdrawal from friends and relatives.

If you see yourself in six or more of the above, you are probably severely depressed. I urge you to take this column to your physician and talk to him about your depression. Ask him to recommend a counselor.

If you cannot afford a private therapist, check the phone book under "mental health clinics." There are many excellent government-funded clinics that cost very little. Moreover, you've already paid for them through your taxes, so *go*.

Dear Ann Landers: Nine years ago in April, I joined a group called Recovery Inc. I owe them my mental health. Today, I live, not merely exist.

Before I joined Recovery, life was a nightmare. I paced the house day and night when I wasn't in a hospital. I slept poorly. My children were very young at the time. I'm glad they don't remember how their mother was then.

I was afraid to be in the house alone. I was nauseated and couldn't eat—sure I would have a coronary because my heart pounded so much. I locked up all the knives—afraid I might kill myself. I was depressed, cried a lot for no reason and was afraid to go out of the house.

When I tried to explain how I felt, I was met by blank stares. No one understood. They just said, "Snap out of it!" Or, "Get a hold of yourself!"

A friend told me about Recovery. She had read about this group in your column. I went, and a miracle happened. Everyone there knew how I felt. They told me to keep coming to meetings and I would get well. They were right. I have been a group leader for seven years. It really works!

—Grateful in Canada

Dear Canada: Yours is about the 10th Recovery Inc. testimonial I have printed. The founders of this terrific organization told me several years ago that I "put them on the map." I couldn't receive a finer compliment.

All you folks out there who sneer when I say, "There is help for you. Find it! And get counseling!" please give this organization a try.

Look in your phone book. There are more than 1,000 chapters, and they have succeeded when expensive private psychiatric hospitals have failed. I can't say enough for this beautiful organization.

If you can't find it in the phone book, write to the national headquarters: 802 N. Dearborn St., Chicago, IL 60610, or call (312) 337–5661.

Dear Ann Landers: Six years ago, I married a divorced man who is retired from the service. Our children are grown and gone, so there are just the two of us.

During the six years we have been married, he has never once gone into the bathroom, if only to wash his hands, without locking the damn door. He has yet to dress or undress in front of me.

He moved into my home when we married, and his trailer is still parked in the yard. (More craziness.) Lots of times, he'll go in there, lock all the doors and take a bath.

I have questioned him about his peculiar behavior. He says he has done this since his kids were small. (His "baby" is now 18 years old.)

There is no one here but us. I think he is crazy as a loon. What's more, it makes him fighting mad when I mention it. Ann, please tell me what you think is wrong with this character.

—Married to a Nut

Dear Married: The "character" has some deep-seated hang-ups about his body and everything related to it.

It would take years of intense therapy to get this clinker out of his thinker. You are not going to change him, so resign yourself to his kookiness and quit knocking your head against the wall.

Dear Ann Landers: I was amazed by the letter from the girl who cut herself with jagged pieces of glass because she needed to feel pain and watch herself bleed. I thought I was the only one in the world who did that.

It started for me when I was 15. I was having a good time at a beach party when suddenly I wanted to hurt myself and bleed. I went off alone with a can of beer, slashed my wrist with the metal edge and enjoyed the pain and the blood.

When the bleeding got heavy, I got scared and asked my friends for help. They thought I had tried to kill myself, but that wasn't true. I was taken to the emergency room of a hospital, had some stitches and didn't try it again for about three months.

The urge hit me again when I was studying for an exam, couldn't understand an equation and got mad at myself. I took a razor blade and carved some designs on my arm. There was a lot of blood, but I put adhesive tape on the wounds and the bleeding stopped.

I want to be a surgeon—sort of combine business with pleasure. Do you think I am crazy? Some of my friends do. Please reply.

—Medford, Ore.

Dear Medford: Your compulsion to punish yourself physically and the pleasure you receive from seeing blood indicate an urgent need for psychiatric help. Tell the school counselor, your parents or the family doctor at once. You are in a bad way, dear.

Dear Ann Landers: I am a 30-year-old mother of two young children. At first, I fell into this frightening habit to get rid of my anger. Now I do it for excitement. My thing is starting fires in trash cans in alleys. No one ever has been hurt, nor has any property been damaged—so it does seem like a harmless way to have a little fun. But in my quieter moments, I worry that maybe I will go further and set fire to a building and cause some serious damage.

When crowds gather to watch the flames extinguished (someone always calls the fire department), I feel very important. Then, there are times when I want to run to the nearest policeman and say, "I did it!" but I'm afraid of what might happen if I confess.

I know I'm a person who needs to feel important or I wouldn't be doing such things. I also get a feeling of power when I see what I can stir up. I admitted all this to my therapist several months ago, and he told me to stop—but I can't control myself.

I am writing to you because you are a level-headed person, and I think you can set me straight. Please try.

—A Harmless Firebug in a Western City

Dear Friend: My first suggestion is get another therapist. Your present one sounds weak and ineffective, to say the least.

You have a mental illness called pyromania, which most authorities believe is related to a sexual problem. People who are emotionally disturbed, as you are, can be extremely dangerous not only to society but to themselves and their families.

I urge you to call the Mental Health Association in your area or the American Psychiatric Association in Washington at once. Describe your problem, and ask that they recommend a therapist who specializes in this illness.

Dear Ann Landers: I am 20 years old and a sophomore in college. Compared to many of my peers, I've had it awfully good.

In high school, I was well-liked and involved in everything: cheerleading, drill team, student council and sports. I was elected to the homecoming court. My home life is fine. I have two successful, loving parents.

Outside of school, I was involved with a church youth group, taught Sunday school and have done some professional dancing.

I entered my freshman year majoring in biology-premedicine and later that year pledged a sorority. I've never been short of fun or friends, and am the most cheerful, friendly, outgoing person you could know. Because of my bright smile and love of making people laugh, you'd never guess that I want to die.

I don't know when I first became obsessed with dying, but every night, I lie awake in my bed and beg God for cancer or some other terminal illness.

The way I see it, I've had the best of everything and I want to die young with all the chips in my corner. Please understand that I'm not suicidal. I would never kill myself. I just wish something would kill me. I've mentioned this to a couple of close friends and they can't understand why I feel this way.

What's wrong with me, Ann? Why is it that I want more than anything to die, when I have had it all? I know very well that if I put my name and city on this letter, my phone will be ringing off the hook, so I'll just sign myself

—Death Wish Sophomore Who Needs Some Answers

Dear Sophomore: Because you already have stated that you know something is wrong with you, I won't belabor the point. You need to find out exactly what is causing you to harbor such bizarre thoughts.

Every campus has counselors. I urge you to discuss your secret longing with a professional. I don't want to get dramatic, but a wish can suddenly turn out to be the father of the deed.

Dear Ann Landers: A letter in your column changed my life.

When I was 13, I began to pull out my hair. I always thought it was a bad habit I could overcome if I just tried hard enough. Try as I might, I never could stop it. I had been criticized, harassed, embarrassed and ashamed about this habit for over 25 years. (I'm 42 now.)

About two years ago, I read in your column about trichotillomania—compulsive hair pulling—an obsessive-compulsive disorder. It was reassuring to learn I was not alone. You gave the address of the Trichotillomania Foundation, and I wrote for the literature. I learned that approximately 25 million Americans suffer from this disorder to some degree. There is no known cure, but drugs prescribed by a physician can be very helpful.

I'm happy to report the drug worked for me and I no longer pull out my hair. Apparently, the hair pulling was caused by a chemical imbalance, and the medication corrected the problem. I am so thankful, I want to pass along the message. Hopefully, it will work for others.

—Golden West

Dear Golden West: Your letter made my day. And you can bet it will be a tremendous help to countless others who have the hair-pulling problem and don't know what to do about it.

Anyone who needs help can get it by writing for literature and guidance. Here's the address: Trichotillomania Learning Center, Suite 2, 1215 Mission St., Santa Cruz, CA 95060 or call toll-free: (800) 227–1033.

Dear Ann Landers: Last year, you printed my letter about panic attacks. I am thrilled to tell you that I have improved enormously.

I became educated about the illness and decided to talk about it with the people who were closest to me. To my amazement, I discovered that several family members and friends also suffered from panic attacks.

I joined a support group and attribute much of my success to talking with people who have conquered the problem. One of my principal comforts is re-reading the Golden Rules for Coping with Panic. Of all the material I have read, this is the most reassuring and helpful. It is not an exaggeration to say these rules saved my life. Here they are.

Golden Rules for Coping with Panic

1. Remember that although your feelings and symptoms are frightening, they are neither dangerous nor harmful.

2. Understand that what you are experiencing is merely an exaggeration of your normal reactions to stress.

3. Do not fight your feelings or try to wish them away. The more willing you are to face them, the less intense they will become.

4. Don't add to your panic by thinking about what "might happen." If you find yourself asking, "What if?" tell yourself, "So what!"

5. Stay in the present. Be aware of what is happening to you rather than concern yourself with how much worse it might get.

6. Label your fear level from zero to 10 and watch it go up and down. Notice that it doesn't stay at a very high level for more than a few seconds.

7. When you find yourself thinking about fear, change your "what if?" thinking. Focus on and perform some simple, manageable task.

8. Notice that when you stop thinking frightening thoughts your anxiety fades.

9. When fear comes, accept it, don't fight it. Wait, and give it time to pass. Don't try to escape from it.

10. Be proud of the progress you've made. Think about how good you will feel when the anxiety has passed and you are in total control and at peace.

—Arkansas

Dear Ark.: I'm sure you've helped many people today. Thank you.

Dear Ann Landers: I believe that I am a typical high school student. I get good grades, teachers like me, I'm happy most of the time, and I have never thought about killing myself. We had an assembly today on suicide prevention, and I couldn't believe it, Ann. One out of every four teenagers will attempt suicide before he or she is 16. Every minute of every hour, a teenager attempts suicide. Every day, 33 kids will succeed. Why? Nobody knows for sure.

The speaker at the assembly gave us the following 12 warning signs. I know that if you print them, Ann, a life somewhere will be saved. Maybe some kid from my school who had been thinking of suicide tonight will show up Monday morning because somebody recognized these signs and got him or her to get help.

—Typical Teen

Dear T.T.: Thank you for sending on a list that is sure to make a difference in someone's life. Here it is:

1. Sudden change in behavior.
2. Dramatic change in appetite.
3. Sleeping difficulties. Some people want to sleep all the time when they're depressed; others can't sleep at all.
4. Poor performance in school.
5. Trouble concentrating, agitation, inability to sit still.
6. Unexplained loss of energy or excessive fatigue.
7. Loss of interest in friends.
8. Increased drug/alcohol use.
9. Constant feeling of worthlessness or self-hatred.
10. Excessive risk-taking.
11. Preoccupation with death, dying or suicide.
12. Giving away personal or prized possessions.

Dear Ann Landers: Last week, my friend's 15-year-old son killed himself. He was a popular student, was involved in sports, and was a patrol leader in the Boy Scouts. Everyone described him as an outgoing, happy young man. His parents, sisters and friends have no idea why he committed suicide. I can find no words to comfort them.

At the service, the boy's mother pleaded with all the young people in attendance to please talk to someone, anyone, if something was bothering them. Ann, please ask your readers to set aside some quiet time, *tonight*, and sit down with their children and ask what's happening in their lives. If the children are troubled about something and don't want to discuss it, they should be encouraged to speak with a teacher, minister, rabbi, priest, relative, friend—someone—so they can get help resolving whatever conflicts they are experiencing. And parents shouldn't just ask their kids one time. Even if they act as if nothing is wrong, you can never be sure.

If this letter can spare just one family the pain and heartache my friends are going through, maybe it will give them some comfort to know they helped save a life.

—E.L. in L.A.

Dear E.L.: Please be assured that your letter will open the doors of communication for countless parents who have felt shut out or distanced from their children. What a great favor you have done them. Thank you.

Dear Ann Landers: I am writing to ask you to print a letter that could make a huge difference in the lives of a great many people. It is addressed to anyone who is considering suicide.

If you decide to end your life, that is your business. But please choose a method that does not involve anyone else. Those who do otherwise are grossly unfair. Let me explain.

My father was driving home in his 18-wheeler when an 85-year-old man deliberately ran directly in front of his truck. It took four hours to scrape that man off the truck and the pavement. The authorities had to return to the scene to find his foot, which was 70 feet from the accident. The officer in charge said he had never seen such a gruesome sight in his 18 years of service.

Over a period of 35 years, my father had driven 1 million miles without a fatality. He will never recover from that horrible experience.

It is unfair to make someone else pay such a price for an act that should be solitary. This letter is a plea for consideration in your final hour.

—Theresa, Roland Heights, Calif.

Dear Theresa: Thanks for a letter that speaks to a problem few people think about. In the same bag of mail was another letter with a similar message:

Dear Ann Landers: This is a plea to those who are thinking about ending it all. If you want to leave this world, no one has the right to force you to stay, but please leave alone.

My daughter, a beautiful, bright young woman of 24, college-educated, engaged to be married, with a brilliant future ahead of her, was killed on a Saturday afternoon when a drug addict, high on cocaine, jumped to his death out of a 22-story window of a downtown office building. The man's body landed directly on my daughter, killing her instantly.

Even though that drug addict didn't mean to kill my daughter, she is just as dead as if he had taken a gun and put a bullet in her heart.

—N.Y. Mother

Dear Mother: My condolences on your terrible loss. Let's hope your letter prevents similar tragedies.

Dear Ann Landers: Ten years ago, everything hit me from all sides. I became depressed and suicidal and started to plan my own death. I attempted to kill myself in March, but a motel attendant saved me.

I came out of the hospital, still determined to end my life. I began saving prescription pills. When I went to church in search of answers, I would look around to see if there was a way I might hang myself from the ceiling.

In June, I headed for a small town where I thought I would not be found and took 300 prescription pills with me.

A friend traced me to the motel. Three other friends flew up and talked me into going to the hospital. I walked into that hospital with the 300 prescription pills, determined to kill myself there.

While seated in the lobby with other patients, I picked up a *Reader's Digest* and opened it without looking at the index. Here is the unbelievable part, Ann. The article I saw was titled "Before You Kill Yourself." It gave several reasons to choose life over suicide.

I called a nurse and handed her all the pills I had hidden in my boot toes and luggage. You should have seen her face.

God, friends and that article in *Reader's Digest* saved me. I know you can't print all of this, but please shorten my letter and find space for it in your column. My reason for writing is to help others. P.S. I am doing just fine now.

—Been There and Back

Dear Been There: What a testimonial! I am pleased to give it the visibility it deserves. Bravo.

Dear Ann Landers: You printed a letter from a reader who said he was desperately unhappy and wanted to kill himself.

He had already started to save up pills and was just about to do the deed when he picked up a copy of *Reader's Digest*. His eyes fell on an article that changed his mind.

Lately, I have been having suicidal thoughts and think maybe that article might be helpful. Will you please print it?

—Zydo

Dear Zydo: I've had more than 500 requests for that article, which originally appeared in June 1985. I know it has saved lives. Here it is:

Before You Kill Yourself

Renée T. Lucero, R.N.

You've decided to do it. Life is impossible. Suicide is your way out.

Fine—but before you kill yourself, there are some things you should know. I am a psychiatric nurse, and I see the results of suicide—when it works and, more often, when it doesn't. Consider, before you act, these facts:

Suicide is usually not successful. You think you know a way to guarantee it? Ask the 25-year-old who tried to electrocute himself. He lived. But both his arms are gone.

What about jumping? Ask John. He used to be intelligent, with an engaging sense of humor. That was before he leaped from a building. Now he's brain-damaged and will always need care. He staggers and has seizures. He lives in a fog. But worst of all, he *knows* he used to be normal.

What about pills? Ask the 12-year-old with extensive liver damage from an overdose. Have you ever seen anyone die of liver damage? You turn yellow. It's a hard way to go.

What about a gun? Ask the 24-year-old who shot himself in the head. Now he drags one leg, has a useless arm and has no vision or hearing on one side. He lived through his "foolproof" suicide. You might, too.

Who will clean your blood off the carpet or scrape your brains from the ceiling? Commercial cleaning crews may refuse that job—but *someone* has to do it. Who will have to cut you down from where you hanged yourself or identify your bloated body after you've drowned? Your mother? Your wife? Your son?

The carefully worded "loving" suicide note is no help. Those who loved you will *never* completely recover. They'll feel regret and an unending pain.

Suicide is contagious. Look around at your family. Look closely at the 4-year-old playing with his cars on the rug. Kill yourself tonight, and he may do it 10 years from now.

You do have other choices. There are people who can help you through this crisis. Call a hot line. Call a friend. Call your minister or priest. Call a doctor or hospital. Call the police.

They will tell you that there's hope. Maybe you'll find it in the mail tomorrow. Or in a phone call this weekend. But what you're seeking could be just a minute, a day or a month away.

You say you don't want to be stopped? Still want to do it? Well, then, I may see you in the psychiatric ward later. And we'll work with whatever you have left.

Dear Ann Landers: You asked to hear from readers who attempted suicide and are now happy they failed. Here is my story:

I was 18 and had a 16-month-old son and a 5-month-old daughter. My 20-year-old husband had just left me for another woman. I felt like a failure at everything and decided to end it all. I took an enormous number of pills, drank a bottle of vodka and prepared to die.

Well, I didn't die. My husband found me, took me to the hospital and had my stomach pumped, and I was home two days later. The story is too long to tell, but after my husband divorced me, I met a marvelous man, and my life is beautiful. My son is now 17, excels in track and is handsome and lovable. My daughter is 16, a talented musician and a real beauty.

When I think that I might never have seen these children grow up, I can't bear it. I'd like to tell your readers something *you* can't because you have never been there. I have. Please, please, don't give up on life. Ann is right when she says, "Everything in life can be fixed—except death."

—Nameless in Pa.

Dear Pa.: Thanks for your uplifting words. Read on for more:

From Los Angeles: Here's my "near-suicide" story: When I was 17, I was madly in love. "Jimmy" and I went steady for three years and then broke up. When I saw him at the prom with a girl I had always hated, I decided to kill myself that night.

My date brought me home at 3 A.M. I got the keys to my dad's car, drove myself to a partially frozen river and was prepared to jump in, go through the ice and drown.

Suddenly, I remembered the next day was Mom's birthday. I thought, "What a birthday gift I would be giving her. . . ." I turned the car around and drove home. I know now I wasn't in my right mind. I was in a deep depression. I got counseling at school and continued with a therapist for three years.

Today, I have a Ph.D. in psychology, a fine husband and three beautiful children. I shudder when I think of how close I came to missing all this joy. Any coward can commit suicide. It takes guts to face life.

New York: In 1929, my father, who was a big man on Wall Street, lost everything in the crash. He tried to hang himself. My mother found him in the basement struggling with the rope. She yelled, "You can't even do that right, you idiot." They both laughed and were happily married for 30 years after that.

Chicago: Here is my near-suicide story. I hope you will print it. When I was a junior in college, my 20-year-old girlfriend died in a car crash. I was driving. I felt so guilty, I couldn't eat or sleep or study. After three months, I was a total wreck and decided the only way to escape the pain was to kill myself.

I was about to jump from the fourth-story window of a campus building when two senior guys grabbed me by the heels. I was sent home and instructed to get psychiatric counseling. Intensive therapy put Humpty Dumpty back together again. That was 15 years ago. Today, I am a clinical psychologist, happily married and the father of two great children.

Tell your readers the combination of good therapy and the right medication can do wonders. Suicide has never solved a problem, but it has made life a living hell for those left behind.

For more information, contact:

Anxiety Disorders Association of America
6000 Executive Blvd., Suite 513
Rockville, MD 20852
(301) 231-9350

National Institute of Mental Health Public Inquiries
5600 Fishers Lane, Room 7C-02
Rockville, MD 20857
(800) 421-4211 (for depression)
(800) 64-PANIC (for panic disorders)

National Alliance for the Mentally Ill
200 N. Glebe Rd., Suite 1015
Arlington, VA 22203
(800) 950-NAMI

Obsessive-Compulsive Foundation
P.O. Box 70
Milford, CT 06460
(203) 878-5669

Mental Health Facility Locater
(800) 262-4444

Recovery, Inc.
802 N. Dearborn St.
Chicago, IL 60610
(312) 337-5661

7

Where in the World Did That Sock Go, and What About My Husband's Shorts?

Not all of the letters I receive can be categorized, as my regular readers know. People ask me which way to hang the toilet paper, how to find a long-lost friend, and whether eating off a friend's plate is tacky. They want my recipe for meat loaf or my opinion on bomb shelters.

So kick off your shoes, and enjoy some of the more offbeat letters that have come my way:

Dear Ann Landers: "Martha" and I have been friends for years. She told me she was sorry she was unable to work with me on a church project because she was going to the hospital next week for "a little surgery." When I asked her what kind of surgery, she cut me dead with one word—"minor." I felt as if I had been slapped across the face.

I thought about it all the next day and decided to telephone her physician in the hope that he would tell me it was nothing serious. Well, Ann, I've never been so hurt in my life. The doctor told me to mind my own business and that under no circumstances would he discuss a patient's condition with a third party. I think he hung up on me.

Why would a person be ashamed of having an operation? And why was the doctor so rude when I was merely inquiring about the welfare of a friend?

—Chopped Down

Dear Chopped: If Martha had wanted to give you any information about her surgery, she would have volunteered it. The doctor gave you good advice. Take it.

Dear Ann Landers: Our daughter, who is a junior in college, is interested in "Sid," a young graduate student. Last week, Sid was a guest in our house. He shared a bedroom with our 13-year-old son.

This morning after our daughter and Sid left for school, our son told us he'd had an opportunity to learn a few things. Sid's suitcase had someone else's initials on it. His driver's license indicated that he is 23, not 24. He owes someone $1,200, according to a note in his wallet. There was a mushy letter in his suitcase from a girl who lives in Buffalo. Also, he carries a picture in his wallet of two girls—our daughter and another girl. What do you make of this?

—Concerned Parents

Dear Parents: You have a right to be deeply concerned—about that little punk you're raising. Teach the kid to mind his own business.

Dear Ann Landers: I've been going with a lovely young woman for about 18 months. "Sara" lives in another city, but we see each other every weekend. We are in love and plan to be married. Sara told me early in our friendship that her husband killed himself.

Somehow, my mother and sisters learned about the suicide, and they are trying to talk me out of marrying Sara. They say when a married man kills himself it means his wife failed him. Sara is sensitive and insecure; her life has been a trying and lonely one. I believe it is unfair to say she failed her husband, and I resent the suggestion that she is a poor marriage risk. I'd like your views.

—Color Me Blue

Dear Blue: First, about your family. Color them vicious. Suicide is an irrational act. A husband or wife who has lived through the nightmare should be spared the burden of guilt. If you love the woman and want to marry her, disregard your family's cruel insinuations. And you might tell your relatives to M.Y.O.B.

The No-Excuse Sunday

To make it possible for everyone to attend church next week, we are planning a special no-excuse Sunday.

1. Cots will be placed in the vestibule for those who say, "Sunday is my only day for sleeping in."
2. Eye drops will be available for those whose eyes are tired from watching TV too late on Saturday night.
3. We will have steel helmets for those who believe the roof will cave in if they show up for church services.
4. Blankets will be furnished for those who complain that the church is too cold. Fans will be on hand for those who say the church is too hot.
5. We will have hearing aids for the parishioners who say, "The pastor doesn't talk loud enough." There will be cotton for those who say, "The pastor talks too loud."
6. Scorecards will be available for those who wish to count the hypocrites.
7. We guarantee that some relatives will be present for those who like to go visiting on Sunday.
8. TV dinners will be available for those who claim they can't go to church and cook dinner too.
9. One section of the church will have some trees and grass for those who see God in nature, especially on the golf course.
10. The sanctuary will be decorated with Christmas poinsettias and Easter lilies to create a familiar environment for those who have never seen the church without them.

See you in church.

Dear Ann Landers: A friend of mine told me something the other day that makes no sense. I am troubled because she is a smart girl who usually knows what she is talking about. The more I think about what she said, the crazier it seems, yet she was so sure of her facts, I decided to write and ask for your opinion.

My friend says that when you pick a leaf off a tree or when you pick a flower, the plant actually feels pain and lets out a high-frequency scream, which can be heard only with a special instrument. She also believes if you talk nicely to one plant and harshly to another plant, the plant you talk nicely to will do much better.

I hope you don't think this is too nutty to bother with. I would like very much to know the truth.

—S.M.

Dear S.M.: It depends on whose word you want to take. A man named Cleve Backster wrote an article for *National Wildlife* in which he described the results of his experiments. Backster wired plants to a polygraph (lie detector) and subjected the plants to various stimuli. He concluded that the growth and general health of plants are indeed affected by the way the plants are spoken to.

A housewife in La Jolla conducted her own experiments for a horticultural group. She reported that her philodendron and sansevieria nearly died when subjected to four hours of rock music for five days. These same plants recovered and flourished when she discontinued the rock music and switched to Debussy and Chopin.

Floyd Swenk of Morton Aboretum in Chicago said, "Others have tried similar experiments and have had the same results. There must be something to it."

Insofar as plants "screaming" when a leaf is plucked or stem broken, sorry, this is fantasy. Plants don't have voice boxes.

Dear Ann Landers: Our home was burglarized last week. We lost a great many valuable items—family heirlooms, jewelry and silver.

Several years ago, you ran a letter written by a convict who was serving time for a series of break-ins. He told people how they might protect themselves against being burglarized. I read that article with interest. I should have torn it out and memorized it.

It's too late for us, but I'm sure it would help a great many people if you printed it again. Will you, please?

—Heartsick in Winnetka

Dear Win: Yes, I will. Sad to say, the topic is as relevant now as when it first ran in 1972. Here it is:

Dear Ann Landers: As you can see from the letterhead, I am in jail in Indianapolis at Marion County correctional facility. I am not asking for help. I am writing instead to offer some help.

As a person who has made a fortune in burglaries and robberies, I have some advice for your readers. Perhaps I can save them some trouble and money.

People spend money on burglar alarms, pick-proof locks and watchdogs, but they encourage break-ins by leaving open garage doors that lead into the house. An experienced burglar knows how to deal with alarms and locks. A hunk of meat or a blast of Mace will quiet the dog.

You might think it unbelievable, but I have ransacked many a nightstand while the owner slept less than 1 foot away. Burglars have discovered that the nightstand is a gold mine of wallets, credit cards, checkbooks, jewelry—and guns.

Once in the wee hours, I actually had to crawl under a bed while the sleepy victim got up and went to the bathroom. When he returned and resumed his snoring, I ripped the place off for a couple of watches, a handgun and $125 in cash.

One thing that worries a burglar is a light in the bathroom. Most burglars do not wish to risk a confrontation with a person coming out of the bathroom. If you want to discourage an intruder, keep the bathroom light on all night and the bathroom door ajar. If you are not at home, the ploy still works—provided you remember to rumple up the bed so it will look as if someone has been sleeping in it.

The important thing to remember is this: If you are in bed and you hear a stranger in the house, stay in bed. Pretend you are asleep.

Don't try to be a hero. Most burglars travel in pairs these days, and they are usually armed.

If a confrontation does occur, keep cool. Remember that about 75 percent of all break-ins today are by people who are high on drugs or pills. They are desperate for money and will kill you if they have to. Don't argue or scream. Don't try to get to an alarm button or a phone. The smart thing to do is fake a faint and stay "unconscious." Nothing you own is worth getting killed for.

The judge has already said I should spend from one to ten years with the Indiana Department of Corrections for my misdeeds. From where I see it—at the age of 21—the immediate future isn't too rosy. I hope when I'm free I'll still be worried about your house. Sincerely,

—D.P.F., Cellblock 3-G

Dear D.P.F.: So do I. In the meantime, thank you for a most informative letter.

Dear Ann Landers: I read your column every day. I especially enjoy letters that inspire, challenge and bring out the best in us.

Here's something that should get your readers thinking. I cut it out of a local newsletter.

—Susan in Miami

Dear Susan: Thanks for your kind words and the enclosure. I liked it a lot and want to share it with my readers. Here it is:

You Can Bank on It

Imagine you had a bank that each morning credited your account with $1,440—with one condition: Whatever part of the $1,440 you had failed to use during the day would be erased from your account, and no balance would be carried over.

What would you do? You'd draw out every cent every day and use it to your best advantage.

Well, you do have such a bank, and its name is time. Every morning, this bank credits you with 1,440 minutes. And it writes off as forever lost whatever portion you have failed to invest to good purpose.

Dear Readers: A Boston student wrote to me and asked, "Here's a brainbuster for you. Four words in the English language end in 'gry.' Two are 'angry' and 'hungry.' What are the other two?"

Responses poured in by the thousands. After checking a mind-boggling number of words submitted by readers from all over the globe, I decided that William Safire, one of the premier wordsmiths of our time, was right when he described word games as "a hoax designed to provoke hours of useless brain-racking." I am ashamed to tell you how many hours I spent chasing down words in seven dictionaries.

Laurence Seits of North Aurora, Ill., wrote to say that the best authority on words in the United States is George Scheetz, head of the public library in my old hometown, Sioux City, Iowa.

I telephoned George, who assured me that there were more than four words in the English language that ended in "gry"—48 to be exact. He promised to send the list pronto, which he did.

On George Scheetz's list were old English words such as ahungry, unhungry, hongry, dog-hungry, meat-hungry, wind-hungry, ever-angry, fire-angry, half-angry, heat-angry, self-angry and tear-angry.

Sorry, George, those words were not in any of the four dictionaries I have at home or the three dictionaries in my office. I'm sure they appeared in some musty old English dictionary, but if I can't find them, I don't count 'em.

Nor can I count the words of French origin whose endings were changed from "e" to "y."

George, dear, if you are still reading this, I also can't count Ballingry, a town in Scotland, nor can I count Hungry-Bungry, a sandwich that was served in a restaurant that is no longer in business in Champaign,

Ill. I also am not counting Wigry, a lake in Poland, or Schchigry, a river in the U.S.S.R.

The original writer was off by one when he said there are four words in the English language that end in "gry." Actually, there are five, according to *The Oxford English Dictionary*. In addition to the two he named, angry and hungry, there is aggry, a glass bead found buried in the earth in Ghana (try to work that into a conversation, kids); puggry, a light scarf wound around a hat or helmet to protect the head from the sun; and meagry, of meager appearance.

I don't know about you, folks, but I have had enough of word games for a while.

A reader once wrote and asked me an off-the-wall question: "Tell me, Ann, if I run from one building to another in the rain, will I be wetter than if I walked?"

The question was raised by a Notre Dame graduate who said he and his buddies had tried to work it out mathematically but never quite made it. He concluded, however, that the faster you run, the wetter you get because the more space you sweep per unit of time. Then, the graphics editor of The Washington Post *got into the act with a mind-bending equation, which I was unable to challenge because I can't keep a checkbook straight, much less follow a double-dome equation.*

I was stunned by the number of readers who wrote to dispute the graphics editor. Here is a sampling, none of which I comprehend, but which I'm printing for you math buffs. I had no idea so many people cared.

Dear Ann: My husband, who teaches physics, plans to use that rain question in his next exam. Here's his mathematical shortcut for solving the problem:

"If you run twice as fast, you cover the distance in half the time. If the rain is falling at an angle, think of it as having a vertical component that affects how much rain you get on your head and shoulders and a horizontal component that affects how wet you get on your front or back. The faster you run, the less rain you will get on your head. If the rain is falling toward you, the faster you run, the less rain you will get on your front. If the rain is coming from behind, the optimal speed to run in order to reduce the amount of rain on your front or back is the horizontal component of the rain's speed, in which case, you won't get any rain on your back. If you run slower than this, you'll get rain on your back. If you run faster, you'll get rain on your front. So run—no matter what."

—JMH

From Redding, Calif.: Here's a simplified way to figure out who gets wetter, the guy who walks or runs: Take Container A with an opening equal to the area exposed by a man from the overhead position. Take Container B, with an opening equal to the area exposed by a man from front view. Have George and Bill each carry one Container A and one Container B. Container A should have an opening to the top. Container B, an opening to the front. George moves forward at twice the speed of Bill, arriving in half the time. Bill's Container A will contain twice as much water as George's Container A. But George's Container B will contain more than twice as much as Bill's Container B.

The containers should be designed to approximate the curvature of the body in running form. Visualize the problem by supporting a string of spaghetti in vertical position. Then, you can take 10 lashes with the wet spaghetti for jumping to a conclusion without the facts.

—Wet

Air Force Institute of Technology, Wright-Patterson Air Force Base, Ohio: The solution of the raindrop problem depends on the size and shape of the man, the speed at which he runs and the direction of the falling raindrops. A fat man will get wetter than a thin man. Also one will get wetter running into the wind than if he runs with the wind. The faster the rain falls, the faster the man should run.

—H. C. Larsen, professor and director, Aerospace
Design Center

Chatham, Mass.: Who needs all that math? The faster you run, the quicker you'll get there and the drier you'll be.

—John L. Rowland

Dear John: Thanks, buddy. Your letter was the easiest to understand. I'm with you.

Dear Ann: Remember the rain problem—whether to run or walk to get less soaked? Well, we seniors at the Missouri School for the Deaf were challenged by our science and math teachers to solve it. So we rigged up some empty cartons, lined the sides with paper towels and gave one carton to a runner and one to a walker.

The two experimenters held the boxes over their heads, left the building at the same moment and went the same distance—240 feet. It took the runner 20 seconds to reach his destination. The walker took 60 seconds.

We wrung out the paper towels and discovered that the walker absorbed nearly twice as much moisture as the runner. The exact measure was 10.1 grams to the runner's 5.2 grams.

—MIT, Here We Come!

My very first editor, back in 1955, was Larry Fanning (rest his beautiful soul)—a patient mentor and a marvelous teacher. He told me, "You can deal with any subject so long as you use the right words—with one caveat: Never take your readers into the bathroom."

Twenty-five years later, I departed from his advice and printed a letter from a woman who was having an argument with her cousins. Should the toilet paper be hung so that it goes over the roll and hangs down in front—or should it go in the opposite direction and hang close to the wall?

When I received more than 15,000 letters from readers with opinions, I knew it was an OK subject.

Although I still harbor a twinge of guilt for going against Larry's admonition, here's the letter that started it all, from 1977:

Dear Ann Landers: I am calling on you to settle matters in a friendly family discussion.

While I was visiting family and other kissin' cousins last summer back in Iowa (near Sioux City, as a matter of fact), I brought up the subject of how they all needed to reverse their paper towels and toilet tissue on the spools since they were placed incorrectly. The paper rolls should be coming from the wall up toward the top, over and out. They all disagreed.

Please settle this for all of us. In the meantime, they are calling me

—Paper Crazy

Dear P.C.: There is no right or wrong way to dispense paper towels or toilet tissue. It's strictly a matter of personal preference.

My preference happens to be the same as your cousins'.

Maybe it's because I'm from Iowa, too, and that's the way my mother used to do it.

And here's what happened:

Dear Readers: Remember the reader who was having an argument with her cousins about the proper way to set up toilet tissue? She was certain the right way was with the paper coming from the top—over the roll. Her cousins insisted the paper should come down under the roll. I sided with her cousins because that's the way my mother did it. Actually, I very nearly didn't print the letter because it seemed so inconsequential. Well, folks, I couldn't have been more mistaken.

In short order, I was bombarded with letters from the four corners—including Samoa, Guadalajara, Athens and Mexico City. I had no idea so many people cared about toilet paper. Here's a sampling of what turns people on these days:

Dear Ann Landers: Obviously, you have never been a maid in a ladies' lavatory, or you would have known that toilet paper should be dispensed from the top over. I've worked in several hotels, and we are taught to set up the rolls in that way. Why? Don't ask me, but it's part of the instruction, and when you work for a living, you do as you are told.

—Need My Paycheck

Dear Ann Landers: That letter signed "Paper Crazy" really got to me. I don't know why your mother thought it was best to have the paper come down close to the wall.

I'll bet you never had any cats or dogs in your house. Well, we do (two of each), and if we ever let the toilet paper hang down—even two squares—it would be all over the place. The little darlings just love to drag the stuff around. So rethink your answer, dearie.

—Tidy in Tallahassee

Dear Ann Landers: Of course you are right about toilet paper being dispensed so it comes down from under the roll.

Those manufacturers must be crazy. Why make it elegant if it's not going to be seen? And who can see it unless it's set up to hang down toward the wall—sort of like a painting? Stick to your guns, Annie.

—Also from Iowa

Dear Ann Landers: I was very happy to see you print that letter about the toilet paper. It so happens I was taught, like you, to put the paper on the roller so it comes from under. My husband (a hot-tempered fellow with a serious booze problem) goes berserk if I don't do it the *other* way. You wouldn't believe the yelling if he should find the tissue "upside down," as he calls it. Thanks to Al-Anon, I have learned to accept what I cannot change, so I go along with it, but I know, deep down in my heart, that I am right.

I am waiting until he is sober enough to read, and then, I will show him your column. He thinks you are very smart.

—Another Admirer

Dear Ann: You are right about the toilet paper—and for a very good reason. The roll of paper pivots about the line of support between the axle and the hollow cardboard tube. To get it to turn requires a certain torque, which comes from the tension in the paper being withdrawn. The greater the distance between the plane of the paper being pulled and the axle support line, the less force is required and the less chance of tearing the paper before you have enough.

—Your Friendly Physics Prof

Two years later, I was asked a related question:

Dear Ann Landers: I remember only too well the international controversy that resulted when you printed various views on whether the toilet tissue should go over the roll or straight down, next to the wall. I certainly don't want to start anything like that again. But—I do have a similar problem that has bothered me for years. Please tell me what you think.

Should the lid of the toilet be left up or down? Please note I'm not referring to the toilet seat, it's the *lid* I am talking about.

In my opinion, the purpose of the lid is to keep it closed when the commode is not in use. I can't understand why otherwise fastidious people ignore this reasoning and keep the lid up. Please comment.

—Faithful Ann Fan

Dear Faithful: Of course, you are right. The lid should be kept down. That is the purpose of it. And since we are back in the bathroom again, I'd like to say, in response to thousands of letters that have crossed my desk over these past several years, that it is poor taste for a man to leave the *seat* up. Please, gentlemen, consider the next person, who may be a female.

Dear Ann Landers: After being a bachelor again for nine years, I was recently married. We both knew adjustments would have to be made, and we settled some of the problems in advance. But one small item was not discussed, and it is creating more trouble than I dreamed possible. It's the toilet seat.

Old habits are hard to break. I am simply not accustomed to flopping the seat down before I leave the bathroom. We started with gentle reminders and then tried taping notes to the wall. From there, we went to good-natured kidding that led to insults. Last week, we escalated from snarling to yelling and screaming.

I have decided it is easier to rebel than to change. I refuse to apologize for my habit ever again. When I enter the bathroom, I have enough sense (and decency) to lift the seat. Does it require of my wife more energy to flop it down than it does for me to flip it up? No! Less, in fact, because I am fighting gravity.

I say if a woman doesn't have enough sense to look where she is about to sit, she deserves the consequences. In my opinion, courtesy is something that is extended. It should not be demanded. Will you settle this, Ann? And if you aren't on my side, please skip the whole thing. I have more trouble than I can cope with right now.

—Up, Up, Up in Grand Rapids

Dear Up: An inherent risk of writing to Ann Landers is that she might use your letter—especially if the problem is one a great many people can relate to. Yours is. I only hope you are not so exhausted from "fighting gravity" that you cannot pick up the paper to read my reply.

I believe it is fair to say that any object that is shared should be left in its normal state. In the case of the commode (that's a fancy name for toilet, buster), the normal state of the seat is *down*. The wife of a well-mannered male should not need to look where she is sitting. She knows he is a gentleman and will return the seat to its proper position.

The only solution I can suggest, if you insist on behaving like a stubborn mule, is an apartment with two bathrooms. You can then leave the seat up in yours, and she can keep the seat down in hers.

Dear Ann Landers: Let's blow the lid off the toilet seat debate once and for all. Equality and liberation may be the order of the day, but Western society still gets its knickers in a twist about who left the toilet seat in what position.

It's phony chivalry to suggest that men leave the commode in the appropriate configuration for the next female visitor. We know that the dainty little hand we're sparing the trauma of a seat adjustment is the same dainty little hand that gave the bowl a vigorous scrubbing yesterday.

So, if common courtesy suggests that one user prepare the facility for the next, it must also enjoin women to leave the seat up for the next standing customer. People sharing a bathroom should sit down together (perhaps in a different room, on chairs) and reach a satisfactory compromise.

Maybe some entrepreneural plumber will finance his retirement with a time-delay, self-closing toilet seat that tucks itself into a standard position after the user leaves the room. Or perhaps each of us could exercise a little common courtesy and close the entire lid and leave the porcelain presence looking its designer best.

—Canadian Throne Thinker

Dear Throne: I was staggered by the number of people who had strong opinions on bathroom etiquette and were eager to express them. Some sent photos. Keep reading:

From Everett, Wash.: Our office has two unisex toilets. We resolved the problem by asking everyone to close the lid when they finish. Now the men don't feel picked on, and no one has to look into the gaping mouth of an ugly toilet.

Carson City, Nev.: The best reason to close the lid is to save the life of a small child or a household pet. Every year, several babies and dozens of kittens are drowned in toilets. You should have taken this opportunity to advise all adults to close the lid and train their youngsters to do the same.

Coral Springs, Fla.: Like most females, you have been culturally brainwashed. You can bet the man who leaves the seat up is making a statement about the way he feels about women. It's not about manners, it's about control, stupid!

Rational Reader, No City: When you use the bathroom, it is your responsibility to put the lid and the seat in the position that serves you best. It is not someone else's responsibility to do this for you. Real class is how you tend to your own needs, instead of carping and whining because other people don't do it for you. In our house, everyone puts the seat and the lid down. It looks nice, nothing falls in, and the dog can't drink the water.

Sioux Falls, S.D.: Regarding the Great Toilet-Seat Debate. There is a solution. Buy a fluffy toilet tank cover and matching seat cover. They are attractive, and the bathroom will look so much better. The bulkiness ensures that the seat will always fall down after use. I discovered this by accident and no longer need to worry about drowning in the middle of the night.

Dallas: I'm a 71-year-old male who does not spend his time writing to newspapers, but this flap about whether the toilet seat should be up or down is just nuts. I would like to know what the hell difference it makes in the first place, and in the second place, I cannot believe that I am taking the time to write this letter.

Dear Dallas: And I cannot believe over 20,000 people did the same.

I thought we were out of the bathroom and on to other topics, but the toilet-paper issue wouldn't go away. Here it is again, in 1992:

Dear Ann Landers: An unforgettable subject in your column keeps cropping up. I'm referring to that seemingly frivolous issue: which way a person should position the toilet paper when replacing a finished roll.

I always place a new roll in the "over" dispensing position and have been known to reverse an "under" roll if someone in my household puts it that way.

Anyone who believes this issue is silly is mistaken. As a student at Union County College in New Jersey, I began doing a radio show on campus. Just for fun, I decided to take a poll—with score sheet in hand—at school, at my place of part-time employment, and everywhere I roamed. What I found was amazing.

After polling several hundred people, the results are as follows: 51 percent preferred "over," 37 percent preferred "under," and 12 percent didn't care as long as it was there.

Even though many people laughed when they were asked, most had a strong preference and responded immediately.

I'd like to share some of the reasons people gave to justify their preferences. They said things such as: "When the paper goes 'over,' it is easier to employ the 'hit and spin' technique."

"I hang mine 'over' so it doesn't touch the wall."

"I like it 'under' because then it rests against the wall, out of the way."

"You will use less paper if you put it 'under,' especially if you have small children or pets."

One respondent said, " 'Over' people are lazy. It takes more effort to reach when the paper is 'under.' "

Several respondents related stories of family arguments at the dinner table. I was told that there was actually an episode of *All in the Family* where Archie yells at Michael for putting the paper "under."

I had a lot of fun with my survey and wanted you to know that after all these years, it's still a topic of discussion.

—T.D.A., Union, N.J.

Dear T.D.A.: I swore I would never print another letter on that subject, but yours was irresistible. It never ceases to amaze me which subject turns readers on.

And now, the absolutely, positively final word:

Dear Ann Landers: You said you would never write another word about the way toilet paper should be hung, but this latest bit of information is crucial. I read it in the *St. Petersburg Times* and I thought it might convince you to reconsider your decision, since we now have some hard data.

At the National Kitchen and Bath Show in Atlanta recently, the attendees were polled on, would you believe, how to hang the toilet paper—over the top or under and close to the wall. The vote was 1,826 for over and 1,256 for under. Interesting?

—Largo, Fla.

Dear Largo: OK. I reconsidered, but I doubt that the Atlanta exhibition will result in any conversions.

An Ode to a Commode, or The Johns of Europe
Bette Wright, Grosse Pointe Farms, Mich.

In London, you pulled a ring
Protruding from the wall,
Heard a monumental flushing sound
And that was simply all.
In Paris, you pushed a button
On the side of the latrine,
Waited 20 minutes
And all was peachy keen.
Lucerne was somewhat simpler,

You merely pulled a chain;
Of this exceptional efficiency,
The Swiss are very vain.
In Munich, first, you find a crank
And then you push a button,
What happens after that, my friends,
Is absolutely nuthin'.
In Venice, you must pull a knob
And then, you push it in;
Good grief, the water won't swirl out—
The canal just comes on in.
When you turn the crank in Florence,
You get a little miffed;
The toilet doesn't flush at all.
The window shade will lift.
In America, we don't have winding roads
Or cypress trees that line it;
But look for the handle on a U.S. john,
And you'll know just where to find it.

Enough with the tissue issue, let's roll on to some other subjects.

Dear Ann Landers: I should have written this letter several weeks ago, but like everyone else, I keep putting things off.

Thousands of children will be depressed on Valentine's Day. While teachers spend time putting up lovely mailboxes and heart-shaped decorations, little emphasis will be placed on love and kindness.

There will be so many disappointed children again this year. The same pretty girls and handsome boys (always popular) will receive a load of valentines, while the plain Janes and Johnnies will be left out.

I am opposed to free choice when it comes to exchanging valentines in school. It creates too much anxiety and heartache.

The teacher ought to match up valentine "couples." They should make valentines for each other during class time. No other valentines should be given at school. This way, no one will be left out. It's the best way to save hurt feelings.

My own child is pretty and popular. She told me in January she hates Valentine's Day because "the same kids get dozens while other kids get none." She gave a valentine last year to every kid in the class.

I thought it was a kind and generous thing to do. It made me proud of her.

If my letter arrives too late for this year, maybe you can print it and plans can be made for next year. Thanks for your time.

—Mother in Dothan, Ala.

Dear Mother: Here's your letter on Valentine's Day—too late to help the plain Janes and Johnnies this year, but I hope the teachers and parents out there will remember your suggestion for next year. It's a good one.

Dear Ann Landers: It's that time of the year, and once again I am going nuts with Christmas shopping. Every year, I promise myself, "This is the last time . . ." But here I am, doing the same stupid thing. Please, Ann, tell me how to get out of this miserable rat race.

My husband, George, and I both come from large families. We have four children and they each have three children—that's 20 gifts right there (including husbands and wives). My mother is still living and so is George's. That makes 22. I always get George a gift, and he gets me one. That's 24.

I see no way to cut that list, and I don't want to. It's the other 40 people I'd like to skip. I am not exaggerating, Ann—last year, we sent 64 gifts. Somehow, we've become involved with sisters, brothers, aunts, uncles, cousins and even second cousins. I can't recall if they started it or if we did, but it's been going on for years, and I am worn out, not to mention broke.

If you can come up with a solution, you're a genius.

—Financially Embarrassed

Dear Embarrassed: There is a solution, but it is not for the timid or the faint of heart.

Starting with that 25th name, drop a line or make a phone call to each and every person on your old list. Ask them not to send you a gift this year. Explain that you are cutting back on gift giving and you hope they will do the same.

Some will send a gift regardless. Your response will determine the success or failure of the entire plan. If you rush out and buy them a gift in return, you are hooked for next year. It may take three years to get your list down to where you want it, but eventually, you'll succeed if you have courage and fortitude.

Back in the early sixties, no threat was more frightening or seemed as immi-
nent as nuclear war. My mail, as usual, reflected the fears of my readers. In
retrospect, my advice seems almost paranoid, but at the time, it seemed per-
fectly reasonable. You can decide for yourselves.
Here's a letter from 1961:

Dear Ann Landers: My husband said you'd laugh at me if I wrote
for advice on something so stupid. I think it's serious.

We've saved $800 for a recreation room. I think we ought to spend
the money on a fallout shelter instead. We have three children. Don't
you feel that parents are obligated to give their youngsters all the protection possible? I went to a civil defense meeting recently and was
amazed at how much the average person can do to protect himself if
there should be a nuclear war.

My husband says if things get so bad that we need a fallout shelter in
Flint, Mich., he'd just as soon not be a survivor. He promised to settle
for your advice.

—Michigander

Dear Gander: Tell the goose that people who fail to take every reasonable precaution are stupid fools. A country wide open to attack
makes a delicious target.

I happen to be one of those optimists who believe Ivan will never
push the button because he knows we've got a button, too. But all the
same, I strongly advocate preparedness. Better to have it and not need
it than to need it and not have it.

Dear Readers: Recently, a mother from Flint, Mich., wrote and
asked me to settle a family argument.

The question: Should they go ahead and spend $800 on a recreation
room, or should they invest in a fallout shelter instead?

I sided with the wife, who felt that parents have a moral obligation
to protect their children as best they can against accident, sickness or
death—whether it means keeping a bottle of poison out of reach, inoc-
ulating children against smallpox and polio or protecting them against
the devastating effects of nuclear warfare.

President Kennedy has urged Americans to provide shelters as a nuclear war deterrent. The president argued that a country that is ill-
prepared makes an inviting target for the enemy.

Heated reactions to my advice have been spouting forth from every state. The mail is fascinating, and it is enlightening. And 90 percent of the writers are in sharp disagreement with me.

Here are some samples of the most provocative letters received by this writer in the six years she has been turning out this column.

From Lima, Ohio: Your advice to the Flint family to invest in a fallout shelter was unrealistic and foolish. The only people who will benefit from shelters are manufacturers and salesmen. They will rake in the shekels from gullible and ignorant saps who believe what the ads say.

Chicago: I love your column, but I wish you wouldn't get involved in matters of defense strategy. Chills ran up and down my spine when you advised that Michigan family to invest $800 in a fallout shelter. If our own beloved Chicago should be a target, the enemy would not aim for the Prudential Building or the *Sun-Times*. The Russians are too smart for that. They would attempt to paralyze the city industrially and then come in later and take over. Their best bet would be to drop the egg right in the middle of Lake Michigan. The tidal wave would be about 14 feet high. That's all, brother.

Los Angeles: Bless you for advocating shelters. Prudent preparation can help diminish the feeling of panic and hopelessness.

Minneapolis: The fallout shelter racket is an unconscionable scheme to part fools from their money. It is the lousiest fraud ever perpetrated against a nation of sheep. Shame on you for falling for it.

Detroit: So you hide in a hole for two weeks. Then what? You have to come up sometime. What's left above the hole where you hid? Contaminated water. Contaminated cattle. Contaminated vegetation. How long could you live, anyway?

Cleveland: Most fallout shelters, particularly the do-it-yourself types, would be death traps. If President Kennedy believes we should have shelters, the government should build them and not let a lot of blood-suckers get rich.

So, my dear readers, this is what my week has been like. And now I will do something I have never done before. I will tell you why I would not take my own advice.

In the last six years, I have demonstrated the temerity, or the innocence, to dispense advice on every imaginable type of problem—both in the newspapers which carry my column and through the mail.

I am not so foolish or so naive as to pretend to know all the answers. Nobody could. Had I been blessed with the wisdom of the prophets, I could not pull out of my hat the solution to all the problems put to me in a single day.

But when I don't know the solution, I never hesitate to call on an authority, in whatever field the problem may be, in an attempt to provide my readers with the best possible answer.

I believe in the advice I give because I know it is carefully weighed and measured—although at times the light touch may betray the hours of research.

When that Michigan mother asked if she and her husband should spend $800 on a recreation room, or if they should build a fallout shelter instead, I consulted the experts and read bales of material on the subject. The key question has not been answered—at least not to my satisfaction: "Will a shelter do any real good?"

Some authorities claim that if a nuclear war should be unloosed on the world there would be no place to hide. They point out that in August 1945, a single U.S. plane dropped an atomic bomb on Hiroshima, Japan. It killed an estimated 100,000 people. In 1952, the United States carried out a test in the Marshall Islands. We exploded an H-bomb of 15 megatons. It vaporized a 12-mile island and left in its place a hole in the ocean floor one mile long.

That single 15-megaton bomb was equivalent in explosive force to 15,000,000 blockbusters. Today, the Russians are talking in terms of a 100-megaton bomb.

Others claim that the nuclear war would last less than 24 hours—that 90 percent of the population could be saved with adequate preparation, that survivors could come out of the shelters within 10 days, "wash things off" and go on living.

To me, however, the most persuasive of the experts are those who refuse to make flat statements on either side. They say, "There are many imponderables. It depends on the enemy's target, possible aiming errors, size of the weapon, type of burst, weather conditions, and the possibility of interception or advance warning."

Many readers—among them scientists, teachers, clergymen and political experts—have denounced fallout shelters as a racket.

One reader said: "It's the lousiest fraud ever perpetrated against a nation of sheep." Hundreds of readers damned the shelter builders for cashing in on the greatest scare in the history of mankind.

I advised the Michigan family to build a fallout shelter. In the light of all the evidence I could gather on both sides of the question, I would do so again. I would do so because I feel that the race should not allow itself to commit mass suicide. We must make an effort, no matter how slim the chances of survival may seem, to save ourselves and our young children.

I believe in this advice, but I would not take it myself. I would not take it because I have no desire to survive in a world of maimed and sick people. Nor would I wish to be confronted with the decision of whether to shoot my neighbor if he tried to get into my shelter because he had none of his own.

I would prefer to stay above the ground and try to live each day with dignity—and take whatever comes.

Even though talk of bomb shelters petered out, the idea of nuclear war loomed ever larger. This letter from 1982 sums it up pretty well:

Dear Ann Landers: If the two strongest nations in the world, the United States and Russia, don't agree to put a freeze on nuclear weapons, your readers won't have to worry about anything because they will be vaporized in a matter of minutes—along with millions of people.

Talk about a limited nuclear war and plans for civilian defense are insane. It would be impossible to evacuate the cities. Where would people go? What would they eat? What would they drink? Who would take care of them? The physicians and hospitals would be blown to smithereens.

You are more than an advice-to-the-lovelorn columnist, Ann Landers. You mold public opinion. People believe in you. For the love of mankind and its survival, please address yourself to this issue.

—Terrified in D.C.

Dear Terrified: Thank you for writing about a subject that is plaguing us all.

Dr. James E. Muller of the Harvard Medical School said, "The horror of nuclear war is so great that many people choose to deny it exists.

"An all-out attack on the United States could kill as many as 150 million Americans. Their immune systems, weakened by radiation, would succumb to fatal diseases. At least 80 percent of the doctors would be incinerated."

As the Rev. Theodore Hesburgh said at a UCLA peace rally, "The living would envy the dead."

The New Republic pointed out in a recent editorial that the global arms budget for all countries is now $550 billion a year. And $100 billion is earmarked for nuclear weapons.

When one considers that $500 billion equals the entire annual income of the poorer half of the Earth's 4 billion people, one begins to grasp the magnitude of that expenditure. Meanwhile, we are cutting programs that benefit the elderly, the handicapped and the poor. More cheery news: Our secretary of the Treasury, Donald Regan, says, "Our economy is dead in the water."

The standard reference is the Hiroshima bomb. It destroyed the city with the equivalent of 12,500 tons of TNT. (This is 12.5 kilotons.) The newest nuclear bomb is not measured in kilotons but in megatons. The yield would be equivalent to approximately 12 million 1-ton trucks filled with TNT.

The Poseidon submarine carries 16 missiles, each with 10 warheads. Each warhead has three times the explosive force of that single bomb dropped on Hiroshima.

We can already kill every Russian seven times. Now we are trying to build our arms supply so we can kill each Russian 14 times. The United States and other major powers are spending themselves broke on a war we dare not let happen.

Jonathan Schell wrote in *The New Yorker*, "The machinery of destruction is in place, poised on a hair-trigger, waiting for the button to be pushed by some misguided or deranged human, or for some faulty computer chip to send out the instructions to fire."

I implore every person to sign his or her name across this column and mail it to President Reagan, the White House, Washington, D.C. An overwhelming response might prevent a nuclear holocaust that would mean the end of all life on this planet.

Do it *today*. Nothing on your calendar can be more important.

I have said many times in my column that my readers are my friends, and when I ask them to do something, they respond, bless them, at once—and in numbers that stagger the imagination. I am happy to report that they did not fail me.

Apparently, the response caught the president's attention because I received a letter from him. Here it is:

Dear Ann Landers: I am writing about your recent column regarding the letter from "Terrified in D.C." I want you to know that I'll take second to none in my concern over the threat of nuclear war. That is why in my April 17th radio address to the nation, I said:

"To those who protest against nuclear war, I can only say I'm with you. Like my predecessors, it is now my responsibility to do my utmost to prevent such a war. No one feels more than I the need for peace."

It is indeed my highest priority to deter and prevent such a war, for its consequences would be disastrous for mankind.

That is why I've called for negotiations leading to major arms reductions, not limitations that only codify high levels. Under the so-called limitations of SALT II the Soviet Union and the United States could substantially add to their nuclear arsenals.

I have instead called for the reduction of the most destabilizing strategic elements, the ballistic missile warheads, by one-third in the first phase of negotiations on strategic arms reduction. In the area of intermediate-range nuclear forces, I have also proposed the elimination of the most threatening systems, the land-based missiles.

During the last decade, the United States restrained its deployment of new nuclear forces while the Soviet Union enormously increased its forces. We, therefore, now face a serious imbalance, which decreases the credibility of our deterrent.

That is why we must modernize our own forces both to reduce the dangerous imbalance and to make clear to the Soviet leaders that they should join us in negotiating the kind of substantial, equal and verifiable reductions in nuclear arms the world demands.

Ann, we have tried many times since World War II to persuade the Russians to join us in reducing or even eliminating nuclear weapons, with little success. Perhaps, instead of sending copies to me, your readers should send copies of your May 17 column to President Brezhnev. Sincerely,

—Ronald Reagan

Dear President Reagan: Like you, I feel that President Brezhnev should see my column of May 17. Perhaps something in it might strike a responsive chord and get a dialogue going between the Soviet Union and the United States.

I have asked our mutual friend, Dr. Armand Hammer, chairman of Occidental Petroleum, to see that my column of May 17 is delivered to President Brezhnev, his close personal friend. He has agreed to do so.

If I hear from Brezhnev, Mr. President, I'll call you. If *you* hear from him, please call me. It would make my day. Sincerely,

—Ann Landers

Unfortunately, I never heard from President Brezhnev.

———

Some of my younger readers may not remember how the American public revered Walter Cronkite when he anchored the CBS Evening News. *He was the Voice of America—everyone's favorite uncle. It was unheard of to criticize Walter Cronkite. You can imagine the uproar when I printed this:*

Dear Ann Landers: Have you noticed how many people, including those in radio and TV, pronounce February as Feb-yooary? Walter Cronkite, no less, is one of the principal offenders. I will be mighty glad when these so-called experts on the English language get with it. I've written to Mr. Cronkite to protest such sloppy usage but, so far, no reply. How about your trying?

—February Freak

Dear Feb: I sent your letter to Walter Cronkite who, incidentally, is a real pussycat. Across the top of your letter, I wrote:

"Dear Walter: The lady is right. I heard you say it. Please clean up your act or get off the air."

Walter Cronkite telephoned his response. He let me know in no uncertain terms that his act doesn't need cleaning up.

Moreover, he said he has no intention of getting off the air. Mr. Cronkite claims the dictionaries are divided as to the pronunciation of February. I checked several reference books, however, and they all give Feb-yoo-ary as second choice. (See *World Book Dictionary, Merriam-Webster's New Collegiate, Funk and Wagnall's, American Heritage* and *Random House.*) One of them even has Feb-yoo-ary as third choice.

So Feb-roo-ary is preferred, but Feb-yoo-ary is acceptable, and that's the way it is, Monday, April 24, 1978.

Dear Readers: Remember the Japanese soldier who hid in a cave on Iwa Jima for 25 years and no one could figure out why?

Well, I think I know the reason. He probably said something uncomplimentary about Walter Cronkite.

Ever since I printed the letter from the woman who criticized Walter's pronunciation of February (he said Feb-yoo-ary), I have been catching heat from Cronkite fans.

They are angry and unrelenting, and the numbers are staggering.

The woman who signed herself "February Freak" had written to Cronkite about his "sloppy pronunciation." She received no reply and asked me to try to get through to him. I said I would. (I, too, shudder when I hear someone say "Feb-yoo-ary," and I had heard Walter say it.)

Cronkite is a dear guy and a good friend of mine. He phoned his response, which was as follows:

"The dictionaries are divided as to the pronunciation of the word. I happen to prefer Feb-yoo-ary."

I then began to check various dictionaries—*World Book, Merriam-Webster's New Collegiate, Funk and Wagnall's, American Heritage* and *Random House.*

Not one gave Feb-yoo-ary as first choice. In fact, one gave it as third. When I politely suggested that Cronkite clean up his act, the feathers hit the fan.

After several hundred letters in defense of Walter, telling me where to go and what I could do with my typewriter when I got there, I finally hit on a letter I could print. It came from Elaine P. Paden, Ph.D., associate professor of phonetics and phonology, University of Illinois at Urbana-Champaign. She wrote:

"Your reply to 'February Freak' perpetuates a common misconception that the pronunciation of a word appearing first in a dictionary is 'preferred' or 'best.' A second-place variant is not to be regarded as less desirable than the one given first. Thus, Walter Cronkite's Feb-yoo-ary is neither 'sloppy' nor inferior to Feb-roo-ary."

The second printable letter was from Virginia McDavid, professor of English at Chicago State University. She wrote:

"Before you tell Walter Cronkite or anyone else anything about pronunciation, you should learn to use a dictionary. What makes you think the first pronunciation is 'preferred' and second or third is merely 'accepted'?

"The first pronunciation shown is generally considered the one used most frequently, but the second and third are not incorrect and are just as acceptable. So tell your audience that if both pronunciations are in a modern dictionary, great—go with them. And let dear Walter alone."

So-oooo, there you have it. What's more, you can be sure that from now on anything Walter Cronkite says is all right with me.

Better I should criticize motherhood, apple pie or the United States Marines.

I thought the Walter Cronkite debacle was finished, but the readers refuse to let me off the hook despite my abject apologies. Are you ready for more? This, I vow, will terminate the self-flagellation. I've had it with the sackcloth and ashes.

Dear Ann Landers: I couldn't believe my eyes when I read that letter of criticism directed at Walter Cronkite. Why would you permit a clod to use your column to attack that dear, sweet man? It's shocking!

Have you ever listened to yourself on radio or TV? If not, you should. You have a definite lisp. So does your sister, Dear Abby. The two of you could use speech lessons. And don't put the blame on Iowa. I've heard some cultivated speakers who hail from that great state. You and your sister should have been hog-callers.

I just showed this letter to my husband. He said, "Don't be so hard on the girls. I think they need dental work." So—why don't you have it?
—Betting You Won't Print This

Dear Betting: You lose. Thanks for my laugh for the day.

———

Dear Ann Landers: Oh, yuk! You have defended the practice of asking for a "taste" from the plate of a fellow diner. Not only that, you make those of us who do not agree sound like antisocial creeps. I wrote this poem for you:

Ode to the Eppie-Curean
There's a habit that I hate:
Swiping morsels off the plate
By friendly folks who only want to share
Their streptococci, my eclair.
"Gimme a taste, gimme a lick."
Those gregarious people sure are quick!
I've barely time to thank the Lord—
My lunch becomes their smorgasbord.
If they're so happy, so well-adjusted,

The kind of people to be trusted,
How come they always seem to feel
There's something special about my meal?

—Take the Whole Thing in Colorado

Dear Take: Your meter is a little off, but the idea is what counts. I confess I received a lot more flak on this subject that I expected.

Dear Ann Landers: A friend sent me something that stopped me dead in my tracks. I don't know what to make of it, so I'm sending it to you for comment. Thank you very much.

How much of it was coincidence? I refer to the assassinations of Abraham Lincoln and John F. Kennedy.

Both Lincoln and Kennedy were concerned with civil rights.

Lincoln was elected president in 1860, Kennedy in 1960. Both were slain on a Friday and in the presence of their wives.

Both were shot from behind and in the head.

Their successors were both named Johnson, were both Southern Democrats, and were both in the Senate.

Andrew Johnson was born in 1808, and Lyndon Johnson was born in 1908.

John Wilkes Booth was born in 1839, and Lee Harvey Oswald was born in 1939.

Booth and Oswald were Southerners favoring unpopular ideas.

Both presidents' wives lost children through death while in the White House.

Lincoln's secretary, whose name was Kennedy, advised him not to go to the theater.

Kennedy's secretary, whose name was Lincoln, advised him not to go to Dallas.

Lee Harvey Oswald shot Kennedy from a warehouse and ran to a theater.

John Wilkes Booth shot Lincoln in a theater and ran to a warehouse.

The names Lincoln and Kennedy each contain seven letters.

The names Andrew Johnson and Lyndon Johnson each contain 13 letters.

The names John Wilkes Booth and Lee Harvey Oswald each contain 15 letters.

Both assassins were killed before being brought to trial.

Both Johnsons were opposed for re-election by men whose names start with G.

—Spooked in New Jersey

Dear Spooked: That makes two of us. I have no explanation to offer. Mighty strange is all I can say.

Dear Ann Landers: I've seen the list of similarities between the assassinations of Abraham Lincoln and John F. Kennedy before. It's not very impressive.

Some of those "striking coincidences" are actually quite common: Both the names Lincoln and Kennedy contain seven letters. Yeah, so does Landers.

Both of their vice presidents were Democrats who had served in the Senate. Many vice presidents have served in the Senate, including Al Gore, Dan Quayle, Walter Mondale and Hubert Humphrey.

Consider all the ways that Lincoln and Kennedy were different. They didn't belong to the same party, come from the same state or even the same part of the country. They didn't have the same first names or even the same initials. One came from a rich family, the other from a poor one. One went to Harvard; the other didn't go to college at all. One was bearded, and one was clean-shaven. One was elected to a second term, and the other didn't finish his first. Neither is there that much resemblance between the two assassinations. One was inside; the other was outside. One president lingered for almost a day, and the other died within a couple of hours.

Coincidences are often the result of sloppy reporting.

—W. W., Greenbelt, Md.

Dear W.W.: Thanks for striking a blow for accuracy. Your research is right on.

Dear Ann Landers: You are supposed to be a smart cookie. Can you figure this out? I bet my wife $10 you'd flunk, just as we did.

The parent of a Houston high school pupil received a message from the school principal concerning a special meeting on a proposed new educational program.

The message read: "Our school's cross-graded, multiethnic, individualized learning program is designed to enhance the concept of an

open-ended learning program with emphasis on a continuum of multiethnic, academically enriched learning, using the identified intellec-
tually gifted child as the agent or director of his own learning. Major
emphasis is on cross-graded, multiethnic learning with the main objective being to learn respect for the uniqueness of a person."

The parent responded: "Dear Principal: I have a college degree,
speak two foreign languages and know four Indian dialects. I've attended a number of county fairs and three goat ropings, but I haven't
the faintest idea as to what the hell you are talking about." OK, Ann,
do *you* know what the principal was trying to say?

—Two Dummies in Fort Worth

Dear Friends: I don't think you are dummies. That principal needs
to learn how to express himself in simple terms.

What he means is: "We are planning a program for students of all
races, which we hope will encourage the brighter ones to move ahead
at their own speed. Grading will be geared to the learning level of the
student. In this way, we hope to teach and grade each student according to his ability to learn." P.S. Pay your wife the $10. Or better yet,
send it to your local Heart Association.

Dear Ann Landers: It is alarming and frightening that increasingly
fewer eligible voters exercise their right to vote or pay attention to the
issues or who is running for office. How many times have we heard
someone say, "My one vote won't matter, so I just didn't bother"?

For several years I was an election judge supervisor at one of the
precincts in our city. The following was copied from a page in *The
Election Judge's Manual.* Since your column is nationally syndicated,
perhaps it will be read by many people who will finally realize how
important one vote can be. If our right to vote in a free election were
ever taken away, there would be utter chaos. Please, Ann, get behind
this.

How Important Is One Vote?

In 1645, one vote gave Oliver Cromwell control of England.

In 1649, one vote caused Charles I of England to be executed.

In 1868, one vote saved President Andrew Johnson from impeach-
ment.

In 1875, one vote changed France from a monarchy to a republic.

In 1876, one vote gave Rutherford B. Hayes the presidency of the U.S.
In 1923, one vote gave Adolf Hitler leadership in the Nazi Party.
In 1941, one vote saved Selective Service—just weeks before Pearl
    Harbor was attacked.

—From Missouri

Dear Missouri: Thanks for bringing home a vital message in a most dramatic way. I hope every one of my readers will remember this column when it comes time to vote. Bear in mind, your vote might be the one that makes the difference.

Dear Ann Landers: I am annoyed, irritated and just plain mystified. For the third time in less than a year, one of my husband's socks has vanished after having been tossed into the washing machine.

I know very well that I would never put one lone sock in the washer. A pair went in, so what has happened to the other one?

People write to you about every imaginable problem under the sun. You must have had this at one time or another. What did you say?

—Edna, Atlanta

Dear Edna: I have indeed been asked the question before. The best response came from Nancy Drechsler of North Carolina:

> Oh where, oh where is the other sock?
> Is it under the bed, or caught in the casters,
> Or clinging to the basement rafters?
> Trapped in the plumbing?
> Stuffed in a shoe?
> In a darkened corner
> Hiding from you?
> Have they gone to camp and returned alone?
> Been kicked off, perhaps, by the telephone?
> An argyle a starling's home,
> Striped sock found its way to Rome?
> Perhaps there is an odd sock elf,
> Who takes them to some woodsy shelf.
> But truthfully, I know their fate
> The dirty ones disintegrate.

Dear Nancy: It's true. Old socks never die. They just fade away.

In a later column, a reader gave me a more logical explanation: Single socks often get caught in the agitator and flip between the drum and the side of the washer. You can find them if you ever take the machine apart. If you lose them in the dryer, then you're on your own.

———

When I first began writing this column, a lot of my mail concerned house-keeping issues—should the sheets be ironed? Should a wife serve her family breakfast wearing rollers and a bathrobe?

Of course, back in the 1950s, no one knew about permanent-press linens nor would anyone consider telling the husband to pitch in—after all, most women stayed at home, and housework was their job.

When I told a reader that she didn't need to apologize for being in her bathrobe when she greeted a salesman at 9:00 in the morning, all hell broke loose.

This is what happened in 1958:

Dear Readers: I've been catching heat from 49 states (including Alaska) plus a beef from Dusseldorf, Germany.

Typical comment: "Ann Landers, what do you mean by backing up sloppy housewives who slosh around in bathrobes all day?" The consensus is that 9:00 A.M. is time enough for any housewife to be dressed in a crisp house dress ready to greet the bright-eyed, enterprising insurance agent. Most of the bleats came from men—naturally.

I still say a woman's home is her castle and there's no reason to get fully clothed to see her family off to work or school—unless she wants to. This is not to imply that women should appear at the breakfast table with knotted hair, looking lumpy in an old beat-up kimono and maribou bedroom slippers. There are attractive housecoats—in fact, they are much like the Hoover aprons of 20 years ago.

Men, of course, are expected to dress the first thing in the morning. They could hardly go to work in their pajamas. On Sunday, however, how many men get dressed as if they're going to work?

Let's face it. Some women are slobs even when fully dressed. And some women can be appetizing in a housecoat. I see no reason for anyone to object if a woman wants to indulge in a shortcut—least of all a guy who comes by to sell insurance.

Then I printed a letter from a man who said: "Why defend the average American housewife, Ann Landers? She's a pig, and you know it." Here's what happened next:

Dear Readers: This column hasn't provoked such a violent response since I suggested that Elvis Presley was a dancer—not a singer.

Hundreds of irate women, indignant husbands, and children wrote to give that reader a verbal pasting and defend the honor of the Average American Housewife.

Such spirited response rates a full day's column—and here it is:

From Dallas: I'd like to tell that idiot what the "average American pig" did this morning.

Got up at 6:30 A.M. Made a whopping big breakfast for my husband, four piglets and a sow (my mother-in-law lives with us). Packed a lunch for "Porky" (my husband) and set dough for four loaves of bread.

By 10:30, the sty was in order, and I ironed yesterday's laundry until noon, when I stopped to make lunch for anywhere from four to eight kids, as each one usually brings a friend. By 2:30, the lunch dishes were cleaned up, a cake was in the oven for a church bazaar, also an apple pie for the family.

Went grocery shopping for the week, spent 40 minutes on the phone for PTA (I'm president), prepared the swill for dinner, sewed together my daughter's dancing costume and ran next door to help give a sick child medicine. (Mother can't handle him.)

This was one of my "light" days, but even at that, I didn't have much time to wallow around in the mud.

I'm not looking for any medals. Millions of American women do as much and more. So, as Ann Landers says, "Put your nose back in joint, buster."

Manitowoc, Wis.: If the average American housewife is a *pig*, it's because the average American male is a *boar*.

—Informed

Mexico, Mo.: I am 10 years old and in the fifth grade. My mother is not a pig. She is a very neat person.

—Allen

Chicago: I never wrote to a paper before, but no jerk is going to call *my* wife a pig and get away with it. She's a wonderful wife and mother and I have yet to pay a laundry bill or eat a frozen pie in the 15 years we've been married.

—Burned Up

So much for the slobs. What about ironing the sheets and the undershorts? Would any wife consider doing this today? I would never suggest it now, but I did in 1959:

Dear Ann Landers: Last week, I put brand-new sheets on the bed. My husband raved over how luxurious they felt. He asked why they weren't this way all the time. He then added, "Mom's bed sheets were always like this."

I explained perhaps his mother ironed her sheets. I simply fold mine and put them away. He then had the nerve to suggest that I iron the sheets from now on. We got into a hot argument, and I refused flatly. I don't happen to believe in killing myself with housework. Am I wrong, or is he?

—Four-Poster

Dear Four-Poster: Did you know the average person spends one-third of his life in bed? Isn't it worth 30 minutes a week to make your husband happy an additional one-third of his life?

If he wants you to iron the bed sheets, iron 'em, toots. Be thankful your marital troubles *can* be ironed out so easily. Not all people are so lucky.

Dear Ann: Something happened which dates back to your column on ironing bed sheets. Now I have a problem.

My husband wrote me a note this morning. It said, "Unless you are sick, dying or dead, I expect my shorts to be ironed and in my bureau drawer when I come home. Love, Lou."

I've never ironed Lou's shorts in the 12 years we've been married, and he never complained—until now. I decided I wasn't going to spoil him at this late date, so I did not iron his shorts. I cleaned out his closet instead.

Tonight when he came home, he kissed me affectionately and headed right for the bedroom to check on the shorts. They were in his bureau drawer, folded neatly but not ironed!

He said nothing, but I could see he was disappointed. You've put me in a bad spot, Ann. Please give me your frank opinion. Should a wife who has never ironed her husband's shorts start after 12 years?

—Kathleen

Dear Kathleen: Well—here we go again! There are all kinds of husbands in this world. Some couldn't care less whether their shorts are ironed or not. Others complain if their handkerchiefs aren't lined up just so.

In my opinion, it is not unreasonable for a man to want his shorts ironed. If your husband has decided after 12 years he'd like ironed shorts—then iron 'em.

You'll burn up less energy ironing seven pairs of shorts a week than arguing about it. I promise, Kathleen, if you begin to iron Lou's shorts, he'll stand on his head to please you.

And this from 1966. (I wonder how much a homemaker would be worth today.)

Dear Ann Landers: All my married life, I've felt like a nobody because I was "only a housewife." My husband made me feel that I should be grateful to him for putting food in my mouth and clothes on my back.

Today, I read something that gave me a lift. If you print it, I'll bet you'll give thousands of housewives a new lease on life.

The home economics department of our state college published a leaflet in chart form. It shows what a housewife is worth per week in dollars and cents on today's labor market. Here it is:

Cooking, table-setting, serving, at $2 an hour . . . $50.
Dishwashing, at $1.25 an hour . . . $17.50.
Child care, at 50 cents an hour (ridiculous since this is what most sitters get for just sitting) . . . $17.50.
Routine housework, at $1.25 an hour . . . $22.50.
Laundry, at $1.25 an hour . . . $6.25.
Ironing, at $1.25 an hour . . . $6.25.

The chart suggests adding 25 cents for miscellaneous work. So the grand total is $150 a week. On a yearly basis, a housewife is worth $7,800.

Believe it or not, this leaflet has given me dignity. I no longer feel like a parasite. Tonight when Mr. Greatheart comes home, I'm going to greet him like a woman who earns almost $8,000 a year because that's what I am.

—Ashamed No Longer

Dear Ashamed No Longer: Housewives of America, unite! Clip this column for your husband. And as for you, Mr. Greatheart, take that—and that—and that.

Dear Ann Landers: As if my wife and I don't have enough arguments about how much work she does and how little she gets in return, *you* had to print that information from some nutty home economics teacher who figured out that the average housewife is worth $8,000 a year on today's labor market. I'm willing to bet that ours was only one of a million fights you caused across the nation.

Has it ever occurred to you that for $8,000 a year a man could live in a beautiful apartment with maid service and not have to put up with a nagging broad, not to mention her miserable mother?

The American housewife has been glorified to the point where she thinks she's right up there with the vice president of General Motors. You make less sense all the time. I think you're getting rocks in your head, granny.

—No Fan of Yours

Dear Ann Landers: How do *you* know what my wife is worth as a housekeeper? Have you ever been inside our home?

I'd invite you over for a look, but I don't think you could get through the front door. Junk is piled to the ceiling—unopened barrels and crates she hasn't gotten to yet. (We moved into this place in November.) The Christmas tree is still up. She says she'll take it down when she has a free afternoon.

I can't say much about my wife's cooking because she hasn't cooked a meal in so long I can't remember it. The last time she did the laundry was in 1956 when she washed my wallet, which was in the pocket of my work pants. The wallet contained my paycheck and every important card and piece of paper I owned.

You may know a lot, Ann Landers, but you don't know what goes on in *our* house. So, please don't try to tell a man what his wife is worth unless you have met her.

—Up to Here

Dear Ann Landers: It's about time you came through for us women for a change. I have been reading your column for years, and you are so prejudiced in favor of men that I'm sure those pictures that run with your column are phony and you are really a man yourself. That estimate of $8,000 was low. I perform all the duties mentioned in that letter plus the following:

I hang wallpaper, repair furniture, serve as my husband's barber, psychiatrist and financial adviser. I interpret his dreams and read his horoscope. I referee the fights he has with his relatives. But the money is only part of it. Most men have such lousy dispositions they couldn't hire help to stay with them. Marriage is the only answer.

—Swampfire

Dear Ann Landers: I just read where some so-called authority has decided a housewife is worth $150 a week. I am a married man who earns only $135 a week. This means I cannot afford to keep this wonderful woman who sleeps until noon and has scorched every shirt I have ever owned. Thank you for making me realize that I don't deserve her. I'm kicking her out tomorrow.

—Stanley Greatheart

Dear Ann Landers: I have read some awfully good poems in your column over the years. Here's a "payback." It appeared in a little publication called "Time-Out" in Greenfield Park, Ohio—author unknown. Thanks for years of great reading.

—A Loyal Ann Fan

Dear Loyal: Thanks for a delightful addition to my column. I loved it and am sure my readers will, too.

Day Off

The dishes are all piled high in the sink.
The garbage pail is filled to overflowing.
The hamper is stuffed right up to the brink.
And the carpets all seem to need mowing.
The dust is as high as a chipmunk's chin.
The den's a disaster zone.
The upstairs smells like a hive of sin.
(Who dropped the eau de cologne?)
The bread box is empty, the ashtrays are full.
There's a gift from the cat in the hall.

The bathtub's a swamp, the kids all missed school.
And dinner, a hard frozen ball.
Yesterday's paper's all over the house.
(The dog decided to chew it.)
What does a housewife do all day long . . .
Today, I just didn't do it!

Dear Ann Landers: I got a laugh from your column that listed the three biggest lies ever told. They were "The check is in the mail," "This is my *last* cigarette," and "I'm from the government, and I'm here to help you."

A language researcher discovered that six of the most heartwarming statements in the English language are: "I love you." "Dinner is served." "All is forgiven." "You can sleep until noon." "Keep the change." "You've lost weight, haven't you?" It was my laugh for the day. Please print it. It may be someone else's.

—From Fresno

Dear Fresno: Laughter is good medicine—even when you aren't sick. Thanks for providing it.

Back in 1979, I wrote that the lyrics to some rock songs were crude and offensive. Here's a response for the younger set:

Dear Ann Landers: I'm really sorry you found that old song of mine crude and offensive. Actually, "Cold Ethyl" is just a harmless number about necrophilia.

The point I want to make is that the kids are not bothered by this—their parents are.

The kids see the song and gruesome antics, like with the guillotine, for exactly what it is—satire, done with a sense of humor to a rock and roll beat.

Kids know I am harmless. It's their parents that make me out to be some kind of a monster. I would like to see you print this in your column, Ann. Sincerely,

—Alice Cooper

Dear Alice Cooper: Thanks for writing.

For those who don't know what necrophilia is, it's sexual intercourse with someone who is dead. You can call it funny if you want to, Alice. I call it sick.

I like satire as much as the next person, but chopping off heads and spurting blood all over the place is not my idea of entertainment.

I caught your guillotine number in Chicago several years ago and almost lost my supper. (Guess I'm an uncool cat.)

You have in your group some exceptionally talented performers and you're no slouch yourself, Alice—I just wish you'd clean up your act.

Dear Ann Landers: During the Carter administration, I decided to collect peanuts as memorabilia of the president.

I have now nearly 350 pounds of peanuts from the Carter years. Since I didn't get started until some time after he became president, I have only 26 pounds of 1977 peanuts, but I have more than 100 pounds for each of the years 1978, 1979 and 1980.

My thought was that these peanuts would in time become very valuable to collectors on the lookout for interesting remembrances of past presidents. I have had little bags printed with President Carter's picture on them and the year of the peanuts.

Each bag holds approximately 2 ounces. For those who want something special, one of my neighbors has embroidered some lovely cloth bags with President Carter's full name and the date the peanuts were packaged.

Recently, the price of peanuts (and peanut butter) has skyrocketed. I could make a very nice profit on my peanuts if I sold them at today's prices. Frankly, I could use the money. However, I have really gotten attached to them.

Please tell me what to do.

—Collector in Modesto

Dear Mod: You have some novel mementos of an era that has passed. My advice is sell the peanuts while the price is still up there, take your profit and invest in jelly beans.

Some of the sweetest, most heartwarming letters I have printed have involved reuniting people through my column. I don't ordinarily use it for this purpose, but every so often, I can't resist. Here are four great stories:

Dear Ann Landers: The American flag is a beautiful symbol of everything we stand for.

My most memorable moment relating to our flag occurred on a Sunday morning, April 29, 1945, at Stalag VII-A, Moosburg, Germany, a POW camp where I was imprisoned along with 30,000 other Allies. (The camp was built to hold 3,000.)

We heard the deep rumble of diesel tanks approaching, but they were in the valley, and we couldn't see them. When the first tank poked its nose over the hill and the column of Gen. Patton's 3rd Army tanks made its way to the main gate of our prison camp, a huge roar went up that drowned out the sound of all those beautiful tanks. This was *freedom* coming up the road!

Shortly after our liberators arrived, a grimy, skinny but smiling GI shinnied up the flagpole by the main gate. He tore down the ugly swastika of Nazi Germany and replaced it with the glorious Stars and Stripes. It was a moment none of us will ever forget.

There were many hardened veterans in that camp. Some of them had been POWs for more than three years, but the tears rolled down their cheeks, and they were not ashamed to be seen crying. Being set free can do that to people when they have been behind barbed wire and don't know if they will ever see their families again.

Although all this took place more than 43 years ago, Ann, the memory of that morning is as clear as if it happened yesterday.
—B. McD. Jr., Lt. Col. USAF (Ret.), Irving, Texas

Dear Colonel: Thank you for jogging loose some thrilling memories for millions of readers. Those old war stories, even after 40 years, can still get the blood coursing through the old veins.

Dear Ann Landers: I was thrilled to see the letter in your column by Retired Lt. Col. B. McD. Jr. He recounted the events that took place Sunday morning, April 29, 1945, at Stalag VII-A in Moosburg, Germany, where he was a prisoner of war, along with 30,000 others.

The writer described his feelings when the first tank poked its nose over the hill and Gen. Patton's 3rd Army tanks made their way to the main gate of that prison camp. A huge roar went up from all of us who knew we were free at last! I was the American security officer at the front gate when that skinny GI shinnied up the flagpole, tore down the ugly German swastika and replaced it with the beautiful Stars and Stripes.

Capt. Dynamite Dunn commanded the tank company that took the camp. He was a fraternity brother (Kappa Alpha) from the University of Maryland, as were two other fellow officers, Lt. William A. Mac-Gregor and Lt. Page B. Pratt. We were taken to headquarters and given royal treatment. What a day!

An interesting aside: Gen. Patton's son-in-law, Col. Waters, U.S. Infantry, was also interned in Moosburg, and later in the day, he was reunited with the general, who made a rousing speech to the newly freed prisoners of war.

Thanks, Ann, for bringing back some memories of that fateful day 43 years ago.

—Robert L. Hartman, Charleston, W.Va.

Dear Robert Hartman: One of the most rewarding aspects of writing this column is providing the thread of humanity that binds us one to the other. I never know, when I print a letter, how many lives I will touch. When I receive feedback, such as the letter you wrote, it gives me a feeling of enormous satisfaction.

Space does not permit the printing of all the letters from "Moosburgers" who were on hand when Gen. Patton's 3rd Army came in and liberated the POWs, but here are two more.

Dear Ann Landers: When that great letter appeared from the lieutenant colonel from Irving, Texas, a whole host of memories flooded my mind.

I was 19 years old, a ball gunner on a B-17. We had been shot down just two months before, over Berlin, and considered ourselves darned lucky to be alive.

I was at Moosburg on April 29, 1945, when Gen. Patton and his men came rolling down the road. I will never forget the smiles on the faces of his courageous men as they rode into our camp. What a fabulous-looking guy Patton was with his ivory-handled pistols gleaming in the sun!

Thank you, Ann, for the best column ever.

—Robert L. Copelin, Lubbock, Texas

Dear Ann Landers: My husband was a POW at Stalag VII in Moosburg, Germany. Unfortunately, he didn't live to see Gen. Patton's 3rd Army come thundering down the road. My beloved husband died of tuberculosis just three months before. He wrote some wonderful letters that were sent to me, along with his medals and personal belongings after he died.

In one of his letters he said, "I hope to God this is the last war we will ever fight. It is such a cruel and senseless way to settle differences. I will never forget the face of a German lad I killed last week. He was handsome and young, somebody's son and maybe a husband and father—like me. War is hell."

—Nameless Please in Northern California

Four years later, this cropped up in my mailbox:

Dear Ann Landers: Four years ago, you printed several moving letters from American GIs who had been prisoners of war in Moosburg, Germany, during World War II. The letters described the feelings of the GIs as Gen. George Patton's 3rd Army tanks made their way to the main gate of that prison camp.

One of the letters was from an American security officer who was at the front gate "when that skinny GI climbed up the flagpole, tore down the ugly German swastika and replaced it with the beautiful Stars and Stripes." Well, Ann, that skinny GI was me.

I was the pilot of a B-26 bomber shot down over North Africa in January 1943. Before I was sent to Moosburg, I was in another POW camp, Stalag Luft III. In 1944, a large American flag was smuggled into the camp and brought to me for hiding. (I was a security officer.) We were supposed to put the flag on the ground in case the planes that we prayed would one day come to liberate us had trouble identifying the camp. I sewed the flag between two old German blankets and slept under it for the next year.

In early 1945, we were ordered to start walking east. Before we left camp, I grabbed my precious blankets and a small transmitter that had also been slipped into camp. Twenty thousand of us walked for nearly six days in the snow to Moosburg. It was rough, but I'm sure the Bataan death march was worse.

When Gen. Patton liberated us, my roommate and I went up to the German flag tower, took down their flag and proudly replaced it with the beautiful American flag I had kept hidden for so many months.

Sorry it took me so long to write, but I've been thinking about this for four years and decided it was time I let you know.

—Dr. Martin Allain, Shreveport, La.

Now that we've learned about shinnying up, *let's find out about falling* down. *Take a look at this letter from 1993:*

Dear Ann Landers: I was working on the Garrison Dam in Riverdale, N.D. At that time, it was the largest earth-filled dam in the world. I was working on top of a 130-foot surge tank when a crane hit me in the back with a cable, throwing me off the tank. I was headed for the concrete below, with no chance of survival, when a man by the name of Floyd Hartman grabbed me around the waist. He had his safety belt on and caught me as I passed by him.

I was taken to the hospital and didn't get a chance to thank him. That was his first and last day on that job, and I don't know where he went. So thank you, Floyd Hartman, for saving my life.
—Roger W. Daub, Center, N.D.

Dear Roger: What a terrific story! I hope Floyd Hartman sees this and writes. Or—if anyone knows where Floyd is, please send him this column and tell him I want to hear from him. He should write to me in care of the *Chicago Tribune.* I'll keep an eye peeled for his letter.

Fortunately, the story didn't end there.

Dear Readers: Remember the letter from Roger Daub?

Roger was working on top of a surge tank when a loose cable hit him in the back. He was headed for certain death when a man named Floyd Hartman caught him.

Roger never had a chance to thank Floyd. By the way, this incident occurred in 1960.

Well, guess what! I heard from Floyd's son, Dennis, immediately after that column appeared in the Birmingham, Ala., *Post-Herald.* His name, incidentally, is Hardiman, not Hartman. Floyd is now 74 years old and a member of the Warrior, Ala., Senior Citizen Center. He was thrilled at the opportunity to speak on the phone to the man whose life he saved 33 years ago.

Deborah Vance, a reporter for the *Birmingham Post-Herald,* interviewed Floyd Hardiman, and I received a copy of the story. Floyd said he remembered grabbing Roger around the waist with his legs. Floyd said if he had not been wearing his safety belt, he would not have been able to save Roger.

"Roger wasn't wearing one," said Floyd, "but thank God I was [or it would have come] down to where I was either going to have to let go or fall to my death with him." Roger said, "He saved my life. I just can't believe I found him. There's no one like him that would have done what he did."

And now, dear readers, writing seven columns a week is a piece of cake when you run into a story like this one. I was amazed at how much interest and concern this letter generated. Readers from all over the country wanted to help locate Floyd. A man in Plano, Texas, looked up every Floyd Hartman he could find and then wrote to them on my behalf. Several other readers sent me computerized lists of all the Floyd Hartmans in the U.S. telephone directories. A number of readers shared the following view:

Dear Ann: That incredible column about how Floyd Hartman grabbed Roger Daub in the middle of a fall while they were both working on a dam in North Dakota was a real thriller.

I'm sure you will get a lot of mail saying it's a bunch of baloney—that such a thing couldn't have happened. Let me tell you that I am a true believer, and there is not a doubt in my mind but that it did happen.

I believe Floyd was Roger's guardian angel. The clue was that line about Roger not being able to thank Floyd for saving his life because it was Floyd's first and last day on the job. I am convinced that some higher power sent Floyd for that one day to watch over Roger.

Most of your readers will think I am some kind of nut, but so many things occur for which there is no logical explanation, and this, dear Ann, is one of them.

—J.R. in Dallas

Dear J.R.: You are not alone in your belief that Floyd was Roger's guardian angel. I received several letters saying exactly the same thing.

So I say hooray! Let the banners wave! These days, when we read so much about man's inhumanity to man, it is reassuring to know something like this can happen. It gives us all hope.

Dear Ann Landers: I missed your first article on Roger Daub, who fell from the Garrison Dam, but I saw the second letter, and it brought back memories.

When I was a 20-year-old engineering student at the University of North Dakota, I got a summer job on the Garrison Dam. I worked as an inspector on the surge tanks, and one of my primary responsibilities was to see that the contractors followed safety standards such as wearing safety belts on the scaffolds.

I had been on the job only about a week when Roger Daub came tumbling down. After that happened, I changed my major from engineering to math. Nobody falls 150 feet in math.

—J.C.H., Dallas

Dear Dallas: I've had lots of comments on that incredible fall, but yours was the funniest.

——

Dear Ann Landers: When I first arrived in Vietnam in July 1968, I was a supply officer for an artillery battery. My clerk was an enlisted man.

His name was Kevin Howard Dugan. He was from Blue Point, N.Y. Kevin was extremely kind and helpful to this young, apprehensive first lieutenant. He was rather shy at first, but after a while, he opened up and was one of the friendliest and nicest guys I had ever met.

He was low-key, understated and extremely competent. Kevin never forgot a thing.

We were stationed at an isolated post, miles from the nearest city, and spent many long hours discussing New York, the Army and sports and, of course, talked endlessly about the meaning of life, death and war.

After 50 days, I was transferred to another artillery battery in a town 17 miles away. Three weeks later, Kevin was coming to pick up supplies, and we planned to get together. I waited. Kevin never showed up.

He was not a guy who would just fold out. I worried and thought about him a lot. I never heard from him again.

Last week as I stood in front of the Vietnam War Memorial in Washington, I prayed that Kevin's name would not be there, but of course, it was.

It is now 20 years later, and I want to let Kevin's parents know that their son is remembered by this lieutenant as a kind, loving young man who went out of his way to be helpful.

Everyone who worked with him respected his competence and willingness to do more than was expected.

Kevin would have made a terrific husband and father. What a shame that he never lived long enough to enhance the lives of so many people. His parents are aware of all this, of course, but I hope they will see my letter and get some pleasure out of knowing how much their son was admired and respected by all the men he served with.

Please, Ann, help me convey this message to Kevin's parents through your column. Thank you.

—Gil Noble, Vista, Calif.

Dear Gil: I called the Blue Point, N.Y., long-distance operator in search of a relative of Kevin Howard Dugan.

I spoke with several Dugans in that area. None was related to or knew Kevin Howard Dugan.

I hope someone out there will recognize the name and alert Kevin's parents to your kind letter.

If it happens, I'd love to know.

Someone did recognize the name, and what happened next kept Ma Bell busy.

Dear Readers: Gil Noble wrote to me after he had been to the Vietnam Memorial in Washington. His fears about what had become of his friend Kevin Dugan were confirmed when he saw Dugan's name.

He wanted to let Kevin's folks know that their son was one of the nicest guys he had ever met—competent, admired and respected by all the men he served with.

A great many people write and ask me to help locate sons, daughters, sweethearts, first-grade teachers and college roommates. I respectfully decline, explaining that this is not what the column is for.

But this request was different. Here was an officer who wanted to tell the parents of a soldier who was killed what a wonderful guy he was. I simply couldn't pass up the opportunity to bring some pleasure to a family that had suffered such a devastating loss.

I printed Lt. Gil Noble's letter and told him that I had phoned the long-distance operator and obtained the numbers of several Dugans in the area of Blue Point, N.Y., which Noble remembered as the young man's home, but none was related to nor did they know a Kevin Howard Dugan.

I had done my best and wished him luck.

The morning the column appeared in print, I was vacationing in Connecticut. My office phoned to tell me that Kevin's mother had read the column and was trying to reach me. She does indeed live in Blue

Point, N.Y., but had been widowed and remarried. Her name is now Mrs. Anne Dugan Brown.

In a wonderfully excited voice, Anne Brown told me that she was still in bed when phone calls about the column started to come in. Within half an hour she had heard from people in three states.

Anne and I spoke for a long time. She has a son, Terry, 10 years older than Kevin. Terry, like Kevin, is 6 foot 5, and both boys loved to play basketball. Anne also has three daughters, 14 grandchildren and two great-grands.

The missing link was Gil Noble. But not for long. Terry Dugan got Noble's phone number from information in Vista, Calif., and called him up. He ran into Gil Noble's answering machine.

Noble, now a business teacher, and his family were vacationing in Hawaii. But a neighbor of Gil's was checking the machine periodically and relaying the messages. Within hours Terry Dugan received a call from Noble. (Friends in Vista had seen the paper, and at least 20 excited pals had called to alert Noble to Ann Landers' column.)

What excitement! Noble also got Anne Brown's phone number and called her from Hawaii. Everyone was thrilled that the lieutenant had at long last located Kevin Dugan's mother. I confess that I was as thrilled as anybody.

What a privilege to have been able to brighten the life of this lovely woman whose handsome son had been cut down at such a tender age. And I made the lieutenant happy, too.

"He was walking on air," Anne told me. "We exchanged addresses and telephone numbers, and I'm sure we will get together one day."

Stories like this one validate the goodness of people. It proves what I have known for a very long time—that most folks are pretty darned OK, and if given the opportunity, they can be downright wonderful. What better evidence than this heartwarming story that came full circle after 20 years?

———

Dear Ann Landers: My wife and I adopted a child from St. Petersburg, Russia, last December. We went through an awful lot to get her, and the trip back and forth was emotionally and physically draining. Of course, it was well worth it, and we are immensely grateful for all the caring and support we have received from family and friends.

On the plane from Frankfurt, Germany, some lovely people moved so the three of us could sit together. Our child, who was not quite 4 years old, was extremely well behaved, but she became upset every time my wife left her seat. By the time the flight ended, half the plane knew our entire story.

When we landed in Atlanta, the lady sitting behind my wife leaned over and handed her a $20 bill. My wife asked, "What is this for?" The woman replied, "I just wanted this to be the first $20 bill your child ever had."

Ann, I would dearly love to get in touch with this woman and thank her and share some pictures of our child. The lady's name was Bea McGraw, but I never asked for her address or phone number. I'm not sure if she lived in Atlanta or was catching a connecting flight.

Maybe Bea will read this and get in touch with you. This was one of the nicest things I have ever experienced, and I would like to show Bea our gratitude. Thanks so much for helping us, Ann.

—Jim in St. Charles, Mo.

Dear Jim: I generally do not put people in touch with one another through the column, but your letter is such a sweet one, I am printing it, and it's up to Bea to take it from here if she chooses. You can be sure she will either read this or someone will tell her about it. Best of luck. (Bea, if you see this, please contact me at the *Chicago Tribune*.)

Dear Ann Landers: I am Bea McGraw, the woman who gave the $20 bill to the newly adopted Russian girl on the plane to Atlanta. I am a teacher for the Department of Defense Dependents School in Weisbaden, Germany.

You were right, Ann, when you said someone was sure to tell me about your column. I heard about it the day the column appeared. I had been out of the building most of the day, so I missed several calls. When I finished practicing with the German-American choir, a teacher friend told me my name was in *Stars and Stripes*, the newspaper for the Armed Forces. I said, "Yeah, right!" and laughed. She elaborated, "You are in Ann Landers' column, and I am not kidding."

I insisted that I had never written to you, but my friend asked, "Did you meet a lady on a plane who adopted a child from Russia?" I couldn't believe my ears. I bought the newspaper at once and read all the details.

Ann, that couple did such a good job with their little girl. By the time we arrived in Atlanta, most of us *did* know about that sweet family because whenever her mother needed to leave for the rest room, the baby would scream. She was otherwise very well behaved.

I wanted to express my appreciation to the adoptive parents for what they had done, but I had only a few seconds because the plane had landed and I needed to secure my luggage, go through customs and make my connecting flight. So I gave the little girl her first $20 bill.

I am planning to come to the United States soon and hope to arrange a visit and see for myself how that little girl is doing. Because of your column, I have received letters from all over the world. Friends I haven't seen in 20 years have written. Many people do good deeds every day and never get recognized. You will never know how many lives you touch, Ann. I am honored that someone remembered my moment of thoughtfulness.

—Bea McGraw, Weisbaden, Germany

Dear Bea: And now, because of this letter, you are going to hear from even more people. How nice! Your 15 minutes of fame is going to last a lot longer. Since your letter reached me, I've heard about your visit with that little girl's family. Watch for a follow-up soon.

Dear Readers: Remember "Jim in St. Charles"? He's the man who wrote looking for Bea McGraw, a woman he and his wife had met on a flight to Atlanta. Bea had given their newly adopted daughter a $20 bill. After Jim's letter appeared, Bea wrote to me and I printed her letter. She said she was making plans to come to Missouri and visit Jim and his family in St. Charles.

I'm happy to say that Jim and Bea connected, and here's what I received in the mail today:

Dear Ann Landers: Thank you so much for the wonderful experience you made possible by printing our letter. When I first wrote to you, all I wanted to do was thank the woman who had been so kind to us. With only her name to go on, I hoped that she or a friend might see your column.

This succeeded better than I could ever have imagined. Bea, a teacher in Frankfurt, Germany, heard from a multitude of friends all around the world, some of whom she hadn't seen in 20 years. She wrote you to say she was coming to see us. Two local TV stations and the *St. Louis Post-Dispatch* covered our reunion. We exchanged gifts, shared remembrances, had dinner and promised to stay in touch.

I am so glad that I was able to share with Bea the joy that I feel having adopted our little girl. Bea is as nice as she seemed when we first met her, and she told us this was the most exciting month of her life.

Please let your readers know that acts of kindness do count for something. They help to make this world a better place. And so do you, Ann.
— Jim, Charlotte and Valla Mielziner, St. Charles, Mo.

Dear Jim, Charlotte and Valla: That cheering you hear in the background is all those readers who were hoping you and Bea McGraw would reunite. And you did—in a great big way. I love stories with happy endings, and this certainly is one.

I was deeply moved when Ogden Nash selected my column as a subject for his verse. When I read of his death in May of 1971, I regretted that I never had the pleasure of meeting him. He was one of my favorites. The opening line of his poem is evidence that he understood what my column is all about, and it pleases me immensely:

But I Could Not Love Thee, Ann, So Much, Loved I Not Honore More
Ogden Nash

Some find the world in a grain of sand,
I in the correspondence of Ann Landers.
I eavesdrop unabashed as she spoons out her acerb sauce with
    even hand
On lachrymose geese and truculent ganders.
Her desk is positively formicating, which means swarming with
    moving beings,
Although I might well employ the other word that sounds like
    unto it.
Because her mail consists mostly of letters from those embittered
    ones
Who have discovered about illicit sex that often there are more
    headaches than fun to it.
A present-day Emma Lazarus, she cries, Give me your huddled
    problems,
The wretched refuse of your wrongs, unwrap for me your
    festering sores and stigmas;

Your poison is my meat,
Be it alcoholism, infidelity, frigidity, satyriasis, premarital
   pregnancy or borborygmus.
Yes, if anyone's Gordian love knot requires a blade more cutting
   than Alexander's,
Let them call on Ann Landers.
No pussy-footer she, no purveyor of admonitions soothing or
   polite;
It's tell the bum to jump in the lake, tell the old bag to go fly a
   kite.
If Anne of Cleves would have written to Ann Landers
I bet Henry would have thought twice before calling her the
   mare of Flanders.
From a human comedy as varied as Balzac's I choose for you one
   excerpt.
The ultimate in walls of poignant woe,
The plaint of a teenager who doubted the affection of her boy
   friend because the only compliment he ever paid her was
You sweat less than any fat girl I know.

And finally, here are my two most-requested recipes:

Best-Ever Lemon Pie

1 baked pie shell
1¼ cups sugar
6 tablespoons cornstarch
2 cups water
⅓ cup lemon juice
3 egg yolks
1½ teaspoons lemon extract
2 teaspoons vinegar
3 tablespoons butter

   Mix sugar and cornstarch together in top of double boiler. Add the
two cups of water. Combine egg yolks with juice and beat. Add to rest
of mixture. Cook until thick over boiling water for 25 minutes. This
does away with starchy taste. Now add lemon extract, butter and vinegar, and stir thoroughly. Pour into deep 9-inch pie shell and let cool.
Cover with meringue, and brown in oven.

Never-Fail Meringue

1 tablespoon cornstarch
2 tablespoons cold water
½ cup boiling water
3 egg whites
6 tablespoons sugar
1 teaspoon vanilla
pinch of salt

Blend cornstarch and cold water in a saucepan. Add boiling water and cook, stirring until clear and thickened. Let stand until *completely* cold. With electric beater at high speed, beat egg whites until foamy. Gradually add sugar, and beat until *stiff* but not dry. Turn mixer to low speed, add salt and vanilla. Gradually beat in cold cornstarch mixture. Turn mixer again to high speed and beat well. Spread meringue over cooled pie filling. Bake at 350 degrees for about 10 minutes.

Meat Loaf

2 pounds ground round steak
2 eggs
1½ cups bread crumbs
¾ cup ketchup
1 tsp. Accent
½ cup warm water
1 package Lipton's onion soup mix
8-ounce can Hunt's tomato sauce
2 strips bacon (optional)

Mix all ingredients together except tomato sauce and bacon. Put into loaf pan; cover with 2 strips bacon if you wish. Pour tomato sauce over all. Bake one hour at 350 degrees. Serves six.

Addictions: The Wrecking Ball of Love, Health and Careers

The human body responds in a variety of ways to what we put into it. Some of those ways are unhealthy and can even kill us.

I am not a drinker and never have been. I have often told my teenage readers that it's better not to take that very first drink than to try to quit when you're hooked. There are those who drink to drown their sorrows. Unfortunately, sorrow knows how to swim.

Dear Ann Landers: Please print the enclosed message that came in the mail anonymously. It was, I am sure, sent by someone who cared enough to let me know he was concerned about my drinking. I am taking the message to heart and hope others will, too.

—Received and Noted in Corning

Dear R. and N.: I like it. Here it is:

Positively Negative

We drank for joy and became miserable.
We drank for sociability and became argumentative.
We drank for sophistication and became obnoxious.
We drank for friendship and made enemies.
We drank for sleep and awakened exhausted.
We drank for strength and felt weak.
We drank to feel exhilaration and ended up depressed.

We drank for "medicinal purposes" and acquired health problems.

We drank to get calmed down and ended up with the shakes.

We drank for confidence and became afraid.

We drank to make conversation flow more easily, and the words came out slurred and incoherent.

We drank to diminish our problems and saw them multiply.

We drank to feel heavenly and ended up feeling like hell.

We drank to cope with life and invited death.

We now know that alcohol and drug addiction is the result of a chemical reaction in the body. Back in 1966, however, the jury was still out on the causes of addiction. Believe it or not, here's what I wrote back then:

Dear Ann Landers: Has it ever occurred to you that your advice may be getting a little moth-eaten?

You ought to re-examine your antiquated approach to alcohol and tone down your insistent lectures on the "evils" of drinking. Recent developments are making you look pretty stupid, Ann.

Just a few weeks ago, I read that a Harvard professor who is an authority on alcoholism believes that children should be taught to drink liquor at an early age. He claims that if children grow up to accept liquor as just another ordinary beverage and not a devil in a bottle, they will attach no special significance to liquor and their chances for developing an unhealthy craving for it will be greatly reduced.

I agree with the professor that the reason there are so many alcoholics around is because liquor was forbidden to them and they never learned how to handle it properly.

I hope you will be big enough to print this letter and your answer. If you can think of one.

—The New Look at Life

Dear New Look: I am well aware of the professor's theory, and I do have an opinion that has been reinforced by a distinguished Washington, D.C., psychiatrist—also Harvard-trained. I think *your* professor's theory is as sappy as a maple tree in April.

The professor recommended that children be taught to drink alcohol at an early age. According to him, a little sherry in the water for elementary school kids would be just dandy for openers.

Now, can't you just see a young mother sending her little tyke off to school, happy in the knowledge that her youngster is going to learn a great many things—including how to hold his liquor?

I do not buy the professor's basic assumption that *everybody* is going to drink so they should learn how early—real early. If this theory is correct, why not teach kindergarten kids to smoke cigarettes and use narcotics—sparingly, of course.

Your professor sets forth another premise that I believe is false—that liquor attracts and finally traps people because it is forbidden.

Excessive drinking is rarely traceable to the forbidden-fruit doctrine. A craving for alcohol is caused by a personality deficiency—a defect in the ego structure.

People who drink too much usually blame outside pressures. The truth is, they reach for the bottled anesthetic because they lack the inner resources to tolerate the pain.

I believe we should teach our youngsters the joy of achieving the rewards that come from meeting a challenge with courage and confidence. It is a crime against humanity to give a child a crutch when he has two perfectly good legs. This is the best way I know to produce a generation of cripples.

After studies done by some of the best authorities in the country, I came to agree with them that substance abuse has chemical underpinnings—that alcoholism is an illness, not a character flaw. Here is some information I hope will help those who need it:

Are You an Alcoholic?

1. Do you need a drink at a definite time every day?
2. Do you prefer to drink alone?
3. In the morning do you crave "the hair of the dog that bit you"?
4. Is your drinking hurting your family in any way?
5. Do you take a drink when you feel yourself getting the shakes?
6. Is your drinking damaging your reputation?
7. Do you lose time from work because of your drinking?
8. Has drinking made you inconsiderate of your family's welfare?
9. Have you, since drinking, become jealous or suspicious of your spouse?
10. Have your initiative and perseverance decreased?
11. Do you drink to relieve anxiety?

12. Has your drinking made you more sensitive?
13. Is it endangering your health?
14. Do you show marked moodiness as a result of your drinking?
15. Has your drinking made you harder to get along with?
16. Is it making your home life unhappy?
17. Is it jeopardizing your job or hurting your business or career?
18. Has it made you irritable?
19. Is drinking affecting your peace of mind?

If you can answer "no" to every one of these questions, and if a member of your family agrees that your answers are correct, your drinking is under control—at least for the present.

Every "yes" answer is a red light, which means there could be trouble ahead.

Dear Ann Landers: Since you seem to be an authority on the subject, will you please attempt to categorize the various degrees of intoxication? People need to know when they are slipping from one category to another.

—Huntsville, Ala.

Dear Hunt: I'm not sure it is possible to classify the various stages of intoxication, but I found a reference that might be helpful. It appeared in a periodical of the Office of Health Economics in England. Here it is:

1. Dizzy and delightful.
2. Drunk and disorderly.
3. Dead drunk.
4. Dead.

Dear Ann Landers: I first met her in high school. She was older than I, and exciting. She'd been around. My parents warned me to have nothing to do with her. They claimed no good could come from our relationship.

But I kept meeting her on the sly. She was so sophisticated and worldly. It made me feel grown up just being with her. It was fun to take her to a party in those days. She was almost always the center of attention.

We began seeing more of each other after I started college. When I got a place of my own, she was a frequent guest. It wasn't long before she moved in with me. It may have been common-law, but it was heart-breaking for my parents. I kept reminding myself I wasn't a kid any-more. Besides, it was legal.

We lived together right through college and into my early days in business. I seldom went anywhere without her, but I wasn't blind. I knew she was unfaithful to me. What's worse, I didn't care. As long as she was there for me when I needed her (and she always was), it didn't matter.

The longer we lived together, the more attached I became. But it wasn't mutual. She began to delight in making me look foolish in front of my friends. But still I couldn't give her up.

It became a love/hate relationship. I figured out that her glamour was nothing more than a cheap mask to hide her spite and cynicism. I could no longer see her beauty after I came to know her true character.

But old habits are hard to break. We had invested many years in each other. Even though my relationship with her made me lose a little re-spect for myself, she had become the center of my life. We didn't go anywhere. We didn't do anything. We didn't have friends over. It was just the two of us. I became deeply depressed and knew that she was re-sponsible for my misery. I finally told her I was leaving for good. It took a lot of guts, but I left.

I still see her around. She's as beautiful as when we met. I still miss her now and then. I'm not boasting when I say she'd take me back in a minute. But by the grace of God, I'll never take up with her again.

If you see her, give her my regards. I don't hate her. I just loved her too much.

Chances are you know her family. The name is Alcohol.

—Robert L. Rodgers, Waco, Texas

Dear Robert L. Rodgers: I have never met her personally, but a great many people who have been intimately involved with your old love have written to say she ruined their lives. She has no class and no character and is totally ruthless.

You didn't mention one of the main problems she creates. It's finan-cial. Almost everyone who becomes a victim of her charms ends up with money trouble. She's an expensive "hobby."

Nor did you mention what your companion of the past did to your health. Many of her close friends develop heart trouble, stomach prob-lems and cirrhosis of the liver.

I'm glad you had the strength to end the relationship. You didn't say whether you had help from Alcoholics Anonymous. Thousands of readers have told me it was the only way they could get out of her clutches.

Incidentally, I heard from a good source that she hated to lose you but she's not lonesome. She's on millions of guest lists around the country. In fact, they wouldn't dream of having a party without her! Funny that someone so evil and destructive continues to be so popular.

Dear Ann Landers: Another terrible accident occurred last weekend. My husband, a state trooper, was so sick when he came home, he had to go to bed. Please print the enclosed column again. Thank you.

—Ohio

Dear Ohio: There was a bad one in Illinois, too. Thanks for asking. Here it is:

How to Make a Trooper Cry

Want to see a state trooper cry? Would you like to see him bury his face in his hands, bawl like a baby and slam his fist into the side of his patrol car? It's easy.

Start by refusing to listen when your wife suggests that she drive.

Don't be a wimp. Assert yourself.

Say, "Aw heck, I can drive the car better with a few beers under my belt than you can cold sober."

Show her who's boss.

Twenty minutes later, you are standing in the dark on the side of the highway with broken glass and spilled gasoline all around.

Your wife is screaming, pinned beneath jagged edges of twisted metal.

Your 2-year-old daughter is silent.

Your 6-year-old son is sprawled face-down 30 feet away.

The highway trooper smelled the alcohol on your breath when you tried to explain, and he's not very gentle as he pushes you into the rear of the patrol car and tells you to shut your mouth.

Then he pauses for a moment to wipe away his tear before he turns his attention to what is left of your car and your family.

Congratulations. You've made a troo'   ry.

Dear Ann Landers: A few years ago, you published an essay that was very thought-provoking. It was called "The Quietest Room in Town" and was written in 1955 by Bill Kiley of the old *Los Angeles Mirror-News*. Would you please print it again?

—Northwestern U. Law Student

Dear N.U. Law: The essay you have requested made a powerful impression on my readers. I'm pleased to repeat it.

The Quietest Room in Town

They have been expecting you. They knew that eventually you'd show up. It won't be possible for you to know what is happening, so I'm going to take the liberty of filling you in.

The beginning for you will be when you stagger to your car. The beginning for them will be when a bulletin goes out on the police radio reporting the location of a serious accident with instructions to "proceed at once."

You won't hear the sirens. The ambulance and the police car will arrive together. They will check you over and pronounce you dead.

A few curious motorists who heard the crash will stop their cars and walk back to look at your broken, bloody body. Some of them will get sick.

The ambulance driver will roll out a leather-covered stretcher. The attendant will stuff your hands under your belt and grab you under the arms. The driver will take hold of your legs. You will be placed on the stretcher and covered with a blanket.

They will drive you to the coroner's office, where a deputy coroner will wheel you over to a big scale. He will remove the blanket, shake his head and say, "Another one."

Your clothes will be cut off with scissors. You will be weighed and measured. The deputy coroner will make a record of your injuries, cover you up again and wheel you to a small room with white tile walls. There are hoses in that room. Traffic victims are almost always a bloody mess.

You will be cleaned up (as much as possible) and moved to a long hall with several stretchers lined up against its pale green walls. In that hall are 41 crypts. If it has been a slow evening, you will have a stretcher and a crypt all to yourself. But if it's Christmas, New Year's or Memorial Day weekend, you may have lots of company.

They will go away and leave you there in the quietest room in town.

In an hour or so, they will come back and move you again. You will be placed behind a large glass window so your wife or your husband or your parents or a friend can identify you.

You won't see the agony and pain in their eyes, and it's just as well. Nor will you hear the screams and sobbing when they lower the sheet and ask, "Is this your husband . . . wife . . . son . . . daughter . . . brother . . . sister . . . friend?"

As I was saying, they are waiting for you—the police, the ambulance crews, the coroners at the morgue and the morticians. They are expecting you.

Remember this tonight, when you toss down that last drink and climb behind the steering wheel.

Dear Ann Landers: My beloved 17-year-old son was one of four young people killed in a drunken driving accident. Many teenagers are not able to make appropriate decisions regarding alcohol, so we must make the decisions for them. By not taking a stand, by doing nothing, we condone their drinking. False identification cards are easily obtainable. It is estimated that three-fourths of all high school students have them.

I need your help, Ann. My ideas are not unique, but they need to be re-emphasized. Here they are:

1. Set a curfew, and enforce it.
2. Seriously consider not allowing 16-year-olds to drive if they are not mature enough to accept adult responsibility.
3. Take the car keys away from your child indefinitely if he has been caught drinking.
4. Don't take responsibility for your child's actions by paying fines or trying to get him off. Part of becoming an adult is assuming responsibility for one's behavior.
5. Do not serve minors alcoholic beverages (pre-prom cocktail parties, etc.). It is against the law. When your child is going to a party, call up and make sure there will be adult supervision and no alcohol will be served.
6. Know how much beer, wine and hard liquor is in the house, and periodically check to see if any is missing. A locked bar is a good deterrent.
7. Check your child for alcohol breath when he (or she) comes home. Inform your teen that you will be waiting up to make sure "all is well."
8. If you leave your teenager home without adult supervision for an evening or a weekend, make it plain that there will be no parties

while you are gone. If you learn he cannot be trusted, get an adult to stay in the house in your absence.

9. Be alert for false identification cards in your child's possession.

10. Talk to other parents about problems and setting limits. You aren't the only one having these problems.

Thanks for your support, Ann.

—Lynne D. Pancoast, R.N., M.S.N.

Dear Lynne: Those are superb guidelines. May I add a suggestion? Teenagers *can* be alcoholics. If you suspect your child has this problem, contact the local chapter of Alcoholics Anonymous and ask if there is a group for teenagers. If not, ask what substance abuse center is available to help.

Dear Ann Landers: You printed a letter from an 18-year-old who drove home drunk and couldn't even remember it. When he sobered up, he vowed never to drive drunk again.

How fortunate he was to have had the chance to make that decision. Several years ago, I left a bar so drunk I had difficulty walking. On the way home, I rolled my car and broke my neck, severing my spinal cord. I'm thankful I was alone and didn't have any passengers. I'm also thankful that I didn't hit another car and murder a carload of innocent people.

I spent my 21st birthday in surgery. The surgeons took two inches of bone from my hip and fused it to a vertebra of my neck. My family spent the next six months visiting me at the rehabilitation center. I am now paralyzed from the neck down and am confined to an electric wheelchair. My fingers and legs will always be paralyzed no matter how much rehab I have. I am typing this letter with an adaptive device that helps hold my wrist and hand in place. On the end of the device is a wooden stick that I use as a finger.

For a very long time, I was depressed and miserable. Life had absolutely no meaning. It took several years before I quit planning my suicide. My life and the lives of all my family members have been changed beyond the average person's comprehension, and it happened in a split second. One minute I was healthy and whole, and then all of a sudden, I found myself confined for the rest of my life to a wheelchair—unable to shower myself, dress myself, curl my hair, put on my shoes, prepare a meal or hold my darling niece. And all this happened because I was drunk when I got behind that wheel.

The only advice I'm qualified to give is this: If you see a friend who is intoxicated, be a *real* friend and drive him or her home. That's the greatest gift you can give.

—D.S., Adel, Iowa

Dear Iowa: Your letter is powerful and moving. I'm sure you made a heavy impact on a great many readers today. Thank you for the time and effort it took to write this letter. Believe me, it was worth it.

For those parents with teen drivers, I hope you will look at this carefully and consider using it in your own home:

Dear Ann Landers: I am sending you a contract I have devised for parents of teenagers about to obtain their driver's license for the first time.

Parents can use this contract to help their children become better and safer drivers, not to mention the possibility of preventing injuries and saving a life. I hope you will print it.

—John Violette, Nederland, Texas

Dear John Violette: Thank you for sharing what appears to be a splendid idea. You have written a contract that sets forth clear, no-nonsense guidelines that are sure to give a teenager a good idea of what is expected of him or her. I urge all parents who have teenagers who are now driving or soon will be to clip this column, discuss it with their teens and get a signature.

Contract for Drivers

It is understood and agreed that having a driver's license and driving a motor vehicle are privileges. Any privilege has to be earned, and it must be earned on a continuing basis. This means that driving privileges may be revoked due to an infraction of the following rules:

1. Breaking the driving laws or abusing a motor vehicle can result in the loss of driving privileges, even if we learn about it from a source other than the police. You never know who may be observing you.
2. You will strive to maintain the grades, conduct and attitude at the same high level as when we first granted your driving privileges.
3. No one else should be allowed to drive a vehicle entrusted to you. This means you may not lend your vehicle to friends.

4. If you are ever in a condition that might render you less than 100 percent competent behind the wheel of a car, phone us. We will come get you. This will not result in the loss of driving privileges.

5. You are never to be a passenger in a car in which the driver should not be driving. A call to come get you will not result in the loss of driving privileges. If you cannot reach us, hire a taxi. We will pay for it, and there will be no punishment.

Signed this ____ day of _____, 19__
Dad _____ Mom _____
Newly Licensed Driver _____

Alcohol doesn't just affect the person who is drinking it. It can also affect a woman's unborn child. Studies show that babies born of alcoholic mothers have lower birth weight, more developmental problems and a harder time learning. Even a small amount of alcohol taken while the fetus is forming can have devastating effects.

Dear Ann Landers: My 23-year-old sister has been divorced for three years. She has been going with about four different guys and is pregnant. She is not sure who the father is and says she doesn't care because none of the guys she has been sleeping with is worth a hill of beans and she wouldn't marry any of them.

The problem is that "Tracy" thinks she is in good shape with her pregnancy because she has given up all drugs. She wants to keep the baby and is anxious that it be 100 percent healthy.

I am glad Tracy has given up drugs, but she has not stopped drinking. This worries me a lot because she's a heavy drinker. Can you put something in your column to educate women who drink while they are pregnant? We read plenty about babies born to crack- and cocaine-addicted mothers but very little about those born to alcoholic mothers. Thanks for your help.

—Her Sister in Topeka

Dear Topeka: I hope your sister will read this column and take it seriously.

In November of 1992, a 24-year-old woman was jailed in Waynesville, Mo., and charged with second-degree assault and child endangerment when her child was born intoxicated.

Every year, about 40,000 babies are born damaged because their mothers drank alcohol during pregnancy. Babies who are born with fetal alcohol syndrome have flattened facial features, their eyes are widely spaced and they have hooded eyelids. Almost all these children are learning-disabled and have varying degrees of mental retardation. They are usually small and short and remain that way throughout their lives.

I urge Tracy to make every effort to stop drinking at once. If she is unable to do it on her own, she should contact Alcoholics Anonymous. It's listed in the phone book and costs nothing to join. If she is not seeing a doctor, she should do so immediately. Good luck to her. She is going to need it. (P.S. You were a loving sister to write on her behalf. I hope she appreciates you.)

People abuse many substances besides alcohol. Here are some others:

Dear Ann Landers: You have given lots of advice to people who write to you about drugs. But you have never touched the main subject that hits me square on the nose. I am talking about the long-term effects of grass.

I am an 18-year-old pothead who is having some firsthand experience. I work in a restaurant on the 11-to-7 shift as a cook, or should I say *the* cook. (There is no manager, just the waitress and me.) I am in charge.

The waitress is also a pothead. Every night, we end up smoking about six joints each. There isn't a day that goes by that I'm not stoned out of my mind. Anyone who thinks the effects of pot are gone after the high wears off might as well hang it up. I really don't know how to say this, but pot affects your head permanently. I now have a severe mental blockage. I'm losing my memory, and it's frightening.

I said I'm a cook. Sometimes when I get an order while I'm stoned, I'll repeat the order and turn around to make it. Then, I'll forget what it was and have to go back and ask.

So, those of you who want to smoke pot or are just starting, ask yourself a few questions. Do you want to lose your memory in your teens and see it get worse every day?

Thanks for listening, Ann, and please keep on printing that terrific column.

—Been There and Still There

Dear Been: You mentioned the long-term effects of pot—well, here's the latest: There is growing evidence that pot does indeed interfere with the memory. Heavy pot smoking also can reduce the testosterone level in males and cause fertility problems. Females may also run into trouble when they want to have children.

Pot damages the lungs more than ordinary cigarettes and, as you pointed out, produces memory loss. Thanks for writing. I'm glad you remembered to mail the letter.

Dear Ann Landers: I am writing this from jail. Your column is the first thing I read every morning. I noticed at the end of one column a mention of your booklet, "The Lowdown on Dope." It started with these words, "Drugs are everywhere, they're easy to get, easy to use and even easier to get hooked on."

These words certainly have the ring of truth, but most people don't know how hooked they can get. I know because I got hooked on crack cocaine the first time I smoked it. I lost my job, I lost my new truck and I lost the respect of many people who loved me. The most painful loss was my fiancée.

More than once, I promised myself I would quit the craziness, and I did quit—for 24 hours. But I couldn't stay away from the stuff. Last January, I was arrested for selling cocaine. I've been in jail since then, and I haven't been sentenced yet. My lawyer says, "The courts are backed up with guys like you."

Will this nightmare ever end? Please let me tell your readers that crack kills. If you are thinking about trying it for kicks, don't. If you are using it, get some help. —Finally Woke Up in Bloomington, Ind.

Dear Bloomington: Your letter did more good than you will ever know. No one could have told your story more effectively.

Dear Ann Landers: I've been on Valium for 17 years, and for the last 7 years, I've wished I were dead. Please tell me how to get off this miserable stuff.

All these years, I've been what everybody wanted me to be instead of what I wanted to be. I can get down to ½ of a 5-milligram pill a day and function OK, but I still feel spaced out and not in control of myself. I think my family likes me better on Valium because I am easier to get along with and I don't make any demands on anyone.

I resisted taking Valium when the doctor first suggested it as a temporary relief for anxiety. The thought that I might not be in control of my behavior frightened me. I wish I had had the courage then to say no to the drug, which was supposed to help me get over a bad time.

Now, I feel completely burned out. I have no self-respect. No matter what I am asked to do, I do it. This damned Valium has made a zombie out of me. I am unable to express an opinion different from that of a friend or a relative. I do as I am told—like a robot. In other words, I am not me. I am the creation of a chemical that can be purchased in a pharmacy. It's a lousy feeling, and I hate it. Can I get off this stuff and be *me* again?

—Disgusted and Tired in Illinois

Dear Tired: You are unquestionably hooked on the stuff. What kind of a doctor would prescribe a tranquilizer for 17 years?!!! I am appalled!

People who know say it is harder to get off pills than booze. Contact a drug abuse center. (Look in the phone book—there are several.) It's a tough battle, but you *can* win it. Others have, and so can you.

Dear Ann Landers: I am writing to alert your readers to a relatively unknown but deadly problem in drug abuse among teens—inhalants.

Inhalants include hundreds of common household products like paint, aerosols, cleaning solvents and gasoline. Increasing numbers of adolescents and young teens are using these products for a cheap, quick high. A recent study by the University of Michigan shows that one in every five or six students in grades 8 through 12 has tried inhalants. Inhalants are particularly frightening because they produce serious health problems in a short period of time. Inhalants are poisons. They work directly on the heart, the nervous system and other vital organs. At best, an inhalant user has impaired coordination and faulty judgment. At worst, inhalants can kill by robbing the body of oxygen.

Parents should be alert to obvious signs like paint stains (especially gold or silver) on a child's hands or face, chemical odors on breath, clothing or rags, or the rapid disappearance of household aerosol or cleaning products. If inhalant use is suspected, parents should contact their local substance abuse or mental health program for help.

Inhalants are legal and easy to obtain. Parents should talk to their children about this *before* it becomes a problem. In spite of all we hear about outside influences, parents are still the biggest influence in the lives of young teens. Sincerely,

—Bob Kustra, lieutenant governor of Illinois

Dear Lt. Gov. Kustra: You have written a very important letter. Let us hope that parents all over the United States, Canada and wherever this column appears will pay attention.

Dear Ann Landers: A boy in my class died a week ago. It was not a natural death. It was an accident that shouldn't have happened. It occurred during lunch hour in the park across from our high school.

"Jason" had been at a friend's house. They were sniffing glue or lighter fluid, maybe both. On the way back to school, Jason kept blacking out. Finally, he fell and never got up. By the time we were able to get him to the hospital, it was too late.

I'm writing this letter to warn everyone who reads your column that sniffing anything from an aerosol can, correction fluid or any kind of solvent can produce brain damage or death.

If Jason had known how dangerous sniffing is, he never would have done it. I just hope that all his schoolmates who attended the funeral learned a lesson. As that dear, sweet boy lay in the satin-lined casket, he looked so innocent. I know he had no idea of what he was messing around with.

It seems such a shame that a young person should have to die to make people realize how dangerous drugs can be. Please print this letter as a warning to others.

—We'll Miss Him, Cleveland

Dear Cleveland: I hope your letter will make an impact on those folks out there who are sniffing stuff for a cheap high. They should know that the fumes can produce irreversible brain damage and, in some cases, death. And P.S. Kids who go in for sniffing almost always go on to harder drugs.

Dear Ann Landers: I am 15 years old, and I read your column in the *Boston Globe*. I have learned a lot from it. Not long ago, a parent asked about the dangers of allowing her children to inhale helium gas from the balloons given out at birthday parties.

I read in the paper that a guy died from inflating helium balloons in the back room of a restaurant. This 20-year-old was showing a 17-year-old girl how to fill the balloons with helium for her birthday party. They began to horse around, taking "hits" from the tank. After only the second hit, the guy fell to his knees and passed out. They tried to revive him using CPR, but he died a few minutes later of "massive pulmonary hemorrhaging."

I realize that people of all ages operate these tanks. I have seen kids my own age working in stores using them to inflate balloons. The common perception is that helium is fun and relatively safe. Obviously, this is not so. Maybe the helium in one balloon is harmless, but the compressed gas in the tanks can be deadly.

A local medical examiner reported to our daily newspaper that the 20-year-old guy literally "blew his lungs out." Everyone in my town was shocked by this tragedy. I hope people who use these machines at work and for parties will realize how dangerous they can be.

—S.C., Newburyport, Mass.

Dear Newburyport: The tragic incident you referred to was widely reported. I received several clippings.

The helium from a single party balloon poses little danger, but the tanks used to fill balloons should not be trifled with. This "sport" can be fatal.

One of the hardest addictions to beat is neither alcohol nor drugs. What could be tougher? Read on:

Dear Ann Landers: If the surgeon general wanted a really effective health warning on cigarettes, she would place the following messages on cigarette packs:

"Warning: Smoking can reduce the enjoyment and frequency of sexual activity."

"Warning: Smoking is a contributing factor to sexual impotence."

These are health risks associated with cigarette smoking. Most teenagers cannot relate to the word "cancer." They do, however, understand the word "sex."

—Kansas City Reader

Dear K.C.: Thanks for the suggestion.

Dear Ann Landers: My brother's wife, Olga, lights one cigarette off the other. I've seen her forget she has one going in the ashtray and then light another one.

My husband and I do not smoke. We find Olga's continual smoking a nuisance.

Last night, we were playing cards, and Olga was, as usual, smoking up a storm. I said, "Please blow it over there. I don't want your lung cancer." She replied, "Secondhand smoke is harmless. You're getting crotchety." I say a person does not need to inhale smoke to be harmed by it, and that being around smoke can be damaging. What do you say, Ann?
—Choking in Sioux Falls

Dear Choking: Never mind what I say. Here's what the Interstate Commerce Commission said in 1972 when it ruled that smokers must sit in the back of the bus: "Secondhand smoke is an extreme irritant to humans, particularly with respect to its effect upon eyes and breathing." Furthermore, Dr. D. M. Cousin of Paris at a recent European council on smoking said: "Non-smokers can inhale smoke equivalent to one pack if they spend a day in a smoke-filled room."

Here's what the Centers for Disease Control and Prevention have to say about secondhand smoke today:

Secondhand smoke has been classified by the U.S. Environmental Protection Agency as a known cause of lung cancer in humans.

Passive smoking is estimated by the EPA to cause approximately 3,000 lung cancer deaths in nonsmokers each year. Nonsmokers who live with smokers are more likely to develop lung cancer than other nonsmoking adults.

The developing lungs of young children are also affected by exposure to secondhand smoke. Infants and young children whose parents smoke are among the most seriously affected by exposure to secondhand smoke, being at increased risk of lower respiratory tract infections such as pneumonia and bronchitis. A baby who lives in a home where one or both parents smoke is more likely to have lung disease serious enough to need treatment in a hospital during the first two years of life.

Children exposed to secondhand smoke are also more likely to have reduced lung function and symptoms of respiratory irritation like coughing, excess phlegm and wheezing.

Passive smoking can lead to a buildup of fluid in the middle ear, the most common cause of hospitalization of children for an operation.

Asthmatic children are especially at risk. The EPA estimates that exposure to secondhand smoke increases the number of episodes and severity of symptoms in hundreds of thousands of asthmatic children. The EPA estimates that between 200,000 and 1,000,000 asthmatic children have their condition made worse by exposure to secondhand smoke. Passive smoking may also cause thousands of nonasthmatic children to develop asthma each year.

Exposure to secondhand smoke causes irritation of the eye, nose and throat.

Passive smoking can also irritate the lungs, leading to coughing, excess phlegm, chest discomfort and reduced lung function.

Secondhand smoke may affect the cardiovascular system, and some studies have linked exposure to secondhand smoke with the onset of chest pain.

Dear Ann Landers: Why is it that when the hazards of smoking are brought up, the only disease discussed is cancer? Why is it that no one ever brings up emphysema?

People who smoke cigarettes *will* get emphysema sooner or later. I am well acquainted with all the stages of this disease. My grandmother, who was otherwise a very healthy woman, died a slow and painful death from emphysema brought on by years of smoking. My stepfather will die the same way. He is now tethered to an oxygen tank that is his constant companion. It is the only way he can keep his windpipe open.

My mother, who is also a smoker, is in the early stages of emphysema. She has a terrible cough that gets worse every year. Younger people who smoke boast that they can jog several miles and never get short of breath. They don't understand that the cells in their lungs are mutating. For my sake and theirs, will you please print another letter on this subject?

—Alaska

Dear Alaska: It is not necessarily true that *all* smokers will develop emphysema. Not enough studies have been done to confirm this.

The surgeon general classifies bronchitis and emphysema together as Chronic Obstructive Pulmonary Disease (C.O.P.D.). Before smoking became common, these were rare diseases. Now C.O.P.D. is the fourth-ranking cause of death in the United States.

According to the American Lung Association, smoking is responsible for 82 percent of the C.O.P.D. deaths in the United States. (The remaining 18 percent are caused by air pollution, environmental factors such as dust and asbestos and a rare hereditary condition.)

The message is clear and irrefutable. Smoking is a crippler and a killer.

My family has not been exempt from this problem. Here's a column from September 1976.

Dear Readers: Please forgive this personal reference, but I must share with you, my millions of friends, what is on my mind and in my heart.

A few weeks ago, our family gathered in Omaha to bury one of the dearest, most gentle people I have ever known. He was David Brodkey, married for 43 years to our eldest sister, Helen.

Dave was a delight. We adored him. He was meticulous about detail, the perfect choice to take charge of any family project. Dependable. Industrious. Thorough. "Integrity" was his middle name.

Dave cherished Helen, and well he might. She was a devoted wife, the beauty of the family, a talented pianist, a superb cook and a leader in community affairs.

But Dave, the Perfectionist, the man who did everything right, did *one* thing wrong. He smoked at least two packs of cigarettes every day for 30 years. This senseless addiction deprived him of the joy of seeing his grandchildren marry. And it will deny those who loved him the pleasure of his beautiful presence.

So often I have heard smokers say, "Well, you have to die from something." True. But please, friends, if you can help it, die from something else, and don't rush the event. Lung cancer is a horrible way to go. While non-smokers, too, die from lung cancer, the evidence is irrefutable that cigarette smoking does cause lung cancer. The more we study it, the more certain we become. Smokers are the leading candidates for this dreaded disease and heart trouble and emphysema as well.

One out of every four Americans alive today will have some form of cancer during his lifetime. One out of six people who get cancer will die from it unless, of course, we learn more about how to prevent this scourge and how to cure it.

The economic cost of cancer in our country is $20 billion a year, to say nothing of the agony and suffering. The life of every person who reads this column has been touched in some way by cancer. It is the second biggest killer in the United States.

Almost the last words Dave uttered to his wife were these: "I should have listened to you years ago when you begged me to stop smoking." But like so many others, Dave believed cancer happens to other people.

And now, all you wives who are nagging your husbands and all you husbands who are pleading with your wives to throw away those filthy killers and all you young people who are turning your healthy pink lungs into tar pits at 65 cents a pack, for God's sake, for the sake of those who love you, *stop smoking today.* Do it for yourself. Do it for the people who care about you.

We *can* conquer cancer in our lifetime if enough people will join hands in this effort. Thank you so much and God bless.

—Ann Landers

Addictions are not necessarily chemical. If you see yourself or someone you love in the next letter, please call Gamblers Anonymous:

Dear Ann Landers: I once heard you say that gambling is just as much a disease as alcoholism.

I think my husband has the illness. He keeps denying it, although I haven't seen his paycheck for seven weeks. (It's a good thing I have a job.) What are the symptoms of a compulsive gambler? How does one tell?

—Wish I Knew for Sure

Dear Wish: Gamblers Anonymous, an extremely effective organization that operates along the same lines as AA, has prepared these 20 questions. If you answer yes to more than seven, your husband is a compulsive gambler.

Here they are—and please keep in mind that women can have the sickness, too.

1. Does he lose time from work because of gambling?
2. Is gambling making his home life unhappy?
3. Is gambling affecting his reputation?

4. Has he ever felt remorse after gambling?
5. Does he ever gamble to get money with which to pay debts or to otherwise solve financial difficulties?
6. Does gambling cause a decrease in ambition or efficiency?
7. After losing, does he feel he must return as soon as possible and win back his losses?
8. After a win, does he have a strong urge to return and win more?
9. Does he often gamble until the last dollar is gone?
10. Does he ever borrow to finance gambling?
11. Has he ever sold any personal property to finance gambling?
12. Is he reluctant to use "gambling money" for normal expenditures?
13. Does gambling make him careless of the family welfare?
14. Does he ever gamble longer than planned?
15. Does he ever gamble to escape anxiety or personal problems?
16. Has he ever committed, or considered committing, an illegal act to finance gambling?
17. Does gambling cause him to have difficulty in sleeping?
18. Do arguments, disappointments or frustrations create an urge to gamble?
19. Does he have an urge to celebrate any good fortune by a few hours of gambling?
20. Has he ever considered self-destruction as a result of gambling?

Most loved ones of compulsive gamblers will answer yes to seven or more of these questions.

For more information, contact:

Alcoholics Anonymous World Services, Inc.
General Service Office
475 Riverside Dr.
11th Floor
New York, NY 10115
(212) 870-3400

Al-Anon Family Groups (for family members affected by alcoholism)
1600 Corporate Landing Parkway
Virginia Beach, VA 23456
(800) 356-9996

Narcotics Anonymous
P.O. Box 9999
Van Nuys, CA 91409
(818) 773-9999

Gamblers Anonymous
P.O. Box 17173
Los Angeles, CA 90017
(213) 386-8789

Parents who want more information on inhalants can call the National Inhalant Prevention Coalition at 1-800-269-4237.

We have to eat to live, but for some of us, eating is not so simple. For those with eating disorders such as anorexia, bulimia or gross overeating, food can be life-threatening:

Dear Ann Landers: I am a nurse who saw a 37-year-old woman die today. She left three young children. That woman didn't have to die. She starved herself to death. They call it anorexia nervosa.

The poor dear weighed 60 pounds. Her body was just a skeleton, but she had the most beautiful eyes I have ever seen. I saw pictures of her when she was 25 and she was truly gorgeous.

I first heard of anorexia in your column. Please continue to tell your readers how dangerous it is to starve, just to be thin. Keep telling them that this insidious practice can turn into a compulsion—a mental illness—and the result can be death.

—Sad in Sandusky

Dear Sad: I've been harping on this subject for ages, urging everyone who suspects she is a candidate to get professional help at once. The same for bulimia—binging and vomiting. Both illnesses can be life-threatening.

Dear Ann Landers: When I was in high school I was fat and miserable. Staying on a diet was impossible and I hated myself.

I read in your column about a girl who had the habit of gorging herself and then throwing up. You told her it was dangerous and to stop it before she ran into serious physical and emotional problems.

I decided I was smarter than you and that it was a neat way to take off weight and stay thin. Since that time I have been forcing myself to throw up three or four times a week. That was 10 years ago. I am still not thin but I have done some awful things to myself. Please let me use your column to warn anyone who may be tempted to try it.

After throwing up, I feel physically exhausted. My skin becomes blotched and greenish in color. My eyes hurt and I get sores around my mouth.

As the years go by it is harder and harder to make myself throw up. When I was 16 I used my finger. Now I use all sorts of instruments and have to stick them farther down my throat. Sometimes it takes me an hour or more to vomit.

I am trapped in this behavior and am so embarrassed I haven't been able to ask for help. It's horrible, just like drug addiction or alcoholism, because it controls me. The more I do it, the worse I feel and the more I want to do it again. I know it's crazy, but aren't all addictions?

Can you tell me more about the damage I am doing to my eyes, ears, stomach, skin and glands in my throat? It might help me stop. Thank you.

—Having a Devil of a Time in Denver

Dear Denver: Telling you more about the damage you are doing to your body will not help you stop. You are trapped in a compulsive pattern of behavior and common sense won't work.

You need the help of a trained professional, and I urge you to get it at once. Look in the phone book under "mental health." Denver has some excellent facilities. You can get counseling for little money or maybe without charge.

Dear Ann Landers: I wonder if you fully realize how women are being sabotaged by the advertising establishment, which tells us we are nothing unless our bodies are perfect.

We are living in a society in which women are being brainwashed to feel imperfect. And why? Because it's a booming business. Americans spend $33 billion a year on the diet industry.

Women have chosen to place importance on their weight and looks because they have been taught that if they look better, they will be more lovable and have more fun.

I was bulimic. After seeing a very good counselor, I realized that I'd chosen to give an insane amount of power to those extra 10 pounds on my body. I know now that my life and my problems are the same whether I'm 10 pounds overweight or 10 pounds underweight.

I bought into the myth that said my life would be better if I weighed less, and I purchased all the diet "products." Well, I choose differently now. I hope that the millions of women with eating disorders stop to realize that they do have a choice.

—C.C., Littleton, Colo.

Dear Littleton: You've written one of the most sensible letters on the subject of weight that I have read in a very long time. Thank you for this wonderfully sane and convincing contribution to my readers.

Dear Ann Landers: I recently attended my niece's ninth birthday party, along with 16 of her classmates. The boys were talking about school and vacation plans and telling jokes. The girls were having a heated discussion on who was "fat" and who was "skinny." They discussed diets and were critical of the girls with weight problems.

I was so disgusted I left the room. I wanted to tell those girls that it's what's inside a person that counts, but I realized there was no way to undo in a few sentences what our culture has done to them since the day they were born.

When will the media and other powerful elements in our society stop insisting that thinness is ideal? Why are women judged by what they weigh while men are judged by what they accomplish and how much money they make?

It is estimated that one out of five female college students suffers from an eating disorder. I do not want my niece or any other young girl to become a statistic. Female students with eating disorders cannot concentrate on schoolwork. Working women with eating disorders cannot concentrate on their jobs. The equality women have fought for won't mean a thing if there are no healthy women around to enjoy it.

These young girls learn from television to emulate supermodels who weigh, on average, 23 percent less than a normal American woman. My 9-year-old niece is not interested in boys. She is trying to be thin because society has taught her that she will not be accepted any other way.

Please address this issue, Ann.

—Concerned Aunt in N.J.

Dear N.J. Aunt: I share your concern that it is unhealthy for a 9-year-old to be so preoccupied with her weight. The current mania to be thin, thin, thin has affected females of all ages.

The only way to lose weight and keep it off is by changing eating habits and incorporating exercise into the daily routine—permanently. Young, healthy girls should not be dieting. If they exercise regularly and eat well-balanced, nutritious meals, that should be sufficient.

I see no realistic solution to this problem, since the obsession to be pencil-thin is inherent in our culture. How unfortunate.

Dear Ann Landers: I have seen many TV talk shows where over-weight people have been guests. On one show, a woman said, "It's my business how much I weigh." These are the people I want to address.

Our oldest son had a weight problem most of his life. We tried everything to encourage him to lose weight. Repeatedly he said, "It's my life. I'll do what I want with it." Well, Ann, he did exactly that and died at age 33, weighing 560 pounds.

He went into the hospital with what everyone thought was a severe case of the flu. A few days later he developed symptoms of hepatitis, but according to the tests he did not have this illness.

The doctors couldn't take X rays because the table wouldn't support anyone who weighed more than 300 pounds. They couldn't do a body scan because he wouldn't fit in the machine. They couldn't do a spinal tap because the nurses were unable to roll him over.

Eight people were required to give him a sponge bath—two to hold the bed down so it wouldn't tip over. He was in the hospital less than a month when he died of congestive heart failure and liver and kidney problems.

No one should ever experience the helplessness of watching a loved one die because it was "his life to do with as he pleased." I know this pain after watching my son die from overeating. How tragic that all the medical knowledge available couldn't save him.

—P.L.W., Colton, Calif.

Dear Colton: This was more than a medical problem—it was a psychological problem. It wasn't so much what your son was eating, but what was eating him. I'm sure you did your best, dear. Some people are beyond help and nothing can save them. My condolences.

For more information, contact:

National Association of Anorexia Nervosa and Associated Disorders
P.O. Box 7
Highland Park, IL 60035
(847) 831-3438

Weight Watchers
(800) 228-2315

Overeaters Anonymous World Service Office
P.O. Box 44020
Rio Rancho, NM 87174-4020
(505) 891-2664

9

The Nightmare of Physical Abuse and Rape

Abuse comes in many forms—and my readers have told me about all of them. I've heard from battered wives, abused children, mistreated parents, and injured husbands. There is now a domestic violence hotline that's open 24 hours: (800) 799-SAFE; TDD: (800) 789-3224.

I have taken a strong stand against all types of spousal abuse ever since my column began. Take a look at these letters, some of which are thirty years old but sound as if they could have been written yesterday.

Dear Ann Landers: What is so terrible about slugging a woman if she darned well deserves it? This United States of America is the only country in the world where the practice is frowned upon. As a result, our women are the most spoiled and certainly the laziest in the world.

As for the pain of a slap, it is nothing compared with the suffering a man must endure from the razor-sharp tongue of an enraged female. In the heat of battle, one sure way of ending the discussion is to give the offending party a sound crack across the mouth.

This is why a policeman carries a gun and why we need an H bomb. We never want to use it, and hope we never need to, but it's a good thing to let the opposition know it's there—just in case.

—Michael S.

Dear Michael: Let's get out the whips and really live, eh? Your reasoning is so filled with fishhooks and booby traps that I won't attempt to straighten you out. If your technique for ending a discussion is to crack the offending party across the mouth, you are doomed to have a wretched life and a lonesome one. Please read the following letter for a fresh approach to the subject:

Dear Ann: I wonder if a man who strikes his wife can imagine what this does to their children. I was a child who lived in fear that my parents would kill each other so I know what I'm talking about. Every night I used to lie in bed shivering with fright. I listened to their angry voices and waited for that awful moment when the first blow would be struck. I used to pray for their lives, my young mind visualizing death as the only force that would put an end to the fighting and screaming.

Often I would creep out of bed, hoping the sight of me would stop the fighting but it never did. I call it a "fight" but it was, in reality, a man beating his wife. My father was a heavy drinker and had a violent temper. I would hear him curse my mother and throw things. Then the sound of crashing objects and her moaning was almost too much to bear.

I pity any man who thinks he's powerful because he can slap his wife around. These men are little boys who never grew up.

I know I am stating this badly but as I write my hand is shaking and my stomach is churning. Remembering makes me literally sick. But please, Ann, fix this letter up in your own nice words like an educated person, so it will be fit to print. For the love of God, let these people know what they do to their children if they have no respect for themselves.

—A Friend

Dozens of male readers thought my disapproval of wife beating was ridiculous. Surprised? So was I. One male wrote, "Ever since women got the vote in this country, they've been crowding men out of jobs and denying them their rightful place as head of the house." But I refused to back down. In the early sixties, women needed as much support as they could get. Here's a letter that will make your hair stand on end:

Dear Ann Landers: You are all wet about wife-spanking. I've been spanking my wife for 10 years and I'm no bully.

I adore the little woman and would never strike her in the face, or cheat on her the way some so-called wonderful husbands cheat on their wives.

Women are not as smart as men and they need guidance. A female who is left to her own devices has a tendency to develop some mighty undesirable traits. A good hard spanking when she needs it is the most effective method of correcting small faults before they turn into serious ones.

I know couples who argue for hours and nothing is ever settled. Long, drawn-out verbal battles can be nerve-wracking and time-consuming. Nothing clears the air like turning a wife over your knee and giving her a good sound paddling. If more men tried it there would be fewer divorces in this country.

—The Boss

Dear Boss: If more men tried it there would be fewer *men* in this country. Not *all* women are lame-brained, lily-livered jellyfish like the pitiful creature you married.

Just where does spanking end and beating begin? And who is to decide if she "needs it"? A husband who would spank his wife places her in the category of a child. A wife who would tolerate such indignity admits she's an adolescent who longs to be punished by "Papa" (poor thing). Such a woman should never have married. She should have stayed at home and played with her dolls.

Here and there you'll find a wife who won't stand for the 3-year-old child treatment. The husband who attempts to "guide" her with a paddle may get a little guidance himself—in the form of a healthy klop in the chops.

Dear Ann Landers: Please excuse the mistakes in this letter. I can't see very well. I have two black eyes and a broken nose, which is why I'm writing.

My husband hits me a lot, but it's always an accident. Usually it happens when Mike is helping me, like a good husband. This last thing was the worst. We were putting away the week's groceries. Mike was standing on a ladder and I was handing him the canned goods. A canned ham fell on my face. The bleeding wouldn't stop, so Mike drove me to the hospital. The doctor said my nose was broken.

Two months ago Mike was mopping the floors. He forgot to tell me the bucket was behind me. I stepped in it, fell and broke three ribs. A week before that, Mike was vacuuming the living room. His elbow caught me in the mouth and I lost a front tooth.

A friend who teaches psychology told me Freud said there are no accidents. What she means is Mike does these things on purpose. Is this possible? I think she is jealous because I have such a nice husband and she is 33 and still teaching school. Please comment.

—Riverside

Dear Riv: It's interesting that all the accidents occur when Mike is performing domestic chores. It might be that subconsciously he resents doing housework. So why don't you excuse him in the future or hire a cleaning lady one day a week? It would be cheaper than the doctor bills.

Women are not the only ones caught in destructive relationships. Men, too, have been abused, and they are more reluctant to seek help because they are embarrassed or ashamed. Our culture has only recently begun to recognize these battered men and provide support. Life for them can be hell. See for yourself:

Dear Ann Landers: You've said that a man who hits his wife is the lowest type of animal. Now—what about a woman who hits her husband? What kind of an animal is she?

I'm married to an active volcano. When she loses her temper (which is often) she hauls off and slaps my face, punches me, kicks me in the leg or throws dishes. We've been married almost three years and I don't know how much more of this I can take. I've never hit a woman in my life but I'm beginning to think maybe it's about time I did. May I have your advice?

—Black and Blue

Dear Blue: A husband who belts his wife in retaliation reduces himself to her primitive level. My advice to a husband who gets hit is to leave the house for several hours. If this doesn't cure your wife, stay away for several days or indefinitely. No man should have to duck crockery or wear a crash helmet in his own home.

Dear Ann: About every three months my wife (we've been married six years) goes off her rocker and picks a fight with me so she can bounce some glassware off my head or kick my shins black and blue. We had a real go-round last night, and she hit me in the mouth and cut my lip with her ring. (The diamond I gave her when we were engaged.)

I don't drink, gamble or run around. The reason she goes off half-nuts is because I like to read or watch TV after dinner, and she thinks I should be talking to her instead.

I do talk to her a lot, but I don't care to spend three or four hours at it, especially when there's football or hockey on the tube. What's the solution?

—Idaho Woe

Dear Woe: Your wife needs counseling. Her behavior is immature and childish. She needs to learn how to get rid of her frustrations and aggressions in a civilized manner. I hope she follows through before you get fed up and leave. No man should have to put up with physical abuse.

My position on spousal abuse has been unequivocal since I started writing the column, but I cannot say the same about spanking children.

Back in 1955, parents followed the admonition "spare the rod, spoil the child." Although I never condoned physical abuse, I felt, as did most parents then, that an occasional swat on the behind was simply good discipline.

I have since revised my views. Some parents don't know their own strength, and, too often, spanking leads to beating. It is not necessary to hit a child to get a point across. In fact, studies have shown that children who are abused often grow up to abuse others.

But in the early sixties, my opinion was less enlightened. Can you believe the following words came out of my typewriter?

Dear Ann Landers: You did millions of young Americans an injustice when you pontificated in a recent column that children should not be spanked.

As a retired general in the U.S. Army, I have had vast experience with young men. We could tell within a week which boys had been raised with discipline.

A strap, when folded, soundly applied to the posterior and thighs, never did a child any harm.

Many a volunteer is alive today because of the discipline instilled in him not by the Army, Navy or the Marines, but by a stern parent.

I hope no one will take your advice and spare the rod, Ann. The next generation has enough trouble in store without being a pack of spoiled brats to boot.

—Retired General

Dear R.G.: How did a man who can't read acquire your rank?

I clearly stated that I am not opposed to spanking but I take sharp issue with you when you advocate the use of a "folded" belt. No child should receive a blow harder than the human hand can deliver—and nature supplied the ideal spot. OK, General, two days of KP for you—and don't leave the base for 48 hours.

Child abuse cuts across all class lines. It is heart-wrenching to read these letters. Fortunately, there are many organizations that will provide support and assistance, and I never miss an opportunity to recommend them. Here's a letter from 1963:

Dear Ann Landers: I'm so upset I don't know where to turn. My mother who lives 22 miles from here had a stroke. I've had to spend a lot of time relieving my older sister who is trying to care for her.

When I go to my mother's my husband takes care of our 17-month-old daughter. Three weeks ago when I came home, I found a note saying my husband had taken the baby to the hospital. She had fallen out of her high chair. Fortunately no bones were broken.

Last night I found a similar note. This time, the baby suffered a broken arm.

When I went to the hospital this morning the doctor questioned me at length. It seems this is the fourth time in a year our child has been brought in. (I didn't know about the other two times.) The doctor suspects my husband has been beating the baby.

Can this be possible? If it's true what can I do? Please help me—I am a nervous wreck.

—Edna

Dear Edna: A University of Colorado team investigated the "battered child syndrome" recently and found 302 cases in a single year. The parents usually deny beating the child. The high chair excuse is the most popular.

A parent who would beat a youngster is deeply disturbed emotionally and the child should be protected against such brutality. Keep your eyes wide open and if there is further evidence, by all means get this man out of your home and into treatment.

This letter touched the hearts of my readers:

Dear Ann Landers: As I write this my little boy is lying on the couch under an icebag. His face is as red as a beet and the skin is broken in a few places where I slapped him.

When he gets stubborn or has a tantrum, I become so angry I can't control myself. I have hit him like this several times before, even though I know it is wrong.

I read your column every day and have read your advice to look in the phone book under child abuse. I looked and there is nothing in this town (population 3,000).

When this boy was born four years ago, I really didn't want him but my husband was crazy about children and insisted that I have a family. I have always hated this kid, which is a terrible thing for a mother to admit, but it is true. His daddy died two years ago and, thank God, I don't have any other children. I am a rotten mother.

Many times I have thought of giving up the boy for adoption. I know there are many couples who would love to have him. He is very smart for his age and darling-looking.

But just when I get ready to put my hand on the phone, I tell myself, "Don't do it. Keep him and learn to be a good mother."

I live 1,500 miles away from my own family. I have a good job and work 50 hours a week.

Please tell me what to do.

—Telling It Like It Is in Kansas

Dear Telling It: My heart aches for that little boy on the couch. And for you, too. I know the guilt must be killing you.

You *must* get help at once. Call Parents Anonymous immediately at (909) 621-6184. They may be able to give you a local number to contact in your area.

The morning that letter appeared in print, the phone in my office began to ring at 8:30 A.M. By noon we had received calls from all over the country. Five phones were going at once. My secretaries lost count of the number of callers who pleaded, "We'll take that little boy. Just tell us where he is."

One woman in Pennsylvania said, "Our children are 2 and 3, and there's another one on the way, but I can't bear to think of that little one being abused. We'll pay his airfare no matter where he is. Please send him to us."

Readers phoned their local newspapers and learned where my syndicate was located. They called and asked how to contact the mother of the abused child.

The mail poured in from all over the United States and Canada. Hundreds of readers were eager to open their hearts and their homes to the boy.

I had to tell them all that the mother's letter was anonymous. She gave us no name or address, and asked that we not try to track her down. The best I could do was beg her to contact an organization that was there to help her learn how to handle her hostility and be a better mother.

But I wanted to let you know there is a staggering number of beautiful, caring people in this world. They don't make headlines because being decent and generous and warmhearted isn't news. But it's a wonderful feeling to know they exist. A million thanks to those who offered to take that little boy. I love you all and God bless.

Sometimes parents do everything right, but things still go wrong:

Dear Ann Landers: This morning I witnessed an unusual case of child abuse. It broke my heart.

I was seated in the reception room, waiting for the doctor, when I noticed a rather young woman engrossed in a magazine. A little boy, about 9 months old, was on the floor beside her. He was such an adorable child with the sweetest smile I'd ever seen. I was captivated at once. Children know when they are appreciated, and this wee one crept over to me and held out his little hands—asking me in his own way to pick him up. I did.

I observed his hand-knit suit—very expensive to be sure—and little stockings to match. Then, I saw the Pablum dried on his sweet face, from ear to ear, and dirt under his tiny fingernails. At the same moment I felt a dampness on my lap. His diaper needed changing.

I carried him to the young woman and said, "Your little boy needs to be changed." She looked up at me, annoyed because I had interrupted her reading, and snapped, "He's *not* mine. I'm the sitter." With that she took a bottle out of her bag, put it on the floor and the child had to crawl about two feet to get it. When the baby finished the bottle, he began to cry. The young woman told him to "shut up," threw a blanket over him and continued to read.

I was just about to take him on my lap when she swooped the youngster up and said in a loud voice, "The heck with this. My appointment was 15 minutes ago. . . ." She left, carrying the baby on her hip into the 40-degree weather without a cap or a coat.

I wonder what the child's mother would have thought had she witnessed that scene.

· How can a mother leave her precious baby with someone so uncaring and callous? Is a second car, or a home in the suburbs, *that* important? Or, if she really must work, surely she can find a better-qualified person to care for her precious baby.

A thoughtful inquiry would certainly turn up a good day-care center.

And then we wonder, 10 years later, why our children have so many problems. Have we offered them a start in life that makes them feel loved and wanted? Did they get the early nurturing that every human needs?

I hope this letter will wake up some of those working mothers. Do they know what quality of care their youngsters are getting while they are out making sure their college education doesn't "go to waste"?

Thank you, Ann Landers, for letting me have my say. I feel so much better for having written this letter. You have my permission to make the necessary changes so that it will be printable. I am not much of a writer. Sincerely yours,

—A Wisconsin Reader

Dear Wisconsin: I didn't cut a word. Your letter is going into the column exactly as you wrote it. Thanks for a most provocative contribution.

Not all abuse is physical. Sometimes a parent can do a great deal of damage in less obvious ways:

Dear Ann Landers: I realize it would be a miracle if this letter made the paper, but I'm going to write it anyway. Getting this off my chest and having someone listen will make me feel better.

The problem is my husband. The way he treats our children makes me sick. I call it child abuse. He says I am crazy. Will you please tell me what *you* call it?

He never says one word to our teenagers (three of them 15, 16 and 18) unless it's to tell them how dumb, useless and ugly they are. It seems they can't do anything right. His constant belittling has hit one of our children so hard she has become withdrawn and afraid to open her mouth. I'm worried sick about her. Her father has made her feel like a fat slob—completely worthless.

He tells her every day that she is ugly, stupid and clumsy. She believes him. The girl cries a lot and keeps her feelings to herself. She refuses to talk to me about her problems although I have tried to open the lines of communication.

Our children have no respect or affection whatsoever for their father. In fact, I'm sure they hate him. If one of the kids makes a mistake, he never lets up until the child is in tears. I call this *emotional* child abuse. He says there is no such thing. He claims abuse means physical beating. Is there such a thing as emotional child abuse? I leave it to you.

—Kalamazoo Reader

Dear Kal: You bet there is such a thing as emotional abuse. Another term is mental cruelty.

Your husband sounds like a bully. He was probably belittled and emotionally battered by his father.

The only way to break this vicious cycle is through counseling. Your family doctor or clergyman should speak to him (privately) and explain what he is doing to his children. Another problem is your relationship with him. I suspect you are at odds with one another a good bit of the time and the kids have been the battleground.

Family counseling would be ideal . . . with everyone involved, speaking his piece and laying his feelings on the line.

I hope you can get someone to intervene on behalf of the children and make your husband see what he is doing to their lives—and yours. Everyone would profit.

Dear Ann: This letter has been written in my head a hundred times. Now it goes on paper and into the mailbox. It is called: "Games Fathers Play."

Pinning: This is a game where the father will want to hold his son down. Son will call time after a few minutes, but father will persist. After a few more minutes, son will scream to be freed, or cry or beg, but father just smiles and berates the boy for being a sissy.

Score—Daddy 10, Son 0.

Boxing: This is a game of self-defense. A few punches, a push, a shove, a loud command to fight back "like a man." Son whimpers—

feels inadequate, knows the odds are against him. So he cries. Father teases him for being a sissy.

Score—Daddy 10, Son 0.

Football: This is a game of skill and kill. Son must have killer instinct at 6 years of age. He must outshine all others and give 110 percent. Daddy gets very angry if son doesn't make the team or turn out to be a star.

Score—Daddy 10, Son 0.

Now, Daddy, after all your guidance and nurturing, son grows to manhood. He is the image of *you*—his instructor and role model. He is critical, abusive and insecure. The score is Daddy 0, Son 0.

This is the story of my son and his father. I say to you dads everywhere that one of the most precious games you can play with your son is "Gentleness," but in a manly way. A kiss, a hug, an approving glance and some kind words. He is sure to become a man among men if you play this game. Score—Daddy 10, Son 10. Sign me

—The Scorekeeper

Dear Scorekeeper: I agree with your observations completely. Thank you for mailing the letter. It packs a real wallop. And now, Dad, if your wife hands you this column, don't get mad. Get smart!

Dear Ann Landers: I am a young mother who just had her third child.

Several years ago—at least six or seven—you printed a prayer that I keep under the glass in my dressing room. That prayer by Marjorie Holmes helped me keep my sanity. I am not exaggerating when I say that.

My copy is getting yellow, and it may fall apart any day now. Will you please print it again, not only for me, but for other young mothers who may never have seen it? It's a beauty.

—Content in Detroit

Dear Content: With pleasure. It's one of my favorites. Marjorie Holmes' book *I've Got to Talk to Somebody, God* (published by Doubleday) has this lovely piece and many others.

Every mother who reads it will see herself. On behalf of the millions of mothers who love their children but are, alas, less than perfect, I thank you for requesting a rerun.

A Prayer for
Cross Mothers

Oh God, I was so cross to the children today! Forgive me. I was discouraged and tired—and I took it out on them. Forgive my bad temper, my impatience, and most of all, my yelling. I am so ashamed as I think of it.

I want to kneel down by each of their beds, wake them up and ask them to forgive me. But I can't.

They wouldn't understand. I must go on living with the memory of this awful day, my unjust tirades.

Hours later, I can still see the fear in their eyes as they scurried around, trying to appease me—thinking my anger and maniacal raving was their fault.

Oh God, the pathetic helplessness of children! Their innocence before the awful monster—the enraged adult.

And how forgiving they are, hugging me so fervently at bedtime, kissing me good night.

All I can do is straighten a cover, touch a small head burrowed in a pillow and hope with all my heart that they will forgive me.

Lord, in failing these little ones whom you have put in my keeping, I am failing you. Please let your infinite patience and goodness replenish me for tomorrow.

Children are our most precious resources. They are vulnerable and deserve our protection from the predators that seek them out.

Dear Ann Landers: I am a professional man (certified public accountant), 40 years of age and the father of four young boys. I am attracted to little girls.

Please do not recommend that I seek psychiatric care because I have already gone that route with two psychiatrists and a clinical psychologist. "Treatment" has cost me more than $6,000, and I received no help whatsoever.

You cannot respond to my home because my wife might open the letter and it would mean the end of our marriage. Please help. I am desperate.

—No City, No State,
Just Dead-End Street, USA

Dear USA: When people are sick the only advice I can give is "See a doctor," and you are among the sickest.

Even though you feel the professionals did not help you, I'm going to recommend that you try still another therapist. Apparently you were "helped" sufficiently so that your activities are kept to a minimum.

The alternative is to keep going along without therapy. Then, one of these days, the father of a little girl to whom you become "attracted" may put a large hole in your head—and no jury would convict him.

Dear Ann Landers: This is the hardest letter I have ever written in my life. I must write it because I am crazy with worry and have no one to talk to.

My son is 16. He was arrested for molesting a 4-year-old girl. He is now awaiting trial in juvenile court. When the officer came and told me about the charges, I was so shocked I just stood there frozen—I couldn't say a word.

My son was always a good boy, hardworking, honest and loving. He was the kind of a person who went out of his way to do nice things for people in need. He never gave me a minute's trouble.

His father walked out on us when the boy was 3 years old. The lad started to take jobs in the neighborhood as soon as he was big enough to mow lawns and rake leaves.

He was well liked by everyone but could never keep a girlfriend for very long. This bothered me, but I figured one day the right girl would appear and all would be well.

My son admits doing the deed and says he doesn't know why he did it. It seems tragic to see a young, promising boy marked for life because of one mistake. Right now I am so sick at heart I wish I could die. Please advise me.

—A Mother in D.C.

Dear Mother: A 16-year-old boy who would molest a 4-year-old girl is obviously in need of counseling. He will undoubtedly get it. So, try to see the good that will come from this heart-breaking incident.

As for you, I hope you will seek out a clergyman and talk to him about your grief. If you don't belong to a church, go to the pastor of a church of a friend—someone you have heard about.

You are in desperate need of emotional support, and I urge you to get it. And please write back and let me know how things go with you.

The aftereffects of child molestation are far-reaching. These children carry the burden of abuse into adulthood:

Dear Ann Landers: I was molested by two relatives when I was 6. I told no one then and later convinced myself that I was the only one. After 20 years, I finally told my parents. Together, we learned that my sister also had been abused.

Within months, both relatives were arrested for sexually molesting little girls. My sister and I were allowed to testify at their trials, establishing that the pattern had persisted for more than 20 years. Many other cousins also came forward to tell of their abuse by these two.

It is important to remember that such abuse is rarely an isolated incident. Men who sexually abuse continue to do so all their lives if not stopped.

The only way molestation can be stopped is by speaking out *now*, before more defenseless children are victimized. You may face criticism and rejection, but rest assured that if even one parent becomes more aware and cautious, you may have saved a child from a lifetime of pain.

—Champlain, N.Y.

Dear Champlain: Thank you for a letter that is sure to make parents more vigilant.

The best protection against this hideous crime being perpetrated in your family is to have a close and open relationship with your children. Let them know that they can tell you anything without embarrassment or fear of being punished. And don't be afraid to ask questions about any situation that arouses your suspicion. A child molester is often the person (male or female) whom you would least suspect.

In expecting children to protect themselves, have we gone too far? I would be remiss if I didn't allow the other side to speak out.

Back in 1991, I printed a letter from "Heartbroken Grandpa in Alton, Ill." Grandpa was holding his 4-year-old granddaughter on his lap and the girl accused him of "touching her body." The grandfather was disgusted that an innocent game of Pattycake could be so misconstrued.

I was surprised by the mail I received both supporting and condemning Grandpa. Here's the best of the other point of view:

Dear Ann Landers: You performed a valuable service when you printed the letter from "Heartbroken Grandpa in Alton, Ill.," whose relationship with his 4-year-old granddaughter was destroyed after she told her mother that he "touched my body." Actually, they were playing an innocent game of "Pattycake, Pattycake, Baker's Man."

As a result of well-meaning efforts to do something about sexual abuse of children, there are now more than 200 "prevention" manuals on the market. A major study by the Family Welfare Research Group (University of California, Berkeley) concluded that these manuals are worthless for preschoolers because the children cannot understand them. After listening to the stories, up to 20 percent of the preschoolers questioned believed that normal parent-child activities such as being bathed and tucked in at night were "bad."

If Heartbroken Grandpa's granddaughter had told her teacher that he touched her body, he might have been reported to Child Protective Services. At the very least, it would have led to an investigation, terrifying the child, and a medical examination—another trauma—for signs of sexual abuse.

You will probably get letters claiming that another study, by David Jones and J. Melbourne McGraw, found "only" 6 percent of child sexual abuse allegations are false. That is incorrect. The study actually found that 6 percent are *deliberately* false. Another 17 percent are false due to honest mistakes, such as Heartbroken Grandpa's case. The study found insufficient information to determine the truth in another 24 percent of the cases. In other words, nearly one-fourth of the allegations are clearly false, and the number could be almost as high as one-half.

Every false allegation is a double tragedy. Child protection workers have enormous caseloads and too few resources. The time, effort and money spent on investigations that traumatize innocent children are stolen from another child who really has been abused and needs help.

The problem of child abuse is serious and real. It's the solutions that have been ineffective.

—R.W., Albany, N.Y.

Dear R.W.: You have given us a clear look at the other side of a volatile issue. I have been swamped with letters of gratitude for printing this "unpopular" point of view. My thanks to all who wrote.

What about children who abuse? It's frightening to contemplate the future of youngsters like these:

Dear Ann: My 5-year-old nephew is very cruel to animals. He choked a little rabbit to death and set fire to our cat. His parents think he'll outgrow it. What do you think?

—San Antonio

Dear San: I think that child should be evaluated by a professional and watched carefully. His sadistic tendencies indicate that he is extremely troubled. He should certainly not be allowed to have a pet.

Dear Ann Landers: Recently, you responded to a reader from San Antonio who was concerned because her 5-year-old nephew had choked a rabbit to death. Your answer was right on, Ann, but I do wish you had said more.

The American Humane Association is this country's oldest child and animal protection organization. We have checked out incidents that are hair-raising. It is frightening how often children and animals are victims in dysfunctional family situations where spousal abuse, sexual molestation and other brutalities are everyday occurrences.

We are well aware that children who are cruel to animals are in desperate need of help. One of the most dramatic examples of what can happen if animal abuse by a child is overlooked took place in New York state. A 13-year-old boy was charged with the murder of a 4-year-old child. The small community was in shock. Yet one year earlier, that same boy had choked a neighbor's cat with a hose clamp, and nothing was done about it.

People still shrug off abuse to animals. "It was just an animal," "Boys will be boys" and "It's just a phase" are classic phrases heard from the judicial benches across the country. But cruelty speaks volumes about the perpetrator, no matter if the victim is human or animal.

Please help us get the word out to parents, law enforcement officers, teachers, prosecuting attorneys and other professionals who can help us break the cycle of violence to children and animals.

—Michael E. Kaufmann, coordinator of education,
American Humane Association

Dear Mr. Kaufmann: You are right when you say this problem should be looked into and these children need help. It is also true that children often abuse animals to release aggression they feel toward abusive adults. Merely knowing *why* they do it is not enough. Society also needs protection against these sick kids. I do thank you for giving me the opportunity to spotlight a problem that needs a great deal more visibility.

As more and more elderly parents are forced to live with their adult kids, my mail has reflected the increase in the physical and emotional abuse of the elderly:

Dear Ann Landers: We need help. My mother, 66 years old, is being beaten up by my brother, who is 34. She is living with him and his wife in Michigan.

This guy has a terrible out-of-control temper and a history of spousal abuse. My daughter saw him hit his wife last year when she visited them. When we realized what was happening, my oldest sister called Adult Protective Services. The people there said they couldn't do anything because we don't have enough evidence and my mother refuses to press charges.

We love our mother and need advice on where to go for help. The woman deserves to live her last years in peace. I am getting to the point where I could do my brother in and feel no remorse. I'm very frightened that he might hurt my mother or maybe even kill her. Please suggest something.

—San Diego

Dear S.D.: No legal action can be taken unless your mother agrees to press charges against her son or someone witnesses the brutality and calls the police.

Since you believe your mother's life might be in jeopardy, why don't you or your sister take her in? You would then know that she is safe from harm.

Abuse of any kind—physical, sexual, emotional—directed toward anyone, whether a spouse, child, girlfriend, boyfriend or parent, is reprehensible. We must all work together not only to prevent such harm from happening but to help those who need it most.

For more information, contact:

Parents Anonymous (for people who are or fear becoming child abusers)
675 West Foothill Blvd., Suite 220
Claremont, CA 91711
(909) 621-6184

National Committee to Prevent Child Abuse
332 South Michigan Ave., Suite 1600
Chicago, IL 60604-4357

National Child Abuse Hotline/Child Help USA
(800) 422-4453

Parents United
232 E. Gish Rd.
San Jose, CA 95112
(408) 453-7616

Rape can scar both the mind and the body. The more information you have, the better prepared you are. Here are some facts on rape from the Bergen County Rape Crisis Center in New Jersey:

Rape is not a crime of lust. It is a crime of violence. No person provokes rape by acting or dressing in a particular manner.

A rapist's motive is not sexual gratification. It is to degrade, control and/or humiliate.

The rapist is not always a stranger. Nearly 75 percent of all rapes are committed by a friend, relative or acquaintance.

Sex is consent between partners. If one doesn't consent, it's rape.

No one has the right to verbally pressure you or physically force you to have sex, even if:

He has spent a lot of money on you.

You are dressed sensually.

You have flirted or led him on.

You are high on alcohol or any other drug.

He says he is turned on and can't stop.

You have had sex with him before.

You have agreed to have sex with him and then changed your mind.

Dear Ann Landers: Your column has provided a refreshingly frank forum for almost every aspect of human behavior. One topic that has been conspicuously absent is "date rape."

It would not surprise me if at least half of the rapes that occur in this country are perpetrated by men who are known to their victims. Thousands of high school and college students are raped every week, but they don't consider it rape because the male is an acquaintance or a friend. What they don't understand is that if a man forces a woman to have sex against her will, he is a rapist.

Law enforcement officials say rape may be one of the most underreported of all crimes. On our campus, this is certainly true.

The woman does not report it because she is ashamed of what happened, doesn't want to be stigmatized and often believes that somehow it was her fault.

A close friend told me yesterday that she was raped six months ago by a student who offered to help tutor her in biology. When I asked why she didn't report him, she said, "Maybe I am crazy but I didn't want to ruin the guy's reputation or get him kicked out of school."

Please print my letter and urge your female readers to (1) recognize what rape is and (2) report it without hesitation.

—My Name Is Woman

Dear Woman: Thank you for an excellent letter.

Dear Ann Landers: With your willingness and capacity to tap the best information sources, I hope you can find an answer to a question I believe is, or should be, of general interest to women.

Let's say an unescorted female is walking alone on a street. She sees an unsavory-looking man walking toward her.

Should she avoid eye contact if he appears to be sizing her up, or should she meet his gaze assertively? And what if a similar scene should occur in a parking lot?

I seem to recall having read conflicting advice on this subject. Two local policemen said they "hadn't thought about it" and gave no answer.

I can't believe that there isn't a right and wrong way to behave in such a situation. Please, Ann, which is safer—to look tough and aggressive, or to look away?

Thanks for a definitive answer on behalf of all potentially vulnerable females from a

—Regular Reader in Houston

Dear Regular Reader: According to Cmdr. Jose Velez at the Chicago Police Department and Cheryl Pearson of YWCA–Metro

Chicago Women's Services, it is best to establish eye contact assertively and let the man know you are aware of his presence. It will also help identify him later.

If a woman does not feel comfortable making eye contact, she should do something else to acknowledge his presence, such as walk to the other side of the street or move her handbag in a way that lets him know she suspects he might be after it.

No matter what she does, it will not provoke an attack if the man has no such intentions, nor will it prevent an attack if he is out to get her.

Dear Ann Landers: I'm a single woman who works as a waitress. I get off at midnight and have to walk three long blocks from the bus to my apartment. Three of the girls I work with have been raped in the last six months. I am petrified that it might happen to me.

I carry a can of Mace in my pocket and an icepick, too. Frankly, I doubt that I would have the nerve to use the icepick. As for the Mace, I don't think I would have the presence of mind to use that, either.

Some articles on rape say if a woman is attacked she is better off to submit—that her chances of being beat up or killed are greatly reduced if she does as she is told and doesn't put up a fight. Other articles say just the opposite.

I am terribly confused and hope you will settle this matter once and for all. I am going to follow your advice, no matter what it is.

—N.Y. Worry

Dear N.Y.: I'm with Dr. Mary Conroy, who teaches at California State University in Los Angeles.

She advises, "Kick him in the scrotum. Gouge his eyes out. Slash him in the Adam's apple. Scream! Shriek!" Conroy says the more noise you make, the better your chances for escaping the would-be attacker.

I consulted with several authorities in law enforcement and almost all agreed that women who were submissive or begged to be let go accomplished nothing. Would-be rapists are mean and single-minded. They do not respond to tears or pleas for mercy. (Also, many are doped-up and off their rockers.)

So, N.Y., and any other woman who is faced with the decision: Put up a fight and yell your head off. It's your best bet.

And now an additional word, in case you lose: I implore you to go at once to the nearest telephone and call the police. They will come and take you to a hospital where you will be cared for immediately. Give as detailed a description of the rapist as possible. And, please, please, accept the offer for counseling.

Rape is a hideous experience that can leave scars on the psyche that never heal unless the victim ventilates her feelings of violation and purges herself of the rage. The sooner after the incident, the better.

Dear Ann Landers: I must comment on your recent advice to women who are attacked by rapists. You quoted authorities who cautioned against submitting peacefully. They urged women to "scream, kick, gouge, scratch" and put the knee where it hurts the most.

That advice may be fine under certain circumstances, but a very important element was left out of your response. No mention was made of the armed attacker. When a gun or a knife is held at the victim's throat, the possibility of being maimed or killed is very real. The March 23, 1981, issue of *Time* magazine on violent crime put it well. Capt. Ephrine F. Leija of the Houston police department said, "Do the best you can under difficult circumstances. Above all, don't try to be a hero."

I am glad you urged all rape victims to report the crime at once and to give as accurate a description as possible. May I add, if he is apprehended, don't be afraid to testify. We must do everything we can to get these sick creeps off the streets.

—Chicago Suburbanite

Dear Suburbanite: I appreciate your additional comments. They are sensible and realistic. In a life-threatening situation, submission is the better choice. Women can and do recover from rape. Death is permanent.

Dear Ann Landers: My husband insists there are police records of women who have raped men. I say a woman can seduce a man, but she cannot rape him. Are there any such rapes on record? I find this impossible to believe, but if you say it is so, I will accept it.

—Confused in Evans, Wash.

Dear Confused: Your husband wins this one.

According to Jane Larson, professor of law at Northwestern University, it is rare, but women have been prosecuted for rape.

In the 1970s and '80s, most states changed their rape statutes to criminal sexual assault laws that are sex-neutral and punish a broad range of offenses including penetration of a person's body by a foreign object and forced oral sex.

As of this writing, most of the women who have been prosecuted participated with a group of men in a gang rape against a male victim.

Dear Ann Landers: The New Orleans *Times-Picayune* runs a column called Working Woman by syndicated columnist Niki Scott. I hope you will find room for this piece in your space, Ann. I think it could cut down on the number of rapes in this country.

—A Constant Reader

Dear Constant: What a splendid contribution. I thank you on behalf of all the women you have helped today. Thanks, too, to Universal Press Syndicate for permission to reprint this column.

A Rapist Tells You How to Avoid Him
Niki Scott

"If you're a working woman, I'm looking for you, and you'd better hope I don't find you. I'm a rapist.

"I'm not going to tell you why I'm a rapist, but I'll say this. I do it because I like it. It's like hunting, but easier."

This is the way the letter began. It had no return address and arrived in an ordinary batch of mail. My heart stopped while I read it.

I'm printing it because it rings true and because although his boasting is frightening and infuriating, we can learn from it. We need all the help we can get.

The letter continues:

"As I said, working women are my game, and they're usually pretty easy targets. Mostly that's because they travel by themselves, work by themselves and are so dumb about taking care of themselves.

"I live in a big city, but I often hunt in the suburbs. Small offices in big buildings or small businesses are good places to find women alone. That's where you might find me at the end of a day. Most of the time, a simple lock on the door stops me, and I stay away from places where I see people coming and going.

"I've never been caught, never even come close, and that's because I don't take stupid chances. I don't break in to get at a woman I want. Most often I can walk right in—or she lets me in.

"The thing is that I look pretty harmless and pretty ordinary. In fact, I try to look like I belong wherever I am. I'm neither big or small. I'm deliberately clean cut. Nobody who knows me would think I'd do such a thing.

"Darkness is my friend, but I don't always hunt after dark. The end of the workday is my time. Everybody's too interested in getting the hell out to pay much attention to what's going on around them.

"Shopping centers around closing time are good, too. Many of the women I've raped came my way because they were dumb. They stayed late and parked a long way from the store. They locked their keys in their cars or left their lights on and ran the batteries down.

"I pick my women because of their situations, which I've studied before I move. Looks don't mean a lot to me, but she's always alone in a place where nobody else will come, or I get her to go to one. You'd be amazed how easy that is.

"About self-defense for women: Don't make me laugh. I don't go after a woman who looks like she'd be able to whip me in a fight.

"The best protection from me you working women have is company or a locked door you're smart enough not to open when I ask. More than that, the best protection from me is to remember there are lots of guys like me out here who are looking for you."

Dear Ann Landers: I am a retired captain in corrections for 32 years and would like to discuss prison rape. When a prisoner complains that he or she has been raped by another prisoner, we send the victim to the hospital for treatment and call in the police. Most of the time, the rapist gets additional time added to his regular sentence.

Movies do not give you the real picture. Rape, no matter where it occurs, is hideous and dehumanizing. When members of the same sex are housed together for long periods of time, rape will occur. The sex drive doesn't turn itself off when a person goes to prison.

In prison, we obtain warrants if there is a complaint. Sometimes, the victims refuse to prosecute. When that is the case, we can do nothing.
—St. Louis

Dear St. Louis: I have received letters from prison guards (and their wives) with the same message. As I see it, the criminal justice department could do a better job of educating and rehabilitating the incarcerated population so they could make an honest living when they are released. Too many revert to a life of crime because they aren't equipped to do anything else.

More than 40 years ago, Dr. Karl Menninger, one of the century's most brilliant minds, wrote a book entitled, *The Crime of Punishment*, in which he reiterated the futility of caging criminals, doing nothing to rehabilitate them and then expecting them to be peaceful, law-abiding citizens when they get out. How prophetic were his words.

Dear Ann Landers: My brother was raped while in prison serving a three-year sentence for arson. He called for help but none came. When he told a guard what had happened, the reply was, "Welcome to prison life."

He tried other avenues to get assistance, but was ignored. Someone must have tipped off the other prisoners because later a "blanket party" was thrown. He was raped again and beaten and told to keep his mouth shut.

My brother was 19 years old. He is now 42. I heard this story for the first time just two years ago. As he told it, he was shaking and crying his eyes out, 23 years later. Where is the American justice we hear so much about?

—Permanently Disillusioned in Arizona

Dear Ann Landers: I have worked for the Wisconsin Department of Corrections for 18 years. During that time, I cannot recall one instance of prison rape being tolerated. Every allegation of sexual assault in this facility is investigated, internally, and often outside authorities are called in to pursue further criminal charges against the perpetrator.

After the internal investigation is completed, the assailant, if found guilty, can receive an administrative punishment of 368 days of segregation and 20 days extension of the mandatory release date.

Rape is a reprehensible act and cannot be tolerated in any setting. Those of us professionals who deal with inmates do "give a damn" and we do everything we can to safeguard society.

—Plymouth, Wis.

Dear Plymouth: Too bad there aren't more professionals who have your lofty principles. The next letter will twirl your turban:

Dear Ann Landers: I have over 25 years of correctional experience, including corrections internal affairs and headquarters administration.

Sexual assaults are considered an "indicator" of the management health and order of a prison. A well-run prison has few sexual assaults because the employees are constantly intermingling with the inmates and supervising them. A poorly run prison will have many sexual assaults.

Budget cuts result in an insufficient number of correctional officers, which means the inmates are allowed to run the prison. The smart ones rise to the top. Prison officials want to look good so very few sexual assaults are reported.

In the worst cases, there are prison administrators who use inmate gangs to help manage the prison. Sex and human bodies are now the coin of the realm. Is inmate "X" writing letters to the editor of the local newspaper and filing lawsuits? Or, perhaps he threw urine or feces on an employee? "Well, Joe, you and Willie and Hank work him over, but be sure you don't break any bones and send him to the hospital. If you do a good job, I'll see that you get the blondest boy in the next shipment."

—Louisiana Corrections Officer

10

Age Is Only a Number, Baby!

Times have changed. Grandmas are no longer tied to the stove by their apron strings—they're out selling real estate, taking aerobics classes and going on cruises.

This is from a speech Nardi Reeder Campion made at her 40th reunion at Wellesley College. I hope you enjoy it as much as I did.

Profile of a Senior

Who is a senior citizen? What is one? A senior citizen is one who was here before the Pill and the population explosion. We were here before TV, penicillin, polio shots, antibiotics, open-heart surgery and hair transplants. Before frozen food, nylon, Dacron, Xerox, Kinsey, radar, fluorescent lights, credit cards, ballpoint pens and Frisbees.

For us, time-sharing meant togetherness, not computers or condos. Coeds never wore slacks. We were before panty hose and drip-dry clothes, before ice makers and dishwashers, clothes dryers, freezers and electric blankets. Before Hawaii and Alaska became states. Before men wore long hair and earrings and before women wore tuxedos.

We were before Leonard Bernstein and Ann Landers, plastic, the 40-hour week and minimum wages. We got married first and then lived together. How quaint!

Closets were for clothes, not for coming out of. We were before Grandma Moses, "The White Shadow," Frank Sinatra, Batman, Herblock and Miss Peach. Girls wore Peter Pan collars and thought cleavage was what butchers did.

We were before vitamins, disposable diapers, Jeeps, pizza, face-lifts, Cheerios, instant coffee, decaffeinated anything and McDonald's. We thought fast food was what you ate during Lent. We were before Boy George and Chiquita Banana. Before FM radios, tape recorders, electric typewriters, boom boxes, word processors, electronic music and disco dancing.

In our day, cigarette smoking was fashionable; grass was for mowing. Coke was a refreshing drink, and pot was something you cooked in. If we had been asked to explain CIA, NATO, UFO, VCR, GNP, MBA, BMW, HMO, SDI, NFL, JFK and MS, we'd have said "alphabet soup."

We are today's senior citizens, a hardy bunch when you think of how our world has changed and the adjustments we have had to make. I'm pretty proud of us.

Dear Ann Landers: I live in Riverside, Calif., and newspapers are my hobby. I ran across something in the Yucaipa, Calif., *News-Mirror* that tickled my funny bone. It doesn't say who the author is but that person is certainly tuned in to what life is like when you get to be 65. I hope you will share this little essay with your readers.

—Ann's Fan

I Have Noticed

Everything is farther away than it used to be. It is even twice as far to the corner and they have added a hill.

I have given up running for the bus; it leaves earlier than it used to.

It seems to me they are making the stairs steeper than in the old days. And have you noticed the smaller print they use in the newspapers?

There is no sense in asking anyone to read aloud anymore, as everybody speaks in such a low voice I can hardly hear them.

The material in dresses is so skimpy now, especially around the hips and waist, that it is almost impossible to reach one's shoelaces. And the sizes don't run the way they used to. The 12s and 14s are so much smaller.

Even people are changing. They are so much younger than they used to be when I was their age. On the other hand, people my own age are so much older than I am.

I ran into an old classmate the other day and she has aged so much that she didn't recognize me.

I got to thinking about the poor dear while I was combing my hair this morning and in so doing I glanced at my own reflection.

Really now, they don't even make good mirrors like they used to.

Medical technology and healthier lifestyles are helping Americans live longer and longer these days. Unfortunately, sometimes the quality of life deteriorates. That means the number of aging parents who are also in need of constant care is increasing. Placing an elderly parent in a nursing home is a difficult and painful decision, and one not easily reached.

It is rare indeed that I get a letter saying, "I just love my 82-year-old mother-in-law" . . . or "Gramps is a joy to have around the house."

Because of the nature of this column, I get the beefs—not the bouquets. People write when things are bad—not good.

Although no two problems are exactly alike, a thread of similarity runs through many of the letters dealing with aged parents. More often than not, one son or daughter is saddled with the total responsibility for one or both parents while several brothers and sisters refuse flatly to help out in any way whatever.

In some cases the parent is meddlesome, crotchety or an out-and-out troublemaker. I've had many letters from harassed daughters-in-law who describe the back-breaking job of caring for an older person who is physically incapacitated, childish and not in control of his or her faculties.

One woman wrote, "I love my father-in-law dearly, but I'm afraid if I don't get some help I'll die before he does. He's 79 years old, has no sight and I must care for him like an infant. He belongs in a nursing home where he can get proper attention. But my husband says, 'My father will die in the home of his loved ones. We'll send him to a nursing home over my dead body.' Well, Ann, I'm afraid it will be over my dead body!"

In such cases I strongly advise the wife to get moral support from her clergyman. Often he can make the husband see the light. No woman should be a 24-hour slave year after year to save her husband from needless guilt feelings.

In some instances the older person has no contact with the world and is unable to identify his surroundings or the person caring for him at great personal sacrifice. Under these instances home care makes no sense whatever.

Not all older folks are a problem. Some are hale, healthy, cheerful, helpful and a source of genuine pleasure to those around them. If they went off to a home for the aged they would be sorely missed.

Dear Ann Landers: I never cease to be amazed at all the fanfare in the newspapers when a person lives to celebrate a 100th birthday. The president of the United States sends a telegram, the governor sends greetings, and there's usually a five-layer cake. And then, the last line of the newspaper report goes something like this: "Mrs. Hawmintosh has made her home with her daughter-in-law for the last 40 years."

I say the president should send the telegram to the daughter-in-law—especially if those last 40 years have been happy ones for the lady who has reached 100.

—Added Word

Dear Added Word: And now may I add a word? *Amen.*

Dear Ann Landers: This is the story of widowhood.

First—numbness. Then busyness. A million things to settle. Endless death certificates and things to sign. Friends are so considerate. The neighbors helpful. Caring support from relatives. You keep busy.

At night you pound the empty side of the bed in grief. Finally you close your eyes and throw his toothbrush in the garbage can and toss out the old work shoes you brought home from the hospital in a plastic bag.

You empty the closet and give all his things away. It's a heartache like you wouldn't believe. Every suit reminds you of a party you went to together—or a wedding or church affair.

A year has passed. You are still in one piece. Then the blow. Your good friends celebrate a birthday. All couples. You are not included because you'd be a fifth wheel.

Please remember us widows. Don't treat us like excess baggage. We've been handed a rotten break, and we need friends.

—Laura in Minneapolis

Dear Laura: Here's your letter—and as poignant a one as I have seen in a long time. I hope it is read by people who can do something about your loneliness—and that they respond to their better instincts.

Dear Ann Landers: It has been 14 months since my husband's sudden death. He was 55.

Ed and I were married 37 years and did everything together. Ed's funeral was the biggest the town had ever seen. But where are all those people now? The couples we socialized with for years have dropped me like a hot potato. Don't they realize that I'm still the same person, only now I don't have Ed?

I joined a golf club. I volunteer one day a week at the hospital. But in the lonely hours I wonder what is the matter with me that no one invites me anywhere.

I went with a female friend to a couple of singles parties, and we both felt out of place and would never go again. I've considered putting an ad in the shopping news to find a male companion to go to a movie with, or out to dinner. I love to dance, but I won't go to a ballroom alone. Men my age want younger girls.

Ann, I'm ready to give up. Can you help me turn my life around?
—Cleveland Widow

Dear Cleveland: Unfortunately, dear, the world is not waiting to entertain and "include" widows. Most people are busy with their own lives.

Have you thought of giving some parties for your old friends? Nothing fancy—Sunday hotdogs and baked beans, TV football viewing get-togethers, anything to get a group together. And don't fail to include three or four extra men. Or, make the first move and invite an unattached man over for a home-cooked meal. Buy an extra ticket to a play or movie or concert and pick up the phone.

This sort of thing is no longer considered out of line. What is needed is some positive forward movement on your part. Have you joined AARP, the American Association of Retired Persons? (Inquire about their Widowed Person's Service.) Cleveland has a fine program. The bottom line is, go for it, and please let me know how you do.

Dear Ann Landers: Your advice to the Cleveland widow who complained about being lonely was worthless. Why don't you wake up and smell the coffee?

You told her to have a party and invite "three or four extra men." Get real, Ann. Don't you know that today there are at least eight widows to every widower?

My husband died two years ago. I would love to go out with a man occasionally, to a movie or a play or a concert or just for a simple dinner, but the question is, where do I find one?

Please don't tell me to join a singles group. I tried that once. There were 17 widows and two widowers. One was 42, the other was 75. I decided that there are worse things than being alone and I had just seen a couple of them.

—Dover, N.J.

Dear Dover: Thanks for the message. I received thousands of similar ones after I printed the Cleveland widow's letter. Read on:

From Lansing, Mich.: I'd like to ask a question of the Cleveland widow who was married to Ed for 37 years and is now whining because her married friends don't invite her anywhere. Welcome to death and divorce, dearie. How many widows did you entertain when you were happily married to Ed? Darned few, I'll bet. The loneliness you are now experiencing is the chickens coming home to roost.

Tacoma, Wash.: May I tell "Cleveland" how to cope with widowhood? Forget about men. What's out there isn't worth bothering about. Oh sure, there are plenty of sponges who would be happy to join you for dinner (at your place, of course) and park their shoes under your bed, but not one is worth a damn. Stick with your widowed friends and enjoy one another's company.

Brooklyn: I was a widow at 50 and positive that there could never be another man in the entire world as kind and loving as my Herman. I was wrong. My sister-in-law nagged me for months to go to a meeting of Parents Without Partners. Finally I gave in so she'd leave me alone. There I met my second Prince Charming. It was love at first sight. We will celebrate our third wedding anniversary in February.

Raleigh, N.C.: That widow in Cleveland who misses her husband so much can have mine. I've been married to this miserable skunk for 51 years. He was a gambler, a drunk and a chaser until he wore himself out. The man was no father and no husband. I pray God will take him first and grant me a few years alone.

Chicago: A spouse should enrich one's life, not define it. I'm 34 and lost a wonderful man two years ago. I had a terrific marriage and hope I'll get a chance to love again. In the meantime, I'm not looking. I'm going to live my life, develop my skills, further my career and cherish the friends I have.

Sacramento: In California, widows are dropped like hot potatoes because they are considered a threat by their women friends. The wisest move for a California widow is to leave the state and go to Oregon, Washington or Alaska.

Newark: When my husband died, I felt like a fifth wheel. Then I joined a group called Widows or Widowers. I had to show my husband's death certificate to prove he died. They don't want divorced people. I met a fabulous man at my first meeting and life is beautiful again. I now know that love can be better the second time around.

Baltimore: The widowers and divorced men in this town are looking for fillies half their age. Any female over 40 is considered "over the hill." The last woman in Baltimore to make a brilliant marriage was the Duchess of Windsor.

Dear Ann Landers: I have never written to you before, but I believe the following might interest you and your readers. I found it in an old magazine. It was written by Rudy Joe Mano.

It Was Grandfather's Birthday

It was Grandfather's birthday. He was 79. He got up early, shaved, showered, combed his hair and put on his Sunday best so he would look nice when they came.

He skipped his daily walk to the town café where he had coffee with his cronies. He wanted to be home when they came.

He put his porch chair on the sidewalk so he could get a better view of the street when they drove up to help celebrate his birthday.

At noon he got tired but decided to forgo his nap so he could be there when they came. Most of the rest of the afternoon he spent near the telephone so he could answer it when they called.

He has five married children, 13 grandchildren and three great-grandchildren. One son and a daughter live within 10 miles of his place. They hadn't visited him for a long time. But today was his birthday and they were sure to come.

At suppertime he left the cake untouched so they could cut it and have dessert with him.

After supper he sat on the porch waiting.

At 8:30, he went to his room to prepare for bed. Before retiring he left a note on the door, which read, "Be sure to wake me up when they come."

It was Grandfather's birthday. He was 79.

Dear Friend: I don't often puddle up when I read letters, but this one did it. Thank you for sharing.

Dear Ann Landers: I'm going to tell you about a love story that I witness every time I go to the nursing home to see my husband who has Alzheimer's disease. Unfortunately, I know firsthand how this terrible illness affects family members, but I would like the world to know what love really is.

I see a man who, I understand, has spent the last eight years caring for his wife who has Alzheimer's. They have been married over 50 years. He cooks and feeds her every bite of food she eats. He has bathed her and dressed her every day all these years. They have no other family. She lost a baby at birth, and they never had any more children.

I cannot describe the tenderness and love that man shows for his wife. She is unable to recognize anyone, including him. The only things she shows any interest in are two baby dolls. They are never out of her hands.

I observed him when I parked my car beside his the other day. He sat in his old pickup truck for a few minutes, then he patted down what little hair he had, straightened the threadbare collar of his shirt and looked in the mirror for a final check before going in to see his wife. It was as if he were courting her. They have been partners all these years and have seen each other under all kinds of circumstances, yet he carefully groomed himself before he called on his wife, who wouldn't even know him.

This is an example of the true love and commitment the world needs today.

—Ft. Worth

Dear Ft. Worth: I don't know when I have read a more touching letter. These days, when half of the marriages in this country fail and the average marriage lasts seven years, it is reassuring to read a letter like yours. Thank you so much for writing.

Dear Ann Landers: You know you are getting older when:
Almost everything hurts. What doesn't hurt, doesn't work anymore.
It feels like the morning after the night before, and you haven't been anywhere.
All the names in your little black book end in M.D.
You get winded playing chess.
You look forward to a dull evening.
You still chase women but have forgotten why.
You turn out the lights for economic not romantic reasons.
Your knees buckle and your belt won't.

You are 17 around the neck, 42 around the waist and 126 around the golf course.

You sink your teeth into a steak and they stay there.

You try to straighten the wrinkles in your socks and find you aren't wearing any.

A little old gray-haired lady tries to help you across the street. She's your wife.

—L.F. in San Antonio

Dear L.F.: Thanks for my laugh for the day—and if I get any beefs from the Gray Panthers, I'm sending them on to you.

Dear Ann Landers: Please urge people to plan ahead while they still have all their marbles. It's a bad idea to leave those decisions for the family to argue about.

I have made a written living will. Copies of it are in the hands of my medical-plan physician and are a part of my medical records. Copies are also in the hands of my sons. They know that if I'm not lucky enough to die in my sleep and must enter a nursing home or hospital, absolutely nothing is to be done to keep me alive.

There will be no "heroic measures" or forced feeding. I make these wishes known before getting into the legal gobbledygook, thus relieving my family of these decisions. My body will be donated to the University of Washington School of Medicine. It is then to be cremated. There will be no funeral.

The reasons for all this planning? My parents lived into their 90s independently in their own home, with Mother failing, but Dad able to care for her. When Dad had a stroke at the age I am now, my brother, who had power of attorney, put them both in a good nursing home with private room and bath.

Dad hated the home and flushed his meals down the toilet. He died 18 months later. Soon after, Mother got pneumonia and had no will to live. Heroic measures were employed, and they brought her back to life. She lived three more years, helpless, flat on her back in the nursing home she hated!

My hearing is poor. I walk with a cane. I am a bit forgetful but still live alone. When I can no longer do that, I want to die. No one looks forward to death, but it is as natural as birth, and I believe most of us prefer it to being a burden. Don't you?

—P.T.M., Seattle, Wash.

Dear P.T.M.: I do, indeed, and I applaud your good sense. You've done a big favor to your children by planning in advance, and I'm sure they appreciate it.

I hope your letter will encourage others to follow your example of preparing a living will now when they are of sound mind. It's the last gift they can give their loved ones and, I might add, one of the best.

Dear Ann Landers: For the last 20 years (maybe 30) my aunt has been saying, "I really ought to make a will." She never did. Last week she died, and before the body was cold my cousins were fighting over her possessions. It was an ugly spectacle.

Some months ago my mother gave me an antique silver service. Later I found out she had promised it to my sister. We are both distressed by mother's forgetfulness, and neither of us wants to hurt her feelings by mentioning her previous commitment. My sister is not greedy and neither am I. We can live with whatever the most recent will decrees.

I realize that making a will is an admission of the inevitability of death. While this understandably is difficult, one of the most thoughtful gestures a parent can make is to draw up a will or simply a handwritten paper designating what he or she wishes done with material possessions. Please urge parents (everyone, for that matter) to ease the burden of their passing by making a will. And do it today—there may not be a tomorrow.

—A Loving Child, Anywhere USA

Dear Anywhere: Most people (about 99 percent) hate to make a will because they are certain they will cash in their chips the very next day. This, of course, is nonsense.

I pose a question to every person reading these words. If you died tomorrow, would your money, home, furnishings, clothing and jewelry go to those individuals you want to have them?

The best way to make sure your wishes are respected is to sit down with a pad and pencil and write down all the objects you want to give away and to whom. Then think about your liquid assets. Do you want to leave specific gifts to special friends and the charities you support or admire? Call a lawyer and have it put in the form of a legal document.

If you die without a will in many states, the court will award one-half of your estate to a surviving spouse and one-half to the children.

The final word from here is: Age is only a number, baby. Forty isn't 40 anymore, and 80 isn't 80 anymore, either.

Life Begins at 80

Frank Laubach

I have good news for you. The first 80 years are the hardest. The second 80 are a succession of birthday parties.

Once you reach 80, everyone wants to carry your baggage and help you up the steps. If you forget your name or anybody else's name, or an appointment, or your own telephone number, or promise to be three places at the same time, or can't remember how many grandchildren you have, you need only explain that you are 80.

Being 80 is a lot better than being 70. At 70 people are mad at you for everything. At 80 you have a perfect excuse no matter what you do. If you act foolishly, it's your second childhood. Everybody is looking for symptoms of softening of the brain.

Being 70 is no fun at all. At that age they expect you to retire to a house in Florida and complain about your arthritis (they used to call it lumbago) and you ask everybody to stop mumbling because you can't understand them. (Actually your hearing is about 50 percent gone.)

If you survive until you are 80, everybody is surprised that you are still alive. They treat you with respect just for having lived so long. Actually they seem surprised that you can walk and talk sensibly.

So please, folks, try to make it to 80. It's the best time of life. People forgive you for anything. If you ask me, life begins at 80.

For more information, contact:

American Association of Retired Persons
601 E Street NW
Washington, D.C. 20049
(202) 434-2277

Alzheimer's Association
919 N. Michigan Ave.
Suite 1000
Chicago, IL 60611-1676
(800) 272-3900

For living wills, contact:
Harvard Health-Medical Directive
P.O. Box 380
Boston, MA 02117
(Send $6 for two copies)

11

Nice Work If You Can Get It

We spend a huge portion of our lives at our jobs. It's only to be expected that a lot of my mail deals with work or lack of it, not to mention annoying bosses and irritating coworkers.

The Secretary's Prayer

Dear Lord, help me to do my work well, to have the memory of an elephant and by some miracle to be able to do five things at once: answer four telephones while typing a letter that "must go out today." When the letter doesn't get signed until tomorrow, please give me the strength to keep my mouth shut.

Dear Lord, never let me lose my patience, even when the boss has me searching files for hours for the report that later is discovered on his desk.

Give me the intelligence of a college professor, although my education is limited to a high school diploma and secretarial training.

Help me to read his mind and his handwriting and carry out all instructions without explanation.

Let me always know exactly where my boss is and when he'll be back, even though he never tells me these things.

And Lord, when the year ends, please give me the foresight not to throw out records that will be asked for in a couple of days even though I was told emphatically, "Destroy these; they are cluttering up the place."

I ask these blessings, dear Lord, in the name of secretaries everywhere. Amen.

Dear Ann Landers: I demand equal time. Will you please print an "Executive's Prayer"? Thank you very much.

Dear Lord: Give me the patience of a saint and the ability to endure my secretary's knack for confusion. Help me keep calm when she reminds me of my morning appointments—after lunch. Give me the strength, Heavenly Father, to keep my anger in check when she takes 30 minutes for a mid-morning coffee break while I take phone messages from her friends. I realize that nobody's perfect, but help me, dear Lord, to keep my cool when she hands me a letter to the company president with two erasures, two strike-overs and a misspelled word. I need extra strength, Heavenly Father, to hold my tongue when she orders her groceries and makes hair appointments on my private phone, which is reserved for incoming long distance calls. I realize that assault and battery is against the law, dear Lord, so please restraineth my hand so that I may not do violence. Amen.

—The Boss

Dear Boss: I believe in prayer but if it's as bad as it sounds, you need to look in the want ads—between prayers, of course.

Dear Ann Landers: I am tired—not just "tired," but bone-weary exhausted. I'm the female of the '90s, a professional woman with a good husband and three wonderful children. I put in 40 hours a week downtown and just as many at home. When people like me are written up in a women's magazine or a newspaper article, you'd think we had the world by the tail. Baloney.

My job as a supervisor is stressful. The demands on me are awesome. Everyone wants something. When I come home I must prepare supper, clean the house, wash clothes, pick up the kids from the activity of the day, help them with homework, see that they are bathed and put to bed. By then, I am totally shot. My body says rest, but my mind says I must get ready for tomorrow.

I am 45 pounds overweight, and every week I add another pound or two. This is another area of my life that I can't seem to control. I know I should go on a diet, but I don't feel like tackling another big job.

My husband helps more than most husbands, and the children are our top priority. I truly wish I didn't have to work, but there's no way we could make it if I stayed home. I'm not working so we can have a Mercedes, a pool or fancy vacations. I work so we can meet our house and car payments, buy decent clothes and put food on the table. We are not extravagant people. Even though my husband and I are both professionals, we don't make a great deal of money. If I quit work, it would cut our income in half.

I miss not picking up my kids after school. I was depressed all summer because I couldn't stay at home with them. Before I know it, these children won't need me and I'll have missed it all.

My point is this: I'm being pulled every which way by people I feel responsible for. I know you will suggest counseling, Ann, but I live in a rural area and the closest counselor is 55 miles away. With my work, family and limited income, counseling isn't possible.

My pastor tells me I should "pray about it." My doctor says other than occasional hypertension due to my weight and stress, I'm as healthy as a horse.

So, there you have it. Each day is busier than the day before. I feel as if I am sinking in quicksand. I know I have a lot of company. More and more women are juggling jobs and families. Are there any answers for us? I'd like to know what Ann Landers has to say. How in the world did you do it?

—Tired in Texas

Dear Tired: Please don't look at me as an example of a woman who "did it." There were no sacrifices and no heroics involved.

I was 37 years old when I started to write this column. I had never held a job before, and my daughter was in high school. I had plenty of household help, a supportive husband, and there were no money problems.

I am awestruck when I read how hard millions of women work at their jobs and then come home to another full-time job. I don't know how they manage. I'm not at all sure I could do it. Tell me, readers, how do you do it?

A woman (professional, married with three young children) described herself as a "female of the '90s." She said she was bone-weary and felt as if she were sinking in quicksand. I said I was awestruck by the number of women who work at their jobs and go home to another full-time job and asked, "How do you do it?"

Thousands of women dropped their computers, brooms and biscuit batter to tell me how they do it. Every female who is working at a paid job and raising a family can learn something from what follows.

From Irving, Texas: How did I do it? I laid down the law. Everyone in the house except the baby is responsible for his or her own territory. (I throw in a little "corporate" territory, too.) The 14-year-old daughter, 11-year-old son and 9-year-old daughter wash, dry, fold and put away their own clothes. I iron. Everyone vacuums his or her own room and one corporate room (living room, dining room, playroom). My husband does the bathroom. I cook. Kitchen duty is divided among the children. I pay the two older ones $1 an hour to supervise the baby, bathe, diaper and feed her. Is my house spotless? No. Are the kids well-trained? Yes. Are we a happy family? You bet. How's my weight? Don't ask, but I'll do something about that eventually.

Houston: I gave up a lucrative career and settled for waitress work three evenings a week so I could stay at home and raise a family. We are much better off financially because I no longer wear designer clothes, have my hair and nails done downtown, eat lunch in fancy restaurants or drive a second car that means insurance, upkeep, parking and garaging. I adopted a whole new set of values and put aside pride, envy, competitiveness and the need for recognition. I am truly content being a stay-at-home wife and a nurturing mother.

Calgary: I'm a divorced father who has custody of three children under 14. Here's how I do it: All the children are in school, so we don't need outside help. We plan menus on Wednesdays and do the marketing Thursday evenings. We buy fruit and vegetables in season and do a lot of canning and freezing. We don't spend money on movies. We rent tapes. The kids get an allowance, out of which they must save something every week for college. They are fine students and I've never had trouble with any of them. The answer: I learned that less is more.

Philadelphia: I was one of those women who ran herself ragged until I finally learned how to say no to family, friends, neighbors, organizations, committees, etc., etc. One day when I realized I was on the verge of collapse, I asked myself, "What would they do if I were dead? How would they manage?" The answer: "They'd ask somebody else." That taught me to say no and reclaim my life. I'm enjoying the newfound freedom and my ulcers are gone. Praise the Lord.

Oakland: Worrying takes energy, so I got smart and cut it out. We strive for neatness and forget about sparkling clean. I discovered that garage sales and thrift shops have terrific bargains. In the last four years, I went from upper middle class to poor, but I am a lot richer than most people, and I'm happier, too.

White Plains, N.Y.: Our lives became manageable when my husband and I quit smoking, quit drinking, started to exercise instead of play cards and finally woke up to the fact that the friends we were trying to impress weren't worth the effort.

———

Dear Ann Landers: We hear a lot about sexual harassment, but I'm not sure I know exactly what it is. I'll bet a lot of others are also fairly vague about this and would appreciate it if you would spell it out. How about it, Ann?

—Undereducated in Charlotte, N.C.

Dear Undereducated: The Chicago Board of Education issued some guidelines for those who asked the same question. Here are some of the offenses the board said constituted sexual harassment, whether intentional or not:

Jokes or comments about sex or explicit invitations to have sex.
Displaying sexually suggestive objects, photos or cartoons.
Remarks about a person's body or sexual attractiveness.
Whistling, gawking or commenting on body parts, pro or con.
Touching, leering, whistling or making insulting, suggestive or obscene comments or gestures.

Most companies will issue a warning after a first offense. If there is a second occurrence, it could mean dismissal.

Be aware that sexual harassment in the workplace can be an equal-opportunity offense. Some men have sued and won. They cited female department heads and bosses who came on to them, and when the men rebuffed their advances, they were demoted or fired. P.S. I just received a bulletin from Harvard Medical School instructing young physicians on what to do when sexually harassed by patients. What a world!

Office problems aren't always serious, but even frivolous ones are still annoying. A lot of these office antics involve feet, although I couldn't tell you why.

Dear Ann Landers: I am writing about a unique problem in the hope that you will tell us what to do.

332 / ANN LANDERS

We are a small commercial bank in Chicago. A gentleman in our office removes his shoes and socks and sprays his feet with something that asphyxiates nearby staff members. He does this *every day*.

The fact that he is situated in a customer contact area does not seem to faze him. When he had his own office and performed this ritual, it was viewed with distaste but tolerated. Now that he is right next to the receptionist, we find it totally unacceptable.

No one has approached him, although many of us have verbalized our disgust loud enough for him to hear. Nothing changes.

Please tell us what should be done.

—Freaked Out in Chicago

Dear Freaked: The man's supervisor should be told about this incredible lack of judgment. I can assure you the boss will put an end to these daily obscenities.

Dear Ann Landers: What can a secretary do about a boss who seems to lie awake nights thinking of small ways to irritate her? When he laughs, the whole building shakes. He pops his chewing gum and cracks his knuckles. Last week he took off his shoes and cracked his toes.

When he talks to me on the intercom, he breathes so hard between sentences I want to scream. Sometimes he coughs and wheezes—all this with a cigar clenched between his teeth so his words are barely intelligible.

Some days when he is extremely busy, he will tell me not to put through any calls. Later in the day, when I give him a list of the callers, he gets mad and yells, "Why didn't you put Mr. X. and Mrs. R. through? You should have known those calls were important!" So in addition to having the patience of a saint, I am expected to be a mind reader. Any suggestions?

—Only Human and That's Not Enough

Dear Only: These small annoyances will loom larger as time goes by. You don't really like this man, and I can tell you he is not going to change. So start now to look for another job, buttercup. You and the boss are incompatible.

Dear Ann Landers: I am a secretary in an academic department at a California state university. I was in my office one morning when a part-time lecturer walked in. This woman was in her early 30s, had a bachelor of arts degree and a master's degree, and was working on her Ph.D.

"Nora" started to complain that her large toenail was making a hole in her pantyhose. She sat down, whipped off her pantyhose and proceeded to trim her toenail with her teeth. I was absolutely speechless when she put her foot up to her mouth and started to perform this incredible act.

I am enclosing my home phone number in case you want to verify this story, but please don't print my name. I would never hear the end of it. Sign me

—Still Stunned in California.

Dear Still Stunned: I don't need to phone you. I don't doubt for a minute that the incident occurred.

I wonder how many woman over 40 who are reading this can get their big toe up to their mouth? I tried it and finally succeeded, but it was one gigantic struggle.

Shortly after this column appeared, I received a letter from an angry woman whose mother tried to put her toe in her mouth and wound up in the hospital with a wrenched back.

What Went Wrong

This is the story of four people.
Everybody, Somebody, Anybody and Nobody.
There was an important job to be done and Everybody was sure
    that Somebody would do it.
Anybody could have done it but Nobody did it.
Somebody got angry because it was Everybody's job.
Everybody thought that Somebody would do it.
But Nobody asked Anybody.
It ended up that the job wasn't done and Everybody blamed
    Somebody, when actually Nobody asked Anybody.

Dear Ann Landers: A hundred years from now, when people want to know what life was like in the 20th century, they will probably point to your column, as you are the bellwether on social behavior today.

I work for a Fortune 500 company and have a terrific job. Through downsizing, we are now working 60-plus-hour weeks. I do the job four other people used to do. When I get home, I'm exhausted.

Of course, I am thankful for my job and am not a whiner. But the pace and hours we work are absurd. This is not only a burden on our families, but what corporate America does not see is that this is not good for the company.

When you are working constantly, your mind doesn't function as well. I am not as productive on the job as I should be. I bring a ton of work home and spend several hours on the phone or checking automated mail on my home computer.

This is not only my opinion. I hear this from friends and relatives, too. It seems that if the work can't be handled during a normal work week, then perhaps we need more people to do the job.

Ann, what you say really affects public opinion. Can you help?

—Burnt Out

Dear Burnt: It's difficult to tell you what to do because I have no idea where you are in the corporate structure. Moreover, I don't know if the company is extremely profitable or struggling. Nor do I know anything about your energy level or the quality of your performance.

Could you get another job with no trouble, or are you lucky to be where you are? One thing is clear, you feel overworked and underappreciated.

Here are your options: Round up some colleagues who share your discontent, and let your boss know that he (or she) needs to hire additional hands.

Work at a slower pace, quit taking work home and see if that makes you more productive.

Look around for a job that is less demanding, even though it means a smaller paycheck. Forgive me for being corny, but money isn't everything. I have never heard of a man who said on his deathbed, "I wish I had spent more time at the office."

Dear Ann Landers: The letter you printed about the downsizing of corporate America hit a bull's-eye. My old company laid off secretaries, engineers, mail clerks and telephone personnel because profits were falling. The same brain-dead management that hasn't had a bright idea or taken a risk in 10 years still calls the shots. They stack the deck so there are more benefits for themselves. They couldn't care less about us working stiffs.

I am now self-employed because I cannot bear to put up with any more management morons.

—Danbury, Conn.

Dear Dan: The letter I ran on downsizing produced a firestorm of angry mail from both management and "the working stiffs." The anti-management responses were especially hostile. Take a look:

From Dallas: Your response to "Burnt Out" tells me that when it comes to corporate America, you don't have a clue. Managers know the company is understaffed, the employees are overworked and morale is low. They don't give a damn because they have the power. If you complain, your name goes to the top of the hit list, and you are out of there.

Moundsville, W. Va.: I am a coal miner. There are weeks in the winter when I don't see daylight. There have been times when I ate my lunch at the end of a 10- or 12-hour day. The only way I can get a weekend off is to be sick or get hurt. The company has downsized to a third of what the work force used to be, and the production has almost tripled. I would love to quit this stinkin' job, but I don't dare. I have a family to feed.

Oklahoma: "Burnt Out" needs to see the other side of the picture. I run a bakery and put in 74 hours a week. My so-called "day" starts at 1:00 A.M. People complain that overworked, unappreciated employees produce poor service, shoddy workmanship and faulty products. I'd like to tell them a thing or two. I spend half my time hunting for help. People say they want to work, but that's a lie. The job I'm trying to fill requires someone who will be polite and helpful to the customers. Sound easy? The last four people I interviewed were hopeless. One young man wore an earring in his nose.

Waterloo, Iowa: I went to work for a large corporation 30 years ago. After several moves and promotions, I took a field position so I could spend more time with my family. I survived several downsizings, the company merged, and my territory expanded. I am now on the road four days a week. I work every weekend just to keep up. Recently our company split from its parent organization, and we now have no retirement benefits or medical insurance. My father told me long ago, "Never work for someone else." I wish I had listened.

Downstate Illinois: I've been called a tough boss and a slave driver because I expect my employees to look presentable, come in on time, be courteous and put in an honest day's work. Is that too much to ask? Apparently it is because I'm trying to fill three jobs now. The first thing applicants want to know is "Am I off weekends, and how much do you pay for overtime?"

Indianapolis: Please tell your readers that downsizing isn't management's fault. Employers are simply trying to be competitive and stay in business. There will be no jobs if there is no company, and there will be no company if some other company somewhere else can do the job cheaper. Tell the whiners to look at the standard of living in China, India and Mexico, because this is our competition.

Dear Ann Landers: I'm sick of the 70-somethings who whine about the Depression. Those people entered the job market during the post–World War II boom—the greatest expansion in our nation's history. You put out your hands and the money rolled in. Mom stayed home with the kids because one paycheck was enough. Dad worked 40 hours a week and got paid overtime if he worked longer. You have fat pensions to get you through your golden years.

Steel workers in Gary collected twice my income even though they didn't have my education. Rather than make wage concessions to allow their employers to be competitive, they voted to close their plants so they could live off generous benefits.

The Depression-era experiences of your parents are no different from the experiences of today's young people. We got "riffed" by Reagan and "bankrupted" by Bush. Our taxes are paying for your Medicare and Social Security. Compared to today, the Depression was a day at the beach.

I started to work when I was 14. I put myself through undergraduate and graduate school by working 60-hour weeks, and graduated summa cum laude. When the first wave of downsizing hit during the early '80s, I liquidated my assets to go to law school, thinking a legal career would provide job security. I worked 90 hours a week, no overtime or time off for holidays or vacations. Yet I was downsized two more times. I have no pension, my savings are gone and I'm reduced to living with family members.

If you have the guts to print this letter, please don't use my name because I'm trying to find a job—again.

—Unemployed MBA/JD

Dear MBA/JD: It didn't take much guts to print your letter, but it must have taken a lot out of you to write it. With your academic background and the effort you made to get an education, I can't understand why you are having so much trouble.

There's a glitch somewhere that needs to be looked into. You ought to invest in a few counseling sessions. It would be well worth it. Good luck.

Dear Ann Landers: I read with interest the letter from "Unemployed MBA/JD." I work in a law firm and her story is one I've heard before. Many times. The market is so glutted with lawyers that our small firm is able to hire Ivy League graduates for associate positions. In fact, they are beating our doors down.

It definitely is an employer's market. We have received a large number of résumés from attorneys who are applying for paralegal positions. Their cover letters state that they have been trying to find positions without success and are willing to work as paralegals to get a foot in the door.

The attorneys we do hire are expected to work diligently and be extremely competent. If they don't measure up, they don't last long. Replacements are a dime a dozen. One thing is for sure—I am not going to encourage my children to be lawyers. Jobs are hard to find, the hours are long and the pay is lousy.

Good luck to "Unemployed MBA/JD." She will need it.

—Sympathizer in D.C.

Dear Sympathizer: The job market is tough not only for brand new lawyers, but fledgling doctors, engineers and business school graduates, etc. When young people write and ask me how to find employment, I don't know what to tell them.

My response to people who are desperate for jobs is the same as Tarzan's comment to Jane: "It's a jungle out there." I know of no magic words to open those doors.

A reader from Issaquah, Wash., wrote about how hard it was to get a job. I suggested that perhaps her negative attitude had something to do with her failure to land something. I caught unshirted hell for that one.

Dear Ann Landers: My husband and I are about to celebrate 25 years of marriage. We are also about to celebrate his employment, because after three years of looking for a job, he finally found one.

After reading the letter from the young person explaining why he can't get work, I'd like to tell him there are a great many middle-aged men who would jump at a job for $6 a hour. That young person said he had to wait for the older generation to retire. He doesn't understand what has happened to the middle class in this country. They have become part of the working poor.

People with one or two degrees can no longer find positions that pay well enough to support a family. My husband has degrees in math and computer science. I also have two degrees, one in music and another in teaching. Last fall I found a job working in a warehouse for $8 an hour.

We have always been very frugal. We bought our car outright instead of on credit. We never buy anything unless we have the money in the bank to pay for it.

No younger person should wait around for my husband to quit his job. He will have to work for the rest of his life. The chance of ever being able to own a home is probably zero. Health care is a joke. Nobody cares about our health but us and Hillary Clinton.

—Issaquah, Wash.

Dear I.W.: Your letter is downright depressing. I don't want to kill the messenger but your negative attitude may have something to do with all the bad luck you've been experiencing. People who expect the worst often get it.

I hope now that your husband has finally found a job, life will be better for you and yours. This could be the turning point. I'll keep my fingers crossed.

Dear Ann Landers: I'll bet you have already received several hundred letters from readers like myself who were stunned by your insensitivity. I refer to your response to the woman whose husband had been looking for a job for three years. You said her letter was "downright depressing" and suggested that her "negative attitude" must have had a lot to do with her bad luck.

Get real. I know Ph.D.s who have lost their jobs and are now working for $6 an hour. You are going to hear plenty about your unsympathetic response.

—Judy S. in Durham, N.C.

Dear Judy: I did indeed "hear plenty," and when 6,000 people write and tell me I'm out of the loop, I'd better take another look. Meanwhile, here's what my readers had to say:

From Wilton, Calif.: You are clearly out of touch with the sinking middle class. I was at one time a corporate president, and now, due to "downsizing," I am working for minimum wage. Welcome to the real world.

Troy, Mich.: My husband worked for an advertising agency for 23 years. He was only 49 when the company decided to "downsize" and suggested he take early retirement. He's been job-hunting for three years. Now do you get it?

Moline, Ill.: My son has two degrees, one in business, another in accounting. He, too, was downsized and can't find a job that uses his talents. He's now delivering flowers for a wholesale florist.

Davenport, Iowa: When was the last time you dipped into your retirement savings to pay the $650 monthly premium to keep your health insurance in force? Do you know what it's like to send out 125 resumes and not get a nibble?

Hartford, Conn.: Dear Marie Antoinette: Millions of people in the United States and Canada are working for little more than peanuts to create millionaires and billionaires. This is the stuff revolutions are made of.

Bellevue, Wash.: Eight families in our apartment complex have been hit with layoffs in the past three years. They are all degreed, middle-aged, and attractive. You're lucky to have a permanent job, Ann. Shame on you.

Peoria, Ill.: There is a new class in America—the Educated Working Poor. They won't be able to retire or leave anything to their children or grandkids. There goes the American dream.

Cincinnati, Ohio: I was "downsized" (a polite word for canned) out the door after 21 years of faithful service. Management had changed hands and my years of loyalty meant absolutely nothing to the new crowd. My replacement was a lad my son's age. Just sign me "Washed up at 47."

Philadelphia: No jobs? Nonsense! The quality of entry level workers is pathetic. I've interviewed hundreds of college graduates who can't read, can't spell and can't do simple math. Worse yet, many can't pass a drug test. That's the *real* picture. Got it?

Dear Phil: The "real picture" often depends on your vantage point. Millions of competent people are out of work. Downsizing is a fact of life and I feel for those who want to work and can't find jobs.

Dear Ann Landers: The older and younger generations seem to be waging a war in your column. I'd like to add my comments.

My wife and I are 30 years old. When the "old-timers" talk about how tough they had it, we don't complain. We listen. Here's why:

The older folks have Medicare and Social Security, which are both nearly bankrupt. It may not last long enough to help them and they worry about it. These programs were meant to keep the elderly from living on dog food and dying in squalor due to poverty and lack of medical care.

My wife and I can afford medical insurance by having a high deductible. We insure only against catastrophic need, not the sniffles.

For retirement, we save and invest those savings carefully. Although we make only about $40,000 a year between the two of us, we own our home and manage to put money in the bank. Our secret is plain, old Yankee thrift—don't buy it unless you need it, don't buy it new if used will do, and don't buy it at all if you have to use credit.

The days of lifelong employment are over. I have been laid off three times and my wife twice because of downsizing. Each time, we tightened our belts, hit the pavement and were working again within a month. We have no special skills or education (I did not finish high school), but we do have the old-fashioned "can-do" attitude that a job—*any* job—is better than none.

We learned these lessons by heeding the advice of the older generation. My advice to others our age is to stop whining and listen to what those who have been there have to say. It could be valuable and it might even give you some wonderful stories for your grandkids.

—Open Ears in California

Dear California: You and your wife have a great attitude, and your warning about buying on credit shows maturity and wisdom. Thanks for writing.

Why I Fired My Secretary

I woke up early feeling depressed because it was my birthday, and I thought, "I'm another year older," but decided not to dwell on it. So I showered and shaved, knowing when I went down to breakfast my wife would greet me with a big kiss and say, "Happy birthday, dear."

All smiles, I went into breakfast, and there sat my wife reading the newspaper as usual. She didn't say one word. So I got myself a cup of coffee and thought, "Oh well, she forgot. The kids will be down in a few minutes. They will sing 'Happy Birthday' and have a nice gift for me."

There I sat, enjoying my coffee, and I waited. Finally the kids came running into the kitchen yelling, "Give me a slice of toast! I'm late! Where is my coat? I'm going to miss the bus!" Feeling more depressed than ever, I left for the office.

When I walked in, my secretary greeted me with a great big smile and a cheerful, "Happy birthday, boss." She then asked if she could get me some coffee. Her remembering my birthday made me feel a whole lot better.

Later in the morning, my secretary knocked on my office door and said, "Since it's your birthday, why don't we have lunch together?" Thinking it would make me feel better, I said, "That's a good idea."

So we locked up the office, and since it was my birthday I said, "Why don't we drive out of town and have lunch in the country, instead of going to the usual place?" So we drove out of town and went to a little out-of-the-way inn and had a couple of martinis and a nice lunch. We started driving back to town when my secretary said, "Why don't we go by my place, and I will fix you another martini?" It sounded like a good idea, since we didn't have much to do in the office. So we went to her apartment, and she fixed some martinis.

After a while, she said, "If you will excuse me, I think I will slip into something more comfortable," and she left the room. In a few minutes, she opened her bedroom door and came out carrying a big birthday cake. Following her were my wife and all my kids. And there I sat with nothing on but my socks.

12

Bury Me in My 1937 Dodge

No one likes to think about dying, but occasionally we need to remember life's limitations. In the midst of tragedy, my readers find the time to educate me about the best way to face this ultimate challenge:

Togetherness
Henry Canon Holland

Death is nothing at all. I have only slipped away into the next room.

Whatever we were to each other, we still are. Call me by my old familiar name. Speak to me in the same way you always have. Laugh as we always laughed at the little jokes we enjoyed together. Play, smile, think of me, pray for me.

Life means all that it ever meant. It is the same as it always was. There is absolute unbroken continuity. Why should I be out of your mind because I am out of your sight? I am but waiting for you, for an interval, somewhere very near, just around the corner.

All is well. Nothing is past. Nothing has been lost. One brief moment and all will be as it was before—only better. Infinitely happier. We will be one, together forever.

Dear Ann Landers: This may be one of the most unusual letters you have ever received. You see, I am dying. But don't become alarmed, and please don't feel sorry for me. After all, we are all dying. From the moment we are born, we are headed toward inescapable death.

Three years ago I learned I have chronic leukemia. (I was 31 then.) The doctor told me the truth at once because I insisted on knowing. The news came at a crisis time in my life. (I had just gone through a divorce and had young children to raise.)

Would you believe I had to move out of town to a larger city because people would not accept me as a normal person? I was devastated, not by the disease, which has been controlled by drugs, but by the way I was treated. Although I could play tennis, ski, dance, hike and take part in community activities, the people at work made my life miserable. (One woman refused to use the same washroom!) Men wouldn't date me. I was treated like some sort of social outcast—a pathetic, hopeless case.

After I moved to this distant city my life changed dramatically. No one here knows of my illness and I am keeping my mouth shut. I work part-time, attend college, have many friends, am involved with community activities and participate in sports. What a pity that I had to move to a town where nobody knew me in order to live a normal life!

Although I feel well, look fine and am managing beautifully, I know it can't last forever. I dread the day my friends must be told of my illness. I don't want to be pitied. And of course I fear that I may be deserted as I was once before.

The purpose of this letter, Ann Landers, is to help educate people, should they encounter someone in their life's pattern who is in the same spot I'm in right now. Yes, folks—you can help. How? Here are the ways:

1. Treat me the same as a well person. Don't ask me, "How are you doing?"
2. Include me in your activities. I need friends just as you do.
3. Stay off the subject of funeral arrangements and insurance. (Relatives are especially guilty of this.)
4. Forget I have a disease. I'll do better if I don't know it's on your mind.
5. Ask me out. Develop a relationship with me. You can even marry me. I might live another 20 years. (Today that's longer than most couples stay together!)
6. Hire me. If I'm productive I will live longer. If I'm forced to go on welfare or disability, it will raise your taxes.

7. Give to the American Cancer Society. They support research and alert the public to cancer signs.
8. Get a checkup this week. Many forms of cancer can be cured if caught early.
9. Treat me as you would like to be treated under the same circumstances.
10. Love me! Enjoy me! I have a lot to give.

—I Could Be Anybody

Dear Anybody: What a beautiful and courageous letter! Thank you for educating millions of people today. You've made an enormous contribution.

Dear Ann Landers: Not long ago, my husband and I experienced a parent's worst nightmare. We were told that one of our children has a medical condition for which there is no treatment and that we should anticipate her death.

The pain we are feeling is indescribable. Although we are pursuing every avenue, hoping to find someone in the medical field who knows more, we must face the possibility of losing our little angel. Although she is still with us, we are already grieving. There is such a cloud hanging over our heads, it is difficult to get through the day without breaking down. We walk around with tears in our eyes.

Please, Ann, help us. How do we plan to give up a child? Although we have always been strong in faith, we are finding it particularly hard to pray.

May we ask your readers, many of whom have been in our shoes, what we should do? Do we pull our children out of school and take a dream trip? Or is everyday living the best gift for her? What about our other children? How do we prepare them for the loss? Can we avoid any traps that may scar them forever? Is there any way we can prepare for what lies ahead? We are heartbroken. Can you help us?

—Arrow Through Our Hearts in New England

Dear Parents: My heart goes out to you. Every parent who reads your letter is sure to feel your pain. Life has certainly dealt you a cruel blow.

You give no clue as to your daughter's age, the nature of her illness or how much time she may have left. In spite of the scant background, if any of my readers have some suggestions, I will pass them along. Please let me hear from you. Over the years, my readers have become like family, and we must help one another.

Dear Ann Landers: This is in response to the parents whose child is incurably ill. They wanted to know how to make her final days happy ones.

Forgive me for being critical, but I'm afraid they are missing the boat. Indulging her with a "dream trip" or other luxuries will not help prepare anyone for the inevitable. It would only add to the tension and drain the energy of the entire family. Since this lovely young girl will not be able to make contributions in future years, you must now help make her brief life as purposeful and productive as possible.

Use the money you would have spent on indulgences, and try to raise additional funds to build something that will provide health, education or recreation for deprived children.

Perhaps an aquarium in a ghetto school, a playground for handicapped youngsters, a nature walk, an immunization clinic or a sports center. Get your daughter's friends and classmates involved in the project she finds most appealing.

Let everyone see that this is her gift to other children. It will give her a great deal of pleasure and might even lengthen her life.

As for help, perhaps the local Rotary, a church youth group or another organization will join in the project and make it larger and more enduring that something you put together on your own.

And please consider arranging in advance for organ donation. It's a marvelous way for your child's beauty to live on.

In short, help her be part of a lasting memorial that will bring other children a more fulfilling life. Purposeful living is the best preparation for dying.

—A Caring Rotarian

Dear Friend: What a beautiful concept. I received thousands of letters suggesting ways to make this child's final days more pleasant, but yours was the most creative and constructive. Keep reading for more on the subject.

Dear Ann Landers: This letter is for the parents who are faced with the loss of a daughter who is terminally ill. They asked for your guidance.

You, dear parents, have incredible strength that you are not yet aware of. Once you get past this horrendous shock and the "why me?" phase, allow yourselves to say, "Why not me, because I have the strength to make each day a good one for her."

Let each day be calm, loving and ordinary. Do the sort of things the whole family would do anyway, as well as other things you may have been putting off. You will get much advice. That's OK, but trust your instincts.

Parents who have lost a child by accident or murder or sudden death, whatever the reason, had no chance to prepare. Use what time there is to the fullest. It will become clear to you what is truly important and what is trivial. May God bless you. You are in my prayers.

—Swarthmore, Pa.

Dear Ann Landers: I was lucky enough to have the son that every mother dreams will be hers.

"John" was the light of my life—handsome, bright, kind, sensitive, talented, generous and funny. He died in an accident that didn't have to happen. His car was hit head-on by a drunken driver.

I have read everything I could lay my hands on, searching for solace and asking the same question: "Why, why, why?" John was only 21 and had so much to give. Maybe there are no answers, but I would appreciate any word of comfort that you might be able to offer. Please try. Thank you.

—A Heavy Heart in California

Dear Friend: I can find no words to ease your pain, but a few days ago a letter crossed my desk and I set it aside for just the right moment. That moment is now. It is the perfect response that I could never have provided. My readers, bless them, always come through when I need them. Here is the letter.

Dear Ann Landers: On October 15, 1983, my 21-year-old son, Kevin, was killed in an automobile accident. At that time I thought nothing could be as painful and devastating as that loss. I was wrong.

On March 3, 1989, my son, Leo, 28 years old, died. The death of this second son reopened the wounds of my previous loss. It was a struggle to hang on to my sanity. I knew in my heart that my sons would not want me to give up on life. They were so full of fun and laughter. They would expect me to pull myself together and carry on. I knew I had to do it for them. The night after Kevin died I wrote some words to be read at his funeral. When Leo died, I reread them. I would like to share them with your readers. Here they are:

If God said to me, "You can choose or not choose to have a son, Kevin. If you choose to have a son, Kevin, he will have red hair and shiny eyes and a great sense of humor. He will be a ray of sunshine in your life and cheer you on when you are down.

"But you can have him for only 21 years. And when he leaves, you must pay a great price for those 21 years. That price will be deep sorrow."

I would choose to have Kevin.

And if God said to me, "When he goes, you can choose for him to have a lingering, painful death, one that would help you adjust to his leaving and give you a chance to say goodbye.

"Or you can choose for him to go quickly and painlessly.

"But if you choose for him to go quickly and painlessly, you must pay a great price, and that price is deep sorrow."

I would choose a quick and painless death for Kevin.

These words were read at Kevin Brown's funeral on October 18, 1983.

—Barbara Brown, N.J.

Dear Barbara Brown: Thank you for giving me permission to share your words with my readers. What you have written will lift the hearts and ease the pain of millions of parents who have suffered similar losses. The service you have performed this day is incalculable. Leo and Kevin would be very proud of their mother.

Dear Ann Landers: I hope you will find room in your column for some "do's" and "don'ts" for people who want to help bereaved parents.

I am a chapter leader of one of the 224 chapters of Compassionate Friends, an organization you frequently recommend. Thank you for telling the world about us.

—Been There in Santa Monica

Dear Monica: Here are the "do's" and "don'ts" prepared by Lee Schmidt. I appreciate the opportunity to pass the word.

DO's

Do say you are sorry about their pain and what happened to their child.

Do allow them to express the grief they are feeling.

Do allow them to talk as much as they want about the child they lost.

Do give special attention to the child's brothers and sisters, both at the funeral and in the months to come. They, too, are hurt and confused and in need of attention—which their parents may not be able to give them.

Do reassure the parents that they did everything they could, that the medical care their child received was the best, or whatever else you know to be true and positive.

DON'Ts

Don't avoid the bereaved because you are uncomfortable. (Being avoided adds pain to an already intolerable experience.)

Don't say, "You ought to be feeling better by now," or anything that implies a judgment about their feelings.

Don't avoid mentioning the child's name for fear of reminding them of their loss. (They haven't forgotten it!)

Don't point out that at least they have other children. (Children are not interchangeable. One cannot replace another.)

Don't say, "You can always have another child." (Even if they wanted to and could, another child would not replace the child they lost.)

Don't make comments that suggest the care in the emergency room, hospital or wherever was inadequate. Parents are always plagued by feelings of doubt and guilt. Family and friends should be careful not to sow seeds of doubt.

Dear Ann Landers: I recently lost a member of my family in a traffic accident. Until then I never had to attend a funeral of someone so close, and young, who had died in such a terrible way. I found out that very few people know how to act at a funeral. After one hour of being "comforted," I was more depressed than ever by the thoughtless remarks of so-called friends.

Examples: "How many bones were broken? I heard he was crushed. I don't think he looks like himself at all. I wish they had kept the casket closed."

I have written down some guidelines. Please print them in your column. There are so many people who have a lot to learn:

Do send a sympathy card.

Do go to the funeral home if it is possible.

Do sign the register. It is the only way the family members will know for certain you were there. When tragedy strikes, their minds are a blur.

Do extend your sympathy to each family member. Simply say, "I'm so sorry." There is nothing more to be said at such a time.

Don't write long letters and slip them in your sympathy card. Wait a few weeks if you feel the need to say more.

Don't ask personal questions about the accident or illness. If they feel you should know more, they will tell you.

Don't hunt down members of the family at the funeral home. If they are not in the main room, they probably would prefer not to see anyone.

Thank you for letting me express myself. Somehow just writing this letter has made me feel better.

—Greensburg, Pa.

Dear Friend: You have performed a useful service today. Thanks for sitting in my chair.

Dear Ann Landers: I am sending on some suggestions that might be helpful for families who will be facing an empty chair at a holiday table:

You are facing the holidays, and someone you love will be missing. You see intact families everywhere—on TV screens, in magazine ads, on holiday cards, joyfully celebrating. You may be overwhelmed with grief as you face an empty chair at your table.

The following suggestions may help you to cope:

1. Change traditions. Have Christmas dinner at a different house this year. It is a paradox that the more you try to make it the same as it was before, the more obvious your loved one's absence will be.
2. Balance solitude with sociability. Solitude can renew strength. Being with people you care about can be equally important. Plan to attend some holiday parties. You may surprise yourself by having a good time.

3. Relive the happy memories. Pick three special memories of past holidays with your loved one. Recall them often, especially if outbursts of grief seem to occur at an inappropriate time.

4. Set aside "letting go" time. Schedule specific time on your calendar to grieve. When you know you have set aside this time, it will be easier for you to postpone your flow of grief in public.

5. Counter the conspiracy of silence. Because family and friends love you, they may think they are doing you a favor by not mentioning your loved one for fear you will be upset. Break the ice by mentioning him or her yourself. Tell your family and friends that it is important for you to talk about your loved one during the holiday season when that missing person is very much on your mind.

6. Find a creative outlet. Write a memorial poem or story about your loved one and share it. Contribute or work with a group that your loved one supported. Use the money that you would have spent for a gift for that special person to buy something for someone he or she cared about.

7. Don't forget the rest of the family. Try especially hard to make it a good holiday for the children. Listen to them. Talk to them. If decorating the tree or buying Christmas gifts is too difficult for you to do this year, ask a friend to do it for you.

8. Utilize available resources. If your faith is important to you, participate in the holiday church services. Some veterans of the faith have a serenity, a kind of healing wisdom. They can help you. Seek out a support group of other victims. Or start your own short-term support group to help you through the holidays.

It is tempting to conclude that life is awful during the holidays. Yes, you will have some difficult times, but you also can experience some joy.

Having a good time does not mean that you have forgotten your loved one or that you loved him or her any less. Let yourself go.

Above all, remember that you cannot change the past. You can, however, take care of the present. Total recovery may never come. But what you kindle from the ashes of your tragedy is largely up to you.

—J.H.L., Mothers Against Drunk Driving,
Hurst, Texas

Dear Ann Landers: In July, 1985, my wife was diagnosed as having terminal cancer. Shortly afterward, your column on "The Station," by Robert J. Hastings, appeared in *Newsday*.

For years we had talked of "someday" going to Paris, a city I fell in love with as a GI. The day after I read the poem I realized that it was time to pull into the "station."

As soon as the doctor OK'ed the trip, we went to Paris and had the most beautiful vacation of our 43 years. My lovely wife passed away a year and a half after the diagnosis.

I since have taken the liberty of passing copies of that column to friends.

One purchased his "someday" car; another went on a long-delayed trip.

But "The Station" also can mean visiting a sick friend, and that "someday" should be now.

There is so much hurt in looking back and remembering those things we intended to do and didn't.

Thank you, Ann Landers, for Paris.

—Irv Gaiptman

Dear Irv: You were dear to let me know what "The Station" meant to your life. Here it is for all the others who haven't as yet learned that lesson:

The Station

Robert J. Hastings

Tucked away in our subconscious is an idyllic vision. We see ourselves on a long trip that spans the continent. We are traveling by train. Out the windows we drink in the passing scene of cars on nearby highways, of children waving at a crossing, of cattle grazing on a distant hillside, of smoke pouring from a power plant, of row upon row of corn and wheat, of flatlands and valleys, of mountains and rolling hillsides, of city skylines and village halls.

But uppermost in our minds is the final destination. On a certain day at a certain hour we will pull into the station. Bands will be playing and flags waving. Once we get there so many wonderful dreams will come true, and the pieces of our lives will fit together like a completed jigsaw puzzle. How restlessly we pace the aisles, damning the minutes for loitering—waiting, waiting, waiting for the station.

"When we reach the station, that will be it!" we cry.
"When I'm 18."
"When I buy a new 450SL Mercedes-Benz!"
"When I put the last kid through college."
"When I have paid off the mortgage!"
"When I get a promotion."
"When I reach the age of retirement, I shall live happily ever after!"

Sooner or later we must realize there is no station, no one place to arrive at once and for all. The true joy of life is the trip. The station is only a dream. It constantly outdistances us.

"Relish the moment" is a good motto, especially when coupled with Psalm 118:24: "This is the day which the Lord hath made; we will rejoice and be glad in it." It isn't the burdens of today that drive men mad. It is the regrets over yesterday and the fear of tomorrow. Regret and fear are twin thieves who rob us of today.

So stop pacing the aisles and counting the miles. Instead, climb more mountains, eat more ice cream, go barefoot more often, swim more rivers, watch more sunsets, laugh more, cry less. Life must be lived as we go along. The station will come soon enough.

In spite of the seriousness of the subject, every now and then, I'll get an outrageous letter or one that strikes the funny bone. Take a look at these:

Dear Ann Landers: People become really upset when airlines lose their luggage. Can't blame them for that, but what do you think about an airline that loses your father? Here's what happened.

Dad passed away while visiting friends in Missouri. He was to be buried in Chicago. The family requested that his remains be sent there, which meant a change of planes in Kansas City. We gathered at my sister's house while my brother went out to O'Hare Airport with an undertaker.

After waiting for what seemed like an eternity, my brother called and said, "The plane came in, but Pa wasn't on it." I asked, "Where could he be?" My brother said: "They don't seem to know. The computers are down and they aren't sure." I asked, "Do they realize what they lost?" My brother replied. "They sure as hell do, and they are really looking."

After four hours of waiting, my brother called to say, "Remember how Pa used to love to travel? Well, he just had a nice trip. He's in

Washington, D.C." I asked, "How in the world did he end up there?" No one knew, but they sent him back that night, and we all had a good laugh. Bless his heart, that was his final gift to his loving family.

—T.H.

Dear T.H.: Your letter is proof positive that a sense of humor can be a tremendous asset in times of trouble. Thanks for writing.

Dear Ann Landers: My sister has been after me for several years to make a will. I hate even to think about where I want my money and possessions to go after I die. This may sound crazy, but I have six large gold crowns in my mouth and I know they are worth a lot of money.

I firmly believe there will be a resurrection and it will come sooner than most people think. I want to be ready. If I leave the gold crowns to a relative, I would then need to have the crowns replaced after I am resurrected.

Dentistry may be a lot more expensive by the time I rise again. Also, the waiting period to get an appointment might be even worse than it is now.

I wouldn't dream of discussing this problem with anyone I know, but it weighs heavily on my mind. You are the only one I can go to for help without looking like a fool. Please guide me.

—Looking Ahead in North Carolina

Dear Head: Since you are certain you will be needing your teeth for your return to Earth, my advice is keep them in your mouth and out of your will. The decision is sure to take a load off your mind.

Dear Ann Landers: My husband was open-mouthed, slack-jawed and almost turned gray overnight when I told him I wanted to hire a wood craftsman to design a beautiful chest to use in the family room and put some cushions on it so people can sit there—then, when I die, I want it to be my coffin. Besides being able to store blankets in this chest, I will know and become accustomed to my final resting place.

I am a practical person. My husband thinks I am crazy. I also told him I want a private funeral, the most inexpensive one available, only wild flowers, and that he should not have me embalmed.

I hate funerals and do not want my friends and family looking at me in that shape.

Do you think I am kooky? If I put this in my will, who should I give it to? If you print my letter, I ask that I remain anonymous. I'm in enough trouble with my family over this. The neighbors don't have to know.

—Need Your Support in Oklahoma

Dear Oklahoma: If this is what you want, I see no reason why you shouldn't have it.

Putting the instructions in your will ensures nothing. You may be buried before the will is read. Your best bet is to discuss the situation with one of your children, your clergyman and your physician. Between the three of them, someone should see to it that your wishes are respected.

Dear Ann Landers: Have you heard of a Viking funeral? I hadn't until two weeks ago. Since then I have thought of little else. Please give me some guidance. I'm all fogged up on this one.

My grandfather has told my brother and me that he wants a Viking funeral. We didn't know what it was until he explained. The deceased person is put in a boat. The boat is set on fire and shoved out to sea.

Grandpa lives in Minneapolis, and there is no sea anywhere around. He says he wants us to use Lake Harriet instead. It all sounds very sentimental, but the other members of the family insist it's a crazy idea, and they will not agree to it.

My brother and I think Grandpa should have his way. After all, when life has gone out of the body what difference does it make what is done with it? Please agree with us. It would make Grandpa happy to know you are on his side. It might also help persuade the other members of the family to grant that sweet old man his last wish.

—Joe from Bismarck, N.D.

Dear Joe: Every state has its own burial laws, and I know of no state where a Viking funeral is legal. Break the news gently to Grandpa. It sounds as if he had his heart set on it.

Dear Ann Landers: I just learned that my wonderful husband has an incurable illness and cannot live more than three or four months.

We have had over 30 grand years together and this is a terrible blow to me. I know I must face reality so I am turning to you for strength and guidance. Please tell me, Ann, what should I wear to the funeral?

I have a navy blue silk dress with puffy long sleeves. It has a high neckline and is conservative in style. Should I wear gloves and a hat? Would it be proper to wear a veil over my face? What about dark glasses under the veil? Would this be correct in church? If I wear dark glasses into the church, should I remove them for the services?

All eyes will be on me during the funeral and I don't want to do anything wrong. Ever since I got the tragic news I've been a wreck worrying about these things. Please put my mind at ease.

—Almost in Mourning

Dear Almost: Why don't you shoot your husband now while your puffy-sleeved blue dress is still in style?

Nobody is going to give two whoops whether you wear a veil *over* your glasses or *under* your glasses. A funeral is no style show. Of all the self-centered women I've encountered in this work, you take the prize.

Dear Ann Landers: In 1926, when I was a youngster, my mother died. I was an only child and the family had quite a lot of money. My dad managed to lose everything by the time I graduated from high school. He is dead now.

A few weeks ago, at a family party, they got to talking about my mother and what beautiful jewelry she had. One of my cousins asked what happened to the jewelry. My great-uncle replied, "They buried her in it."

When we got home I mentioned to my wife that we could sure use some money and I would like to have my mother's grave dug up and sell the jewelry. She looked at me like I was crazy. Would this be such a terrible thing to do? After all, I am entitled to whatever worldly goods my parents had. My wife says the thought of it makes her skin crawl. May I have your opinion?

—Practical Man

Dear Man: How practical can you get? You've managed to get by this long without digging up any graves, haven't you?

If you are so nuts about money, why don't you dig up a second job?

Dear Ann Landers: Are people crazier today than at any time in the history of man? I believe the answer is "yes." The item I just read in the newspaper is pretty good evidence.

It seems a Mrs. P. Haverland of Charleston, W.Va., has nothing better to do with her time than to try to break the record for being buried alive. The record is held by some flea brain who lay in an underground casket for 75 days. Mrs. Haverland is sure she can set a new record.

I would like to suggest that anyone who has 75 days to blow ought to go to some hospital and volunteer to break a record visiting the sick or writing letters for the disabled or just cheering up the lonely people in the nursing homes. Do you agree, Ann?

—Chicago Reader

Dear Chicago: People usually enjoy doing what they do best. Perhaps this is Mrs. Haverland's greatest talent.

Dear Ann Landers: I'm not on my deathbed, but I'm getting on in years and I realize I don't have too many left. I beg of you not to think I'm crazy or that I'm putting you on. My question is real.

I have a modest collection of antique automobiles—nothing great, but a few of my favorites. The car I love best is a 1937 Dodge. It holds so many pleasant memories that whenever I look at that great automobile, it makes me feel good all over.

What I want to know is this: Would it be possible for me to be buried in that 1937 Dodge? Instead of a casket I'd like to be sitting at the wheel and lowered into the ground. I can't see where it would hurt anybody. It's just something I want very much. What about it, Ann?

—Muskogee, Okla.

Dear Mus: If you want to be buried in your 1937 Dodge you'd better inform your next of kin, a lawyer and a mortician. Also, the cemetery people should be informed. Each has its own "constitution." If they agree, you'll need three or four plots to accommodate the Dodge, plus special equipment to lower the car into the ground. If it's what you want I hope you get it.

Dear Ann Landers: I was surprised at your response to the man in Oklahoma who wanted to be buried in his 1937 Dodge. You said, "If that's what you want, I hope you get it."

You must be just as nutty as he is. Don't you know we are running out of ground? There isn't enough room for people, much less a 1937 Dodge. Get with it, Granny.

—A Realist

Dear R.: I checked with Rosehill Cemetery in Chicago (founded 150 years ago) and they have enough ground to last for at least another 100 years. (Of course, they've been burying people out there, not cars.)

Atlanta, however, is getting into high-rise mausoleums, which is another way to go, if you'll pardon the expression.

The ultimate solution could be cremation, although some religious groups are opposed to it. Time alters customs, however, and it may well alter this one.

Dear Ann Landers: I have a suggestion for that man in Oklahoma who wanted to be buried in his 1937 Dodge.

You said if he could get the OK from the cemetery, you saw nothing wrong with it. And then you reminded him that he might need three or even four plots.

Why doesn't he have himself cremated and put in the ashtray? Then he could have a crusher (which is used to compress old cars into scrap metal) reduce the size of his car to a neat little block. He would need only one plot, and save a good bit of money.

—Galt, Mo.

Dear Galt: Here's your letter, for whatever it's worth. I hope the man in Oklahoma sees it. Then he can decide.

For more information, contact:

Compassionate Friends
P.O. Box 3696
Oak Brook, IL 60522-3696
(Support group for parents, siblings, relatives, and friends of a child who dies)

Widowed Persons Service
601 E Street NW
Washington, DC 20049
(202) 434-2260

National Association for Uniform Services/Society of Military Widows
5535 Hempstead Way
Springfield, VA 22151

13

Pssst! Want to Buy a Porsche for $50?

Every so often, a letter will arrive that cracks me up. My readers remember these letters and periodically ask me to repeat them. Here are a few of my favorite chucklers:

Dear Ann Landers: I am a homemaker, age 30, have a good husband and three fine children. We are upper middle-class folks who live in an upper middle-class neighborhood and have upper middle-class friends. When I'm in the house alone in the morning, after the children go off to school and my husband leaves for work, I like to do my housework with no clothes on. Yes, you read correctly—with no clothes on. I pull the shades and draw the draperies. No one can possibly see me.

Last week I confided this to a friend, and she said I must be off my rocker—that there is something immoral or sick, or both, about a person who would walk about the house nude. I don't know why I do it. All I know is I enjoy it. Please give me your opinion, Ann Landers.

—Lady Godiva

Dear Lady: I can only guess that you enjoy doing your housework with no clothes on because you like the feeling of total freedom—the same way some swimmers get extra pleasure from swimming in the nude.

If you choose to work around in your own home naked as a jaybird, or wearing a raccoon coat, whose business is it? It may be unusual but this doesn't mean it is immoral or sick.

Dear Ann Landers: I could kiss you for printing that letter from Lady Godiva, the woman who enjoys doing her housework in the nude.

For years I thought maybe I was a freak because I do the same thing. Naturally I've never breathed my secret to a soul—not even my husband. I was greatly relieved when you said it was neither immoral nor sick, and that so long as she kept her shades down it was nobody's business.

I'm a woman in my 40s who also enjoys the freedom of doing her housework in the nude. I can bend and stretch, unencumbered. Now I zip right through this eight-room house in less than two hours. Thank you, Ann. You've made me very happy.

—Another Jaybird

Dear Bird: Apparently I made a great many women happy. A staggering number of housewives wrote to confide that they, too, enjoy cleaning house in the altogether. Here's another Jaybird from Memphis:

Dear Ann Landers: Tell Lady Godiva she's not crazy and she's not alone. I've been doing my housework in my birthday suit for 20 years. I consider myself normal and intelligent.

As a bride I was forever sewing torn seams and restitching pockets which had caught on knobs. One day I took off my housedress when I got soaked to the skin. (A frying pan plopped into the dishwater.) I so enjoyed the feeling of freedom that I've been cleaning house in the nude ever since.

I can report only one minor mishap. Several months ago while ironing a bedsheet I stood a little too close to the board and burned my stomach. Nothing serious—just painful. Please warn the girls.

—Me, In the Flesh

Dear You: Sorry about your stomach, dearie. Take note, Jaybirds.

Other hazards of prancing about unclothed are described in the next letter from Louisville.

Dear Ann Landers: I used to do my housework in the nude but a recent experience cured me. Our minister expressed the wish to see our new baby. The time set for his visit was 2:00 P.M.

I was fresh out of coffee cream and phoned my neighbor to ask if she'd bring over half a bottle. She said, "I'll be there in a few minutes."

I was rushing around (in the nude, as usual) trying to get the house tidied up when the doorbell rang. I grabbed a face towel to wrap around my middle so I could reach out for the coffee cream. I opened the door quickly and shouted, "Boy, am I glad to see you, honey!" To my everlasting shame it was the minister. He was so startled his glasses almost fell off. He mumbled, "I'll be back next week when I can bring my wife."

I slammed the door shut and just sat there and shook for 20 minutes. To this day I'm unable to look him in the face. (P.S. You can be sure I'm no longer a nudist.)

—Still Blushing

Dear Blushing: The next letter from Kansas City may be a comfort.

Dear Ann: I wonder if Lady Godiva saw the news item in the paper about an Ohio housewife. She was doing her laundry in the basement and impulsively decided to take off the soiled housedress she was wearing and throw it into the machine.

Her hair had just been set in pin-curls and the pipes overhead were leaking. She spotted her son's football helmet and put it on her head. There she was, stark naked (except for the football helmet), when she heard a cough. The woman turned around and found herself staring into the face of the meter reader from the gas and electric company.

As he headed for the door, his only comment was, "I hope your team wins, lady."

Dear Ann Landers: You recently published a Gem of the Day: "Sign on the door of a curio shop in Hong Kong: Teeth extracted by latest Methodists." I recognized that phrase from a collection I have of similar linguistic follies. It was originally published in *The International Educator*.

Here is the complete list. I hope you and your readers get a laugh out of it. I do, every time I read it.

—Amused in Vermont

Dear Vermont: A few years ago, I ran some of those humorous translations in my column, but I'm happy to run them again. Laughter, it is said, is good medicine, and if ever the world needed more laughs, now is the time.

According to *The International Educator*, these are reported to be signs in English collected by Air France employees, but I wouldn't bet the rent.

Tokyo hotel: It is forbidden to steal hotel towels. If you are not a person to do such a thing, please not read this notice.

Leipzig, Germany, elevator: Do not enter the lift backwards, and only when lit up.

Paris hotel elevator: Please leave your values at the front desk. If you lose them in your room, we are not responsible.

Athens hotel: Visitors are expected to complain at the office between the hours of 9 and 11 A.M. daily.

Yugoslavian hotel: The flattening of underwear with pleasure is the job of the chambermaid.

Japanese hotel: You are invited to take advantage of the women who are employed to clean the rooms.

Moscow hotel: You are welcome to visit the cemetery where famous Russian and Soviet composers, artists and writers are buried daily except Thursday.

Hong Kong tailor shop: Ladies may have a fit upstairs.

Bangkok dry cleaners: Drop your trousers here for best results.

Paris dress shop: Elegant dresses designed for street walking.

Rhodes, Greece, tailor shop: Order your summer suit. Because of the big rush we will execute customers in strict rotation.

Japanese hotel: Cold and Heat: If you want to condition the warm in your room, please control yourself.

German camping site: It is strictly forbidden on our Black Forest camping site that people of different sex, for instance, men and women, live together in one tent unless they are married with each other for that purpose.

Rome laundry: Ladies, please leave your clothes here and spend the afternoon having a good time.

Czech tourist agency: Take one of our horse-driven city tours. We guarantee no miscarriages.

Swiss mountain inn: Special today—no ice cream.

Copenhagen airline: We take your bags and send them in all directions.

Moscow hotel: If this is your first visit to the U.S.S.R., you are welcome to it.

Norwegian lounge: Ladies are requested not to have children in the bar.

Tokyo car rental firm: When passenger with heavy foot is in sight, tootle the horn. Trumpet him melodiously at first, but if he still obstacles your passage, then tootle him with vigor.

Acapulco hotel: We are pleased to announce that the manager has personally passed all the water served here.

Dear Ann: I have a friend. (I'll call him Maximilian.) Max has a dog. (I'll call him Phido.) Phido has fleas. (I'll call them Igor, Ramon, Jeremiah, Amos, Valentino, Pancho, Christopher, Gart, Tiny Tim, Kismet, Ardeshir and Lucinda.)

After Max and Phido had been to my house for a visit, I found Valentino and Lucinda had stayed behind. I noticed they were making love on my Oriental rug, which I will call Karambastan.

My question: What shall I call their numerous offspring? Or should I just call an exterminator? And if so—what?

—Love Your Column Otherwise

Dear Otherwise: By all means call the exterminator. (He won't care what you call him so long as you pay him.) And while he's there, please ask if he has a highly potent flea powder that will eliminate pests like you.

Dear Ann Landers: Nine of us girls belong to a poker club. We've been meeting every Tuesday night for almost 15 years. The stakes are not high enough to hurt anyone and we all have a good time.

The newest member of the club is causing trouble. I will call her Zelda. We took her in last year when her husband died. Zelda has two artificial teeth in front. They are on a bridge. When Zelda is in a big pot she takes her teeth out and puts them on the chips for luck.

You know as well as I do, Ann Landers, that the cards are going to fall where they are going to fall, but it is amazing the way Zelda's luck improves the minute she puts her teeth on the chips.

The girls in the club don't like it—not because she wins, but because it is a disgusting sight. Please tell me what should be done.

—Yesterday's Hostess

Dear Hostess: It is in bad taste to dismantle one's self in the presence of others. Tell Zelda the ladies would appreciate it if she would keep her choppers off the chips.

Since Zelda seems to be compulsive about removing things, suggest that she put her earrings, beads or wristwatch on the chips and leave her teeth in her head.

Dear Ann Landers: A good friend of many years' standing came with her husband to spend a couple of nights in our home. Although she has always been terribly vain about her looks, I am very fond of her and value her friendship.

In the middle of the night, after we all returned from a party, I heard her get up and go to the bathroom. I soon realized that she was ill and throwing up. I asked her if she needed any help. She said, "No, I feel much better now. It must have been the fish."

The next morning she did not join us at the breakfast table. Her husband brought her a cup of tea in the bedroom. They left around noon—she didn't want any lunch—and she kept a handkerchief over her mouth when she mumbled "goodbyes" and said something about having broken a tooth.

Immediately after they left, my husband said there was a problem with the toilet in the guest room. It kept overflowing, and a few days later we decided to call a plumber. He informed us that it was a bigger job than he thought and he would have to remove the toilet from the floor. Lo and behold, he found the problem: a set of false teeth.

My husband and I are undecided as to what we should do. I think we should send our guest her teeth and tell her where we found them. Do you agree, Ann Landers?

—Incredulous in Stockton

Dear Stockton: If you value her friendship, resist the temptation. You didn't say where the woman lives, but this column appears almost everywhere, and if she reads it she'll know you've got her number.

Dear Ann Landers: It is obvious by your unsympathetic response to a recent letter that you still have your own teeth. I refer to the letter about the overnight house guest who accidentally lost her dentures in the toilet. They blocked the drain and a plumber had to be called.

The question was whether to return them or keep quiet about the discovery. Your support of the no-return decision—to protect the friend from embarrassment—was full of cavities, Ann. Properly fitting, attractive dentures can be extremely costly. Frequent replacements are not looked upon kindly by dental insurers. It is possible that the dentureless friend is still toothless. You certainly were no help.

The return of those dentures, with or without a kind note, would have been greatly appreciated.

—R.S., Riverside, Calif.

Dear Riverside: A great many readers wrote to say I had given the wrong advice. Like you, they felt I should have advised the hostess to return the teeth.

I am still not totally convinced. It seems to me that the woman who lost her teeth down the toilet surely was aware of it. Apparently, her embarrassment was so great that she preferred to say nothing and sacrifice the dentures. Let's hope the poor dear had an extra pair at home.

In 1960, a woman wrote about her mother-in-law, who insisted that she frequently received secret radio messages through her bridgework. The situation became critical when the mother-in-law announced at a dinner party that she was listening to an exchange of secret information between Russia and Red China and wanted to notify the FBI. I suggested psychiatric help.

This is what my mail was like for the next few days. You can draw your own conclusions.

From Charleston, W.Va.: I am a research engineer who wishes to comment on the woman who says she is bringing in radio messages on her bridgework. It is entirely possible that she is receiving radio programs, but if she's getting Russia, she is the first person in electronic history to bring in an overseas signal in this way.

Yonkers, N.Y.: There is an established case of a Carborundum worker who retained enough of the dust so that it acted as a detector in his mouth. He had a great deal of gold work, plus a sensitive jaw bone. This man did bring in Station WOR in New Jersey.

Little Rock: I'm a ham and hold a second-class radio-telephone license. I've known people who have received radio signals through the fillings in their teeth—particularly when they have two different types of metals in the mouth. The teeth carry the vibrations to the brain by bone conduction, as in a crystal-tuned circuit.

Lexington, Ky.: My aunt wore metal frame glasses and used a copper-handled cane to help her get around. She once swore she was receiving radio waves from the planes overhead when she was waiting for me at an airport.

Grand Rapids, Mich.: During the war we had lots of fun listening to radio messages by attaching a safety pin to a rusty razor blade and a little piece of copper wire. We actually got Tokyo Rose.

Abilene, Kan.: My grandmother wears a hearing aid. She gets radio messages all the time—especially when she's eating with stainless steel silverware.

Sandusky, Ohio: My uncle once sat in the corner of the living room smiling and tapping his foot rhythmically. When I asked what he was listening to (he had his ear cocked slightly), he replied, "Lawrence Welk is coming through my teeth." We thought the old guy was balmy, but since I've read the one about the woman and Red China, I'm not so sure.

Richmond, Va.: I work in a small plant. For several months I thought I was going out of my mind because I imagined I heard voices. I was afraid to tell anyone for fear they'd put me away. One day the voices became so clear I decided to see the plant doctor. You can imagine my relief to learn that small particles of metal filing were getting between my teeth and I was receiving radio waves.

Traverse City, Mich.: The steam radiators in our apartment give us better dance music than the radio, especially when it's raining.

Stamford, Conn.: One question please. Did that woman who said she was receiving secret radio messages between Red China and Russia understand Chinese or Russian? Surely the messages were not being transmitted in English!

Dear Ann Landers: As I was snitching a bit of potato salad from the bowl in the fridge before supper last night, my wife caught me and insisted that I read your column about the "hog-mouth" husband who was too lazy to get a plate.

Now that I have been properly chastened, I will, of course, give up this foul habit. Thanks to 25 years of Ann Landers' brilliant counseling, my wife has molded me into a model of perfection. I no longer dance at parties with a lamp shade on my head, nor do I pinch the fannies of pretty waitresses. Furthermore, I have given up spitting in the eye of smokers who blow the stuff my way. The list of bad habits you caused me to drop goes on and on.

But, dear woman, the pressure of being perfect is getting to me. You and I must be the only two perfect people in the world. How do you deal with it, Annie Baby?

—Dudley Dull from the Midwest

Dear Dud: It's easy. I wear my hair in a bouffant style so the halo doesn't show and my clothes are cut to allow extra room for wings.

And now may I ask you a question? Do you brush your teeth with gunpowder? Since you do such a good job of shooting your mouth off, I thought I'd ask.

Dear Ann Landers: You've often said that truth is stranger than fiction. Here's a lulu from your own backyard—the *Chicago Tribune:*

A man in California saw an ad in the paper for an "almost new" Porsche, in excellent condition—price $50. He was certain the printers had made a typographical error, but even at $5,000 it would have been a bargain, so he hurried to the address to look at the car.

A nice-looking woman appeared at the front door. Yes, she had placed the ad. The price was indeed $50. "The car," she said, "is in the garage. Come and look at it."

The fellow was overwhelmed. It was a beautiful Porsche and, as the ad promised, "nearly new." He asked if he could drive the car around the block. The woman said, "Of course," and went with him.

The Porsche drove like a dream. The young man peeled off $50 and handed it over, somewhat sheepishly. The woman gave him the necessary papers, and the car was his.

Finally, the new owner couldn't stand it any longer. He had to know why the woman was selling the Porsche at such a ridiculously low price. Her reply was simple: With a half-smile on her face, she said, "My husband ran off with his secretary a few days ago and left a note instructing me to sell the car and the house, and send him the money."

—Still Laughing in Wilmette

Dear Still: I checked with Bill Jones, the managing editor of the *Chicago Tribune.* He, too, had read the story and thought it was hilarious, but his researchers could not find it in their paper. However, the incident did happen as reported and was a news story somewhere.

Dear Ann Landers: I don't think my new husband is very sensitive to my feelings. He insists on calling me "Babe" instead of using my real name.

He calls me Babe when he phones from his office. He refers to me as Babe in conversations with others and I'm Babe when we're in bed. "Jay" has been married before—three times. I often wonder if he called his other wives Babe as well.

Every time he calls me Babe, I have the feeling that he can't remember my name, or I wonder if it's because he doesn't want to get mixed up and call me by the name of one of his ex-wives. I've asked him several times to please call me Jane, but it hasn't done one bit of good.

What do you make of this, Ann? Am I super sensitive or what? Should I keep harping on this or shut up?

—Babe No. 4 in Virginia

Dear Babe No. 4: You might as well shut up, because this guy is going to keep on calling you Babe, whatever the reason. My best hunch is that it is a term of endearment, so accept it as such. I've had letters from women whose husbands have called them a lot worse.

Dear Ann Landers: I have always called my husband "darling" or "sweetheart." Although he loves me and is a wonderful husband and father, he has never used terms of endearment.

After 16 fabulous years of marriage, I realize this is just his way, and my feelings don't get hurt. Nevertheless, after reading your column, I decided to try one more time. I asked him, "Why don't you ever call me by a pet name?" His response was immediate: "I love you, Lassie."

We held hands and laughed until we fell asleep.

—Learning to Leave Well Enough Alone

Dear Learning: What a darling man you have! I hope you two enjoy many more fabulous years together.

Dear Ann Landers: Most of us have endured the confusion of traffic accidents and then had to summarize briefly the event on those pitifully inadequate insurance forms.

The following was published by an insurance company for internal distribution. These are summaries submitted when policy-holders were asked for a brief statement describing their particular accident.

Your readers may enjoy them.

—Raleigh, N.C.

Dear R.: What a hoot! Thanks for passing them on.

"The other car collided with mine without giving warning of its intention."

"I thought my window was down but found it was up when I put my hand through it."

"A pedestrian hit me and went under my car."

"The guy was all over the place. I had to swerve a number of times before I hit him."

"I pulled away from the side of the road, glanced at my mother-in-law and headed over the embankment."

"The accident occurred when I was attempting to bring my car out of a skid by steering it into the other vehicle."

"I was driving my car out of the driveway in the usual manner, when it was struck by the other car in the same place it had been struck several times before."

"I was on my way to the doctor's with rear-end trouble when my universal joint gave way, causing me to have an accident."

"As I approached the intersection, a stop sign suddenly appeared in a place where no stop sign had ever appeared before. I was unable to stop in time to avoid the accident."

"The telephone pole was approaching fast. I was attempting to swerve out of its path when it struck my front end."

"To avoid hitting the bumper of the car in front, I struck the pedestrian."

"My car was legally parked as it backed into the other vehicle."

"An invisible car came out of nowhere, struck my vehicle and vanished."

"When I saw I could not avoid a collision, I stepped on the gas and crashed into the other car."

"The pedestrian had no idea which direction to go, so I ran him over."

"I saw the slow-moving, sad-faced old gentleman as he bounced off the hood of my car."

"Coming home, I drove into the wrong house and collided with a tree I don't have."

"The indirect cause of this accident was a little guy in a small car with a big mouth."

Dear Ann Landers: I really enjoyed those traffic accident reports from the insurance company. We all need a good laugh now and again, and that column was mine.

I am sending on some honest-to-goodness excerpts from letters written to a public assistance office by applicants seeking financial aid.

—Janet, Your Travel Agent Friend in Milwaukee

Dear Janet: The best humor comes straight out of the lives of everyday folks. Funny, you bet, but sad, too, in a way. Thanks for sharing.

"Dear Sir: You asked me to forward my marriage certificate and six children. I had seven, but one died and was baptized on the half sheet of paper here."

"This is to let you know that Mrs. Jones has not had any clothes for a year and has been visited by her minister regularly."

"I cannot get sick pay. I have six children. Can you tell me why?"

"Please find out for certain if my husband is dead. The man I am now living with can't eat or do anything until he finds out."

"I am very annoyed to find that you have branded my son as illiterate. This is a lie. I was married to his father a week before he was born."

"I am forwarding my marriage certificate and my three children, one of which was a mistake, as you can see."

"My husband got his project cut off two weeks ago, and I haven't had any relief since then."

"You changed my little boy to a girl. Will this make any difference?"

"In accordance with your instructions, I have given birth to twins in the enclosed envelope."

"I have got to have my money as quick as I can get it. I have been in bed with the doctor for two weeks, and he doesn't do me any good."
(Compiled by Connon Barclay, freelance writer, Holland, Mich.)

Dear Ann Landers: My wife and I soon will be celebrating our 30th wedding anniversary, and although we've been quite happy together, I can't bring myself to tell my wife something that's been bothering me since our honeymoon. When we unpacked our things in a nice little resort hotel, my wife opened a large suitcase and took out an accordion.

"Louise" had never told me she played the accordion and that she took it with her everywhere. I was flabbergasted that night as I sat through three recitals of "Lady of Spain" and an old English madrigal with some surprisingly ribald lyrics. Those are the only tunes she knows.

Our social life has always been rather quiet. Our only close friends are "Bernice" and "Murray." They come over quite often and join Louise in a rousing chorus of "Lady of Spain." Murray plays his head—that is, he raps his knuckles on his head while opening and closing his mouth, which produces changes in tone. Bernice clacks two spoons together and hums the harmony.

Ann, I've had about all I can take of this. How can I tell my wife after so many years that she is no musician and the racket is driving me crazy? Any suggestion would be greatly appreciated.

—Had it on Long Island

Dear Long Island: You've been truly wonderful. Please don't blow 30 years of sainthood by losing your temper.

Surprise Louise with a dozen accordion lessons and several pieces of sheet music. Sorry, but I can't think of a thing you can do about Bernice and Murray.

Dear Ann Landers: That letter about Louise who played the accordion accompanied by Bernice and Murray put me away. I nearly split my sides laughing. I made copies and sent them to friends on both coasts.

This morning I received a letter from my sister-in-law in Clinton, Iowa. She wrote: "You don't believe that letter was real, do you? Ann printed it as a joke. Get with it."

Ann, I do believe it was real. Am I naive? Please set me straight.

—Another Ann in Rockford, Ill.

Dear Rockford: Every letter that appears in my column is for real. No way could I contrive anything to compare with the mail that crosses my desk.

Tell your sister-in-law in Clinton that after 26 years I'd be pretty hard to fool. Or better still, let her read this in the *Clinton Herald.*

After that letter appeared, a reader wrote in with this to say: "Where is your sense of humor, Ann? While Louise plays 'Lady of Spain,' Murray plays his head, and Bernice clacks spoons, her husband should join in the fun and play his armpit."

A Dog Named Sex
Morty Storm

Everybody who has a dog calls him "Rover" or "Boy." I call mine "Sex." He's a great pal but he has caused me a great deal of embarrassment.

When I went to city hall to renew his dog license, I told the clerk I would like a license for Sex. He said, "I'd like one, too!"

Then I said, "But this is a dog." He said he didn't care what she looked like. Then I said, "You don't understand, I've had Sex since I was 9 years old." He winked and said, "You must have been quite a kid."

When I got married and went on my honeymoon, I took the dog with me. I told the motel clerk that I wanted a room for my wife and me and a special room for Sex.

He said, "You don't need a special room. As long as you pay your bill we don't care what you do." I said, "Look, you don't seem to understand, Sex keeps me awake at night." The clerk said, "Funny—I have the same problem."

One day I entered Sex in a contest, but before the competition began, the dog ran away. Another contestant asked me why I was just standing there, looking disappointed. I told him I had planned to have Sex in the contest. He told me I should have sold my own tickets. "But you don't understand," I said, "I had hoped to have Sex on TV." He said, "Now that cable is all over the place it's no big deal anymore."

When my wife and I separated, we went to court to fight for custody of the dog. I said, "Your honor, I had Sex before I was married." The judge said, "The courtroom isn't a confessional. Stick to the case, please."

Then I told him that after I was married, Sex left me. He said, "Me, too."

Last night Sex ran off again. I spent hours looking around town for him. A cop came over to me and asked, "What are you doing in this alley at 4 o'clock in the morning?" I told him that I was looking for Sex. My case comes up Friday.

I published a letter from a reader who was convinced that Elvis Presley is still alive. He said: "Elvis got so fed up with people following him around, pestering him and writing all those awful stories because he had put on a few pounds, that he faked his own death so he could have some peace and quiet. It all adds up."

I told the reader that there was some pretty convincing evidence that Elvis Presley died on August 16, 1977, and his funeral was one of the most incredible displays of hero worship that this country has ever seen.

After that column appeared, I was swamped with letters from readers who said I was mistaken. Pull up a chair and look at my mail.

From Stanford, Conn.: There seems to be some disagreement as to whether or not Elvis Presley is alive. Let me settle it once and for all. "The King" lives! I attended his funeral and lingered at the casket for quite a while before the guards made me move on. Elvis was not in that casket. It was a wax dummy. I stood very close and had the opportunity to look at him for a long time. I would bet my life on it.

Albany, N.Y.: The man they buried was an Elvis look-alike. I recall that a young guy in California was so obsessed with Elvis that he paid a plastic surgeon $20,000 to make his face look like Presley's. The results were fantastic. That's the fellow they buried.

Bay City, Mich.: I have seen Elvis in the supermarket. Once he gave me a wink as if to say, "Don't tell anybody." Several people in Kalamazoo know where Elvis lives, but they respect his privacy and are protecting him from the media.

Nashville: My cousin was president of the Elvis fan club about 100 miles from here. When they announced that "the King" had died, his father, Vernon Presley, called all the fan club presidents and told them not to come to the funeral. My cousin suspected something was fishy. She went to Memphis anyway but couldn't get near Graceland. Finally she gave up in disgust and went home, convinced that the funeral was staged and that Elvis hadn't died at all.

Henderson, Ky.: My uncle works in a place that manufactures coffins. The elaborate coffin that Elvis was buried in can be obtained only by special order because it takes a long time to construct. Elvis' coffin was ordered several weeks in advance, which proves that his "death" was planned long before the public was told that he died.

Bismarck, N.D.: My sister's niece works in the courthouse where Elvis' death certificate was processed. The original certificate stated that the body weighed 170 pounds. The paramedics who picked him up said he weighed at least 250 pounds. Looks like there were two corpses, doesn't it? To add to the mystery, the first death certificate disappeared and was never found.

What you have just read is a small sampling of the mail that poured in. Amid all the "Elvis is still alive!" hysteria, I saw a glimpse of sanity in the words of Rabbi Ben Kamin of Cleveland, who wrote the following in The New York Times:

Elvis Presley, brilliant, stunning, original, became as sick in spirit as he was sublime in song. His music may have been good, but his lifestyle was bad. Elvis

died from an addiction to drugs and alcohol. The end of his life was a cacoph-
ony of indulgence and irresponsibility. He was not martyred, he was stoned.

Dear Ann Landers: While riding the bus to work, my friend glanced at the man seated opposite her. He was reading a newspaper. Suddenly she noticed the man's zipper was open and the gap was most embarrassing. She managed to get his attention when he turned a page. Using gestures, she directed his attention to the problem. The man was horrified and set about to close the gap at once.

The very moment he yanked up his zipper, the bus lurched and the woman seated next to him flipped the tail of her fox fur over her shoulder. The fur got stuck in the man's zipper and they were hopelessly entangled.

The woman, furious and not at all accepting of the man's apologies, suddenly yelled, "This is my stop!" She got up to leave and of course, the man had to get off the bus with her. The last my friend saw of this ill-fated couple was the two of them on the street corner, struggling to get free from one another.

—Vera R., Hemet, Calif.

Dear Vera: Thanks for a hilarious story. That's enough to make a man want to go back to buttons.

Dear Ann Landers: Your column on zippers made me laugh. It also reminded me of my favorite story. Perhaps you'd like to share it with your readers.

Last year we had a banquet to install the new officers in our organization. Everyone was in formal attire. There were 200 people in attendance.

When the chairwoman raised her baton to quiet the crowd and open the meeting, the zipper on her gown broke. That zipper went from the back of her neck down to her hem. She gracefully finished her speech and walked over to where the other officers were seated. They all removed their name badges and pinned her gown closed. She then proceeded to chair the meeting without missing a beat.

My husband, who is usually very reserved, said in a loud voice, "Now that's what I call a classy lady!"

—I.K., Seattle

Dear Seattle: The lady is not only classy, but cool-headed in the face of disaster. She gets my vote for woman of the year.

Dear Ann Landers: Your zipper story reminded me of one that made the rounds 50 years ago when zippers first became popular.

A mother was buying a pair of trousers for her young son. The clerk showed her the newest style with a zippered fly. The horrified woman exclaimed, "Oh, no! Don't show me any trousers with a zipper!"

"But, madam," the clerk continued, "this is the very latest." The mom quickly replied, "I know, but I bought him a sweater with a zipper a few weeks ago and you should see what it did to his tie."

In 1940 this joke was considered quite naughty. Today it could be part of a TV sitcom. Print it, will you?

—Also from Iowa

Dear Also: You bet. Here it is.

Dear Ann Landers: Now that tax time looms large on the horizon, we are reminded that tax laws are regulations that must be obeyed.

As a law-abiding citizen, it is my responsibility not only to follow the laws of the Internal Revenue Service but to adhere to those laws when I prepare tax returns for my clients.

What appears below is an interpretation of the Internal Revenue Code by the U.S. Treasury Department. It is designed to help establish guidelines for professionals.

Best regards from a suffering accountant.

—M.L., N.Y.

Passive Loss Regulations, Part II

Section I, 469-4T (f) (4) (iii) (C) (2):

If paragraph (f) (4) (iii) (A) of this section applies to a supplier undertaking, the supplier undertaking shall be treated as similar to undertakings that are similar to the recipient undertaking and shall not otherwise be treated as similar to undertakings to which the supplier undertaking would be similar without regard to paragraph (f) (4) (iii) of this section.

If paragraph (f) (4) (iii) (B) of this section applies to a recipient undertaking, the recipient undertaking shall be treated as similar to undertakings that are similar to the supplier undertaking and shall not otherwise be treated as similar to undertakings to which the recipient undertaking would be similar without regard to paragraph (f) (4) (iii) of this section.

Dear Ann Landers: My morning mail brought multiple requests for donations to worthy causes, free offers (if I buy $40 worth of junk), four catalogs offering everything from pantyhose to government surplus Army blankets and real estate bargains, and then I ran across this jewel of an essay. Want to share it with your readers?

—Mr. R. in Des Moines

Dear Des Moines: The piece is a hoot. If you find out who wrote it, let me know so I can give proper credit.

A Pauper's Plea, or Gimme a Break

Dear Sir: In response to your request that I send a check, I wish I could, but the present condition of my bank account makes it virtually impossible. My shattered financial condition is due to federal laws, state laws, county laws, city laws, corporation laws, liquor laws, mother-in-laws, in-laws and outlaws.

Because of these laws I am compelled to pay a business tax, an amusement tax, a head tax, a school tax, a poll tax, a gas tax, a light tax, a cigarette tax, income tax, and—I almost said carpet tax. I also must buy a business license, car license, hunting license, truck license and dog license.

I am required to contribute to every charitable, fraternal and maternal organization the genius of man is capable of putting together for the purpose of extracting as much money as possible from every person, living or dead, who has a mailbox and a city address.

I am told that for my own safety, I am compelled to carry life insurance, property insurance, liability insurance, burglar insurance, tornado insurance, accident insurance, termite insurance, unemployment insurance, old age insurance, hurricane insurance and fire insurance.

My business is so closely supervised by the government that it is no easy matter for me to figure out how much is mine and how much belongs to Uncle Sam.

I have been inspected, expected, suspected, disrespected, rejected, examined, re-examined, informed, required, summoned, fined and commanded until I have provided an inexhaustible supply of money for every known need, desire, hope and dream of humankind. And because I refuse to go out and beg, borrow or steal money to give away, I'm cussed, discussed, boycotted, talked to, talked about, lied to, lied about, held up, held down and robbed until I am plum ruined.

I can tell you honestly that, except for the miracle that happened just yesterday, I could not enclose this check. But the wolf that has become a stationary fixture at our front door just had pups. I sold them this morning and here is the money I owe you. Yours truly, Mr. Any Person, USA

As one who has been lumped, bumped, jumped, stumped, pained, strained, maimed and brained by the IRS, I am able to empathize. However, I would gladly sign an I.O.U. P.D.Q., rather than live anywhere but in the U.S.A.

The Stress Diet
Pamela Pettler

STRESS DIET BREAKFAST

1/2 grapefruit
1 slice whole-wheat bread
8 ounces skim milk

LUNCH

4 ounces broiled chicken breast
1 cup steamed zucchini
1 Oreo cookie
1 cup herb tea

MIDAFTERNOON SNACK

Rest of the package of Oreo cookies
1 quart rocky road ice cream
1 jar hot fudge sauce

DINNER

2 loaves garlic bread
Large pepperoni and mushroom pizza
Pitcher of beer
3 candy bars
Entire frozen cheesecake eaten directly from the freezer

Another reader sent in these diet tips:

1. If no one sees you eat it, it has no calories.
2. If you drink a diet soda with a candy bar, they will cancel each other out.
3. Calories don't count if you eat with someone and you both eat the same amount.
4. Food taken for medicinal purposes does not count. This includes toast, hot chocolate, brandy and Sara Lee chocolate cake.
5. If you fatten up everyone around you, you'll look thinner.
6. Snacks consumed at a movie do not count as they are part of the entertainment. For example: Milk Duds, popcorn with butter, red licorice, and M&M's.
7. Pieces of cookies contain no calories. The process of breaking causes a calorie leakage.
8. Late-night snacks have no calories. The refrigerator light is not strong enough for the calories to see their way into the calorie counter.

14

No B.S., No M.A., No Ph.D., but I Got the J.O.B.!

From time to time, readers ask me personal questions—"How did you get started writing the Ann Landers column?" or "Do you write all those columns yourself?" and "Are you really a man?"

In October 1995, I celebrated my fortieth anniversary as Ann Landers. With the exception of my recent vacation columns, which are reruns, I have written seven columns a week, 365 days a year, since October 16, 1955.

Here are some direct answers to your most often asked questions:

Dear Ann Landers: My wife and I heard you speak at a convention last year [in 1965]. When you said you work 10 to 12 hours almost every day, I gave my wife a nudge. She didn't believe it and neither did I.

Who do you think you are kidding? Half of your work is done by the goofs who write to you. Some of their letters don't even ask for advice. Often they merely comment on a letter that appeared previously and you say, "Thanks for writing" or "Why don't you take a long walk on a short dock?"

So how do you figure the 10 to 12 hours a day? How about an explanation—if you can come up with one.

—Mr. and Mrs. Doubting Thomas

Dear Mr. and Mrs. Thomas: This question has been raised by others and I am going to try to answer—again.

If it were possible to "get" me for anything, I assure you I would have been "got" years ago. I would not have been in this work for 11 years.

There is more to producing a column than grabbing a few letters out of the mailbag. I read thousands of letters in order to make an appropriate selection. Some days I read as many as 500 letters before I find one that is suitable for use in the column.

Almost every letter must be trimmed because people write too long, especially when they are distressed. Often the language must be laundered. The copy goes through my typewriter at least twice, usually three times. Then I sit at my editor's elbow as he slashes away. He frequently asks me to rewrite an answer or he'll kill a letter simply because it's dull or because I've dealt with a similar problem recently.

So far all I've done is produce the column. But I keep several secretaries busy helping with personal replies to readers who send self-addressed, stamped envelopes. We direct thousands of people to physicians, lawyers, psychiatrists and clergymen. We refer thousands more to service agencies.

This is my mission—to help those who ask for it. Why thousands of people sit down and write to an advice columnist in the first place is an interesting question. But the fact is they do—to the tune of approximately 1,000 every day. [Today, in 1996, over 2,000 letters are in my mailbag each day.]

We have a complete file of service agencies for every city in which this column appears. We send readers to Legal Aid, the Family Service Association, homes for unwed mothers, mental health clinics, Alcoholics Anonymous, the YMCA—the list is a long one. We mail huge numbers of booklets. We respond to hundreds of requests for speaking engagements. (Usually, "Sorry, no.")

This work is immensely satisfying and it is enormously demanding. When I take a vacation or go on a lecture trip the columns are written in advance.

To maintain the quality I strive for 365 days a year is a back-breaking job, and there are no honest shortcuts. As Red Smith put it, "Writing a daily column is easy. All you have to do is sit at a typewriter until small drops of blood form on your forehead."

Dear Ann Landers: A few nights ago we were sitting around with a group of extremely intelligent people and someone quoted you. As a rebuttal (and I'm sure in jest) one of the chaps said, "They ought to get her for practicing without a license."

I am not trying to be impertinent, but would you please explain how and why you can give advice on legal, medical and emotional problems? Is it sufficient to quote from the authorities?

Let me repeat, I do not mean to be arbitrary. I am merely inquisitive.

—Nosey Parker

P.S. It was significant to me, at least, that every person in the room was a reader of your column.

Dear Parker: I do not pretend to be what I am not. I despise the phony and dishonest. Legally, I could use the title "Dr." but I wouldn't dream of doing so since my doctorates are all honorary.

No one needs a license to listen. No one needs a license to provide a shoulder to cry on or to direct the troubled and the uninformed to service agencies, or to give a word of encouragement to the heavy-hearted, or a swift kick in the posterior to the arrogant. There's more to getting the job done than having a license—as any fisherman will tell you.

Dear Ann: Love your column. Heard you speak in Huntington, Long Island, and can attest to the fact that you are a dynamite lady. Let there be no mistake about it. I'm on your side. But I wonder if you have a clear picture of what your column is all about?

You have said, "Superior people talk about ideas. Mediocre people talk about things. Little people talk about other people." Surely you must realize that each and every one of us enjoys a little gossip. In fact, your column is the most widely read gossip column in the world. People can't wait to see what their neighbors, friends, relatives, colleagues and fellow workers are up to. The saving grace is that all who write in are protected by the merciful cloak of anonymity. At least nobody is hurt. Just sign me

—A Little Person Who Loves to Talk About
Other People

Dear Person: If one considers other people's problems "gossip" then I am guilty as charged. But I view this column in quite a different light.

To me, it represents an opportunity for anyone and everyone to unload anger, fear, hostility, guilt, frustration—the full gamut of human emotions. I try to print letters that deal with every aspect of life. Although some of them may seem bizarre, let me assure you nothing is so outrageous or crazy that somebody won't do it.

Of course there are those who read Ann Landers for laughs and I have no objection to this. (It may be their only laugh for the day.) Humor can take the sting out of misery. Laughter can be good medicine.

Anyone who reads this column regularly cannot help but recognize himself—or his son, or his wife, or his daughter or his boss—eventually. Trouble is the common denominator of living. It is also a great equalizer. When we share the same kind of trouble we become brothers and sisters under the skin. That, to me, is what this column is all about.

I have been asked repeatedly if it is true that my twin (who writes as Dear Abby) and I do not speak. The answer is "No. It is not true." We do speak—a lot. And often to each other.

For many years my sister and I celebrated our wedding anniversaries and birthdays together. We were born on July 4, 1918.

We were married in a double wedding ceremony at Sha'are Zion Synagogue in Sioux City on July 2, 1939.

Now we fax each other constantly—at home and at the office. The Good Lord willing, I hope we will do so for many years to come.

———

I once mentioned in the column that I knitted socks for the American Red Cross to help the war effort during World War II. My supervisor at the time suggested I could better serve my country by knitting for the Germans.

That inspired someone to send me this:

Dear Ann Landers: You must be the person to whom the GI wrote the following ditty:

> Socks received. Some fit!
> I use one for a helmet
> And one for a mitt.
> I must say, dear lady,
> You've done your bit.
> But where in the hell
> Did you learn to knit?
> —Buster in Bismarck

Hello, Buster: I plead guilty as charged. But happily the damage was limited. I knitted only one pair of socks and then turned in my needles.

During the Vietnam War, I had the privilege of visiting our troops overseas. It made quite an impression on me and I shall never forget that trip. Apparently, neither did some of the GIs. Here's a letter from 1986:

Dear Ann Landers: Eighteen years ago, Ann, you sat on the edge of my bed in the 17th Field Hospital in Saigon. You held my hand and we talked mostly about our common roots in Iowa. What I remember most about the visit was your undivided attention. Your eyes were on me and me alone. You made me feel as if I were special. You cared.

You asked questions about my life and my family. Your ability to put me at ease and make me feel comfortable made a profound impression on me.

When it came time for you to visit the guy in the next bed I held on to your hand, hoping I might prolong our visit just a few more minutes. It was the nicest thing that had happened to me in a long time. I hated to see it end.

Today I am a counselor in a substance abuse center back home in Iowa. I try to make every one of my clients feel special. I learned the importance of this from you. I don't know how to sign off, so I'll say, Sincerely yours,

—Wayne, New Hampton, Iowa

Dear Wayne: I can think of few things in my life that have given me as much satisfaction as that trip to Vietnam to visit our men in the hospitals. It was Vice President Hubert Humphrey who made it possible. I shall be eternally grateful to him for the privilege. Thank you for letting me know my visit meant a lot to you. I feel good about that.

Dear Ann Landers: I live in Tokyo and am writing to you for two reasons:

The first is to let you know that I spend $1.20 per day for the *Asahi Evening News* because my day would not be complete if I did not read your column.

My second reason for writing is that I am concerned about what will happen to your column when you leave this planet for a more celestial life.

I don't want to sound morbid, Ann, but no one is immortal. Are you, by any chance, training an apprentice to take over after you depart? Or would you consider an arrangement whereby the newspapers could reprint 30 years of reruns? They would still be fresh to a new generation.

Whatever the solution, Ann, I urge you to think seriously of a way your column could continue ad infinitum. It provides a much-needed anchor to a world ever more adrift.

—Don't Leave Us on the Boat Alone

Dear Don't Leave Us: Thank you for your concern. I have, indeed, pondered the question you have raised and am pleased to share my thoughts with you.

I love my work in spite of the fact that it is enormously demanding, and I feel that I am making a meaningful contribution. After 40 years, it is still exhilarating and exciting. My energy level has not declined, and only one or two shingles have fallen off the roof.

Am I training an understudy? No, I am not. I wouldn't know how to teach anyone to do what I do. Nobody taught me, though I was lucky to have had a terrific editor, Larry Fanning, for the first 10 years of my career. My column is more than a vehicle to dispense information. It's at the heart of an intensely personal relationship with my readers.

I'm sure that there are many talented people around who could do a very good job and that one day you will be reading another column in the space I now occupy, but I am not ready to pack it in.

I own the name Ann Landers, and I will never sell it for any amount of money. When I go, the column goes with me. There are bound to be many good advice columns after I have left the scene, but there will never be one that carries my byline. And you have my word on it.

Dear Readers: I love you all and would do anything in my power to help you; however, there are some things I simply cannot do. I hope you understand. I am unable to:

1. Find a husband for your daughter or wife for your son.
2. Lend you money to start a new business.
3. Get you an appointment with Mayor Daley.
4. Give you my home telephone number so you can call after work.
5. Read your manuscript and tell you if it is marketable.
6. Have dinner with all of you.

7. Translate your letters into Spanish so you can correspond with relatives in South America.
8. Get you on Phil Donahue, Oprah Winfrey or Joan Rivers.
9. Offer you a position in my office.
10. Send a check to help you though college.
11. Attend everyone's wedding, bar mitzvah or parents' 50th wedding anniversary.

Sincerely yours,

—Ann Landers

Dear Ann Landers: My cousin has kept an Ann Landers scrapbook for 20 years. Recently she showed it to me. I was surprised when I ran across a color photo of you on the cover of *The New York Times Magazine* section dated October 13, 1974.

There, for all the world to see, was the advice goddess (literally in the flesh) luxuriating in a marble bathtub with nothing between her and all those bulging eyes but a zillion blue and pink bubbles.

How did you find the nerve, Ann? Were you really naked? Was the photographer a female? What reaction did you get from the public? Did you receive many complaints? Dare you print this letter and respond to my questions?

—Sightly Square in Newark

Dear Slightly: That color photo by Elliott Erwitt on the cover of *The New York Times Magazine* section created quite a sensation.

I was wearing a strapless bathing suit and used three bottles of bubble bath. The first reaction was from Clifton Wharton Jr., then president of Michigan State University in East Lansing, and his lovely wife, Delores. They thought the photo was smashing.

My readers, family and friends were delighted, not only with the photo but the splendid interview by the late Judy Wax. The only negative comment came from Father Ted Hesburgh, president of the University of Notre Dame. My friend, the Reverend, considered it "out of character and inappropriate, but not indecent."

Once in a great while, something truly momentous happens in my life and I feel I must share it with you, my readers. You have been my loyal friends for forty years.

Here are a few of the special columns where my personal and public life came together:

Dear Readers: There will be no letters and answers in the column today. My heart is heavy, and I am not up to giving advice. Last night, I lost my lovely mother-in-law.

Gustie Lederer of Detroit passed away quietly in her sleep. She was 81. God gave her 11 years more than the Biblical three score and 10, which, according to the Scriptures, is the rich, full life. And rich and full it was. Gustie attended the weddings of nine grandchildren, and she lived to hold in her arms 10 great-grandchildren.

This remarkable little woman, only 4-foot-10, was widowed at the age of 37 when her husband was killed in an auto accident near Jackson, Mich. She was left with seven young children. My husband, Jules, was her eldest son. Jules knew what had to be done, and he did it. Immediately after his 16th birthday, he left high school to go to work and help support the family.

Gustie was no chicken soup mama. She was loving and gentle, but she was also determined that her children be self-reliant and independent. There was neither the time nor money for the pampering and multiple choices that so many children today find frustrating. Everyone did his and her share. Gustie once told me that she never set up any house rules and she had very few disciplinary problems. Her children knew what was expected of them, and they did it.

Not one of the seven went wrong, although, had they done so, the psychiatrists and psychologists could have come up with many plausible "explanations." The situation was classic—teenagers without a father, severe economic hardship, etc. "We were what you might call disadvantaged," Jules once told me, "but we weren't actually poor. We just didn't have any money."

Gustie was my mother-in-law for 34 years, and as God is my judge, we never exchanged one unpleasant word. Her five daughters, each one blessed with a delightful sense of humor, often chided me about being Gustie's "favorite." It was only natural, they allowed, since I had the good fortune to live in Chicago and they all live in Detroit. Gustie called me "Eppeleh with the Keppeleh" which in Yiddish means, "Little Eppie with the good head." But there was more to our relationship than appeared on the surface. Apart from the obvious affection and many good laughs we enjoyed, there was a quiet understanding—my unspoken gratitude for the wonderful son she raised for me—and her deep appreciation for my being a good wife to him.

After her second attack of congestive heart failure, we knew the end was in sight. The time had come for Ann Landers to take some of her own advice. I telephoned the doctor in charge and asked that no extraordinary measures be used—no needles, no tubes, no machines that might deny Gustie the right to die with dignity. I asked that she be kept comfortable and left in God's hands. She was tired and weary, her work was done, and she deserved to go in peace. The doctor assured me that he was in complete accord, and he kept his word.

Fifteen years ago, I ran a contest in search of the world's best mother-in-law. The winner was a woman in Kansas City. Her nomination was sent in by her daughter's husband. The prize was a gold medal on which was engraved "To the World's Best Mother-in-law." When I sent the Kansas City woman her medal, I sent a duplicate medal to Gustie Lederer in Detroit. Today, as I said my final farewell to that dear little person, I was glad I had done it, because she was, unquestionably, the real winner.

This column appeared in 1969:

Dear Readers: This may be just another day to you, but it is a very special day in my life. Thirty years ago, on a sweltering Sunday afternoon in Sioux City, Iowa, Jules Lederer slipped a plain gold band on my finger, and I became his wife.

Honesty forbids me describing myself as a student at Morningside College, so I'll simply say I was enrolled there. Jules had had one year at Northwestern—High School, that is. He was a product of Detroit, handsome, energetic, imaginative, a born optimist and eager to take on the world. He had a good job and a promising future. He was also broke.

I was an effervescent, fun-loving girl, hopelessly square, driven by a crusading spirit to save the world—sort of a Jewish Joan of Arc. I had accepted a ring and was engaged to marry a law student in California. But Jules, never one to be discouraged by small obstacles, asked me to marry him anyway. I said yes, and the wedding took place three months later.

We were blessed the following year with a baby girl, Margo. From then on, I saw more of the moving van than I saw of Jules. When an opportunity for advancement arose, he took it. And it seemed always to be in another city. We moved from Sioux City to St. Louis, from St. Louis to New Orleans, from New Orleans to Milwaukee. Then came World War II, and Jules served in the infantry. In 1945, we moved from Little Rock to Los Angeles, from Los Angeles to Eau Claire, Wis., and from Eau Claire to Chicago.

Time, that subtle thief of youth, is often cursed by those who long to stop the clock, or turn it back, but we want none of that. Each year has been better than the last because we have grown together. A good marriage, it is said, is made in heaven. This might be true, but the maintenance work must be done right down here. A successful marriage is not a gift, it is an achievement. No real marriage can exist without differences in opinion and the ensuing battles. But battles can be healthy. They bring to marriage the vital principle of equal partnership. If there is a secret to making marriage work it is "Never go to bed mad."

Our 30 years together have been blessed with good health, good fortune, good friends, good times and success. Jules says he could not have made it without me. I am not sure he is right. But I could not have made it without him, and of *this* I am certain. He taught me how to be alone without feeling sorry for myself. He taught me never to back away from a challenge—that it is better to try and fail and then to try again. He taught me how to use my time productively. His work habits are impeccable. I learned mine from him.

Being Mrs. Jules Lederer has been superb training for Ann Landers. Thirty years with this unselfish, supportive, responsive man has enabled me to live life as few people get the opportunity to live. Being Ann Landers' husband could pose a terrible problem, but Jules has met the challenge with dignity and incredible good humor. My husband is my best friend, and I am his. I consider it a privilege to be the wife of this beautiful guy, who took on the world with a ninth-grade education and a hole in his sock.

Who knew that six years later I would be sharing this news with you:

Dear Readers: In my 20 years as Ann Landers this is the most difficult column I have ever tried to put together.

I do so after many hours of soul-searching. Should it be written at all? Would it be appropriate? Would it be fair? I have decided yes—because you, my readers, are also my friends. I owe it to you to say something. There should be some word directly from me. The sad, incredible fact is that after 36 years of marriage Jules and I are being divorced. As I write these words, it is as if I am referring to a letter from a reader. It seems unreal that I am writing about my own marriage.

Many of you may remember the column that appeared in 1969. It was in honor of our 30th wedding anniversary. You may also recall the column I wrote when my beloved mother-in-law, Gustie Lederer, passed away. On both occasions I gave you some intimate glimpses of our life together. Thousands of readers were kind enough to write and say they considered those columns my best.

Every word that appeared in those columns was true when I wrote them, and very little that was said then could not be said today—in complete honesty.

Jules is an extraordinary man. His nickname for me was "The Queen." He was loving, supportive and generous. He is still all those things and I will always cherish our wonderful years together.

That we are going our separate ways is one of life's strangest ironies. How did it happen that something so good for so long didn't last forever? The lady with all the answers does not know the answer to this one.

Perhaps there is a lesson there for all of us. At least, it is there for me. "Never say, 'It couldn't happen to us!' "

Please, don't write or call and ask for details. The response would be, "Sorry, this is a personal matter . . ." Time will not alter my position. I shall continue to say, "No comment." There will be no compromising . . . no exceptions. Just wish us both well.

Not only is this the most difficult column I ever have written, but also it is the shortest. I apologize to my editors for not giving you your money's worth today. I ask that you not fill this space with other letters. Please leave it blank—as a memorial to one of the world's best marriages that didn't make it to the finish line.

—Ann Landers

One of the most heartwarming letters I have ever received was this one. I hope you don't mind my including it:

Dear Ann Landers: I've read your column since I was 7. Now, I have a daughter that age. Reading about other people's problems has made me realize how small mine are.

You guided me through a difficult childhood and adolescence. I could pick up the paper every day and learn how others solved problems similar to mine. And I knew I wasn't alone.

I also learned from you that most problems aren't so serious that you can't have a sense of humor about them.

Many of your columns are so good they should be read over and over. I have even gone to the library to find the columns you wrote before I was born. I didn't want to miss anything.

You've been a strong, positive influence in my life, and I'd like to say thanks by sending you this essay. I hope you'll print it.

Lessons Learned from a Lifetime of Reading Ann Landers

You are responsible for your own happiness. No one can diminish your self-esteem unless you give them permission to do so.

People won't stay mad at you long if you can say, "I blew it, and I'll try to make amends."

When something is troubling you, tell people you trust instead of trying to cover it up. You'll be surprised to learn that they've been through something similar.

Don't pass up an opportunity to tell people you care about them. You may never get another chance.

Reserve judgment until you know all the facts. Even then, keep your mouth shut if no useful purpose is served by adding your two cents' worth.

Be grateful for your good health and the health of those you love. Be aware that without good health, wealth and success mean little.

If you enjoy your work and your life, you are rich. If you aren't happy with either, how can money help?

If you're having a rotten day, don't take it out on others. Simply say, "This is a rotten day. Tomorrow is sure to be better." This attitude can save a lot of relationships.

Don't be afraid to try something you think you can't do.

There's no such thing as the perfect man or woman. Look for the best overall package of ambition, kindness, consideration, self-esteem and intelligence. Otherwise, you'll spend your life alone.

Spend time with your children.

You can respect and learn from people even if you don't like them. You can learn something from everyone—because every person in the world knows something that you don't.

—Nancy Line Jacobs, Omaha

Dear Nancy: Your letter is a wonderful example of how my readers learn, not so much from me as from one another. And that is the real value of this column. Thank you.

15

Play It Again, Sam

Scattered throughout this book are many of my readers' favorite poems and essays. No book would be complete, however, without including the rest of my collection. I hope everyone will find that cherished poem or essay in here.

Just for Today

Just for today I will live through the next 12 hours and not tackle my whole life's problems at once.

Just for today I will improve my mind. I will learn something useful. I will read something that requires effort, thought and concentration.

Just for today I will be agreeable, I will look my best, speak in a well-modulated voice, be courteous and considerate.

Just for today I will not find fault with friend, relative or colleague. I will not try to change or improve anyone but myself.

Just for today I will have a program. I might not follow it exactly, but I will have it. I will save myself from two enemies—hurry and indecision.

Just for today I will exercise my character in three ways. I will do a good turn and keep it a secret. If anyone finds out, it won't count.

Just for today I will do two things I don't want to do, just for exercise.

Just for today I will be unafraid. Especially will I be unafraid to enjoy what is beautiful and believe that as I give to the world, the world will give to me.

What you are about to read was sent to me by a reader from Tennessee. The author is Jim Stentzel.

This little essay drives home the point, in a forceful manner, that each of us is an important part of a bigger picture.

Keep this handy and reread it when you get to feeling insignificant. You do count. And if you doubt it, read this a second time.

Am I Really Needed?

Xvxn though my typxwritxr is an old modxl, it works swxll xxcxpt for onx of thx kxys. I'vx wishxd many timxs that it workxd pxrfxctly. Trux, thxrx arx 42 kxys that function, but onx kxy not working makxs thx dif-fxrxncx.

Somxtimxs, it sxxms to mx that our organization is somxwhat likx my typxwritxr—not all thx pxoplx arx working propxrly. You might say, "Wxll, I'm only onx pxrson. It won't makx much diffxrxncx." But you sxx, an organization, to bx xfficixnt, nxxds thx activx participation of xvxry pxrson. Thx nxxt timx you think your xfforts arxn't nxxdxd, rxmxmbxr my typxwritxr, and say to yoursxlf, "I am a kxy pxrson and thxy nxxd mx vxry much."

Dear Ann Landers: Here's a story told to me by my father, who heard it from his father. The moral of this story is a lesson we all need to learn.

—R.S. in Detroit

Dear R.S.: How right you are! Thanks for tossing it my way.

A Mule Called Hiney

An old farmer and his grandson owned a mule called Hiney. Things weren't going very well on the farm and the bills were mounting. They decided it would be best to take Hiney to the city to be sold.

The old farmer and his grandson started to walk Hiney down the road. A woman saw them and shouted, "You foolish people! Why are you walking when you have a mule you could ride?" They decided she had a point and climbed on the mule.

Down the road a way another woman called to them, "What fools you are! With both of you riding that mule, he will become exhausted and drop dead!" So the old man climbed off.

A little farther down the road a farmer shouted, "You foolish lad, making your old grandfather walk while you ride! Aren't you ashamed?" The boy climbed off and urged the grandfather to get back on.

A short time later an old woman called out, "You foolish man! That poor mule looks as if he is going to drop dead. Get off and carry him for a while!"

Thinking that she had a point, the grandfather dismounted, hoisted the mule onto his back and headed toward the city. When he came to a bridge he lost his footing and dropped the mule into the river. Of course the poor animal drowned.

The moral of this story is this: If you try to please everyone, you will lose your Hiney.

Dear Ann Landers: My sister sent this to me. It appeared in the church bulletin in a small town in Oregon. I hope you will think it is good enough to print. I got a lot out of it.
                                          —Edna D. in Eugene, Ore.

Dear Edna: So did I. Here it is. Sorry we don't know who wrote it. I like to give credit when it's due.

Be

Be understanding to your enemies.
Be loyal to your friends.
Be strong enough to face the world each day.
Be weak enough to know you cannot do everything alone.
Be generous to those who need your help.
Be frugal with what you need yourself.
Be wise enough to know that you do not know everything.
Be foolish enough to believe in miracles.
Be willing to share your joys.
Be willing to share the sorrows of others.
Be a leader when you see a path others have missed.
Be a follower when you are shrouded by the mists of uncertainty.
Be the first to congratulate an opponent who succeeds.
Be the last to criticize a colleague who fails.
Be sure where your next step will fall, so that you will not stumble.
Be sure of your final destination, in case you are going the wrong way.
Be loving to those who love you.
Be loving to those who do not love you, and they may change.
Above all, be yourself.

Dead at Seventeen

John Berrio

Agony claws my mind. I am a statistic. When I first got here I felt very much alone. I was overwhelmed by grief, and I expected to find sympathy.

I found no sympathy. I saw only thousands of others whose bodies were as badly mangled as mine. I was given a number and placed in a category. The category was called "Traffic Fatalities."

The day I died was an ordinary school day. How I wish I had taken the bus! But I was too cool for the bus. I remember how I wheedled the car out of Mom. "Special favor," I pleaded. "All the kids drive." When the 2:50 P.M. bell rang, I threw my books in the locker . . . free until tomorrow morning! I ran to the parking lot, excited at the thought of driving a car and being my own boss.

It doesn't matter how the accident happened. I was goofing off—going too fast, taking crazy chances. But I was enjoying my freedom and having fun. The last thing I remember was passing an old lady who seemed to be going awfully slow. I heard a crash and felt a terrific jolt. Glass and steel flew everywhere. My whole body seemed to be turning inside out. I heard myself scream.

Suddenly, I awakened. It was very quiet. A police officer was standing over me. I saw a doctor. My body was mangled. I was saturated with blood. Pieces of jagged glass were sticking out all over. Strange that I couldn't feel anything. Hey, don't pull that sheet over my head. I can't be dead. I'm only 17. I've got a date tonight. I'm supposed to have a wonderful life ahead of me. I haven't lived yet. I can't be dead.

Later I was placed in a drawer. My folks came to identify me. Why did they have to see me like this? Why did I have to look at Mom's eyes when she faced the most terrible ordeal of her life? Dad suddenly looked very old. He told the man in charge, "Yes, he's our son."

The funeral was weird. I saw all my relatives and friends walk toward the casket. They looked at me with the saddest eyes I've ever seen. Some of my buddies were crying. A few of the girls touched my hand and sobbed as they walked by.

Please somebody—wake me up! Get me out of here. I can't bear to see Mom and Dad in such pain. My grandparents are so weak from grief they can barely walk. My brother and sister are like zombies. They move like robots. In a daze. Everybody. No one can believe this. I can't believe it, either.

Please, don't bury me! I'm not dead! I have a lot of living to do! I want to laugh and run again. I want to sing and dance. Please don't put me in the ground! I promise if you give me just one more chance, God, I'll be the most careful driver in the whole world. All I want is one more chance. Please, God, I'm only 17.

Maturity

Maturity is the ability to control anger and settle differences without violence or destruction.

Maturity is patience. It is the willingness to pass up immediate pleasure in favor of the long-term gain.

Maturity is perseverance, the ability to sweat out a project or a situation in spite of heavy opposition and discouraging setbacks.

Maturity is the capacity to face unpleasantness and frustration, discomfort and defeat, without complaint or collapse.

Maturity is humility. It is being big enough to say, "I was wrong." And, when right, the mature person need not experience the satisfaction of saying, "I told you so."

Maturity is the ability to make a decision and stand by it. The immature spend their lives exploring endless possibilities; then they do nothing.

Maturity means dependability, keeping one's word, coming through in a crisis. The immature are masters of the alibi. They are the confused and the disorganized. Their lives are a maze of broken promises, former friends, unfinished business and good intentions that somehow never materialize.

Maturity is the art of living in peace with that which we cannot change, the courage to change that which should be changed and the wisdom to know the difference.

Dear Ann Landers: My husband and I were amazed and delighted by these words written by my 88-year-old father, who is a guest at the Masonic Homes in Elizabethtown, Pa.

It truly displays his own philosophy and lifestyle. He wrote it for his "Poetry Corner" discussion group. Perhaps you may find it worthy to share with your readers.

Definition of a Real Man
R. Nelson Valentine

One who has self-confidence but does not show it.
One who can be courteous in the face of discourtesy.
One who keeps his word, his temper and his friends.

One who wins respect by being respectable and respectful.
One who has a steady eye, a steady nerve, a steady tongue and
    steady habits.
One who is silent when he has nothing to say.
One who is calm when he judges and humble when he
    misjudges.

That defines a real man and a gentleman and by these standards my
father is indeed a "real man."

—Proud Daughter in Harrisburg, Pa.

Dear Daughter: Thanks for sharing that beautiful essay.

Class

Class never runs scared. It is surefooted and confident and it can handle whatever comes along.

Class has a sense of humor. It knows that a good laugh is the best lubricant for oiling the machinery of human relations.

Class never makes excuses. It takes its lumps and learns from past mistakes.

Class knows good manners are nothing more than a series of petty sacrifices.

Class bespeaks an aristocracy unrelated to ancestors or money. A blue blood can be totally without class while the son of a Welsh miner may ooze class from every pore.

Class can "walk with kings and keep its virtue and talk with crowds and keep the common touch." Everyone is comfortable with the person who has class because he is comfortable with himself.

Dear Ann Landers: I enjoyed your definition of "class." And now will you please give us another definition? What is charm anyway?

—MG

Dear MG: Charm walks on art-gum soles. It is gentle. But it packs a wallop like a bag of wet cement.

Charm is a magical quality that defrosts, disarms, delights and fascinates. It is not a sudden attack of sweetness that can be turned off and on like a faucet. It is woven into the fabric of the personality like a silver thread. It glistens. It shines and it wears well. For months. For years. Forever.

Youth

Samuel Ullman

Youth is not a time of life; it is a state of mind; it is not a matter of rosy cheeks, red lips and supple knees; it is a matter of the will, a quality of the imagination, a vigor of the emotions; it is the freshness of the deep springs of life.

Youth means a temperamental predominance of courage over timidity, of the appetite for adventure over the love of ease. This often exists in a man of sixty more than a boy of twenty. Nobody grows old merely by a number of years. We grow old by deserting our ideals.

Years may wrinkle the skin, but to give up enthusiasm wrinkles the soul. Worry, fear, self-distrust bows the heart and turns the spirit back to dust.

Whether sixty or sixteen, there is in every human being's heart the lure of wonder, the unfailing child-like appetite of what's next, and the joy of the game of living. In the center of your heart and my heart there is a wireless station; so long as it receives messages of beauty, hope, cheer, courage and power from men and from the Infinite, so long are you young.

When the aerials are down, and your spirit is covered with snows of cynicism and the ice of pessimism, then you are grown old, even at twenty, but as long as your aerials are up, to catch the waves of optimism, there is hope you may die young at eighty.

Dear Ann Landers: A great many readers were furious because you advised a wife to "forgive and forget" when she learned her husband had been unfaithful. I'm on your side, Ann. Your advice was, as always, mature, practical and wise.

Too few people understand the true nature of forgiveness. Forgiving does not mean the offender goes free. He often suffers untold tortures.

Obviously, all of us make mistakes. Each of us knows the warmth that fills our hearts and the deep sense of gratitude when we are forgiven.

Forgiveness can spell the difference between a life of bitterness and hate and a life of compassion and understanding. When we are forgiven by those we have wronged we are then able to forgive those who wrong us. Your column teaches this beautiful philosophy. Thank you for it.

—No Stranger to Trouble

This definition of success was written in 1904 by Bessie Anderson Stanley.

Success

He has achieved success who has lived well, laughed often and loved much; who has enjoyed the trust of pure women, the respect of intelligent men and the love of little children; who has filled his niche, and accomplished his task; who has left the world better than he found it, whether by an improved poppy, a perfect poem, or a rescued soul; who has never lacked appreciation of Earth's beauty, or failed to express it; who has always looked for the best in others and given them the best he had; whose life was an inspiration; whose memory a benediction.

Whenever possible, I give credit to the authors of the pieces that appear in my column. However, sometimes it's not that simple. Here's an example of the chaos that can occur:

Dear Readers: Remember the poem that began, "If you think you are beaten, you are. If you think you dare not, you don't. If you like to win but think you can't, it's almost a cinch you won't."

I asked if anyone knew the author. I wanted to give him (or her) credit. The response was staggering—and strange.

Here's a sampling:

From High Bluff, Manitoba, Canada: My uncle, A. W. Shaw, wrote the poem. He was an amateur philosopher but much better than many who get paid.

Richmond, Va.: My father, S. W. McGill, wrote it. He was too modest to claim credit.

Panama: I wrote that poem when I was in high school. It was quite a shock to see it in your column after all these years.

Detroit: Any fool knows that poem was written by Edgar Guest.

Treasure Island, Fla.: That poem you inquired about was the work of Napoleon Hill. People steal from him all the time.

Racine, Wis.: The unsung hero is C. W. Longenecker. It's high time the world knew.

Dallas: The author you should praise is Paul (Bear) Bryant. he was a great football coach at the University of Alabama. I knew him well.

Fullerton, Calif.: That poem was written by Vince Lombardi, you dummy. How come you didn't go look it up?

Crestwood, Ill.: A magazine editor named Wesley Potlook wrote "If You Think You Can," which is the correct title, not "It's All in a State of Mind."

Rabbi Sidney Greenberg, Dresher, Pa.: Walter D. Wintle is the author of the poem "It's All in a State of Mind."

At least 500 others also credited Walter D. Wintle, and I decided he was probably the real author.

Well, imagine my surprise when, years later, I found out that the author was really C. W. Longenecker, and the title of the poem was "The Victor." Here's the poem in its entirety:

The Victor
C. W. Longenecker

If you think you are beaten, you are.
If you think you dare not, you don't.
If you like to win but think you can't,
It's almost a cinch you won't.
If you think you'll lose, you're lost.
For out in the world we find
Success begins with a fellow's will.
It's all in the state of mind.
If you think you are outclassed, you are.
You've got to think high to rise.
You've got to be sure of yourself before
You can ever win a prize.
Life's battles don't always go
To the stronger or faster man.
But soon or later, the man who wins
Is the man who thinks he can.

Dear Ann: I was surprised and flattered to discover my poem at the end of your column in today's *Washington Post.* It was sent in by Sonja Lawson. Does this mean that Sonja clipped it and sent it in, or did she say that she wrote it? If it is the latter, I fear she is mistaken, because I wrote it in 1985 and it was published in *Guide* on August 16, 1986.

—Marlen E. Neumann

Dear Marlen: "Sent" means she sent it in. Sonja didn't say she wrote it. Sorry it was unclear. I regret the misunderstanding and am pleased to set the record straight. Here's your "gem" again:

> Be careful of the words you speak.
> Make them soft and sweet.
> You never know from day to day
> Which ones you'll have to eat.

Are you still with me? Get a load of what piled up on my desk that week:

From Omaha: Maybe Marlen Neumann managed to get that little poem about keeping words "soft and sweet" published in *Guide* in 1986, but she certainly did not write it. My mother has been reciting those lines since I was a child, and I'm in my 40s now. Mom said she learned them from her mother when she was growing up in Scotland. Strange, eh?

—J. Barnes

Chanute, Kan.: Marlen Neumann the author of that little poem? I seriously doubt it. I first remember seeing it as a pressed cardboard motto, hanging on the iron headboard of my mother's bed. That was at least 65 years ago. I later discovered it in another part of the country, framed and hanging in my dentist's waiting room.

—R. M. Smith

Portland, Ore.: In September 1967, I stopped in a restaurant in Ontario, Ore., and there on the wall was the framed poem about "soft and sweet" words. I thought they said a great deal and copied them in my notebook. How then could that woman possibly have written them in 1985???

—R. E. Knapp

Tallahassee, Fla.: I am 57 years old. My mother was a school teacher who was always quoting little poems to make a philosophical point. One of her favorites was the one about keeping words soft and sweet because one day you may have to eat them. I transcribed it in the family Bible in about 1945, which was 40 years before Marlen Neumann said she wrote it.

—M. Edwards

Hillsboro, Ore.: My father, Andrew Haugen, carried a small notebook in which he copied bits of wisdom that appealed to him. He gave me that book in 1978, before he passed away at age 85. I am enclosing a photocopy of the page on which my father transcribed the poem about "sweet words."

—V. Lacy

Houston: My great-grandmother, the daughter of a Cherokee Indian chief, died in Texas in 1922 at age 84. She taught me that poem when I was a toddler about 1915. To Marlen Neumann, who claimed authorship of a poem she did not write: Please take note of the old adage, "Many things are opened by mistake, but none so often as the mouth."

—L. D. Peterson

Gossip—Remember Me?

My name is Gossip. I have no respect for justice.
I maim without killing. I break hearts and ruin lives.
I am cunning and malicious and gather strength with age.
The more I am quoted, the more I am believed.
I flourish at every level of society.
My victims are helpless. They cannot protect themselves against
    me because I have no name and no face.
To track me down is impossible. The harder you try, the more
    elusive I become.
I am nobody's friend.
Once I tarnish a reputation, it is never the same.
I topple governments and wreck marriages.
I make innocent people cry in their pillows.
My name is Gossip.

Cross the Street

Ola Byrd

Mrs. A called Mrs. B on the telephone. "Hello, Mrs. B," said Mrs. A. "How are you today?" Mrs. B replied, "I'm doing fine, how about you?" "Well, Mr. A and I are thinking of going to Hawaii. We realize that we've been far too busy with our careers and haven't spent much time together." Mrs. B said, "That sounds great. You both deserve a vacation." They chatted for a few minutes, and Mrs. B invited Mrs. A to come across the street for a cup of coffee.

When Mrs. A returned home, Mrs. B got on the phone and called Mrs. C. The conversation went like this: "Don't breathe a word of this, but Mr. and Mrs. A are having problems. Mrs. A has decided to leave Mr. A." Mrs. C replied, "No kidding? Is she going home to her mother?" "No," said Mrs. B. "She told me that she is moving to—let me think for a minute—it starts with an H."

"Is it Holland?" asked Mrs. C. "Yes," said Mrs. B. "She's moving to Holland."

Mrs. C called Mrs. D and told her that Mr. and Mrs. A were getting a divorce and Mrs. A was moving to Hong Kong. Mrs. D told Mrs. E that Mr. A hadn't paid enough attention to his business and things got bad so Mrs. A was leaving him to live in Havana.

Well, this went on and on until the story got to Mrs. Q. She called up Mrs. A and repeated her version. Mrs. A was more amused than angry. Her only response was "Well, it appears that the women in this town have taken me around the world when all I did was cross the street!"

Golden Rules for Living
Miriam Hamilton Keare

1. If you open it, close it.
2. If you turn it on, turn it off.
3. If you unlock it, lock it up.
4. If you break it, admit it.
5. If you can't fix it, call in someone who can.
6. If you borrow it, return it.
7. If you value it, take care of it.
8. If you make a mess, clean it up.
9. If you move it, put it back.
10. If it belongs to someone else, get permission to use it.
11. If you don't know how to operate it, leave it alone.
12. If it's none of your business, don't ask questions.

Dear Ann Landers: Please tell me why normally intelligent people seem to take leave of their senses at Christmas time? I refer to those individuals who sit down and compose interminable chronicles of the year's activities, have them mimeographed (usually a poor job) and proceed to send the drivel to everyone whose last name they can spell.

Isn't this the height of egocentricity? What makes these people think anyone (save a special few) is interested in wading through all that stuff?

For several years, we have been receiving family newsletters, and I've had it up to here. I guess what really galls me is the way everyone tries to paint such a glowing picture of affluence and success. I have before me a fistful of chatty little Christmas letters. I'm going to lift a few sentences from each to illustrate the point (the names of persons and organizations have been changed for obvious reasons):

Dear Friends: What a wonderful year we have had! Jim was named vice president of the bank so we celebrated by buying a Mercedes and taking a trip to the Orient. In addition to his Boy Scout work, Jim served as chairman of the United Fund Drive. He is still on the hospital board and president of Kiwanis. Just for laughs, he played the lead in the Little Theater production last June and everyone said he was better than the star who did it on Broadway. His first love, however, is still conservation and he continues to work hard as chairman of the Committee to Fight Dutch Elm Disease.

After completing my term as Junior League president, I swore I would take life easy, but it seems I am more involved than ever. I accepted the vice presidency of the Garden Club and am still active in the DAR. Our church organist became ill, and they asked me to substitute, so I accepted. I ran the rummage sale for the Eastern Star again this year and managed to take a course in flower arranging which was offered by a Japanese exchange student.

Jim Jr. was elected class president and won his letters in football and basketball. He is on the all-state debate team and placed third in the national oratory contest last May. We were surprised when we read in the paper that he had won a $100 prize in an essay contest sponsored by The American Legion. We didn't even know he had entered! He has already been accepted by Harvard.

And so it goes—until you could up-chuck.

Next year, Ann Landers, I am going to send a newsletter to all the people who have been sending *us* newsletters. It will read something like this and I hope they get the hint:

Dear Friends: We had a perfectly rotten year. Hal was passed over for promotion again, so he got mad and quit. He hasn't lined up a new job as yet, but he has his name in at two agencies and he looks in the paper every day.

Hal Jr. was defeated for homeroom monitor. He flunked French and will have to go to summer school.

Billy has not had a haircut since August and had to hock his guitar to pay for repairing his Honda which he wrecked.

My mother-in-law's annual two-week visit in May turned into two months, and my migraines got so bad I had to go back into therapy.

As I write this, the whole family is down with the flu, and I don't feel so good myself. We hope next year is better. It couldn't be much worse. Love to all.

—Mary

Over the years, I've printed brutal assaults on mimeographed Christmas let-
ters. I've said I don't care for them and that they are nothing but brag sheets,
and 80 percent of my readers agree. The 20 percent who disagree have bom-
barded me with obscenities. One year, a friend from Reno wrote, "Since you
and Herb Caen of the San Francisco Chronicle *are opposed to mimeo-*
graphed Christmas letters, I thought you might consider quoting something
from Herb's column." Here it is:

I don't care for Christmas letters, but Bruce Bliven's are different. Now 86, the onetime editor of *The New Republic* (for 30 years) lives with his wife at Kingscote Gardens, Stanford. He wrote:

"At 86 Rosie and I live by the rules of the elderly.

"If the toothbrush is wet, you have brushed your teeth. If the bedside radio is warm in the morning, you left it on all night. If you are wearing one brown shoe and one black shoe, you have a pair like it somewhere in the closet.

"Try not to mind when a friend tells you on your birthday that a case of prune juice has been donated in your name to a retirement home.

"I stagger when I walk and small boys follow me, making bets on which way I'll go next. This upsets me. Children shouldn't gamble.

"Like most elderly people, we spend many happy hours in front of the TV set. We rarely turn it on."

I wrote: "There's a Christmas letter that warms my heart. Not a single word
about Jim's promotion, the children's stellar achievements, the dog's litter of

puppies, Mother's arthritis, or the new Rolls-Royce. I hope Bruce and Rose see this and put me on their list for next year."

Well, folks, I'm happy to report that Bruce and Rose did put me on their list. Here's a condensed version of their 1976 Christmas letter:

Dear Friends: Rosie and I are now 87. Would we care to try for 174? The answer is no. I'm 46 percent as old as the United States, and still can't spell 'seize.'

Rosie has aged some in the past year, and now seems like a woman entering her 40s. She chides me about the little elf who regularly enters our house in the middle of the night, squeezes the toothpaste tube in the middle and departs. Last May we celebrated our 63rd wedding anniversary.

As for me, I am as bright as can be expected. I remember well the friend who told me years ago, 'If your I.Q. ever breaks 100—sell!'

I walk with a slight straddle, hoping people will think I just got off a horse. On my daily excursions I greet everyone punctiliously, including the headrests in parked empty cars. Dignified friends seem surprised when I salute them with a breezy 'Hi!' They don't realize I haven't enough breath for a two-syllable greeting.

When we are old, the young are kinder to us and we are kinder to each other. There is a sunset glow that radiates our faces and is reflected on the faces of those about us. But still it is sunset.

[signed] Rose and Bruce Bliven

Dear Ann Landers: Like everyone else, I am flat broke from overspending at Christmas time. But I need to go shopping again soon, because I am completely out of self-respect. I've said some things I wish I could take back and I am not feeling too good about myself.

I also want to exchange a load of self-righteousness I picked up during the year for an equal amount of humility. I hear it is less expensive and wears well. And while I am at it, I am going to check on tolerance and see if there is any available in my size.

I must remember to try to match some patience with the little I have left. My neighbor is loaded with it, and it looks awfully good on her. I was told the same department has a repair shop for mending integrity. Mine has become frayed around the edges from too much compromising and not enough self-discipline. If I don't get it refurbished soon, there won't be any left. I almost forgot the most important thing of all—compassion. If I see some, no matter what the color, size or shape, I'm going to stock up heavily, regardless of the price. I have run out of it so many times and always feel ashamed of myself when it happens.

I don't know why it's taken me so long to get around to shopping for these items. They don't cost nearly as much as some of the frivolous things I bought at Christmastime and I'll get a lot more satisfaction from them. Yes—I'm going shopping today, and I can leave my checkbook and credit cards at home!

—Pueblo, Colo.

Dear Pueblo: Thanks for the wonderful idea. I hope you find the store crowded.

United Technologies Corp. has from time to time run a series of messages. I hesitate to call them ads—they are far too classy. These essays by Harry J. Gray of Hartford, Conn., contain more common sense per square inch than anything I have ever read. The man is a genius. Here's one of my favorites:

Do You Remember Who Gave You Your First Break?

Someone saw something in you once.

That's partly why you are where you are today.

It could have been a thoughtful parent, a perceptive teacher, a demanding drill sergeant, an appreciative employer or just a friend who dug down in his pocket and came up with a few bucks.

Whoever it was had the kindness and the foresight to be in on your future. Those are two beautiful qualities that separate the human being from the orangutan.

In the next 24 hours, take 10 minutes to write a grateful note to the person who helped you. You'll keep a wonderful friendship alive. Matter of fact, take another 10 minutes to give somebody else a break. Who knows? Someday you might get a nice letter. It could be one of the most gratifying messages you ever read.

For All Parents

Edgar Guest

"I'll lend you a little time, a child of mine," He said,

"For you to love while he lives, and mourn when he is dead.

It may be six or seven years, or twenty-two or three,

But will you, till I call him back, take care of him for me?
He'll bring his charms to gladden you, and shall his stay be brief,
You'll have his lovely memories as solace for your grief.
I cannot promise he will stay, since all from Earth return,
But there are lessons taught down there I want this child to
    learn.
I've looked the wide world over in my search for teachers true
And from the throngs that crowd life's lanes, I have selected you.
Now will you give him all your love, nor think the labor vain,
Nor hate me when I come to call, to take him back again?
I fancied that I heard them say, 'Dear Lord, Thy will be done.
For all the joy Thy child shall bring, the risk of grief we'll run.
We'll shelter him with tenderness, we'll love him while we may;
And for the happiness we've known, will ever grateful stay.
But shall the angels call for him much sooner than we planned,
We'll brave the bitter grief that comes, and try to understand.' "

Dear Ann Landers: This stew keeps extremely well. We've had it in our family for years. Will you please pass the recipe on to your readers?
—P.H.P. in Kansas City

Dear P.H.P.: You bet I will. It sounds delicious—and fail-safe, too.

Family Stew

Take one large pot.
Mix together assorted sizes, shapes and temperaments of Mom and Dad.
Add children gradually with care and love.
Sprinkle on dreams, encouragement, patience, honesty and pride.
Stir in work, friends, pets, schools, life's ups and downs, church, picnics, parents, grandparents, brothers, sisters, nuts and bolts.
Don't forget some craziness, kisses and hugs, fanny pats and more patience.
Tooth fairies, Santa Claus, angels, witches, gremlins and goblins.
Take a large scoop of luck, an abundance of energy. Keep blending constantly with all the other ingredients.
Bring to a boil—then simmer for 20 or more years over a very moderate flame.
If the stew becomes too thick after 15 years or so turn heat off (teen years). Stew can turn unpredictable at this time. All stews are original and need generous amounts of imagination, fortitude and tolerance to

keep from turning rancid. The magic of this incredible stew is that after 50 years the aroma still lingers and the pot never empties, although the flavor may vary depending on taste, preference and seasoning. Bon appetit!

Dear Ann Landers: This essay warmed my heart. It was written by a third-grader and appeared in the newsletter of the Saint Andrew's Society of Washington, D.C. If it moves you as it moves me, will you print it?

—Your Friend

Dear Friend: It did and I will.

What Is a Grandmother?

A grandmother is a lady who has no little children of her own. She likes other people's. A grandfather is a man grandmother.

Grandmothers don't have to do anything except be there. They are old, so they shouldn't play hard or run. It is enough if they drive us to the market and have a lot of dimes ready. When they take us for walks, they slow down past things like pretty leaves and caterpillars. They never say "hurry up." Usually grandmothers are fat, but not too fat to tie your shoes. They wear glasses and funny underwear. They can take their teeth and gums out. Grandmothers don't have to be smart, only answer questions like, "Why isn't God married?" and "How come dogs chase cats?" When they read to us they don't skip, or mind if we ask for the same story over again.

Everybody should try to have a grandmother, especially if you don't have television, because they are the only grown-ups who have time.

What's a Mother?
Wanda Beal

Mothers look different from other women. Their hair isn't always done in the latest style, and sometimes, it isn't done at all.

A mother is a woman who can bake a cake with six other hands helping her and still have it turn out fine.

A mother's shoulders sometimes smell of sour milk, and if you are very observant, you'll notice safety-pin holes in her clothes—even her Sunday best.

Mothers frequently have runs in their stockings. Likely as not, Junior didn't park his trike off the sidewalk.

A mother is different. She likes chicken wings and backs and the hamburger that is slightly burned—things the kids and Daddy don't care for. She never takes the last chop on the plate, and she always saves the candy from her tray at the club to bring home to the children.

A mother may not have ulcers, but she has versatile tears. They show anger, weariness, hurt or happiness. Once, when Daddy forgot an anniversary, Mother cried. One Saturday, he brought home chocolates when it wasn't her birthday or anything, and she cried then, too.

A mother is someone who can repair the kitchen sink with only her hands—after Daddy has spent a lot of time trying with tools and plenty of cuss words.

When a mother dies, she must face Him with her record of accomplishments. If she's done a good job of caring for her children, she'll get the most sought-after position in heaven, that of rocking baby angels on soft white clouds and wiping their celestial tears with the corner of her apron.

Dear Ann Landers: This article by Paul Harvey has meant so much to me through the years. Will you please print it in your column? I feel it is something that should be shared.

—A Fan of Paul's and Yours

Dear Fan: With pleasure. I regret that the original won't fit into my space, so here is an abbreviated version.

What Are Fathers Made Of?

A Father is a thing that is forced to endure childbirth without an anesthetic.

A Father is a thing that growls when it feels good and laughs loud when it is scared half to death.

A Father is sometimes accused of giving too much time to his business when the little ones are growing up.

A Father never feels entirely worthy of the worship in his child's eyes. He is never quite the hero his daughter thinks he is and never quite the man his son believes him to be. This worries him sometimes, so he works too hard to try and smooth out the rough places in the road for his son who will follow him.

A Father is a thing that gets very angry when school grades aren't as good as he thinks they should be.

He scolds his son although he knows it's the teacher's fault.

Fathers grow old faster than other people.

While mothers can cry where it shows, Fathers have to stand there and die inside.

Fathers have very stout hearts, so they have to be broken sometimes or no one would know what is inside.

Fathers give daughters away to other men who aren't nearly good enough so they can have grandchildren that are smarter than anybody's.

Fathers fight dragons almost daily.

They hurry away from the breakfast table, off to the arena which is sometimes called an office or a workshop . . . where they tackle the dragon with three heads—weariness, work and monotony.

Fathers make bets with insurance companies about who will live the longest.

Though they know the odds, they keep right on betting.

Even as the odds get higher and higher, they keep right on betting more and more.

And one day they lose.

But Fathers enjoy an earthly immortality and the bet is paid off to the part of him he leaves behind.

I don't know where Fathers go when they die.

But I have an idea that after a good rest, wherever it is, he won't be happy unless there is work to do.

He won't just sit on a cloud and wait for the girl he's loved and the children she bore.

He'll be busy there, too . . . repairing the stairs . . . oiling the gates . . . improving the streets, smoothing the way.

The following was translated from a Dutch magazine. This nostalgic little piece appeared in the Danbury, Conn., News-Times.

Father

4 years: My daddy can do anything.

7 years: My dad knows a lot, a whole lot.

8 years: My father doesn't know quite everything.

12 years: Oh, well, naturally Father doesn't know that, either.

14 years: Father? Hopelessly old-fashioned.

21 years: Oh, that man is out-of-date. What did you expect?

25 years: He knows a little bit about it, but not much.

30 years: Maybe we ought to find out what Dad thinks.

35 years: A little patience. Let's get Dad's assessment before we do anything.

50 years: I wonder what Dad would have thought about that. He was pretty smart.

60 years: My dad knew absolutely everything!

65 years: I'd give anything if Dad were here so I could talk this over with him. I really miss that man.

Your Name

Edgar Guest

You got it from your father, 'twas the best he had to give.
And right gladly he bestowed it. It's yours, the while you live.
You may lose the watch he gave you and another you may claim.
But remember, when you're tempted, to be careful of his name.
It was fair the day you got it, and a worthy name to bear.
When he took it from his father, there was no dishonor there.
Through the years he proudly wore it, to his father he was true.
And that name was clean and spotless when he passed it on to you.
Oh, there's much that he has given that he values not at all.
He has watched you break your playthings in the days when you were small.
You have lost the knife he gave you and you've scattered many a game,
But you'll never hurt your father if you're careful with his name.
It is yours to wear forever, yours to wear the while you live,
Yours, perhaps, some distant morning, another boy to give.
And you'll smile as did your father—with a smile that all can share.
If a clean name and a good name you are giving him to wear.

Dear Ann Landers: My grandmother gave me a copy of this poem a few months ago. No matter how many times I read it, I am always moved to tears. The author is Truman P. Reitmeyer. Please print it, Ann.

—New York State

Dear New York: Thank you for that tender but disturbing poem. I say "disturbing" because it is sure to make every bird hunter who reads it stop for a moment and question the sport. Here it is:

A Hunter's Poem

Truman P. Reitmeyer

A hunter shot at a flock of geese that flew within his reach.
Two were stopped in their rapid flight and fell on the sandy
beach.
The male bird lay at the water's edge and just before he died,
He faintly called to his wounded mate and she dragged herself to
his side.
She bent her head and crooned to him in a way distressed and
wild,
Caressing her one and only mate as a mother would a child.
Then covering him with her broken wing and gasping with
failing breath,
She laid her head against his breast, a feeble honk . . . then death.
This story is true, though crudely told. I was the man in this
case.
I stood knee-deep in snow and cold, and the hot tears burned my
face.
I buried the birds in the sand where they lay, wrapped in my
hunting coat.
And I threw my gun and belt in the bay, when I crossed in the
open boat.
Hunters will call me a right poor sport and scoff at the thing I
did,
But that day something broke in my heart, and shoot again? God
forbid.

Dear Ann Landers: I want to share with you something I saw in the *Cincinnati Post.* I know you will find it as inspiring as I did.

—J.S.K., Atlanta

To Remember Me

Robert N. Test

The day will come when my body will lie upon a white sheet neatly tucked under four corners of a mattress located in a hospital busily occupied with the living and the dying. At a certain moment, a doctor will determine that my brain has ceased to function and that, for all intents and purposes, my life has stopped.

When that happens, do not attempt to instill artificial life into my body by the use of a machine. And don't call this my deathbed. Let it be called the Bed of Life, and let my body be taken from it to help others lead fuller lives.

Give my sight to the man who has never seen a sunrise, a baby's face or love in the eyes of a woman. Give my heart to a person whose own heart has caused nothing but endless days of pain.

Give my blood to the teenager who was pulled from the wreckage of his car, so that he might live to see his grandchildren play. Give my kidneys to one who depends on a machine to exist. Take my bones, every muscle, every fiber and nerve in my body and find a way to make a crippled child walk.

Explore every corner of my brain. Take my cells, if necessary, and let them grow so that, someday, a speechless boy will shout at the crack of a bat and a deaf girl will hear the sound of rain against her window.

Burn what is left of me and scatter the ashes to the winds to help the flowers grow.

If you must bury something, let it be my faults, my weaknesses and all prejudice against my fellow man.

If, by chance, you wish to remember me, do it with a kind deed or word to someone who needs you. If you do all I have asked, I will live forever.

The tragedy of the Space Shuttle Challenger *brought forth an outpouring of mail. In time of sorrow people feel a need to express themselves. Many letters were extremely poignant and sensitive. I selected this one to share with you. Stacey O'Brien of Massachusetts sent it with a note attached:*

Dear Ann Landers: We are all devastated by the explosion of the Space Shuttle *Challenger.* I want to express my sadness to the families who lost loved ones and to the nation as well.

Here's a beautifully comforting poem I clipped from your column several years ago. It is not only for those seven brave people who lost their lives, it is for all of us.

Sadly Hollow
(Prayer of the Makah Indians)
Do not stand by my grave and weep.
I am not there. I do not sleep.
I am a thousand winds that blow.
I am a diamond glint on snow.
I am the sunlight on ripened grain.

I am the gentle Autumn rain.
When you awake in the morning hush.
I am the swift uplifting rush.
Of quiet birds in circling flight.
I am the soft starshine at night.
Do not stand by my grave and cry.
I am not there. . . . I did not die.

Footprints

Margaret Fishback Powers

One night I dreamed a dream.
I was walking along the beach with
     my Lord.
Across the dark sky flashed scenes from
     my life.
For each scene, I noticed two sets
Of footprints in the sand,
One belonging to me
And one to my Lord.
When the last scene of my life shot
     before me
I looked back at the footprints in the sand.
There was only one set of footprints.
I realized that this was at the lowest
And saddest times of my life.
This always bothered me,
And I questioned the Lord
About my dilemma.
"Lord, You told me when I decided to
     follow You,
You would walk and talk with me all
     the way.
But I'm aware that during the
     most troublesome
Times of my life there is only one set
     of footprints.
I just don't understand why, when I needed
     You most,
You leave me."
He whispered, "My precious child,

I love you and will never leave you,
Never, ever during your trials and testings.
When you saw only one set of footprints,
It was then that I carried you."

Everyday Thanksgiving

Even though I clutch my blanket and growl when the alarm rings each morning, thank you, Lord, that I can hear. There are many who are deaf.

Even though I keep my eyes tightly closed against the morning light as long as possible, thank you, Lord, that I can see. There are many who are blind.

Even though I huddle in my bed and put off the effort of rising, thank you, Lord, that I have the strength to rise. There are many who are bedridden.

Even though the first hour of my day is hectic, when socks are lost, toast is burned and tempers are short, thank you, Lord, for my family. There are many who are lonely.

Even though our breakfast table never looks like the pictures in the magazines and the menu is at times unbalanced, thank you, Lord, for the food we have. There are many who are hungry.

Even though the routine of my job is often monotonous, thank you, Lord, for the opportunity to work. There are many who have no job.

Even though I grumble and bemoan my fate from day to day and wish my circumstances were not so modest, thank you, Lord, for the gift of life.

I run the following essay every New Year's Day but I think it can apply to every day of the year.

Make this coming year better than all the others. Vow to do some things you've always wanted to do but "couldn't find the time."

Call up a neglected friend. Drop an old grudge and replace it with some pleasant memories. Share a funny story with someone whose spirits are dragging. A good laugh can be better than any medicine.

Vow not to make a promise you don't think you can keep. Pay a debt. Give a soft answer. Free yourself of envy and malice.

Encourage some youth to do his or her best. Share your experience and offer support. Young people need role models more than they need critics.

Make a genuine effort to stay in closer touch with family and friends. Resolve to stop magnifying small problems and shooting from the lip. Words that you have to eat have no nutritional value and can be hard to digest.

Find time to be kind and thoughtful. All of us have the same allotment—24 hours a day. Give a compliment. It could provide someone with a badly needed lift. Think things through. Forgive an injustice. Listen more. Be kind.

Apologize when you realize you are wrong. An apology never diminishes a person. It elevates. Don't blow your own horn. If you've done something praiseworthy, someone will notice eventually.

Try to understand a point of view that is different from your own. Few things are 100 percent one way or another. Examine the demands you make on others and lighten up.

When you feel your temper reaching the boiling point, ask yourself, "Will it matter a week from today?" Laugh the loudest when the joke is on you.

The sure way to have a friend is to be one. We are all connected by our humanity and we need each other. Avoid malcontents and pessimists. They drag you down and contribute nothing.

Don't discourage a beginner from trying something risky. Nothing ventured means nothing gained. Be optimistic. The can-do spirit is the fuel that makes things go.

Go to war against animosity and complacency. Express your gratitude. Give credit when it's due—and even when it isn't. It will make you look good.

Read something uplifting. Deep-six the trash. You wouldn't eat garbage, why put it in your head? Don't abandon your old-fashioned principles. They never go out of style. When courage is needed, ask yourself, "If not me, who? If not now, when?"

Take better care of yourself. Remember, you're all you've got. Pass up that second helping. You don't need it. Vow to eat more sensibly. You'll feel better and look better too.

Don't put up with secondhand smoke. Nobody has the right to pollute your air or give you cancer. If someone says, "This is a free country," remind him or her that the country may be free, but no person is free if he has a habit he can't control.

Return those books you borrowed. Reschedule that missed dental appointment. Clean out your closet.

Take those photos out of the drawer and put them in an album. If you see litter on the sidewalk, pick it up instead of walking over it.

Give yourself a reality check. Phoniness is transparent, and it is tiresome. Take pleasure in the beauty and the wonders of nature. A flower is God's miracle.

Walk tall and smile more. You'll look 10 years younger. Don't be afraid to say, "I love you." Say it again. They are the sweetest words in the world. If you have love in your life, this new year can be the best one ever.

Ann Landers

Permission Acknowledgments

Grateful acknowledgment is made to the following for permission to reprint previously published material:

CURTIS BROWN LTD.: "But I Could Not Love Thee, Ann, So Much, Loved I Not Honore More" from *The Old Dog Barks Backwards* by Ogden Nash (Little, Brown and Company, 1972). Copyright © 1971 by Ogden Nash. Reprinted by permission of Curtis Brown Ltd.

THE ESTATE OF SAMUEL ULLMAN: "Youth" by Samuel Ullman. "Youth" is found in *Samuel Ullman and "Youth": The Life, the Legacy* by Margaret E. Armbrester (University of Alabama Press, 1993), a biography that includes all of Ullman's poetry. Reprinted by permission.

HARPERCOLLINS PUBLISHERS LTD (CANADA): "Footprints" by Margaret Fishback Powers. Copyright © 1964 by Margaret Fishback Powers. Reprinted by permission of HarperCollins Publishers Ltd (Canada).

ROBERT J. HASTINGS: "The Station" by Robert J. Hastings. Copyright © Robert J. Hastings. Reprinted by permission.

MARJORIE HOLMES: "A Prayer for Cross Mothers" from *I've Got to Talk to Somebody, God* by Marjorie Holmes, published by Doubleday. Copyright © 1968, 1969. Reprinted by permission.

ROBERT S. LAUBACH: "Life Begins at 80" by Frank Laubach. Reprinted by permission courtesy his son, Robert S. Laubach.

RENÉE T. LUCERO, R.N.: "Before You Kill Yourself" by Renée T. Lucero, R.N. Reprinted by permission.

EDNA MASSIMILLA: "Heaven's Very Special Child" by Edna Massimilla. Copyright © 1956 by Edna Massimilla. Adapted to music ©1990 by Publications for Disabilities, P.O. Box 21, Hatboro, PA 19040. Reprinted by permission.

PAMELA PETTLER: "The Stress Diet" by Pamela Pettler. From *The Joy of Stress* by Pamela Pettler. Reprinted by permission.

VERONICA A. SHOFFSTALL: "After a While" by Veronica Shoffstall. Copyright © 1971 by Veronica A. Shoffstall. Reprinted by permission.

HENRY SOBELL: "Your Name" and "For All Parents" by Edgar Guest are from the collected works of Edgar A. Guest. Reprinted by permission.

MORTY STORM: "A Dog Named Sex" by Morty Storm. Reprinted by permission.

UNITED TECHNOLOGIES CORPORATION: "Do You Remember Who Gave You Your First Break?" by Harry J. Gray. Copyright © 1979 by United Technologies Corporation. Reprinted by permission.

UNIVERSAL PRESS SYNDICATE: "A Rapist Tells You How to Avoid Him" by Niki Scott. Taken from the "Working Woman" column by Niki Scott. Distributed by Universal Press Syndicate. Reprinted by permission. All rights reserved.

UNIVERSITY OF PITTSBURGH PRESS: "Frankenstein's Wife Writes to Ann Landers" is the first part of the poem "Help Is on the Way" from *Disguises* by Herbert Scott. Copyright © 1974. Reprinted by permission of the University of Pittsburgh Press.

JUDITH VIORST c/o LESCHER & LESCHER, LTD.: "The Other Woman" from *When Did I Stop Being 20 and Other Injustices* by Judith Viorst, published by Simon and Schuster. Copyright © 1968, 1987 by Judith Viorst. This usage granted by permission of the author.

CHUCK WELLS: "Dogs Don't Have Souls, Do They?" by Chuck Wells. Reprinted by permission of Chuck Wells, Wells Insurance Agency, 628 East Main Street, Palmyra, NY 14522.

Index

About the Author

According to the *Guinness Book of World Records*, ANN LANDERS is the most widely syndicated columnist in the world. According to the *World Almanac*, she is the most influential woman in the United States. She has received honorary degrees from thirty-two colleges and universities, and was the first journalist to receive the Albert Lasker Public Service Award. She lives in Chicago, and has a daughter, three grandchildren, and three great-grandchildren.